"By breaking a public silence, Professor Rose and her storytellers here have done us all a great service. This is one of the first brave steps in beginning to fill in the obliterated stories of black women's many sexualities."

—Naomi Wolf, author of *The Beauty Myth*

"If Freud called woman 'the dark continent of man,' then the sexuality of black women has truly been the dark continent of the African-American tradition. To read so very much of African-American literature before 1970 is to presume that black women did not experience sexual intimacy, or even discuss it. This pioneering collection by Tricia Rose is as significant to the African-American autobiographical tradition as the depiction of Janie's evolving sexuality in *Their Eyes Were Watching God* was to African-American literature."

—Henry Louis Gates

"In *Longing to Tell,* Tricia Rose shares something all too rare: a good conversation with trusted women friends. The emotional power and raw poetry of these candid accounts compels our attention while gently nudging us to contemplate the larger narrative of race, class, color, sexuality, and gender within which each intimate story unfolds."

—Lani Guinier, Bennett Boskey Professor of Law, Harvard Law School

"Rose, a professor of African-American history, interviewed hundreds of black women in the course of her research for a scholarly book on black women's sexuality, then came to the realization that the women's voices deserved book-space of their own. The result is a collection of twenty first-person narratives from a cross section of black women speaking frankly about a range of topics, such as coming of age, sexual abuse, drug addiction, marriage, divorce, AIDS, and interracial dating. Rose provides the broader context of social, racial, and gender issues, including concerns about perpetuating the stereotypes of black men and women as sexual animals and American standards of beauty that often exclude black women. The women themselves speak candidly in their powerful—sometimes painful, sometimes amusing—portraits. . . . Readers interested in race and gender issues will appreciate this revealing book."

—*Booklist*

"Brave, disturbing, cathartic. *Longing to Tell* adds to our knowledge of the enduring impact of slavery and reminds us that we have to be the shepherds of our own healing. Rose has given us an important work."

—Lisa Jones, author of *Bulletproof Diva*

"*Longing to Tell* is a landmark book in black letters and scholarship. In its pages, for the first time, we hear the loving, bracing, hurting, humorous, wise, angry, hopeful—and above all honest—voices of black woman speaking about sexuality and intimacy. Rose's introduction and epilogue brilliantly chart the challenging terrain that black women must navigate in embracing healthy and mature sexual selves. *Longing to Tell* is bound to be a classic of its kind: It dispels myths, stereotypes, and tales about black women while giving us the truth in all its glorious and grievous colors."

—Michael Eric Dyson, author of *Why I Love Black Women*

"Professor Tricia Rose's is a brave, honest, groundbreaking book on black women's sexuality, from their own vantage points. If there is one book you must read on the subject, *Longing to Tell* is certainly the one. The intimate lives of African-American women have been shrouded in secrecy or wrapped in myth. Tricia Rose's oral histories capture the complexity of an aspect of our lives about which there has been too much silence. We need more stories like these."

—Beverly Guy-Sheftall, Anna Julia Cooper Professor of Women's Studies, Spelman College, and coauthor (with Johnnetta Betsch Cole) of *Gender Talk: The Struggle for Women's Equality in African American Communities*

"Tricia Rose has bravely opened the door to honest discussion among black women about who we love and what we desire in the deepest places in our lives. *Longing to Tell* is a treasure."

—Barbara Smith, author of *The Truth That Never Hurts: Writings on Race, Gender, and Freedom*

"In *Longing to Tell,* Tricia Rose enables us to listen as black women from diverse backgrounds candidly discuss, in narratives that range from humorous to shocking and heartbreaking, the effects of racism and sexism on their intimate lives. This valuable book breaks a silence we can no longer afford to ignore."

—Derrick Bell, author of *Faces at the Bottom of the Well: The Permanence of Racism*

"This provocative book delves into the sexual lives of contemporary African-American women. . . . Rose places these sexual tales in the theoretical context of race and gender in American society, [providing] a stimulating basis for dialog on sex and race in America as well as [giving] voice to women who have felt forced into silence."

—*Library Journal*

# LONGING TO TELL

# LONGING TO TELL

Black Women Talk About Sexuality and Intimacy

*Tricia Rose*

PICADOR
FARRAR, STRAUS AND GIROUX
NEW YORK

Note to Readers: All names and identifying characteristics have been changed, as have dates, places, and other details of events depicted in this book.

www.picadorusa.com

Picador® is a U.S. registered trademark and is used by Farrar, Straus and Giroux under license from Pan Books Limited.

For information on Picador Reading Group Guides, as well as ordering, please contact the Trade Marketing department at St. Martin's Press.
Phone: 1-800-221-7945 extension 763
Fax: 212-677-7456
E-mail: trademarketing@stmartins.com

*Designed by Lisa Stokes*

Library of Congress Cataloging-in-Publication Data

Longing to tell : Black women talk about sexuality and intimacy / [compiled by] Tricia Rose.
        p. cm.
    ISBN 0-312-42372-1
    EAN 978-0312-42372-8
    1. African American women–Psychology. 2. African American women–Sexual behavior. 3. African American women–Interviews. 4. Intimacy (Psychology). 5. Love–United States. 6. Interpersonal relationships–United States. 7. Sex roles–United States. 8. Racism–United States–Psychological aspects. 9. United States–Race relations–Psychological aspects. I. Rose, Tricia.

E185.625.L66 2003
306.7'089'96073–dc21                                                    2002032541

First published in the United States by Farrar, Straus and Giroux

First Picador Edition: April 2004

10  9  8  7  6  5  4  3  2  1

*For believers of justice in intimacy*

# Contents

# Foreword

THIS BOOK BEGAN as an attempt to answer a scholarly question: How has the history of race, class, and gender inequality in this country affected the way that black women talk about their sexual lives? It also began as an effort to take on the call made by many black feminists for more reflection on black women's sexuality in modern American society. Over time, though, the stories I had gathered as only one facet of this project seemed to yearn for space to stretch out and wander; it was as if the women stayed in conversation with me long after we parted. They had questions of their own that seemed pressing and in need of a wide public hearing. I began to question the merit of referring only indirectly to such rich and complicated stories without making them available to readers of my imagined book.

Although I had not intended to write an oral history, I began to realize just how valuable it would be to have these stories in print, in as full and dynamic presentation as possible for readers far beyond scholarly ones. As you can see, the women's stories became the heart and soul of this book. My hope is that readers will be as awed by these stories as I was, inspired by the courage of these women in laying bare their lives, and encouraged to tell stories of their own.

Santa Cruz, California
October 2002

# Acknowledgments

MANY PEOPLE have been crucial to making this book a reality. Along the way, several people helped make connections and passed the word about the project, especially J. Adams, E. Miller, and Ronald Aubert. Thanks also to Ronnie for being such a good friend, listener, and cheerleader. A sustaining core of women friends and colleagues, most especially Lisa Duggan, Serene Jones, Liz Fitzsimmons, Genny Palmieri, Alondra Nelson, Thuy Linh Tu, Farah J. Griffin, and Ann duCille, gave strategic support and generous intellectual advice and critique, shared good meals, provided much-needed distraction, and just plain kept me going when I truly thought about giving the whole thing up.

I am grateful to my agent, Geri Thoma, for her enthusiastic representation and good cheer. I am also indebted to my editor, Ayesha Pande, for her attentive support and patience. Many thanks also to Kalbryn McLean for her expert editorial help and to Alyssa, Madala, Aimee, and others who gave a helping hand along the way. Also, special thanks are due to Kristin Elliot for her painstaking transcriptions. Thanks, too, to Craig Levine for his keen eye and generous help. Funding from the Ford Foundation during an early stage of this project gave me the time and resources to sort through the direction it would take.

On the home front, many family members have kept the love flowing. For this, heartfelt thanks are due to my parents, George and Jeanne Rose, and my parents-in-law, Herbert and Irene Willis; and to Chris, Stephanie, Evan, Stephen, Jason, Clark, Coleman, T.J., Ebony, Sarah, and Billie. Finally, immeasurable thanks to my bighearted husband, Andre C. Willis, who has made this journey far richer, more fun, and more meaningful than I thought possible at the outset. It is hard to imagine what would have come of this book, and of me, were it not for his courageous love, insight, support, and joyous spirit.

LONGING TO TELL

# Introduction

*"We compare our lives to the stories we know."*

$F$EW THINGS are as gratifying as a good conversation with trusted women friends. Finding time for it, though, is a struggle. Unscheduled time is such a luxury that when I do manage to connect with my women friends, we usually work it around something else we both have or want to do: eating a meal, exercising, shopping, getting a manicure, scheduling a book club session. But no matter where or why we meet, we end up talking about sex, intimacy, and relationships. It is as if since the last time we spoke with each other we have been holding our breath, and only with each other do we have a proper place to let it go. We desperately need to hear and tell. We are always surprised at how similar some of our intimate circumstances are and hang on each other's every word to find out how the other has handled it.

We are looking not only for reflection but also for affirmation, advice, and a space to hear our side of the story told without taking into account someone else's agenda, needs, or expectations. And yet the stories we tell and the frustrated questions raised by us and by many women are not without connection to these surrounding forces. Why can't I find a decent partner? Why is it that I work forty hours out of the house and another twenty at home and then he wants to know why I don't feel like having sex at 11 p.m.? How is it that even the over-forty women on TV, straight and gay, are considered attractive only when they weigh 120 pounds or less? Why does it take me thirty minutes to have an orgasm (now that I know what it is) while he can have one during commercials? Was that fight we had really domestic violence? Why does enthusiasm for my career take away from my children but my partner's career enhances them?

As numerous black women know, many of these heartfelt concerns have racial dimensions. How is our sense of sexual belonging affected by the fact that the desirable women over forty on TV are all skinny and almost always white? Why can't I find a black man to date? Should we break up over his cheating, and if we do, will I ever find another decent black man? Will my family disown me if I date outside the race? How will I find another black gay lover in this town, since I already know them all? Why did my doctor assume I was a single mother when I went in for prenatal care? I know my man has it tough out there as a brother, but why do I feel that I always have to absorb and care for his injuries as well as my own to keep this relationship going?

The stories behind these questions are rarely heard in our everyday lives, even though our society is fixated on issues of race and sexuality. In our popular culture, we are bombarded by stories about sex and romance, but we almost never hear what black women have to say. The sexual stories that black women long to tell are being told in beauty parlors, kitchens, health clubs, restaurants, malls, and laundry rooms, but a larger, more accessible conversation for all women to share and from which to learn has not yet begun. As will become evident in the stories that follow, sisters have kept quiet in public for ample reasons, even though there is so much to be gained from sharing these stories widely.

*"Audre Lorde is one of my sheroes, and I don't believe that silence will save us . . . I work at the juvenile court, and daily I see sisters dying*

*from the silence, and it's painful. So my belief is that the more of us talk about it, the better."*

—*Rhonda, 35*

Many of the women whose stories are gathered here discuss their fears of being sexually misseen and misheard. As twenty-two-year-old Veronica says, "At times I question being open about sex. I question whether people compute that and use words like 'promiscuous' that I think are linked to this idea that black women are jungle things, that we are sexual people, the way we dance, the way we move."

Simply telling one's story isn't simple at all. Black women's sexual lives, like those of many women, sometimes involve abuse and mistreatment at the hands of men. For black women, though, this means making public statements about black men that might serve to support stereotypical images of black men as violent, dysfunctional, and criminal. Black women's sexual lives are pinned between the powerful uses of distorted myths about black sexuality to fuel racist, demeaning stories about black men and women and the sexuality myths used to maintain the subordination of women as a whole. The afterword explores in greater depth some of these myths and the silences they have provoked.

How silences are broken is as important as breaking them. Sexual story-telling generally follows two approaches, neither of which can properly counter the historical forces that shape black women's sexuality. In the first, the author-expert frames bits and pieces of women's sexual stories around a central thesis. In this approach, we can see how a selected group of women has grappled with a specific issue or circumstance. While this helps us to see similarities across a wide group of people and provides insight into our similarities and differences, it breaks up the stories into fragments that are animated through the analysis the author provides, rather than appreciating them for their own logic and form. We do not hear the women's voices in all their glorious, sometimes contradictory, complexity. Nor do we see how elements of the story work together or come apart. Cutting up such intimate stories into bits and pieces repeats a kind of silencing even as it claims to give voice.

The second approach involves placing sexual stories in what I call "story containers"—such as "rape victim," "incest survivor," "married woman," "single mother," "lesbian," "virgin," and "prostitute." Aspects of sex or sexual parts such as stories about "the vagina" or "losing one's virginity" have also become popular framing devices. Although they have been helpful in bringing denied experiences, quietly held sexist stigmas, and crimes into public view by isolating and illuminating them, they give us a neat and sometimes one-dimensional understanding of how sex and sexuality are experienced. Defining a sexual life by enclosing it within any of these containers may be reassuring, but makes it difficult to understand the complexity of women's sexual experiences.

It is impossible to understand a woman's coming-of-age experiences without having a sense of the larger contexts that shape them, such as family dynamics, expectations surrounding gender and sexuality, economic and educational circumstances, religion, race, color, and weight. If a woman tells the story of losing her virginity, then aspects of her life such as how she was raised, how expectations were communicated, and perhaps what her religious beliefs were become crucial to any understanding. Using simplistic categories may also encourage women who are looking for a way to express difficult experiences to grasp at the most socially acceptable label for their experience, thus collapsing complex and important aspects of their sexuality into this master narrative. It could be the case that a "single mother" might also be a "rape victim"—and she was also likely at some point a "virgin." How do we tell a story that moves across so many labels, as all of our lives do? And, most important, how can we—given the histories of manipulation, fragmentation, and denial of space for black women's own sexual stories—in good conscience subject black women's sexual narratives to these fragmenting strategies?

The stories you will read in *Longing to Tell* are presented to limit this kind of fragmentation, to allow the stories to move relatively freely, and to link sexuality to everyday life. Rhonda, for example, a lesbian/dyke who survived incest abuse, has also survived drug addiction, is finishing law school, has had an abortion, hopes to be a mother, is in a loving relationship, and is a committed social activist. It is my hope that such an approach makes it more difficult to caricature black women's sexual lives, or to force these women's stories into powerful yet destructive images and assumptions. It is my hope, too, that readers will be able to see just how central race is as a defining force in black women's sexuality and yet also see similarities among women despite racial differences. Unable to rely on easy labels, the reader, I hope, will come to the stories with fewer assumptions.

I approached my conversations with these women as an open process that generally centered on their sexual experiences and reflections. My questions were primarily about their individual experiences, but I also asked them about their perceptions of larger issues in society relating to race, gender, and sexuality. I deliberately avoided using a fixed list of questions, and chose a topical, conversational style that touched on key areas. I asked questions about their background and why they wanted to participate in such a dialogue. Then I asked questions about intimacy, how they learned about sex and sexuality, masturbation, orgasms, the experience of first menstruation, virginity, pregnancy, and motherhood; about sexual abuse, race and its import for sex, sexism, sexual fantasy, and regret. The shape of the actual questions emerged from the conversations; many times, the women told stories that included these topics long before I thought to ask.

Some women talked easily, requiring little prodding from me. Others took awhile to warm up to the conversation, and a few remained somewhat aloof throughout. Some topics were unexpected and were difficult for the women to discuss (especially masturbation and orgasm), and other topics, such as the male/female double standard and sexism among African-Americans, seemed quite familiar and well considered. Each woman remembered clearly her experiences surrounding virginity and first menstruation. Motherhood was another landmark experience, as were the traumatic experiences of sexual violence and physical abuse. Questions about sexism in society and its impact on them frequently provoked intense responses, especially in relation to the expectations that confine and define women's sexuality. Many women described the frustrating feeling that many sexual behaviors are good for men but a terrible stigma for women.

Our conversations lasted about two to three hours and took place in private. As part of their agreement to participate, I guaranteed complete anonymity, promising to change all identifying information while preserving the substance of their stories. For example, if a woman grew up in Chicago, I changed this city to a similar-sized midwestern city to preserve some characteristics of the story. At my request, many of the women provided names that they wanted to use as pseudonyms. Although not every woman came up with an alternate name—in which case I provided one—I made the request so that the women would easily be able to find themselves in print and feel a greater connection to the published version of their stories.

One of the most interesting things I learned from listening to the women is how much sexual experience is intertwined with every facet of life and level of society. Their parents' marital relationships, their own career goals, their religious training, medical racism, poverty compounded by racism and sexism, images of black women in society, sometimes their own drug problems, all are part of the sexual story being told, not diversions from it. These sexual stories, when allowed to unfold in the context of women's lives, call out to us to see that black women share important contemporary social, political, and cultural histories with one another and share other histories with women from diverse backgrounds. Their accounts are both compelling personal narratives and extraordinary, socially relevant, collective stories. Sexuality is considered a private matter; yet it has a powerful and volatile public social life.

I hope that the black women's sexual testimonies in *Longing to Tell* will make an important social and political contribution in two ways. First, simply having a collection of such stories may help counter the powerful distorted representations that abound. As the legal studies scholar Richard Delgado has noted, "Stories, parables, chronicles, and narratives are powerful means for destroying mindset—the bundle of presuppositions, received wisdoms, and shared understandings against a background of which legal and political discourse takes place."[1] The kinds of stories that have worked to marginalize, pathologize, and condense the lives of black women cannot simply be legislated out of circulation. They have to be replaced by other stories—ones that make it clear that Mammy, Jezebel, and other entrenched images are not representative *of* black women but symbolize a violent disregard *for* black women. The writer and historian E. Frances White has rightly observed the important role storytelling plays in black families to prepare its members for life in a racist world.[2] These stories are vital in helping black people rewrite widely held dehumanizing ideas about black people. Where are the stories that help prepare black women for life in a racist *and* sexist world?

Second, it is crucial to have access to more stories by black women, told in such a way that they not only illuminate the lives and social forces that shape them but also allow a given story's messy seams to show, let the many life threads that run through them remain visible. These stories are not intended to be read as kernels of social science evidence for what *really* constitutes all black women's sexual experiences. My hope is that, to the contrary, the sheer diversity of experiences and ways of thinking that emerge from even a mere twenty or so stories will prevent a monolithic, objectifying reading of all black women.

How people tell stories is almost as important as what they say. In *Longing to Tell* I have presented oral narrative to allow the flavor of each woman's language and thought processes to be preserved as much as possible. Seeing the seams and threads makes commonalities much more apparent, linking these women's stories to each other, and to black women collectively. By laying bare the amazing similarities in experience between women of different ages, religions, background, education, color, and orientation, this collection enables readers to witness the fact that black women as a group, despite crucial differences among them, are subjected to powerful social conditions. This recognition discourages the kind of naive, individualistic, apolitical reading to which personal storytelling sometimes succumbs. Understanding these similarities among black women should not hinder white readers' ability to recognize important similarities of experience across race; the challenge lies in being able to see simultaneously themes that relate only to black women and themes that relate to all women.

There are significant differences among the women, such as class and sexual orientation, but I have deliberately chosen not to flag them. These factors are highly relevant, yet understanding of the definitions of sexual orientation and class status tend to be extremely rigid: you are either working class or not; you are either straight or gay. In reading through these narratives, it struck me that the ways that class and sexual identity play out are far more complex and sometimes muddled. These complexities would be rendered invisible if the stories were separated into class and sexual orientation categories. I am more interested in seeing how these factors are important in the narratives themselves. For example, there are a few women who identify themselves as heterosexual and yet describe lesbian sexual experiences. The reverse is also true: women who identify themselves as lesbians but have had sexual experiences with men.

Similarly, how do we define class status and how does race complicate it? Income, job status, quality of life in a given community, relative security, cultural literacy, and education are all possible markers of class status. Some women begin in families who would likely be characterized as working class but have jobs that their families perceive as middle class despite the limited pay associated with them. In some cases, women were raised in middle-class neighborhoods until a certain age and then found that they were scraping by for a while. None of this is to say that such identity markers are meaningless; instead, I want to allow the meanings to emerge, to see how they are lived. Furthermore, race complicates class markers significantly. Measures of middle-class status in a black community do not often require generally presumed mainstream middle-class markers, such as home ownership, income, and job status. For instance, some women whose parents had what are often thought of as working-class jobs, such as firemen, postal workers, and secretaries, considered themselves middle class in the context of their mostly black communities. Success and failure were often defined in racial, class, and gender terms, and with acute awareness of how much larger societal sexual expectations matter. As twenty-two-year-old Anondra points out: "How I define myself as a black woman is, I've overcome the odds—I wasn't supposed to make it this far. I wasn't supposed to get a high school diploma, I wasn't supposed to not have kids at an early age, I wasn't supposed to complete one degree and be finishing up another one. I feel that I am satisfied with myself and the choices I made in life and the consequences I've had to deal with."

All the women identify themselves as black, but even this should be understood as a real but not fixed aspect of their identities. Blackness is not a monolith, despite popular notions that race is a uniform and permanent identity. Some of the women are biracial; others have Dominican, Jamaican, or Puerto Rican roots. All of the women understand themselves to be part of the African diaspora and its history and have experiences distinctly shaped by that history.

Once "blackness" is the assumed backdrop for women's sexual experiences, new issues emerge. For example, as you will read, color is an enormously important factor in many black women's lives. Skin color and its relationship to desirability are poignantly discussed by many of the women, especially the darker-skinned women. But it also provokes anxiety among lighter-skinned women. In a society that has assigned an excessive, distorted value to whiteness as a sign of beauty, black people—and especially black women (given the importance assigned to women's beauty)—have an acute awareness of their color and how others perceive it. As thirty-seven-year-old Cocoa says, "The dark skin/light skin thing [is] so crazy; I never understood it. It has affected my self-esteem a lot of times. My being dark-skinned has made me think I'm not pretty or that I have to do things for guys to like me, or for people to like me . . . People, especially men, have told me, 'You're pretty for a dark-skinned lady.' "

Most of the women speak passionately about the continued existence of the sexual double standard and the irony of sexism in the black community, a community that knows intimately the cruelty of double standards. Almost all the women believe that men, including black men, have much greater sexual freedom and that their sexual behavior is under far less scrutiny. Men's abundant sexual experience is considered necessary while similar kinds of experience in women is frequently stigmatized. Thirty-year-old Audrey laments, "If guys knew how many men I slept with, they would think less of me. They'd say, 'Oh, you're kind of slutty, huh?' But in reverse, it wouldn't be like that." Some also reflected angrily on the sexually exploitative ways that black women are frequently represented by black men in popular music, especially in rap music. As twenty-two-year-old Sarita says, "Why is it that you can represent me like that? Why are you representing me like that to the world? It really pisses me off, because I feel like, 'Damn, I birth you, I raise you, and I break my back to feed you all your life'—which I am sure every single one of these rappers' mothers did—'and then this is the thanks I get?' I have a lot of anger about it; it directly affects the way black men treat black women because we're seen as objects, commodities."

On the highly charged question of dating outside the race, the women were divided but all had formed opinions about it. Some felt that race didn't matter and that finding a man or woman who would treat them right was paramount. Other women who identified themselves as heterosexual felt that black men, warts and all, were far better able to understand them as black women than men of any other racial background, especially given how much race still matters. Those who had been sexually intimate with men or women of other races frequently expressed concern about having been desired as exotic. Some women felt that the larger society's celebration of white women's beauty was alienating and hurtful, while others said they didn't notice or care about this exclusionary standard.

A clear and impassioned longing for fairness, more sexual freedom, an end to mistreatment (in the form of lying, betrayal, cheating, and abuse), and indirect calls for full recognition ran though virtually every story. These concerns—ones that are surely important to women across the racial spectrum—have important racial dimensions for black women. Within the history of slavery, Jim Crow, and especially post–Civil Rights retreats from racial justice, are instances of profound societal betrayal, deceit, and abuse. It would be a mistake to imagine that black women's longing for intimate fairness and honesty is not impacted by these larger social desires for racial social justice; each magnifies the other. Hearing so many women ask clearly and directly for honesty and justice within their relationships was a bittersweet experience. I was empowered to hear such lucid and heartfelt expression but also knew that making these requests public, without anonymity, would put these women at enormous risk within and beyond black communities.

Despite black and white feminist efforts to give women more knowledge about their own sexuality over the past thirty years, many silences seem to remain. Most of the women with whom I spoke learned about sex and menstruation from peers, siblings, feminine-product and contraceptive pamphlets, and popular culture. Very few ever spoke with their own mothers about it, and none with their fathers. The few conversations about sex between mothers and daughters addressed the risks of sex and included various forms of putting the fear of God into them. Daughters' coming of age was defined mostly by stories of adult fear and containment. In keeping with this spirit, no one seemed to recall learning about female orgasms as part of her sexual development. Many women had sex for years before having an orgasm or even knowing what it was. As thirty-eight-year-old Luciana reflects, "I was thirty-one or thirty-two and I already had my kids when I had my first orgasm . . . I was like, Damn, all this time I've been missing this. Then I had this rewind of the tape in my head, Why haven't I been having this before?"

Sexual and physical abuse were more common than I expected. A few women told stories of extended and harrowing forms of childhood sexual abuse. Most of the women, however, recalled relatively isolated but nonetheless traumatic incidents of sexual abuse. There was also a good deal of physical violence at the hands of men. Perhaps women with these experiences were more likely to want to participate in this project. Still, it seems to me we need to take seriously the possibility that this is not the reason, and that abuses faced by black women is a highly underreported crisis.

We are all influenced by the prevailing ways of thinking about the world and our lives. In keeping with this, none of these stories present a unified, seamless, consistent perspective. The women draw on several kinds of seemingly incompatible social languages here: religious languages, therapeutic self-help languages, pro– and anti–black men, pro- and antifeminist ideas, and patriarchal fantasies. Linda Rae, for example, speaks about her recovery from drug addiction in self-help language, but also attributes her success to God. It is interesting to find both highly religious and self-help language intertwined within the same paragraph, the same sentence even, since the one depends on placing one's ultimate faith in oneself, the other, in a higher power. Similarly, ideas about women's sexual purity that are associated with their religious upbringing are radically challenged by some women, even while they maintain reliance on other aspects of Christianity as sources of strength and connection with other women. Several women are outraged at the way they feel they have been treated by black men—enough to say they are through with them—and yet also express poignant recognition of the common plights both black men and black women face. Hearing these multiple sources of belief, points of view, and approaches to life from black women from such diverse backgrounds works to undermine the limiting stereotypical and one-dimensional visions of black women that circulate in the public realm. In these stories, we are able to see how women's sexual lives, and their lives in general, are both despairing and victorious at the same time. These are not cozy tales of triumph with easy answers, nor tales of absolute hopelessness. The ways these women talk and reflect fundamentally challenge the easy categorization and segregation of experiences and people. The stories gathered here call out for a more complex understanding of sexuality, intimacy, and its place in our lives.

What can be culled from so many themes and wide-ranging experiences? As I reflected on these stories alone and with a group of women friends, I began to notice that through all of these experiences, most women expressed a sense of how to think about their lives, past, present, and future. They took what they had experienced and fashioned a prism through which they view their sexual lives. Three central dispositions emerged. The first one, which I have called "Through the Fire," emphasizes the difficult, unpredictable, and ongoing process of negotiating sexuality. "Guarded Heart" expresses a heightened need to remain self-protective in the face of a given challenge. Finally, "*Always* Something Left to Love" is meant to capture the sense of possibility that always remains, despite—or perhaps because of—the pains that have been endured. It is about a marked hopeful commitment to loving and being loved, no matter what has gone before. Each of the women has been through the fire and each has a guarded heart, at least to some degree, and each maintains a sense of possibility; where I have placed the women's stories is more about emphasis than absolute difference.

Almost all the women with whom I spoke believed that by allowing their stories to be read by a wide audience, they were making an important contribution to the underdocumented story of black women's sexuality in America. While their motives were various, most explicitly stated that they wanted to help bring this book to fruition because they themselves had longed many times to read such a book. Twenty-six-year-old Rita said, "There is virtually nothing out there as far as black women talking and dealing with the issue of sexuality. And reading *Essence* isn't enough. I thought it would be nice to read something about what it means to be a black woman in this country and all the different dynamics that go along with it. Even though I love fiction, I wanted stories about everyday real women and to have a chance to be a part of it." I hope the stories gathered here will meet this need, and inspire dialogue. Perhaps the collection will also serve as an archive, one that inspires more collections and helps us develop new and more productive ways of thinking about how black women's sexual lives are lived.

The process of collecting each story and then reflecting on the stories as a whole created myriad and conflicting emotions in me. First and foremost I remain honored that these women, none of whom knew me personally, trusted me to bring their intimate lives into print. Thank you, to all of you, especially those whose stories could not be included here. Your courage is abundant and inspirational. Your stories also created tidal waves of emotion in me. Tales about violence and abuse stunned, paralyzed, and enraged me all at the same time. Less vividly horrible stories about the effects of silence, fear, and confusion were overwhelming in a different way. At times, too, I was fearful about sharing these stories. Despite my efforts at camouflage, would some women somehow be identified and would it injure them? The fact that such risk is associated with women's openness about their sexual lives is a disgrace, one that should no longer be accepted.

Some days—many days, really—the collective weight of these accounts made them impossible for me to pick up. Perhaps, I frequently wondered, this is why there are so few published collections of this kind. But always, eventually, I returned. I revisited the stories for reasons as confusing and emotionally complicated as the subject itself. Sometimes I was motivated by my commitment to gather and think through these narratives and my recollection of the women who shared them with me. I did not want to let them down. I often felt this inchoate tug toward silence and had to will myself to remember that my silence, now, in the face of so often ignored injustice and suffering, would be unconscionable.

Other times, I returned, in part, looking for "the" answer to this very troubled terrain of sexuality. At various moments, all of us find ourselves caught up in variations of distinctly American cultural myths about "overcoming the odds," about looking for an unmitigated victory. Fairy tales about women, love, and romance almost always revolve around rescue and an imaginary future with a perfect love where loss, pain, and scarring cannot follow. Black women are similarly influenced by these powerful stories. A small part of me wanted to find a perfect future, one that some might call a more feminist imaginary future, one that held the answer that would open up spaces of sexual freedom and affirmation for black women, and perhaps all women. Nevertheless, these stories show that there is no right choice, no having it all, no getting through this world unscathed.

Even more difficult was my remembering that these very longings, no matter how distant, have an uncanny ability to obscure the heart of women's courage. Once we let go of these pernicious fairy tales, strategies for developing intimate justice reveal themselves not only in victories and exhilarating discoveries but even more so in heartfelt reflections on loss, inequality, and disappointment, in women's ingenious strategies for making it work. Cocoa, reflecting on her own process, captures this when she says, "You just have to constantly work through it. It's not like all of a sudden you just unpack it all and you recognize it . . . You just keep working through it." Indeed. Good, bad, and in between—these stories have in each of them fine but strong threads of courage and possibility, often where you might least expect it.

# one | THROUGH THE FIRE

*A*T FIRST GLANCE, it could be difficult to see what Sarita, a twenty-two-year-old ex-Muslim biracial woman, has in common with Linda Rae, a forty-eight-year-old woman with AIDS whose life has been significantly shaped by sexual abuse, drug addiction, and prostitution. But if we look closely at the emotional currents that drive them, a theme emerges: while vastly different, these women share a sense that victory lies in how they grow from the pain involved in coming into one's own. They carry their desires and hopes through and beyond difficult, sometimes traumatic, experiences, sexual self-doubt, trauma, and confusion. Inspiration emerges from how they struggle through the fires, not from imagining a world in which there is no flame.

Sarita tries to negotiate her intense love of black men and her profound disappointment over how many black men treat black women: "Why should I love you?" she says. "Men have hurt me as a black woman for so long, so why should I put down my anger? Why do I always have to sacrifice for you? So *you* can feel loved?" Later she says, "Black men are so full of love and life. They really are amazing people and they go through so much and it's hard to cut them out." Rita painfully questions her desire for white men over black and their seeming lack of interest in her: "I used to think, Why am I so ugly, why don't they like me, what is wrong with me that I always seem to like white guys, or those were the guys that I seemed to pursue?"

Linda Rae has struggled through a lifetime of catastrophic violence, sexual abuse, drug addition, and prostitution that resulted in her contracting HIV/AIDS. Reflecting on the notions of sex and womanhood that shaped her life she says, "You know, sex was a thing for me to do to make you love me. And nothing else in life was important to me but to have somebody to love me. . . . I didn't even have a clue of what it was to be a woman. And having no idea how, no sexuality of my own, I always took on 'the man's the leader of my life' to show me how I was supposed to act." Now a fierce activist, Linda Rae deals with that history by sharing it with others, educating young women about sexual agency, and encouraging the black community to fight AIDS.

Comic moments, sometimes even more than the sorrowful ones, illuminate and affirm the truth of life's bittersweetness. After years of unfulfilling sex, thirty-eight-year-old Luciana finally has a handle on her desires but can't yet find a partner: "I'm peaking, and"—*bam*, she smacks the table—"somebody needs to do something here! This should be illegal sometimes, the way I'm walking around here."

There are no hollow reassurances, no unblemished success stories here. There is no "Ah ha" moment after which all conflicts are resolved, all lessons are fully learned, and pain is finally conquered. Instead, these reflections offer a more complex sense of how some women navigate life while remaining committed to the possibility of deep connections with others.

# Sarita

*E*VER SINCE I was born, my life has been one big drama. I feel lucky in a way just because I've dealt with so much in the short span of time that I have lived on this earth; and when I think that I have twenty more years to go, I think, what could possibly come? Do you know what I'm saying? Okay, I am twenty-two years old. When I was growing up, we were living in a really good neighborhood in Providence, Rhode Island. Everybody played together. People on the outside would have called it a ghetto, but I never felt poor. We were on food stamps and all that, but I never felt any different than anyone else, because everyone else was poor, too. My father was a black man. He died when I was three. He was a heroin and cocaine addict. My mother is a white woman. She came from a rich family in New England. My grandmother did our family tree and we are related to two presidents, John Adams and John Quincy Adams. My mother's family lives in a rich white suburb and she grew up there. She never even met a black person until she was thirteen. All of her maids were Irish Catholic. Her *maids* weren't even black. So, she met my father and it was like jungle fever at first. He was a jazz musician. He played the piano. And back then, for a black man to have a white woman—a lot of them thought that was a big deal. So they met and then they really fell in love.

My father was Muslim and he already had one wife. And in the Muslim religion you can have as many wives as you want as long as you can support them all. So-called support! So my mother married my father, converted to Islam, and moved to the, quote, ghetto. Her family disowned her, and that's where I come in. He already had a few kids with his other wife. Then my mom had me and my older sister with him, and then he took on another wife, a third wife, Khadijah. So there was Fatima, and my mother, who changed her name to Nadia, and Khadijah. Then he had kids with Khadijah. We all lived in this big old rundown Victorian house. . . . Khadijah lived on the first floor, my mother lived on the second floor, and Fatima lived on the third floor, and my father would spend time on each floor. And meanwhile, he was supporting his habit of cocaine and heroin by selling marijuana and doing whatever illegal things he could get into. My father convinced the three wives to go and rob a bank for him. He didn't even go. It was just crazy!

They robbed the bank and got caught. My mother was driving the getaway car, so she took off. Khadijah got caught, and she went to prison. So my mother ended up taking care of her kids. Then my father died; the doctor had told him, "If you don't stop doing drugs, your heart is going to give in." He couldn't stop. He died in his sleep. The third wife was still there, but she had a drug problem also. My mother didn't have a drug problem. She smoked marijuana all the time, but in relation to the others, it wasn't as bad. So she had to take care of all of these kids. And we were on welfare, but still we were really poor. She didn't know what to do. So she married this guy, Hamid. Evil man. Evil, evil man. He was part of the Muslim community too. He was also a jazz musician, but see, my dad was like the leader of a group of Muslims, and they all looked up to him. They thought he was the spiritual leader. He was really tall, golden brown, and he had a big beard and thin and long, long fingers for playing the piano. That's all that I remember. He was one of those people that, when he walked into a room, had some magic quality to him. Even though he was doing all this messed-up shit, he was just such a lovely person that you couldn't help but love him. That's what everyone says. But this other guy that my mother married wasn't like that. He was a jealous type of person. But she married him because he offered to marry her and in her mind she had no other choice.

That was the next phase in my life: living with him, under his rules, in his house. With my father it was a free-for-all. We could do whatever we wanted. It was like one big playground. We just all had the best time. At that point there were ten kids with only three adults. They were high most of the time. So we did whatever we wanted. And then with Hamid, he had a drug problem too, but he dealt with it in a different way. He was more controlling, and dominating. And there were very strict little rules for every little thing, like when we were eating you had to clean your plate; you had to lick all the food off your plate, and if you didn't eat it all, he would spank you. And you know, when you're a kid, if you don't like asparagus, you do not like asparagus! You're not going to eat it! So I would take my food and ball it up in a napkin and put it behind my chair and hide it under the radiator. One time my mother found all this food under the radiator; and he saw it, and he knew it was me, and he gave me the whupping of my life for it. Peeled my ass.

My mother left him and the religion when I was eight. She just couldn't take it anymore. By that time, Khadijah had gotten out of jail, and Khadijah married Hamid also because she's always had a jealous thing with my mother, where she's had to have everything my mother had. So she married my mom's husband, twice. And my mother's like, "I'm out of here! You take your kids. I can't do this anymore." So she took me, my little sister Latifah, and my mother also had a white baby from a previous relationship, and her new baby, Ahmad, from her second husband, and we left. And we moved to my grandmother's house.

Now this house was *huge*. To me, it seemed like a mansion. My grandmother had all this land surrounding it in a place called Something Estates—this rich, rich place—and there was a pond and swings. It seemed like heaven to me. But we had been ripped out of the old neighborhood—I can't even explain what it was like—it was like a little womb. In the new place, we didn't know anyone, since we hadn't had any friends that weren't

Muslim. There was a Puerto Rican family we used to play with but they never came in our house. In the old neighborhood we went to Muslim schools. So we were ripped from that and from all my sisters and brothers. There was no differentiation, like "You're her mother, and you're his mother and he's your son." We were all of the same thing. If my mother was busy, there were two other mothers that I could go to. That's just the way I grew up, so to be ripped away from that and put in this white world was really traumatic for me. There were no black people whatsoever. And my grandmother was a completely different type of person, and that was really, really hard for us. Also, we went through a lot of trauma because all the people in the Muslim community shunned us after we left. I remember one time, my mother and I went downtown to go take care of some business, and we saw a part of my family on the street; and their mothers said, "Don't look at them." They had to keep walking, they wouldn't look at us, and they wouldn't even say hello.

The religion completely shaped me as a child. First of all, your gender role: when we were little, come free time, especially when we were living with the second husband, Hamid, the boys could go out and play. But the girls weren't allowed to go outside and play; we would have to stay and have classes on sewing and cooking. Then we could finally go out for a little while. And even then, we had to cover all of our hair, and we had to cover down—the only thing that can be showing is your hands and your feet and your face, when you're a little girl. So that made me feel like I had to be always covered up—and it really affects the way you feel. You don't feel very free, and you feel very dominated, or colonized, by these men who decide everything for you. And to be a good woman is to be really submissive and do everything they say, and to do things even before they ask. For instance, you notice that his cup is getting down and you refill it, just like a waitress or servant.

I looked up to the women. They were what a good woman was. The women wore a burkah, which is the thing that covers all of your face, except your eyes. Those women were considered the most feminine and beautiful and the thing to look up to the most. Not all women wore a burkah; they didn't have the discipline. Imagine in the summertime? You're

not going to put that on. You have all this clothing, plus something cover-
ing your face? You can't even breathe? You're going to be like, "Fuck it. I'm
not doing it." So the women who had the discipline were considered so
high up. If you could wear a burkah and exist that way, you were considered
the end-all be-all. I remember we looked up to those women so much.

My mother would make our clothes for us, and we would go to the
store and pick out the fabric; we enjoyed it. It's ironic that we enjoyed our
own prison in a way. We would pick out pretty fabrics for our headpieces
and make sure they matched our pants. I never thought anything was
wrong with it until I moved out of there. We would see the television, and
a naked woman in a bikini would come on in a beer commercial, and my
father would say, "That's the devil; you see that? That's what the devil puts
out for you to see." That's how I was raised. The woman's body is associated with bad things. You're supposed to cover it. They're telling you that
in order to respect yourself, you have to be fully covered, and if you're not
fully covered, then you're bad and you're going the way of the devil. And
the opposite culture seemed to be saying, "You're only beautiful if you take
your clothes off." There's no good choice! I'm fully covered now, pretty
much, and I feel fine about myself, but I also feel fine about myself when I
go to the beach and wear a bikini!

I met a lot of people, especially women, who really helped me out.
When I moved to my grandmother's area, some parts were really, really
white, but the part we lived in was closer to the city. Her town is really in
the middle of the city, but it's a town to itself that the white people took
and said, "We're going to make a town and create our own school system
apart from the city." But it's surrounded by the city. So there's a lot of different types of people around that area, and one person I met was my best
friend, Jardah. She was from Brazil, and she moved to this town in seventh
grade. Her mother was a black woman who grew up in the South in the
sixties. When everybody was going through all that stuff, she went down to
Brazil. She didn't speak a word of Portuguese, and she fell in love with Jardah's father and he fell in love with her. He didn't speak a word of English.
They fell in love and had Jardah. Then her mom learned how to speak Portuguese and they realized they weren't meant to be together. [*Laughs.*]

They lived there all that time, and then they came back up here. In Brazil, you're supposed to show off a woman's body. You go on the beach and you're supposed to wear a topless G-string bikini. People love to look at a woman's body. So she was raised in the exact opposite way from me, and she became my best friend.

I was a freshman in high school when we met. By that time, I'd lived long enough outside of the Muslim community to fully assimilate the way people dressed and the way people acted about their bodies. But still, inside I didn't feel pretty, I didn't feel attractive at all. I felt that I was just passing, just okay because of the way I dressed. But when I met her—she's an amazing person—she showed me that it's okay to love your body. She is really skinny on top, and she has this huge ass, and we used to always tease her, and she used to tease me because my ass was flat. We grew up and learned about puberty together, learned about boys. I knew her the first time I had sex, and she knew me her first time, so we explained the world to each other. She explained to me that the woman's body is whatever you want it to be. It can be like a playground, you can have fun with it, or you can disguise it.

She told me that she feels that I'm a very sensual person. I never really saw myself that way, but I think now she was right. What she meant was that I'm very open to men—'cause she's very closed up to men. That has to do with how her and her father acted toward each other. Her boyfriends would say, "You know, I've gotten to this point, but then there's this wall I can't get past." And she would say, "I don't know what's wrong with me. I don't know how to let them in." I was the opposite, because I craved attention and love from men, so I would be wide open. I had this ability to love that is special and that I think I was born with. So I think that I taught her that it's okay to love, in terms of men. It's okay to open yourself, because giving love is not something that can ever hurt you. It's only something that can help you. It's like a well; it's never-ending.

Once we hooked up, this became the most special relationship I have ever had in my life, and she is still right here with me now. We just became like two sisters. She is one of the only people in the world that I've completely, fully trusted. I looked at her, and she has no ill will for me whatsoever or me for her. Anything she tells me for my own good, I listen to her 'cause I know that she has only my best interests in mind and vice versa. We formed this bond when I met her in high school, and we were just so confident with each other that boys were our playthings. We had no need for them, really, because we had each other, and she gave me everything I needed; I gave her everything she needed 'cause we weren't really into sex yet. I didn't even know what it was about.

I had first kisses, and I had little sexual escapades with boys, but it was never because I really felt the urge. It was just to say, for example, "I went to second base." She was the same way. Plus we were beautiful. She's unbelievably beautiful, and she's cunning and brilliant. But then when you get to know her inside, her outside is almost ugly compared to what she's like on the inside. We just hung so tight, and the boys followed us around 'cause they wanted to be near us. But we had no need for them, so we would play with them, like little toys. We would go to parties outside of our high school where older people were and people that didn't know us, because we loved adventure and mischief. We would be walking down a street in the city and would see a party up in someone's apartment, and we would just go in and pretend that we knew everybody, and make jokes and laugh around, like, "Oh, you know so-and-so?" And then steal a bottle of their wine and run out and just be crazy. So we would go to these parties and we would think up plans to manipulate people. She would be like, "Okay, see that guy in the corner? I'm going to go over to him and tell him that I think he's really cute, and then you go over and say the same thing, and we'll play off of him." We would play mind games on people! We were cruel to some people, but it was just a way to entertain ourselves.

Our relationship was sisterly. I've had friends since then, where it went over into the sexual realm; but with her, it's always been just sisterly. She filled a place for me that needed filling. And she is an only child, but I grew up with all these sisters and brothers. She's never really had that camaraderie with another person her own age so I filled that place for her.

But for the sexual thing, when I got a serious boyfriend, and she got a serious boyfriend, we started spending more time with them. We would still tell each other everything about the sexual things we did with them, but we spent more time apart. And then when it came up about having sex for the first time, it was because my boyfriend asked me, "Do you want to have sex?" We had been dating, I think four or five months, and I didn't know what I wanted to do. So I went to her and said, "What should I do?" because I was confused. In high school that's such a big topic: Have you or haven't you? It was such an issue that all the girls in high school were defined by that standard. I must have been seventeen. Jardah and I were walking home from school, and I was saying, "I don't know what I should do because if I give it up to him, then he'll have had it, and he might not want to be with me anymore." And she practically yelled at me. "Listen to what you're saying! Give it up to him? Give what up to him? You're you—you're a person. Just because you have sex, you're not giving him anything. You're sharing an experience with him, and if he disses you afterward, that's his fault, but that has nothing to do with you as a person. That's because he couldn't hang." I had never thought of that before. She was very confident. I didn't really have that self-esteem; I think it had a lot to do with the religion I was raised in, to feel that I needed men. And she never felt that need.

At this point I had never had an orgasm, whether through oral sex or anything like that. I'd gone down on him, he'd gone down on me, you know. So to me, there was no desire in it until I had an orgasm—and then I was like, wow! This is really pleasureful. And then I had the desire to do it again. Before I thought, This is interesting, but, you know, it doesn't really feel that good. So I wasn't about to go have sex when I knew I could get pregnant. There was no reward in my mind because I never had an orgasm. I thought I had one with him, until I had a real one with someone else! [*Laughs.*] So anyway, I did have sex with him, and he was really in love with me. That took out the whole fear that he was going to leave. I wasn't all excited and into it; I was like, "Let's just go ahead and do it." And my mother came and knocked on the door, and she called me, "Sarita?" I was like, "Shit, shit." We had to hide under the bed. Which we did because *he* was afraid, because I guess that's a real fear for men, to be caught by the parents of the girl. I yelled out, "Mom, don't come in," and she took the hint. My mother is not one to pry. She really just lets us do our own thing.

When I was little I used to take it that she didn't care about me. I really thought she didn't care about me because I never had a curfew. I never had to call her and tell her where I was going or who I was going to be with. The first time I smoked pot, it was with my mother. A lot of bad things that you supposedly hide from your parents, I did with my mother. So, for her to catch me having sex wasn't even really a big deal.

She didn't tell me anything about sex. We used a condom, and that's because he said, "Let's use a condom," 'cause he'd had sex plenty of times before. Afterward, I called Jardah and said, "Guess what? I did it!" She said, "You bitch! You did it before me!" And then she told all of our other friends; and they called me, and they were singing songs to me on the phone. I didn't feel bad at all, and I didn't feel that different, either. It didn't hurt. It was a little uncomfortable because it was this new thing I never felt before, but it didn't hurt. The only thing I wished was that it had been with someone else. The summer before, I had fallen in love with someone for the first time, and he wanted to be my first, but I told him no. And then I was with this other guy that I didn't even really love. He loved me. And I told him yes, but I regretted that.

I went through a really promiscuous period. During my first few years of college, something was coming to a head in me, and I just acted it out in sexual terms. I was having a lot of family problems. I moved out of the house when I was still in high school, and I think I was craving love and affection. And I was getting it through sex. It wasn't that I was being taken advantage of; I was a full participant. But in the sense that I had a deeper need than they did, I was being taken advantage of. But I didn't feel that way at the time. And I wasn't classified as a slut or anything because I only did it with select people, and the "sluts" did it with anyone. For me, it wasn't always tied to relationships. They would want a relationship afterward. But I didn't really have a need for them. Everyday interaction can be quite annoying when you have to deal with problems with someone and the compromises. . . . I wasn't into that. I just wanted to be affirmed by the process. I wanted to have the initial fun part, like they're chasing me, and they're paying all this really nice attention to me, telling me I'm pretty, and all of that, until the sexual act, and then I would just lose interest. I would move along to the next person. That's why I know it was about something else.

I never got pregnant. I really thank my lucky stars because looking back on it, I didn't have unsafe sex a lot, but still, it doesn't really matter, you know? I heard about so many people who were pregnant, and so many people who had already gotten an abortion. In my family and in my friends at school. That to me seemed so scary. And there were two students in my high school that had AIDS. My high school was a very, very sexually liberated type of place. People were having sex a lot.

I stayed with the guy I first slept with for eight months, but I hated five of the months. He would say, "Oh, please, stay with me." I didn't want to be with him, but he was totally enthralled. I got a lot of attention, plus he bought me things. [*Laughs.*] It was on that level. Now I'm so different with the way I view men and relationships. But, at that time, I was like, "Well, shoot, what is he doing for me? He's buying me new clothes, he takes me out, he has a car, so I guess I can put up with him." So I stayed with him until I thought, This isn't worth it. I'm just sick of you.

I recently tried to count how many guys I had sex with, but I got so depressed that I stopped counting. But it was around twenty different people in my whole sexual time from then until my current boyfriend, which is five years. That was really a lot of people. I'm so lucky. I've been tested for AIDS three times, and I don't have AIDS and I've never been pregnant. There were shallow relationships, where I knew it wouldn't go past a certain point and it was because of who they were as a person, or who I was. I didn't really want to be with anybody.

The point that marked the end of that period was when I had an experience—I wouldn't call it date rape, but I would call it rape by mental force. I was completely manipulated and made to have sex through my own mental shortcomings—by a person that I trusted. When that happened, the promiscuous period stopped. He was fifty years old. I was a dancer all my life, and at the end of high school and the beginning of college, I started doing African dance. I was really loving it because I loved ballet all my life, but I had always felt somewhat out of place. In African dance I felt so at home, and I loved it. It was a place I could go and get all of my tension out and just really be myself—and also be proud of my body, 'cause ballet teaches you, again, to be ashamed of your body. In African dance, many women had big hips, big breasts, and they would dance with their babies on their hips, and it was just a woman's thing. And the guy who did this to me was one of the drummers. The drummers in African dance, you look up to them; and you dance for them and they play for you, and it's a symbiotic relationship. I was going to take drumming lessons with him. I think this is how he got to me. He'd always watched me, and then he offered to teach me drumming so I could learn the patterns of the drums and I could do it with my feet too. So he took me to learn how to do it, and that's the night that it happened.

That was the first time I'd been played like that. Never before. I was always the player. I wanted to kill myself. The next few days, I would be at the subway, looking at the train and having to hold myself from jumping in front of the train because I felt so disgusting and dirty. That's how I know it was sort of a rape experience, because I'd never felt that way after sex before. You know what I'm saying? When I got home that night, I went in the shower and scrubbed my body, because he put this oil on me that smelled. It was fragrant oil, and the smell was all over me, and I could not take it. I tried to go to sleep but couldn't. I got up and I scrubbed my whole body to get the smell off me. I felt disgusting. He called the next day and said, "I hope you're okay, because nothing happened last night, right? Nothing happened." He was trying to make me believe nothing happened? He was really trying to mess with my mind. So that made me realize, he knows he did something wrong, or else he wouldn't be calling up saying this.

He took me to his house, and he was feeding me wine, and—he just— it was like, I mean, I still have a lot of shame about it because deep down I feel like I played along with it. But now I realize I was so needy for love and affection because I wasn't getting it at home. My home situation was hell. It was the first year of college, when I came back that summer. I hadn't lived at home for two years of high school, and this was the first time I was going to try to live at home again. There was a situation going on at my house that was awful, and I was escaping into dance. I would go every day, spend hours at the dance studio, and then come home and go in my room and read and stay away from everybody. Now, in retrospect, I know I was really depressed; I wasn't eating and I was getting really skinny. He took major advantage of me. He didn't use a condom and he'd been a drug user before. I just took my mind away into another place. I thought, Fine, I'm not going to get out of this situation. I've had sex plenty of times before, let me just let him have sex with me. It's just so ironic 'cause on the one hand, I spent all that time manipulating men, but on a deeper level, I never felt, when it really came down to it, that I could stand up to a man, and really force my own strength over his. I think because as a child I was undermined by my stepfather so much, and he was really physically abusive to me. And so I think that really gave me a fear of men.

I never went back to that dance studio. Never went back. And I haven't danced since then. I want to dance, but, I just cut it out of myself and threw it out. I found a new way to express myself. Afterward, I had a really rough time, and I had to go into the hospital because I was suicidal, and then everything came crashing down with my family. When I came back from college, my sister from Khadijah was staying with us. She had a baby when she was fifteen. And she hadn't a place to stay, so she came to stay with my mother. My older sister was staying there with her boyfriend, who was a complete fuckup and asshole person. He raped my younger sister and told my older sister that she seduced him and everyone in my family believed him. They didn't even ask my younger sister. My mother believed him. I came back from college before the thing with the older guy happened, so that was the situation at home. And I was the only person saying, "Wait a minute. This is crazy."

I sat down with her one day and said, "Okay. What happened?" And she told me the whole story, and I said, "He raped you." And she was just a mess. She was just crying. His story was that he was drunk, that she snuck into his bed, which is unbelievable. I mean, just not true. And I went to my mother and I said, "Look, this is the situation. She didn't seduce him. That's ridiculous." My mother was in complete denial. My older sister was insane. Every time she went into the room where the younger sister was, she was like, "You bitch, you filthy slut." They couldn't even be in the same room together. And then that other thing happened to me. I was spending as much time away from my house as possible.

I just broke down. I broke down. And I went into the hospital, stayed there for a while. I got back on my feet. But I wasn't eating. I didn't eat or drink anything for ten days. I lost so much weight, I was like a skeleton. I had no will to live. I was so depressed. And Jardah was in Brazil, and all my other friends—when you feel that low, you don't think that anyone understands you, you know? So then I went back to college and did a lot of thinking and lot of growing and I came back because I realized I wanted to do film.

I lived at this lady's house and worked and saved money and left town. I've been back a few weekends here and there, but I'm a really alone person. When I went to the hospital, things with my mother and me got so much better—I came to understand why she put us through all of that as a child. She grew up with a father who was an alcoholic, and he was terribly abusive to them. It made her feel just awful about herself, so she had to get out of that situation. And then she went to a similar situation. That's just what people do. Because they were rich and white, his abuse was different from the way I experienced it, but it created the same sort of effects.

There were two women who I had sexual relationships with. And one is a really funny story. [*Laughs.*] I had a friend named Anna in high school. She was white and she was the sweetest girl. She was one of those kids who grew up in a white liberal household, and her parents were the most well-meaning people you could ever meet. They were so ashamed of what their race does to people and they have spent so much time in their life trying to do the opposite. And I really appreciate that; one thing I'm glad about being biracial is that I've gotten to know white people who really are cool. A lot of black people never meet white people, and they just see white as evil. But there are a lot of white people who are just human beings.

She was one of those people. We became really close friends. Plus, she was into hip-hop and the whole black scene, so we could hang. And one time we sort of . . . I don't even know how to explain it. We didn't really even kiss, but we were hugging each other and holding each other and caressing each other in a sexual way. It was definitely sexual, but we never kissed. The next day she was like, "That was weird." And I said, "Yeah, that was kind of weird. I think I was kind of experimenting." And she said, "Yeah, me too." That was basically all we said about it. Then later on she ended up having a lesbian relationship with someone. So we talked about it again, and she was saying, "I think what we had was a little different" because she was comparing it with her relationship and saying, "You know, this person really wants a relationship with me." But she was torn; she didn't know what to do. She didn't know if she wanted to be in a relationship, or if she was really just experimenting with this person.

Then last summer—this really did torment me a little bit, but now looking back I can laugh at the situation. I have this friend named Lucy, and Lucy is Miss Ghetto. She's very street and rough and tough. She's very smoothed-out looking, but she's rough in the way she deals with life. She's a singer, and this summer we became friends. We would go to clubs together with our group of girlfriends and have a really good time. She had a boyfriend named Sam. This past summer me and her and Sam went to a club. This was the first time I'd met Sam, and he comes and picks me up with her. First thing he says to me is, "Oooh, she's beautiful." Lucy was sitting in the front seat of the car, and he said it to her, not to me. And I was like, whatever. "Thanks." It was kind of strange. Anyway, we're in the club and we're dancing, and he's dancing with me, and he's starting to grind, and I'm feeling weird because that's her man. She was dancing with someone else, and I was looking at her and I was starting to get kind of stiff; and she came over to me and whispered in my ear, "You can be loose with him. I don't care, girl." She was saying, "Do your thing, do your thing." But I was thinking, "He's your boyfriend!" You know what I'm saying? To me, that's just not appropriate. Me and her went to the bathroom, and I said, "What is up with you and Sam?" She's like, "Well, we see other people, you know. We do what we want to do. He does what he has to do, I do what I got to do." They lived together at this point. So I just said, "All right, whatever." Then she says, "You know, he really likes you." And I said, "Oh, I really like him too. He's nice." 'Cause I took it on that level. But in retro-spect, she was saying, he really *likes* you.

So then we all go back to my house. And we're drinking, and smoking cigarettes, and smoking joints, and just chillin'. Where I was living then, my apartment faced out into another apartment building. We're on the roof, and we're looking down into windows, and I say, "One time I saw some guy masturbating in the window," and Sam said, "Oh, really?!" We went downstairs, and he brought it up again. He asked, "What would you do if I started masturbating in front of you?" and I was like, "What?" And he kept on, "I'm serious, what would you do?" I said, "I don't know." He was like, "What would you do if I took off my clothes right now?" And I said, "Tell you to leave." And he was like, "Ha, ha." So he stood up, started unbuttoning his pants, took off his shirt, pulled down his pants, pulled down his shorts—in front of me and Lucy. I'm looking at him, and I look at Lucy, and she's sitting there smiling—I'm still incredulous about it even today. I mean, just . . . just . . . this does not happen to me. I was saying, "What are you doing?" And he takes off his underwear and starts feeling on his penis!

I looked at Lucy, and she looked at me, and all she did was smile! And then I started to feel weird, and I was asking, "What are you two up to? What's going on here?" So he was like, "You don't want me?" Then he came over to me and kneeled down on the ground and put his hands on my legs and started rubbing them. And I was like, "What are you doing? Put your clothes back on." And he was like, "You don't want me to do this?" Like all sexy and soft. And I'm like, "No!" And Lucy said, "What's wrong? Are you scared?" I said "No." I felt like I was in kindergarten or something! And they're like, "You chicken."

Then Lucy was asking, "Well, what's wrong with you? I thought you wanted to." I was like, "What are you talking about?" This was completely beyond me. And she said, "Well, is it that Sam's here? Do you want to just do it with me and you?" And I was like, "No." I was like, "Lucy, I just met Sam. I would never sleep with anyone I just met." By this time I had changed, I felt good about myself, and I wouldn't just sleep with anyone.

And she came back, "Well, I feel like you're being a tease, you're being a flirt because you led us on." I was like, "I didn't lead you on. What are you talking about?" I started to feel really scared and nervous because I trusted her. I mean, I didn't *trust* her trust her, but to me, it was a double shock, because she was just so "ghetto." And most girls I know like that, if you even mention the word "lesbian," they'll be like, "Eehh, that's nasty!"

Anyway, they stayed until about five in the morning. I could not get them to leave because they kept trying. He finally put his clothes back on, and then we were just talking. I really wanted to find a conclusion to this because I knew if they left with it all weird like that, I wouldn't be able to deal with them the next day, and I really, really liked Lucy. I wanted to keep her as a friend. In hindsight, I don't know if it was the best idea, but I wanted to resolve things. I was saying, "Can we be friends after this? I don't feel any ill will toward you, you know. I don't feel that it's disgusting or whatever to be with a girl or to be with two people or whatever, but I'm just saying it's not right for me." They were like, "Yeah, I guess we can still be friends, but I just feel really embarrassed." So finally, we worked it out, and they went home. I'm still friends with Lucy. She's made jokes about it, like, "I'm not coming to your house." [*Laughs.*] She's just like that; she's a freak. She likes to do freaky stuff with people.

I would say there's three people in my life who I really have that intimacy with. Everybody else, our friendship only goes so far. They are my hanging partners; they're my girl at school, the girl I sit with at class, but I don't get intimate with people like that because that taught me a lesson last summer. Especially in the city, you can't just trust people like that; you can't just bring someone back to your house in the middle of the night and hang out if your roommates aren't there because you've only known her for two months. You don't know shit about her. And even though she's a black girl, she's a sister, she seems cool, you don't know shit about her. I have had to learn that for myself; and it's hard for me because I'm a very open person and I constantly have to hold myself back from telling people how much I like them, and opening up what I have to give to them. Intimacy is just a look; it's just a knowing thing. To me intimacy is when that person has your back no matter what. When you've reached that point where they know what you're about; they know the essence of you. Like with me and Jardah, she knows what's up with me. All she needs is one look in the face. And I'm getting to that place with Malcolm, but I don't think you can really be intimate with someone until they meet your family 'cause they don't know you fully until they know your family. That's how I feel about it. I haven't yet taken him to meet my family. I've wanted to, but I'm really sensitive about my family and it's really hard for me to bring someone to them. I guess I just haven't wanted to scare him away. He'll meet them soon enough.

I thought I had an intimate bond with my mother, but deep down inside I knew we didn't have it because I was going through all this turmoil and she would look at me and she wouldn't see it. She would look at me every day and wouldn't see shit. She would say, "Have a good day," and smoke her little weed. I told myself that she's my mother and on some deep level she feels what's in me. But then when that thing happened with my sister's boyfriend, and I begged her to get him out of the house and I begged her and begged her; and I said, "Look, you're going to lose me if you don't get him out of this house because I don't feel safe here. I don't feel safe in my own house because I am living with a rapist." I'm very dramatic, you know, but still that's what it was. Plus I'm my mother's daughter and I felt like it was my responsibility and not my half sister's. My mother said, "I can't choose over you two. I can't choose between you and him. I love him just as much as I love you." She said that to me. She loves my sister's boyfriend as much as she loves me? And that's when the intimacy broke. She chose him over me, basically. And I was like, I'm out! I just couldn't take it anymore.

Now I know that she was just in such bad denial that for her to confront him, she would have had to confront all the other men in her past who had hurt and abused her and abused people she loved and who she hadn't been able to stand up to. He was just another version of that. We went from her father to my father, to my stepfather to David. David was with my sister for eight years and he lived in our house for a long time, you know what I'm saying? He was a presence in our house. So, in hindsight I can see the whole cycle, but at that point I was just done with it.

I don't remember the first orgasm that well, to tell you the truth. I just know that it happened. I think I just realized I had as much power in the sexual situation as they did to achieve my goal, to fill my needs. Before I felt as though men loved and adored my body and they could get close to my body and touch it and do things to it that they wanted to do; and they could achieve something for themselves that they needed. I wasn't myself an active participant in getting something for me. I enjoyed being the source of desire for them; it was a turn-on for me. But not until the first time I had an orgasm did I really understand that now I could be on an equal level with men. It really changed my perception about sex. And I think that's why I started becoming so promiscuous. I hate that word "promiscuous," because it makes you sound like you're a bunny or something. I really like having sex and if I was a boy, no one would have said anything—they would have patted me on the back and said I was great. I am not ashamed of it; it's just that there's all the social norms that say you should be ashamed of it.

I am one of those women who can have orgasms in intercourse very easily. I've never had a problem with having an orgasm. I have a lot of friends who are not like that, who can't have orgasms during intercourse. But I've never had one during oral sex. That's not where I have it. So I'm very motivated to take the situation into my own hands and being the one to move the way I need to move and to set the pace that I need to set rather than having them do it. I'm just now coming to my own sense of sexuality. I'm reaching a place where I really define it for myself. It has a lot to do with my body image, loving my body for what it is. It really starts for me with my body, 'cause my body has been such a big deal in my life as a dancer—staring in the mirror for hours every day and making your body do these movements and trying to be in the space a certain way. And so things have always presented themselves in terms of my physicality. When I was upset and sad, I got really skinny and didn't eat and changed my body that way to make my mind feel better. Now I've gained all the weight back that I lost, plus a little bit, and I have a round belly, down where my womb is. And I used to never have a butt, and that's because I have a white mother. They used to call me Poster in high school because my butt was so flat you could hang a poster on it. But I'm starting to get a little butt, and I have thighs now. Sometimes I think I'm getting fat and then sometimes I think I like how my body feels. I like this roundness down here; it's really just comforting. I enjoy being able to eat with my boyfriend and stuffing ourselves and cooking with each other. I'm feeling more comfortable with myself naturally. I haven't worked out at all—I haven't danced at all—and this is just the way I am at rest, at peace, without forcing myself to do anything else.

I think it's translated into the sexual realm of feeling that whatever I need or is normal to me, is good. My boyfriend hasn't truly reached that. I find myself teaching him a lot and freeing him up a lot sexually. He's spent a lot of his time doing the same things to women that I did to men—just running away from the relationship and being on a shallow level of sex. So he's learning about his own sexuality at the same time as I'm learning about mine. For instance, right now we haven't had sex for two weeks. And it's fine 'cause I feel like when I'm ready to have sex again, I will. I just haven't wanted to have sex—I've been in a real mind space and real critical space about us. Sex really clouds things sometimes and you use sex to wash over problems, and I don't want to do that right now. And I feel okay about that. A lot of times I feel like, Oh, God, we haven't had sex for two weeks. Something must be wrong. But maybe that means something is afoot that we have to deal with. Just in terms of that, I feel like I'm more in control of my sexuality.

I have had sex mostly with black men, and a few white men. I have never slept with an Asian person. I've slept with Hispanic men. When I was younger the issue of color was more out in the open. I think it's masked now that I'm older. I'm very light-skinned and so I'm sought after a lot for that very reason. That never made me feel good; I always knew it was something fake. I think people try to mask the whole light skin/dark skin thing, but I see it more. I've always liked people to like me for me. I think I am beautiful, but I think it's a "me beauty"—it's not a light-skinned beauty. I've always been really sensitive about that. I always made sure the people I was with were really with me for me. I've never slept with someone who was with me just for looks. And I think I am really proud that I've always had a connection with the people that I've slept with, whether we were really good friends, or just had fun together, and we decided to take it to that level. But it's never been just a looks or lust type of thing.

I think more about race now because I am starting to realize that I'm going to be having children and settling down at some point and I don't want to have children with a white man. I don't want to settle down with a white man. When I was younger and I was just playing around it didn't matter. It's that I don't feel comfortable with a white man and I don't feel like I can be my true black woman self with a white man. I feel like I have to do so much explaining about myself. Me and Malcolm are so much more familiar. With someone who's black, it's just a level that you begin at that you don't begin at with a white person. You have to do some explaining about the race issues—where you're coming from—but most of the time it's really just there. I think they see me as a black woman but they also see me as a prize. It's like they have the best of both worlds. They have the black body and attitude that only black women have, which white women can never compare with. I'm not trying to say it in a negative way, but we are our own selves and there's no one on earth that is like a black woman.

But if you are dark, people don't want to look at you, they avert their eyes from you. When you're light people want to look at you because that means you have an extra something good about you. God has given you a gift that hasn't been given to the rest of our race. So I think, especially among white men, they get the best of both worlds, and I'm very aware of that. I don't blame them for wanting to be with black women because why wouldn't you want to be with us?

I like black men's bodies more because they are stronger and thicker and more reliable. A black man's body is more durable and the color is like security to me. Darkness to me is something that envelops you and wraps

you up and keeps you safe and warm, and the lightness makes me cringe
and makes me want to go away from it. My mother has really blue, blue
eyes and they have seemed cold to me all my life. Brown eyes seem so
much warmer to me. Malcolm is my complexion, so when I say "black
men," it doesn't necessarily have to be about skin tone; it's more about the
body shape and the way he carries himself.

A black man is under so much pressure. To be with a black man is almost like living life with a spy because he's constantly ducking things and
he's aware of this whole level of people that are out to get him that I'm not
aware of as a black woman. A lot of them think being a black man is more
oppressive than being a black woman. But it's not; I'm really strong against
that idea. A few days ago, I had this argument with my boyfriend. He was
saying black men are more oppressed than black women. And I was like,
"How can you say that?" And he said, "Well, we die more than you do,
don't we? We're the ones dying out on the streets." And I came back, "But
we're the ones suffering as a result of your death. So is your life more important than mine? You're dead, but I'm suffering a lot. So what does that
mean? That your life is more important than my life?" He says there is a
way he walks through life: when he sees police officers and different people, there's little bells ringing, little signals. I don't live that way; maybe
other black women live that way but I don't live that way. I don't have fear
of people. I really feel like it's just life. But we are constantly battling something and running to something with each other, and we have so many
goals to fulfill. Life with a black man is just so adventurous, I feel like a kid
all the time. We also just try to chill, trying to be together; and sometimes
we just can't get there. But when we do get there, our down time is so
good. I think I am also bringing him a lot of peace and security in his life
that he doesn't have on his own. I don't know what the future will bring.

It's kind of weird, but there is definitely the essence of both of my parents
in me. If someone asks me my race, I always say, "I'm black." My mother
said, "Now look, I'm white but you're black." I know some kids that grow
up biracial, their white mothers are like, "Oh, honey . . . you're mixed.
You're this and you're that." My mother was like, "Make no mistake, be-

cause you're black!" So I never thought I was white. You look at me and I'm black so I haven't really received the same benefits or bad things that come with being white. In fact, my mother never felt that white people had a real culture. She felt like white society was just all fake. I think that's partly why she went to the black culture.

I feel that being biracial has given me a chance to experience so much more than anyone who is of only one race. I can get access to places because my mother's white or because my father is black. I want to be a filmmaker so I'm very curious and I love watching people. It's just been a great way to watch people, to see all these different nooks and crannies in the world that I never would have gotten to see. Sometimes it makes me feel a little bit like I'm not really anywhere. I feel like more of an outsider among whites than I do among blacks because black people are more forgiving and encompassing. We have so many trips going on with us, it's like, "So what if your mother's white anyway?" I always felt more accepted among blacks. When you're black and you have some white look in you, you're still black; you haven't escaped us. But when you're white and you've got some black blood in you, you're black, so you're out of the game now.

Racial images are such powerful things. I realize that every image you see is created for a specific purpose. Every single image, down to the shadow on someone's face, is constructed by people who have motives; and that is mind-blowing to me. Seeing black women treated so disrespectfully in black film and music videos in particular really bothers me. It really affects the way girls see themselves and carry themselves in the world; and it dictates what femininity is for black women and to a lot of young girls. I see them acting out these patterns, especially among the hip-hop community, and it really makes me sick.

In this music video by the rapper Redman, he is on his rooftop, and down on the street there are scenes of prostitutes. They are black with blond wigs on, short shorts and halter tops and really slimy outfits. The camera is showing their asses and their breasts. They are propositioning men in cars and talking to police in very sexual ways; and the video really bothers me because usually in hip-hop videos, you represent who you hang out with. All their boys are up on the rooftop with them and they are rep-

resenting each other the way they are; but then when it comes to representing us, they represent us like hookers. But they don't hang out with
women who look like that; the women they hang out with look just like
them. They wear baggy jeans, big sweatshirts and whatever. They have
their hair and nails done, but they are just average everyday girls. The
groupies that hang around Redman may be sexual but they don't dress like
that. That's not what we look like; and when I go into any black neighborhood I don't see prostitutes. I don't see women dressed like that in any
black neighborhood I've been in, in my entire life.

I don't understand that. Why is it that you can represent me like that?
Why are you representing me like that to the world? It really pisses me off,
because I feel like, "Damn, I birth you, I raise you, and I break my back to
feed you all your life"—which I am sure every single one of these rappers'
mothers did—"and then this is the thanks I get?" I have a lot of anger
about it; it directly affects the way black men treat black women because
we're seen as objects, commodities. Like when I'm hanging around Malcolm's house, guys drop by all the time from around the way and just shoot
the shit and then leave. So they'll come in, completely ignore me, shake
Malcolm's hand, and sit down. If Malcolm doesn't introduce me, they can't
come to me as an individual and say hello. They have to do it through a
man because in their eyes, I'm his bitch—I'm his property. For instance, it
was hot in his apartment and one of them was like, "Malcolm, is it okay if
I take off my sweatshirt?" To him that's respecting Malcolm, but he could
have easily said, "Do you mind?" to me. But he can't communicate with me
as an individual, he has to communicate through another man.

It was the same thing when I was walking down the street and this guy
was disrespecting me. He was crawling on the ground in front of me pretending to lick my vagina—licking the air and being disgusting in front of
me. Malcolm was across the street and he came over and said, "Yo, man,
what are you doing?" And the other guy said, "She's with you, man, I'm
sorry, no disrespect," and gave Malcolm a pound and started to go on his
way. I was like, "What the fuck was that?" I said to Malcolm that I was not
pleased at the way he handled that. And he was like, "What did you want
me to do—get in a fight? He had six guys," because the only recourse in his

mind is to fight someone. I said, "No, but you could have said, 'Hey you shouldn't be apologizing to me. You should be apologizing to her,' " 'cause I'm the one he offended. I told him that I can't make that guy apologize to me because there are six guys there. I've seen girls get their asses kicked by guys who to tried to proposition them. The girls go, "Please, I don't have time for you," and the guy chases her down the block and kicks her ass. I've seen that happen and everybody knows it happens. I need my man to ask for me to get my respect. Do you know what I'm saying? It's not great, but at least it's better than him apologizing to Malcolm as if I was Malcolm's property. As if he spit on Malcolm's car and was like, "Oh, I'm sorry." That type of shit happens all the time and it affects the way black women deal with each other.

Another time we were sitting around in Malcolm's apartment and one of the guys came in with his girlfriend. Malcolm was out of the room, but his roommates were there; his roommates are very rude, and they don't care about anyone. So the guy came in, and he didn't get introduced to me. Nobody said anything. So I said, "Hi, I'm Sarita. Nice to meet you." But the girls, they couldn't say anything to me and I couldn't say anything to them because of the way things were. We were property of these men in this social setting, so we couldn't say hello to each other. We had to be introduced through our male owners. But my male owner wasn't there, so I did a breach of etiquette by even saying hello to this man; and then when my male owner came in the room, everything was okay again, but I still didn't get to meet the girls. So I'm sitting here trying to braid Malcolm's hair, and I'm making a mess of his braids, and I look over to a girl, and I see a way to try and talk to her. So I said, "You see what I'm doing, girls? I'm making a mess on his head, huh?" And she looked at the braid, and she started laughing. She said, "I don't know what you're trying to do," because I don't know how to cornrow, and I was experimenting. I was like, "Come and show me how to cornrow." She said, "I know how to cornrow," because her man has three kids, and she's tellin' me, "I have to do their hair every morning." So, she came over and started to show me how. That's how I made a little connection with her. And then we started talking. It's like we're not even respected enough to get introduced to each other. It's like,

"You all don't even matter. Just sit by us and let us have a conversation. Stand on the wayside." We're not individuals on the same level as you to get introduced to everybody the way you get introduced to everybody.

All these images of black women as objects of black men directly affect the way our social etiquette works. And it really fucking pisses me off. It makes me sick because then I have to take it upon myself to breach the social etiquette all the time if I want to be an individual in a situation. And if I want to join a conversation? I'm as smart as anybody else in that room, most times smarter. Why should I sit by the side when they're talking some bullshit they don't even know about when I could sit there and school all of them on stuff? Malcolm is fighting with this, and it's so hard because this is all he knows.

I think that whole being skinny image problem might be more true for white women—the whole body thing and self-esteem. But the black body aesthetic is more natural. It's more the way women are really meant to be, with big hips and big breasts and thighs. A lot of black women I know—even my friends that are big, that are size fourteen, size sixteen—still have no problem. They really don't torment themselves about it. They get just as many dates as I would get from black men. I wouldn't say that it really affects us that much. I think skin color does much more in that same regard, in terms of self-esteem. A lot of dark sisters that I know had problems with self-esteem growing up because the images of beauty for black women were all of light skinned-women with straighter hair. I think that's much more of an issue than body type.

I read *Waiting to Exhale* by Terry McMillan last year, before I even knew the movie was coming out. I didn't really like the book that much. It was like a beach book; you read it, and it's cool. If I could ever make a movie out of any novel, it would be Zora Neale Hurston's *Their Eyes Were Watching God*. I really would love to get the rights to that screenplay because that is just the bomb. That book is my favorite novel of all time. Anyway, I just felt like the story in *Exhale* is kind of shallow; at the same time that it addresses the issues of how black women need to be self-sufficient and not have to depend on men, it almost perpetuates the idea that our lives revolve around black men. I had a real problem with that fundamental motive of the film. The message was really unclear, because it was saying, "Don't do this," but it was also affirming the idea that you should be looking for a man—like, that's *the* goal in life. You don't have anything until you have a man. Whitney Houston's character was a career woman, and she had a beautiful house, a beautiful car, and she owned things. That's the goal in this capitalist society, right? If that was a man, he would have been a success. He would have had everything in the world. He's a bachelor; he doesn't have any ball and chain on his ass. But for a woman, that's the worst thing in the world, not having a man to share that with. Also, I felt like a lot of the moments between the women were cut off and premature or music was played underneath their dialogue. It made it trivial. It's like, "We are talking here. Hello? Can you cut the music off?"

I had an argument with my boyfriend the other day. He was saying, ("Black women are so angry at us. They are so angry. Why can't you just put down the anger and love us?" So I said, "Why should I love you? You've hurt me. Men have hurt me as a black woman for so long, so why should I put down my anger? Why do I always have to sacrifice for you? For *your* good. So *you* can feel loved. Why do I have to do that?" All these things were mind-blowing to him—he never thought of those things before. But I am really about liberating myself as a black woman.

We need black men, and at the same time we don't need black men. We need them and they need us to further our race, but we are always the ones ending up making the sacrifices and I'm starting to have a real problem with that. That's why I see black women as so complex because we fight racism just as strongly as black men do, but then we have to come home and fight black men and still hold on, you know. We take so much and we let so much slide because of what black men face in terms of racism. We hold down our own pain to hold on to all that we have. I think this is born out of fear that we don't have anything unless we have a black man. It's so much a part of me and when I look into a black woman's face, I see that in her. No matter where she is. Because if she doesn't act that way in her life, chances are her sister acts that way or her mother acts that way.

Or she has gotten over it and moved on from it. But that is at the core of us. And yes, it's unhealthy, but for a lot of us, that's the only thing we know. We just have to pray that the man is going to treat us good.

Listen to how we are talked about in our music. Even if that man treats black women so bad, we will still love him so much; and that's messed up because he, a lot of times, is not loving you back. That's the thing, though . . . I just love them so much. It's like I can't help but love them. Every black man I see, I see so much love in him even if he is doing wrong; I still feel so connected to him. Black men are so full of love and life. They really are amazing people and they go through so much and it's hard to just cut them out. I try, but they have this look on their face that makes you remember all the joy that they have brought you to. So it's just hard to say, "I am not going to do this anymore" and move on, because you are afraid of what's in the future, and sometimes the love feels so good that you think, Well, nothing in the future can compare to what this feels like, so I'm not going to move on. I have struggled with this so many times. But that's the catch because unless you move on, you're never going to find someone who will really love you all the time.

# Luciana

SEX IS INTIMATE, and I think it's secret with a lot of people. It's something that no one talks about. If women have a problem with it, they don't have anyone to talk about it with. Unless they have a real good partner—which most of us unfortunately have not been so lucky to find. So you walk around with your problems, you sleep with your fears, your hopes, all by yourself. And sometimes they're just not pleasant to walk around with; I figured, well, to talk about it a little bit with anyone other than my conscience, I might find something out about myself. I think it's a good way to just step back from myself, to actually give myself voice, and then see what I think about it later.

I'm thirty-eight, I work for an arts festival. I moved to Dallas from Mississippi, and I was doing modeling there. My permanent job was utilities collection. Just before moving here, I went to a modeling convention in New York. There were a lot of agencies there, but they didn't care for my look. They thought that Dallas or Atlanta was the better place for me to find work. So I came to Dallas. I've got a girlfriend here, and she helped me get started. I've been here since '87. I was doing a lot of modeling and acting on my own after I got here. Then the agency found me a job at the arts festival, and they said they'd be willing to work with my schedule—I could come in and out and it would be okay. And that's what I've done. I'm in front of the camera, and then work at the festival.

I was raised in a very small town in Mississippi—if you blink, you'd miss it when you drive on the highway. It took me about five years to leave, preparing my psyche, letting my kids grow a little, until I felt sure that I could make that move by myself because none of my family is here. I was raised just with my mom. She and my dad split up shortly after I was born, but he was still in the same town. I lived with my mom, my grandmom, and her two sisters. They had a family café where they sold food and lunches to the local community. So I was just raised in there. Learned my ABCs on the jukebox. Most of my upbringing was there with my mother's sister's kids and I growing up together; and then eventually she got her own place, and it was just Mom and I. I got to see my dad every now and then, but mostly it was his mother who kept me a part of their family. My Aunt Janice would come and get me just so we could keep a connection. But he didn't do it. His mom kept me in church when I didn't want to be in church.

We were Catholic, so we did the Communion, the Confirmation, and all those good things. I went with my grandmother, or I went alone or with other friends. Had my grandmother always trying to teach me to be a little lady, while on the other side, my mom let me just be the tomboy. She just let me be me. As long as I did my chores or my schooling, she was okay if I wanted to go outside and climb a tree or wrestle with the boys. Whereas my grandmother always wanted me to sit down and be pretty, and make sure I didn't get dirty, and keep my hair neat. So I had a little double life. I had to be a good girl with her and then be me with my mom. It is such a very small community: everybody knows everybody, and you can walk from one end of town to the other in an hour. We still had roads we hadn't paved; it was real country.

The café is still the family business. When my mom got tired of doing that, then she started working in a clothing factory. She did that up until I was eighteen. It was the only steady work in the town, unless you were in an office, and then not many blacks had the opportunity to do that. There was still sort of racial segregation. When I got my first job at city hall, I was the first black there. It was quite an experience. I got this job when I was sixteen. It had just come about where they allowed black students to take the civil service test. I got in through the city councilman who used to be my band teacher in high school. I passed the test, got in, got the job. And the white people just went berserk. They picketed the place and everything. Didn't want a little black girl in there.

My mother had a daughter when I was twenty-five. I was already gone. My half sister and I know each other mostly by telephone; every now and again we see one another. And my dad has a family on his own. He married shortly after he and my mother split, and we have a whole bunch of family on the other side. I have extended family on both sides. I have two boys, a seventeen-year-old and a twenty-two-year-old. The twenty-two-year-old will be graduating next month. And I have a grandbaby.

Intimacy to me is when you share things that you just don't tell everybody; when you talk about your hopes and your dreams and when you really want to know each other beyond the surface. When you talk about things that make you afraid, your failures, your dreams of success—I consider that to be intimate; everybody doesn't talk about that because you're afraid someone may put you down or criticize you or just tell you, "Don't do that. You're wrong." When you can actually sit and talk with someone and don't have that fear, I consider that to be intimate.

I don't have nobody that I would consider myself to be close to. Well, kind of with my mom, but she's not here and we don't communicate often. Most of the time when I call her and it's an odd time, if it's not a holiday or special occasion, she goes, "What's wrong?" "Nothing's wrong. I just called to say, 'Hey, what's up?'" But when we do talk, we're closer now than we were when I lived with her because I have the freedom to say what I want to say without the fear of her reprimanding me. I used to have a best friend, and she betrayed me a long time ago; and I've never had a best friend since. I just no longer trust anybody.

We were best friends all the way up to ninth grade. Then I got pregnant and I told her everything. And while I was pregnant, she had an affair with my boyfriend. I never got over that. I never, never got over that. She was still talking to me; we were hanging out and everything. And she was being with my boyfriend. From that point on, I just dismissed best friends. There's nobody now who I tell my secrets to. I don't trust anyone. No more best friends. To this day I still don't like her. I'm still bitter. And I've gone on. I'm friends with my ex-husband. He's gone on now, remarried, and has another family. But this one particular girl—I am through with her forever and a day.

I've had friends or acquaintances since then, and each time I've let my guard down, they've done the wrong thing. So no more. No. I've had friends betray me on all different kinds of levels. Most of the time the betrayal has been in reference to a relationship. Either I was just starting one or they were part of the beginning, and they tried to get into it themselves—which really I always find out because I'm so nosy. I consider that a betrayal because if you're in at the beginning and you know I like this person, and I think that this person likes me, and you seem to be okay, why in the world do you want to disrupt it? What do you gain from this? I can never come up with a satisfactory answer. A couple times where I have actually approached people to find out why, they always lie. And it just pisses me off that you lie to me, straight in my face, when you know you're lying.

It happens mainly with women. I get along pretty good with men. I don't have that good of a relationship with females, outside of my professional world. I think they just look at me and can't stand me right off the bat! I've had a bunch of guys where it's not an intimate thing, but we clicked. We can sit down and talk trash and hang out, and tomorrow I don't have to worry about who's coming back to rehash what we talked about or where we went, or anything. Whereas with women, there always seems to be an issue, over and over, for nothing. I kind of avoid them whenever possible.

I feel comfortable with my sexuality to an extent. There's just problems of unfulfillment in relationships. The men in my life have been a little bit more selfish than I when it comes to the loving. It's like, get mine, get yours if you can. It never seems to be about a give and take. I've only had one man in my entire life where I actually felt it was balanced, and unfortunately that just didn't work out. Most of my relationships ended on a funny note. I don't think there's anyone out there who's actually angry with me. When we disagree, it's usually, You state your case, I'll state mine, and we'll agree on that, or we will go our separate ways. I can't stand yelling or cursing and not really addressing the issue. I like to talk, and I like to get the details, so I'm not content with just saying, "I'm mad at you; you need to get away from here." We need to find out why we are mad, and why we are feeling we have to split up.

I learned about sex too young, I guess. Reading, TV, movies, conversations. I'd say mostly reading because I read everything, and I'm very interested in how people think, and why they think what they think, especially sexually. I was really curious, so anytime I saw an article or heard about something, then I'd definitely read that. But early on, I learned mostly from my friends. I was always a little old for my age, so all my friends were older than me. They were doing things way before I was able to think about it. And they would talk about it in my company. I was able to ask, "And what else? What d'you do? Why'd you do that?" And then watching my mom and her sisters and my grandma, watching how their relationships went. In my family, I think, we don't do too well with the guys. My grandmother's husband died when her children were young. My mom got married and the marriage didn't last. Each of her sisters got married and both marriages didn't last, and it was always them leaving, not the man leaving. They just seem to end, and maybe that's why I do mine the way I do mine. Because I usually leave first.

But it leads one to wonder, Is there something wrong with us? None of us have a relationship that lasts for a long time. We all are rather headstrong, and we have our ideas about the way things are, and we all like to talk. If you can't explain it, then as far as I'm concerned, my explanation is the one we're going to work with. I've got to be straight. If you're not going to be straight, then there's no point in doing this. And I can walk away first. Like my guy that I loved so dearly, I walked away from him. I'm great at that.

My mom talked a bit about sex with me, but not as much as she should have. More or less just the friendly parental reminder. "Don't let those boys get under your dress. Don't bring no babies here. If you get a baby, it's going to be hard; you're going to have to mind that baby"—that kind of stuff. But never sitting down to talk about how you're going to have a relationship, or what you want to look for in a boyfriend. My grandmother was fifteen when she had my mom; that was back in the day when that's what folks did. And then my mom was fifteen when she had me. Then I came up being fifteen when I got pregnant with mine. So it was like, Let's break this cycle somewhere. Don't continue it. I guess my mom had a fear of having this cycle repeated. I've never really asked her. It's broken now because my boys didn't do it. And my grandmother on the other side, she always did talk about it, but it was like a secret subject about that quiet stuff that's just for grown-ups. I was never grown up in my grandmother's eyes until I brought my own baby. Then I was a grown-up.

So the most information I received would be from my fifth-grade teacher. We had this little booklet called *Very Personally Yours*. It talked about the menstrual cycle, and what happens before you start, and what happens to your body during it, how you start getting these feelings, and how to deal with it. The teacher would actually allow us to ask questions. And at that time I was kind of a teacher's pet, so I used to go to her house sometimes after school and read, and she tried to teach me to play the piano, which I never caught on to. But she was the first person, and the only person, that allowed me to ask questions about those kinds of things.

The first time I got my period, I went to the store and got my things, came home, fixed myself up, and when my mom came home, I told her. My mom just went on saying that I was a little old lady, and she didn't worry about me too much because I was pretty responsible. She told me, don't do this or don't go there, and I didn't do it. She noticed early on that she didn't have a discipline problem with me, so she didn't worry about me too much. Then when my period came along, she goes, "Wow, now you're a big girl." Because that was the term, "You're a big girl now." She would say, "You know now when I go to the store, you can't be having Mama bring you something back. You're not my little girl anymore, you're a big girl." And she told me, "Now that you are a big girl, you can have a baby if you want. Go ahead (and let those boys look under your clothes)." Then she asked me if I had already let anybody do that, and at that time I hadn't. She reminded me that if I wanted to talk about it before I did it, to come and tell her, that she wanted to know, and for me not to be scared to come and tell her about it. She gave me an open door to talk with her, but she wasn't always as forthcoming with information as one would have expected her to be.

I guess my mom had me before she really wanted to. Her sister was my confidante, she almost was like my surrogate mom. She was the one who'd take me and comb my hair and dress me pretty, and talk with me and show me how to cook and all that stuff. Mom was working and partying and going on with life. She just always tried to tell me, be responsible, don't do anything I didn't want to do, stand my ground. If a boy asked me to do anything and I said no, to not let him talk me into things. She gave me all the good points that I really should have taken into account, and we chatted and I understood her.

Everybody I talked to said you should try to stay a virgin until you get married. But I saw so many relationships around me that were not marriages. A lot of them were good, some of them were not good. But I didn't see any shining examples of this virginity thing that everybody held so highly. I didn't see any examples of any benefit to anyone. Everything just seemed to be running rampant. You got married, you got babies, you didn't have a husband. You're with this man, you're not married, you're not even talking about marriage. You already had a boyfriend and you're with him.  So what I learned in my textbook, in my classes, in my catechism, virginity had its place there. But where I lived, it wasn't there. I learned about virginity from church, religion, and through my school. My books and my teachers. I looked upon that as my choice, if I wanted to save it, not because of what I was actually seeing. And at one point I did want to save it, but curiosity got the better of me. I just had to find out what all the madness was about.

I remember one time I asked my mom for birth control, and she brought me to the doctor and the doctor wouldn't give it to me. That was when I was actually becoming curious. He told me no, and the next year I decided to satisfy my curiosity. He said I was too young for birth control pills. I was fourteen. At the time, the clinics weren't giving them to you on your own, like they do now. And the very next year, of course, I was pregnant. At the time I was of the mind-set that the first time I did it I wouldn't get pregnant. I did. I guess it was just a very immature way of thinking.

He was seventeen. We didn't talk about birth control. He was a shy guy, and I'd been a tomboy since I was a little girl. We'd had this little play relationship for the longest time. We played around a couple years, stealing a kiss here and there, hugging and all that, but we would never go that far. And we didn't even talk about it because it wasn't even an issue. We weren't thinking about that. At least it didn't seem we were thinking about it. And then we went to this party one night, and we just had so much fun. I don't know if he drank or what, but it just seemed as though that night, things were a little more heated than usual. And he was like, "Let's try it, let's try it." And I was like, "No, no, no, no." And he was like, "Yeah, yeah, yeah, yeah." So the baby factor, you know, it just wasn't in our minds. But of course, he continued to play around. "Okay, just a little bit, just a little while." And a little bit, little while was too much. Too long! And lo and behold, baby came forth.

I was attracted to him, I wanted to marry, I wanted to be with him forever. And I actually ended up marrying him later on, and I really did want to keep that marriage; it just turned out that I was a little bit more ready than he was. He's married and he's started a family now, but with me, he really wasn't ready to be a husband, a father. We got married right after my sixteenth birthday. I had my baby in December when I was fifteen, and I turned sixteen in January, and I got married a week after that. We stayed married for one year to the day. We had things going on. He was still catering to his mom, putting his mom before us every time. She used to borrow from us, and we didn't really have money to loan. He had a little job, he had a check, and he kept giving money to his mom and she wouldn't pay us back. I would get upset, and he didn't understand why. I kept trying to explain, "You have a wife now. We're supposed to be first. And if she's going to borrow money from us, she should give it back." We never came to an agreement on that.

But on our anniversary night we were at a party. He thought someone was flirting with me across the room, and he threatened to hit me, and that was enough. That was one decision I had in my head a long time, that I would never, never allow a man to hit me. And he threatened to hit me; that was all I needed. I did not go home. He began to put his hand on me to try to shake me, to begin this exchange of whatever it was going to be. I got away. I ran. At that time we did not have a car, so he ran down the street, all the way home. We lived on this street, and the next block over was where my mom lived. I just went right to my mom's. And I didn't go back.

We played around, and the next summer I took him back because everybody influenced me, saying that we should try, I shouldn't have left like that, I got a baby, and we're married and all that stuff. I took him back against my better judgment, and he wasn't with me but a few months when just looking at him made me mad. He would come home after work, and my whole demeanor, everything would change. It was like, You just need to go away. One particular day I just told him, "This is not working. You need to go ahead and move. I don't want you to be here anymore."

He wouldn't take care of us, and I guess finance has always been a big issue with me because I just never had enough. I've never had enough to satisfy my basics let alone going beyond. And I was tired of having trouble with basics. If I am going to do all this struggling and you're not going to help me, then you can just go. And I made him leave. He still kept in touch with my son, and his family did. But it just didn't work between us anymore.

I was thirty-one or thirty-two and I had already had my kids when I had my first orgasm. It was with this guy that I met up with. The one that got away. It was around the same time I slept with the woman who worked with me. It was absolutely wild. For the longest time, I fought myself, not wanting to satisfy that curiosity.

When he and I broke up, I was a mental case. Even though I left him, I just felt that I wasn't worthy, and I really felt bad about myself. I went into this real bad depression for three months, stayed home, just ate, slept, and gained fifty pounds. I have not shaken that whole fifty since. But the woman from work was good for me at that time because she helped reaffirm that I was okay just being me; I didn't need him to affirm who I was. That took a long time because I really felt that I needed him, and I had messed up bad by just walking away from him. But up to that point, I just had sex. It was no tenderness involved, no real passion. All the stuff that I want it to be, that when you think about it, you go, "Oooh!"—it just wasn't that. In my head, that's what I wanted it to be, and I kept searching and searching. And I said, "I must be the oddball because obviously nobody else is thinking like me. What's up?" But when I met this guy, it was such a fairy tale. I guess that's why it didn't work—because it was really a fantasy. I went out to this club by myself, and he was sitting at the bar, and I walked in the club, and I just stopped to look around, and I thought, Oh, he is just so fine! Whoo! How can I get over there?! And we got together, and it was like we knew one another. It was so comfortable right off the bat. We waited a very long time—for me it was a very long time because I would have had him right there on the spot, he was just so fine. Yes, but we were very good. He has a son, too. Just the sight of him would just excite me. He would send love letters every day, and I love that! A guy who's romantic—Oh! He would come to see me and it was like Christmas. When we finally did decide to make love, I was beside myself. Sparks were going off everywhere. Oooh! When we made love, he paid attention to me and my responses, so it was more of an exchange instead of just him trying to get off or me trying to get off. It was more touching and talking and caressing and all the elements that I had stored in my head that I wanted when I would make love. It was perfect. And when I had my orgasm, I almost went into shock. I was embarrassed to confess that that was my first time feeling that. And what made it even better was that he picked up that I felt a little embarrassed. I didn't really have to come out and explain. Then he just held me and talked softly in my ear. He didn't go anywhere, he didn't jump up, and he just made it so sexual.

I was like, Damn, all this time I've been missing this. Then I had this rewind of the tape in my head, Why haven't I been having this before? Why did it not work out like that with anyone else? It was a vaginal orgasm from just straight-out, plain old sex! And it was amazing. Absolutely amazing. The oral sex came afterward and I was in heaven, thinking, This is getting better and better. Before this, I had given but never received oral sex. I never even asked for it. At the time, being the little kooky person that I am, I wanted to be good at it, so I wanted to practice. And giving it to me, well, I was just kind of weird about it. Then when I finally did get it, that's when it all came out. This is a requirement now.

When I first had the experience of giving it, it was with a friend of mine, and he was just so fine. I called him my mentor, told him I wanted to learn how to do that. Of course, he was all for it. "You want to learn how to do that? Yeah!" We just were real tight. Real tight. And we had not crossed that bridge. We would talk about past experiences with other people, but we had not talked about it with us. I just threw it out, so I more or less initiated that part of the relationship. And he was pretty gung ho for it. "Anytime you want to, let me know." We did that for a long time. He asked about giving me oral sex—he actually asked—and I said no, I wasn't ready for that yet.

I just discovered masturbation with myself in the last couple years. Before that, I wouldn't even try and no one talked about it. I guess my sexuality came into being after I moved here to Dallas. Because in Mississippi I couldn't be me; I was kind of odd. I just know I was always different, and my way of thinking, acting, didn't fit. But moving here was a real help for me because I was able to get away from all the influences that made me want to hide or hold back. As a matter of fact, when I started working for the arts festival, I learned so many things. [Laughs.] They were quite an eclectic bunch, to say the least. There was a girl who was a lesbian, a guy that was gay; and although I had homosexual friends in Mississippi, we never really talked sexually. But coming here I met these people on my job. They were so free and so open with themselves, I was like, "Damn! This is cool. People are okay with themselves. It's all right to be like that." They reeducated me. I had lots of questions. And they didn't mind answering. The girl and I became very good friends. We went out together; my kids baby-sat her kids. She introduced me to a whole new world.

I did actually have a lesbian thing. It was scary and it was nice at the same time. I was kind of confused for a while. I didn't know if I was going the other way, or what I was doing. Oh! Matter of fact, she was the first person to talk to me about masturbating. She asked me, "You don't do that?" I said, "No! You do that?!" And she said, "Yeah. All the time." I asked her, "Really? How do you do that?" And she told me all kinds of things. I was like, "Really, and that's enough?"

Well, mentally it was a big hurdle to be with a woman; but when it actually came, it didn't seem that big of a deal. Because it felt so natural, so comfortable to when the time actually came and we did it I didn't have all the hang-ups that I thought I had. Which struck me as odd because usually I'm kind of rigid in my thinking. Anyway, the first one wasn't with the girl at work. I was hanging out with her, and feeling how people do it. It actually occurred with a girl from home that came visiting.

She was kind of out there, too, in her thinking. Her husband, myself, and her used to watch porno movies together. They were the oddest little couple, and I think that's why I liked it—because they seemed so damn odd. She used to tell me about how she more or less perfected her technique of oral sex by watching the movies. When she came to visit, she told me that her and her husband had broke up and the whole sob story. She began to talk about some sexual things they had went through, and about when they were splitting up; and I was just like, Yeah, interesting. She asked me, "Have you ever thought about a woman?" And she kind of put her hand on mine as she was talking. You know, hand on my leg, and then she put her hand on my hand and continued talking very softly. I started talking about, "Well, I never thought about it." And she said, "Well, it's really natural," and she was giving me her little textbook talk—now that I look at it, it's funny. As she talked she continued to touch. I consider myself to be highly sensitive. I can't have people touching me or I get hot, so don't touch me like that. She was talking to me, and touching, and caressing, and one thing led to another and another and another, and it happened. We had oral sex, touching of the breasts, and the kissing and the hugging. The whole nine yards, I think. I didn't have an orgasm with her, and I'm not sure why I didn't. I'm not sure if I was just satisfying curiosity and still holding something back, or exactly what I was doing.

It was okay. I enjoyed it, as a matter of fact. I was quite excited; I couldn't wait to tell my girlfriend at work. "I did it! I did it!" And of course, she's like, "You did?" I said, "Yes, girl, I have to tell you all about it." So I'm telling her all about it, and she goes, "Good. Do you think you're going to do it again?" I said, "Probably. I'm not really sure. I don't think I could actually go and initiate it because I don't think I'm that comfortable with it." So she and I began to go out; she began taking me to lesbian clubs, which I thought was real cool: "Oh, wow, I like this."

It was just a bunch of women, and everybody was okay with themselves. I guess I'm a closet les—a closet freak. I'm not sure which. But it really felt good to me to be able to see people being comfortable with who they were. They were hugging and kissing each other and dancing real closely. That wouldn't be acceptable in my town. It was good seeing that people felt like that, and thought like that. They weren't hiding, they didn't seem to be ashamed. So that was good for me. I've never had it in my family to say that this one's a lesbian, or they're bad people, or people I shouldn't associate with. I never had that type of upbringing. So these people were always okay with me in my mind, but I never saw them and seeing them here was really good.

And that was another thing I'd never had, a black and white relationship. The woman from my office was white. I had one relationship with a white man; it was a really nice relationship that gave me a different opinion of white men. It was someone on the job, and we had a secret affair for the longest time. He was a very nice man, and he treated me very kind. He was like pillar-of-the-community kind of thing. Married, kids, the wife was a schoolteacher. He was a city councilman, school-bus driver, worked in the sheriff's department. Very, very considerate of my feelings, remembered little things, you know, birthdays. Very nice. Good love. Didn't do the orgasms, but we made good love. I still call him every now and then when I'm passing through my hometown. But we haven't been together in quite some time.

The woman from work and I started going out a lot, and she has MPD (multiple personality disorder). I'm still struggling with accepting that because it doesn't add up to me. She's been clinically diagnosed as that. I personally think when she's had enough with life, she just goes, "I don't want to deal with stuff." As far as that goes, I got MPD, too. 'Cause when I get enough, I can turn off. We used to go out all the time and have big fun. I mean, she's a totally different person; she's like Mother Nature at work. Cool but reserved. When we would go out, she would let loose, she would dance, and you could see her letting herself go in the music, just getting free. And she would drink—the whole nine yards. We went out one night to a party. I think perhaps she had a little too much to drink, and I had to take her out of there for a second because she was getting a little bit wild. We went outside to sit in the car and started talking, and she was so tipsy. I guess she was hot at the same time and didn't know what to do with herself. And she just came at me. Just grabbed me with a hug and a kiss, and it kind of surprised me. I went with it, but it wasn't a planned evening, so to speak. We didn't really, really go all the way because of the restrictions of the car; but had it not been for the car in that particular circumstance, it would have been all the way there. But it was more or less just the touching, feeling, kisses, hugging kind of thing. We didn't actually have oral sex together. And I think after she did it, she was embarrassed that she did it because I don't think she had actually planned it with me.

I think her conscience began to bother her because we worked together—not being really, really sure if this would ever come back to haunt her. But of course, her fears were unfounded because it was a fifty-fifty thing. I couldn't bring it to work without it catching me too. So it was like, "No, this is staying right here. When we step out of here, it's right here where we left it." And I wasn't worried about my friend from home saying anything 'cause it'd come back to bite her if she did. My coworker no longer works with me. She's moved up north in the mountains. We still keep in touch. She's my sexual buddy for talking about anything way out there because she's kind of out there. So now, sexual things that I just thought about or read about, that I'm curious enough about, I'm more comfortable now to address on my own.

I was always curious about three people, and I satisfied that. Actually, the guy's a good friend of mine; we've been friends for quite some time. He travels a lot on his job, and we used to always talk about his relationship. He was married when I first met him. They were having problems, and we used to talk about the problems, and I used to be his Dr. Ruth. Go back home and try this, say that, and see what happens. But they eventually broke up, and he got another lady, and he was telling me about her. We were friends, and he said, "Luciana, she's hot." I was like, "That's why you like her then, 'cause your ass hot." He goes, "No, but she's really hot." And I said, "What you mean she's really hot?" He said, "You know, I think she might like to be in a threesome." And I asked him, "How do you know that?" He said, "Because we've been talking about different things, and we've done it a few times." So finally he asked me if I would. And I was like, "I don't know. Let me meet her first." Because if she ain't nice, to hell, I won't do that. So he brought her to town. And she was really nice, and she appeared to be conservative [*Laughs.*] and we had a good time out. Then he asked if I would come on and spend the night over at his place. I said okay. So we went. He can push people, he can just go ahead and lead everybody on; if you're scared, he'll push you on in there, sink or swim.

We went over to his place and we all went to the bedroom and had a drink. And we got to talking, and he had told me before that he was going to get her started first. [*Laughs.*] So he started kissing on her, and hugging her, and getting her all worked up. While he was doing all his thing, I was sitting to the side, and he was still kissing her and he kind of reached for my hand and pulled me over, and put my hand on her. And just the touch of my hand was her signal—she wasn't shy anymore. She took my hand, and before you know it she turned away from him, and turned to me, and things just took off from that point. And it was fun. It was fun.

Being with her was like almost being with me in a weird sense. You know, the soft sense. She kissed like I kissed. Which surprised me. You always think your own stuff is special. But she kissed like I kissed and put her hands on me, which was different from his hands being on me. How she moved along my body was different—it was more tender. More loving.

As if we had already had a relationship. It's a weird way to describe it, but it just felt really . . . okay.

With my girlfriend from home, it was totally different. She was just my bud. And she was out of sorts because she had broke up. It wasn't the same as this. I didn't think of it as being as much of a sexual experience as I did this other thing with my friend and his lady. Maybe it was my mind that really was different. I just felt it was more or less like my girlfriend; I thought she needed comforting. And I know so much about my friend, my male friend, because we had talked about so many things, his relationship, his sexual problems, his financial problems, what he liked and didn't like. Long before I met her, he told me different things about her, what they did sexually, what excited her. And I did find her attractive when I met her.

He let us go at it for a while. I think he wanted to see her let herself go. He felt that from the information that she had given him, she fifty-fifty wanted to and didn't want to. So he let us go at it for what seemed like a long time before he joined in. He just came into the middle of it during an embrace and he began to perform oral sex on her, and kind of like just . . . very gently separated us. And while he performed oral sex on her, she and I were kissing and touching and caressing. Later on she performed oral sex on me.

I didn't feel left out the first time. There was a time afterward that I felt left out. And I told him. I didn't tell him during, but I said, "Of course, you know this is not going to become a habit, 'cause if I don't get mine, y'all ain't gettin' y'alls.' " I guess we've gotten together about three, four, five times total. She's called me a couple times when he was out of town. We had one experience just she and I. That was when he wasn't home. She's such a little firecracker. [*Laughs.*] She's such a little closet lady; she's much more closet than me. But she called one time to go to a fashion show together. Of course we played around before we left. We got involved and we performed oral sex, and we were hugging and kissing and holding; and when it was over, she jumped on the phone and called him to tell him. [*Laughs.*] I was sitting there; I couldn't do anything. I just sat there in non-belief. She actually got on the phone to call him and tell him how much fun she had just had. "And then Luciana came over, and you'll never guess what we were doing." So that kind of shook me. Being with her didn't bother me because I liked her, and I spoke of this with my girlfriend from work: "I'm like, am I bi? What am I?" I'm having a problem right now. I don't know what I am.

I'm not sure if it matters. I really don't know. At times there are women that I feel attracted to, but I won't act on it. I'm not quite sure I'm comfortable with being bi—if I am bi. I don't know if I'm really bi, or if I'm just curious, or if maybe it's the time of the month when I'm really hot or what. My girlfriend tells me, "Just don't worry about it. Just do what you want to do." I have not defined myself, but the interest is here. Part of me wants to act upon it because it would be a confirmation that maybe I am. I'm not sure that I want it to be because in my head I actually do want to get married again and hopefully find the kind of fulfillment that I thought I had discovered with the guy I broke up with. And unfortunately, I'm not having very much luck with that.

I need the passion, I need the extra hugging and kissing, I need that. And I'm finding the men that I meet don't necessarily want to give me as much as I want. It's like, touch, touch, kiss, kiss, touch, touch, whew! And that's just not enough. Maybe that's what feels good to be with a woman. No matter how brief the exchange or the encounter is, it is what I want to feel, that tenderness, that real passion. But I want the man to give that to me. And I'm not finding that. I'm in a very difficult place right now because I'm thirty-eight, and, as they say, I'm peaking, and [*bam!—she smacks the table*] somebody needs to do something here! This should be illegal sometimes, the way I'm walking around here. So I'm really hoping that at some point very soon, I will meet someone that stirs that feeling that I so desperately want to find and keep. I don't want to keep having fly-by-night things that I just stumble upon and hit and miss.

Race doesn't really matter to me, but it's been mostly black partners. As far as white goes, I had two, one real relationship and one very brief affair. With the ladies they've been black, except for my experience with my coworker. But race really doesn't matter to me. I judge people just on how they present themselves with me. I actually try not to associate too much with people who have a problem with race because I think we're all alike; we just all look different. Basically we all have the same needs and desires and just all go about fulfilling them differently. But I don't have a problem with black or Hispanic or white, blue, green, whatever. The white man that I had my relationship with, he just made me feel special as a woman. I don't think he treated me different because I was black, because we had the hiding type of relationship. I don't think that was because I was black; he would have had to do that with anyone because he had a marriage. But he didn't treat me different; he looked out for my kids and looked out for me on my job. He was very good to me. Up to that point, he had been better to me than most black men had been.

Since I've come to Dallas I've met so many different types of men, which has made me glad I left home. It let me see how little of the world I had actually seen while I was there. I've never traveled much; I've gone from Mississippi to live in Dallas, period. I've had a couple trips to New York, a couple to Atlanta, places like that. I've never really vacationed or lived anywhere else.

It was getting raped that really made my decision to move here. I was raped on the New Year's before I moved here. I had gone out to meet one of my friends who was coming from Dallas for the holidays. They were late, and there was this other guy that I knew. At the time I was smoking marijuana, and we left to go outside. And—it's really silly—I let him take me back to his place to pick up something. Now, hindsight is twenty-twenty: that was a dumb move. But I knew him and I didn't even think in that direction, that he might cause me harm. That just didn't register beforehand. Of course, I'm suspicious of everybody now. He ended up taking me to what was a hotel instead of his place and asked me to go inside with him; and when I did, he was searching around as if he was actually looking for something. My original decision was, "I'll wait for you right here." He said that he would just be a minute, I shouldn't just sit out in the car. And like a dummy, I went in with him, and he more or less went from looking into the desk, digging around, to just being all over me. And that hurt—it makes me more mad than anything else. Not even so much that he raped me, but for the fact that I was dumb enough to have let him put me in that position. I have blamed myself because looking back on it now, it was just so textbook. I should have known all of that. I should not have fallen for that. I just should not have done that. We fought, we struggled—the whole nine yards. Then he left me there. And I didn't even have a way to get back. Luckily the hotel manager was kind enough to give me taxi fare. I didn't call the police because I was too ashamed to admit that I had allowed myself to get in that situation. And I knew if I went to court, and I would have to say this, the whole town would know.

My friend's brother had already been to prison for killing a man. And I didn't know how far he would take it. I just didn't want to put them in that spot on my behalf. It was just a little bit too much. So I just kept it to myself. I only have two girlfriends who know about it. My family never knew about it; I never told. It was just before my twenty-seventh birthday. So that really made my decision to move final. I couldn't see myself staying in that town and having to run into him again. I didn't want to have to see him on a regular basis. A couple weeks later my friends found out he had done this to several other women in the community. And they wouldn't press charges either because they were afraid. One girl had reported him, and he went back and—you know—real bad. So the police did not pick him up. I didn't want that kind of madness either.

Most of my decision was based on the fact that I had my kids, and I was by myself, and it was too easy to catch me. Too easy to get my kids. So a lot of things I kind of swallowed because I didn't want it to come back where I couldn't handle it. He ended up being one of those things that I couldn't tell, I couldn't act on because it was bigger than me. So I let that go. Of course, now I don't ride in anybody's car, I have very few dates. It still lingers. Now I'm kind of weird with all my friends who do know me, because I still won't go anywhere in their car. I'm trying not to repeat that again. I felt that I was through with some things, but I find that they really are playing a role in things that I'm doing now, to where I'm really not as over them as I thought I was. The friendship thing, the rape thing, the relationship thing. They all have their lasting effects with me. And sometimes that's not very pleasant, because I really do want to shake some of the things that are following me.

A few years before, when I was on a visit to my mom in San Antonio, I was out with a cousin of mine, and he introduced me to people out at a club, and as it turned out, one of the guys wanted to talk to me but didn't believe that my cousin was my cousin. So they lured my cousin away from me, beat him up outside, and wouldn't let him come back in the club to get me. I was thinking he was outside talking to a lady he'd met. But I stayed in the club because we came together, we're leaving together. The whole night passes, and he never comes back. So the one guy he'd introduced me to—was supposed to be a distant cousin—offers to give me a ride back to my mom's, and he takes me to I don't know where. He attempted to rape me and couldn't, thank God, because he was drunk. And I had a little more stamina than he did and we fought and fought and fought and fought and fought and we fought. Until he just passed out. He had had that much alcohol. And I wasn't drinking; I was having Coca-Cola at the time. Thank God for that. I think I just wore him out. But he had me in the middle of San Antonio, and I didn't know where I was. He had no phone, and I had no money because I had my purse locked in the car with my cousin. I didn't even have a quarter to make a phone call. After he passed out, I looked outside and I just had absolutely no idea where I was. So I just sat there on a chair and cried. I was in some apartment place where he had taken me. I just sat there crying and rocking. And there were no people when I stepped outside the door.

Luckily he had an uncle that came to his place in the morning because he picks up another gentleman in the area and they go to work together. He saw me, took me from there, and brought me back home to my mom's. My mom had been getting ready to call the police because my cousin hadn't showed up. He showed up shortly before I did, and they had beaten him to a pulp. His eyes were closed, and his face was all swollen. I don't know if my cousin pressed charges or not, but I didn't because I was just visiting. So of course, I was ready to go. And to this day I don't visit my mom for any length of time. I'll visit her just a couple of days, and I don't go anywhere while I'm there. I tell her, "I don't like San Antonio. I'm not coming there, I don't want to stay there." No, no, I'm through with them.

This makes me more cautious. It takes me longer now to allow myself to open up again—a few weeks, a few months. I may want to but I won't because of that. And I feel like I'm missing out. I'm still single, but I don't really date in the traditional sense of the word "date" because I have this underlying distrust, or I feel I'm being shortchanged with men; and perhaps that's part of the reason I haven't met anyone that suits me. I haven't really given anybody the opportunity. I won't let them take me out; I won't invite them home for dinner. "You can come so far, and you can stay right there." I haven't been able to go beyond that. I'll meet with them elsewhere, or we'll just talk wherever we are. But it's always on my terms. 'Cause I have had men indicate their interest in going further at a particular time, and I will just say, "I'll let you know; not right now." That's really not the way I feel it ought to be, but I have not come up with a solution for myself as to how to get beyond that point.

I don't think it affects how I feel sexually at this time. When it first happened, I felt that I should keep more to myself, not have people be sexually interested in me. Did I dress a little too provocative? For a while I wanted to dress a little more conservatively and not be me. The "me" is really not all that conservative. But I like wearing short dresses. When I was heavy, my boobs were big, and I liked wearing stuff that showed off my boobs. I like that, and it wasn't for them, it was for me. I like when I look in my mirror and I feel, "You look good." I don't like to feel that I need to cover up because of what somebody else is going to think.

I think in these last couple of years, I'm beginning to feel more comfortable with me, all the weight that I had gained. I've just begun to decide that I want to get rid of it, and I want to get back to me, so that I can feel happy and perky and confident. Because I was really, really feeling low, and no matter how many times someone said, "You still look good," or "You're all right," "You still do your job well," all of that's not enough. I still wouldn't feel good with me. I don't think my kids changed my sexuality. I think they helped to put me in check, more or less. This curiosity that I always had sexually, having my kids has made me not pursue it. Now that they're almost out of the house—one is gone—I'm feeling that if I want to pursue any sexual curiosity, I can more freely. You don't want your kids to think of you in any weird manner. My younger son follows me around when we go out. He can't stand other guys watching me. He'll say, "They ain't lookin' at you, Mom." And he'll stand and block the person's view. He'll say, "Look at them, Mommy, runnin' off the road lookin' at you." And being so close to their age is hard; my older son, his friends used to come home and say, "Your mom looks like your sister." So they had to make me keep in the mother look, more or less, whatever that was supposed to be. I've always had to tinker with that.

Things I wish I hadn't done: trusting in those two experiences. Had done: I wish I had stayed with my guy that I really, really liked. I regret that. He was the closest thing to what I imagine I want. Although sometimes I feel perhaps that what I want is a little too close to perfect. I'll probably never find that, but my relationship with him was the closest thing. I feel we had the possibility of making it last because it meant so much beyond just the bedroom. We did things close. We did window-shopping. I never had a guy go window-shopping. I used to be in pageants, and he would run around with me choosing my clothes and come and cheer me on. And we'd exercise together, work in the yard together. I like to sing those old songs, and he did too, and we used to do that. Just fun things that were not pretentious. I didn't have to always be dressed up to be with him; he was just as happy to see me in tennis shoes and cut-offs as he was to see me in the suit I wear to work. I didn't always have to have my hair permed; it could be in a pony tail or just all over my head. Those were intimate personal things that I loved and that made me feel good about myself.

James was taking too long to make his decision about marrying me. He proposed real early in our relationship because things seemed to be going so well. And we were living together about a year, and he still couldn't come up with a wedding date. It wasn't like I wanted him to marry me tomorrow, but at least give me a time frame you're considering. But he could never give me that. My grandmother always told me that I should never move in with anybody because the old saying was, "Why buy the cow when you can get the milk for free?" He always told me that this was not the case with us. I said, "Well, I want to believe it's not the case, but the fact is you can't come up with a time, and I'm here. It seems that is the case." And he had nothing to say. We talked and we talked and we talked, and he never came through with anything. And I felt that it wasn't right for me to have to make him marry me. It didn't feel right to me, and December 25 I just packed up and left. On Christmas Day I was so filled with emotion, opening presents, that the tears were right here. I loved him, I loved being with him, but he just wasn't giving that last piece.

He let me leave. We continued to see one another a little bit for about six months after that. But you can't fight someone. And just this February, Valentine's Day, is when I was finally able to get closure to where I could really think about him and not want him. I left him in '92. And for the longest time he was in my mind. I was still hung up with him. He would still write me letters every now and again. They were wonderful letters.

Well, he's married now. He married someone else, named Luciana, and she actually kind of favors me. When he first got married, I thought, You couldn't have the real thing, married a copy, huh? And he tried to profess that he still loved me, but he apologized that he couldn't meet my time line. I said, "I didn't have no time line. I just wanted you to give me one that I could work with." So the last few times, I wouldn't even let him see me. He wanted to come to the festival, and I said, "You all can come to the festival, but I advise you strongly, don't even bring your little lady near me. It wouldn't be a very pretty scene for either of you. So don't come. Don't come." He said, "I just want you to meet her." I said, "I don't want to meet her. You've made your choice, that's the person you want, so you keep her. I don't want her, don't bring her by me. Just pissed me off, you took her and had the wedding with her that you described you'd have with me. And you want me to be happy to meet her? She's sleeping in the bed that I helped you decorate. And you want me to meet her?" I just went off. He knew I meant what I said, but he didn't take it in the context where he felt that it meant we were angry and we could not continue to associate.

But we would still talk on the phone. I guess I set myself up to continue to hurt that way. He calls on the radio a lot, and most of the time I hear him on the radio and I call him and talk about his comment. We kept this exchange up for a long time on the phone and through letters, and I would not let him see me. He used to write and say, "We need to get together and talk." And I said no. I'd gotten fat, and I didn't want him to see me fat—he met me during my modeling time when I was just so. But this February, I wrote him a really heartfelt letter to tell him how many problems I was having with him still in my consciousness. I was blocking my other relationships because I was comparing other guys to him, and I needed to get over him. It was like, "If you really love me like you say you love me, you'll help me reach my closure. Because you've gone on, you've married, you have someone. And you're happy, and you're going on with your life and I'm still stuck in time. Because I still love you and I still want to be with you. And I can't cut you off."

On Valentine's Day, I don't know why, I just called him. I said, "Would you meet me?" He said, "Yeah." I said, "Okay, meet me at the mall." He came and met me and it was so strange when I saw him, I was over him. When I saw him, I knew right there. And that was really cool. I didn't have any animosity toward him or anything. Just when I saw him again, I just knew he wasn't my James anymore. When he was mine—I could look at him and see in him and on him, however you want to describe it. But when I saw him on Valentine's, he wasn't my James. He was her James, I guess. And I was able to just talk to him like a bud. "What you gonna get her for Valentine's?" "Well, I'm getting her some lingerie." "Well, let's go shopping for it—can I go with you?" That was a big step for me. I think now the door's about to open for me. I'll be better able to move on and find the love and the experience that I think I really want. I miss that kind of love; I miss that because whatever it is that I think of sexually, I want to be able to do with that person. I want someone where I don't care how far out it is or how dull, I want to be able to do it with that person. And closing the door on him will allow me to at least consider that possibility with someone else. Hopefully I can continue to work on getting over the other hurdles that are keeping people away from me. I want to just be. There was this article in *Essence* that said "Dare to Be." I kept it for a very long time because I felt that I needed to dare to be me, especially sexually. I wanted to have sex a lot and that just didn't seem right because people are telling you not to. There's a lot of times when I want to have sex, and it just seems like a little bit too much, where I say, "Luciana, you got to put yourself in check,

girl. You're just a little too hot for yourself. You better calm yourself down."
I need to have me somebody so when I feel that I'm just going beyond beyond, I got somebody who can calm me down instead of having me just
running rampant, wanting to find a release. And with this masturbating
stuff, I'm still a novice. It's just every now and then I can have an orgasm by
myself. I haven't gotten to the point where I really know my spot and my
peaks and all of that. I'm not there yet. But I feel I'm thirty-eight years old,
what is the problem here? I should know this. You know?

I keep telling myself that after my kids are grown, then I'll have a
chance to be just a woman. Because I've never had that opportunity. I went
from being a child to a mother, to a wife, and to being a parent. And
nowhere in there did I just get to be a woman. To where I worry about my
concerns, my sanity, my well-being, my happiness. I have always been second, third, fourth, fifth on the list. I've never been the number one priority
in my life. There's always been something else that has taken my focus, my
attention, my extra energy. I've never given all of those things to me. I've
never had anybody for me.

# Rita

*I*'M TWENTY-SIX YEARS OLD—I'll be twenty-seven in a few weeks. My parents are originally from Detroit. I was born there, but we moved to a small mostly white town when I was two years old. So we moved from a predominantly black city to a predominantly white city. I was two so I really didn't feel the culture shock. I'm an only child, which I think explains a lot of my quirks. But I love it. My mother started off working for the phone company; she worked there for about twenty years, and then she was laid off. My father worked for the auto industry for twenty-five years. Me and my mother started going to church when I was nine. Dad had a nervous breakdown. And that was part of a kind of mental instability that went on for most of my life. I grew up pretty much afraid of my father. He had the breakdown and my parents got divorced, but they got back together within a few months. That was a whole bag about relationships that I have yet to figure out. When they got divorced, I was happier because it had been a miserable situation. And then when they got back together, I remember being very disappointed.

After college, I took a year off and moved to Seattle, Washington, and worked at a women's bookstore. I had a friend out there, and I just wanted to be somewhere where I was still riding along on my college political high, a let's-go-to-rallies-and-vigils thing.

I feel intimate with someone when I feel I can say the bad things that I'm thinking and they don't judge me for it, or think, "God, you're such a bitch." Instead, they might agree, they might disagree, but at the same time they just accept what I say as part of my opinion or who I am. And I've come to look at intimacy as something that I have with my friends more so than with my family just because I feel like my friends are my family, and a lot of that has to do with my feeling displaced a lot. To tell the truth, I've only had one lover, my current one. I feel like I can say the bad things that I'm thinking with him; with lovers and boyfriends, saying the bad things is an aspect of intimacy.

To lose intimacy happens when the other person isn't reciprocating, isn't carrying their weight in a friendship. I tend to be one of those people, like my mother, who sends cards, remembers birthdays, and if they have something important going on, gives them a call. But sometimes I feel like I'm not getting that same kind of attention in return. That usually takes me awhile, but then something clicks in my head that says, I'm doing all the work here, and that needs to stop. So if so-and-so doesn't call me within the next two weeks, I'll just consider that friendship done. But it's not really something that I've ever been able to do easily, let go of friendships. I'd say there's two friends from college that I feel closest to. And maybe one friend from high school. None of them live near me, but we talk three or four times a month; I make trips to see them. But I think it's just because they've known me for so long, and we have history in common, so we know what each other's been through. When these new episodes come up like new boyfriends, they have context for it, and there's not a lot of having to go back and explain.

I feel sexuality is very important, but it's not a part of my life that gets the same amount of attention as other parts of my life. I feel like part of my upbringing has made me abnormal. The other day I thought, Maybe I'm just a hybrid because I was African American in this very, very white town, and I went to predominantly white schools. In my high school, there were only forty-five students—it was a magnet school—and five of us were African American; all of us in that group had mostly white friends and our closest friends were white. But now that we're out of high school, we seem to have gravitated toward each other. So that meant that I didn't date in high school, and then in college there might have been a couple of one-night stands. It is not that I wouldn't date white guys; I would, and I liked them, but they just never were attracted to me. And then the one African American male in my class that I had a crush on for the longest time was dating a Latina woman. There were two other guys, and I was very close friends with one of them; he was like a brother to me. And then the other one I never really interacted with. Now that I reflect on it, there were two boys that I kissed, and turns out they were both gay, and they were both seeing each other. Then there was another one who was younger than me who liked me, and he was very odd; and now that I think about it, maybe he was gay too. There were older men outside of my high school that I had crushes on who I later found out were gay. I've never quite figured out what that was about, because now from college, a lot of my white male friends are gay also. But the men who I had one-night stands with weren't gay. I don't know what it is in me that attracts gay men, or what in me is attracted to them. I went to some event and ended up meeting this boy, who, now that I think about him, was nasty. He was seventeen and I was thirteen and stumbled across him somehow, and we ended up going in the woods to make out. And I wouldn't go much further, like I didn't want him going up my shirt or down my pants or anything. That was my first kiss. And after that it seemed like the boy who lived next door was constantly hounding me about making out with him; and he was gross, so that wasn't going to happen.

Even now, I am at a mostly white university in graduate school. I have more black friends here than I've ever had, but we're still all in the same boat where we've been raised in these predominantly white environments; and then a lot of the black men that I know here are gay, too.

Not to make excuses for why I am still attracted to white men, but I think a large part of it is that the black men I am attracted to are dating white women. And if I go to a club—which I don't do very much anymore—it seemed like the white men are afraid to date black women, and black men are all dating white women. So I always felt like I was in this gap between everything else that was going on. I never encountered men of other races in my hometown or in college; that's why I think it boiled down to being black or white. It's really lonely, and I think it's had a big impact on my self-esteem. But at the same time, it's hard to separate out everything that I feel is "wrong" with me. Because I'm very tall—according to my family, big-boned—and I wasn't immune to media influences that were putting mousse in my hair in the eighties when really, mousse was not a good thing to be putting in my hair. You know, trying to look like the white girls who were new wave—very petite women. And being tall and overweight—I've lost some weight—and having to go to places like The Avenue or the Big & Tall Girl shop to get clothes, and then trying to feel better about it by saying, Well, I wear the smallest size in this store; at least I don't wear a thirty-two. But still having all these self-esteem things going on with my personal appearance, and race is part of that, and gender. It's always been this mixed bag that I tried to sort through pretty unsuccessfully.

In advertising I think it's sort of moved away from women being seen as animalistic and exotic, but I really only have the seventies as a reference point for that, when the blaxploitation thing was happening—I'm thinking about black television shows where women are wearing this skintight clothing, and their appearance is very sexualized. But what they do or the things they say, they're not supposed to be sexy, they're just supposed to be sort of rough and, you know, sassy—I'm thinking of *Martin*, really. Like the woman in that show, Pam, I think she's beautiful, and yet Martin is always putting her down. And when she is sexy, it's with this sort of forcefulness which I don't think is necessarily bad—you know, to show women being assertive—but when you add race to it, it's as if black women don't need tenderness or don't need anyone to be gentle.

I used to read a lot, I was the cat burglar in my mother's book shelf. There was one book I remember in particular that was very 1970s; that's my reference point for childhood. It looked like one of those Time-Life books, and it was about women's bodies. I remember one picture very clearly; it was a lithograph of these people in various states of undress. It looked like an Italian Renaissance picture. The women in the pictures were being very coy, and the men were lifting up their little towel things they had draped over them and reaching between their legs, and then other people would be doing other things. I remember sneaking to look at this book a lot and trying to figure out what was happening and who was doing what to whom and why they were doing it.

I remember this at seven, or eight maybe. And then once I could read, I don't think I ever went into the adult section to look at dirty books or books that had anything about sexuality, because that's what I considered them then; anything to do with sex was a dirty book, or a dirty movie. But I think a lot of it was just through culture, really, through popular culture. We had HBO, when cable first came out, and the movie *Body Heat* was on. I don't know what year that was, but I remember sneaking and watching that, and every time my parents came down to the basement, turning the channel really quickly and then turning back when they were gone. But as far as getting details about it, there was one girl on my block who was older than myself and my best friend. I was ten or eleven, and she was in junior high; and she spilled the beans about everything and told us who she liked and who she had kissed and who had done what to whom, and about fingering and French kissing. I remember we just sat there with our mouths open. My parents thought she was fast. She was known as the fast girl on the block.

My parents never talked about sex. I don't think they ever sat me down and had any sort of birds-and-bees talk. Maybe they just relied on school to do it, where we had our little sex ed movie, in grade eight, and they talked about chickens hatching. I learned about getting my period through reading Judy Blume books, *Are You There God? It's Me, Margaret.* That was the book. But it didn't help, because when I did get my period, I remember just crying. I remember going to the bathroom, and there's blood and I just start crying, and my mother comes and says, "Why are you crying?" and I said, "I got my period and I don't want it." And she's like, "Oh, stop crying, it's fine," and she just left, went to the store and got some maxipads and came back and showed me how to use the tape; and we talked about how it's lucky because when she had it, they had to use these belts. Dad said, "Oh, I hear you're a woman now." And that just was mortifying because my mother told him that I had my period. So I was just embarrassed and that was the end of that.

People will think it's really perverted, but I was an early masturbator. I don't know how I figured it out, but I remember we moved when I was four or five into a different house. And I remember that room was brown and yellow. Hideous. I remember being in bed and I might wind up a towel or a blanket and put it between my legs and then do something until . . . I don't know, it wasn't an orgasm, I know that now, but I felt some sort of relief. And I remember seeing the walls, and my mother coming into the room and me pretending like I was asleep. And it continued probably through high school but not being very sophisticated about it. Then in college it was my feminist phase, you know, talking about vibrators and stuff with people. I would have had no idea where to buy a vibrator in my hometown, so I just talked about it in college; and then when I moved to Seattle, there was a store that has all the sex toys and all this really great information so you can read about what's happening and what's stimulating and what's not.

I felt ambivalent about virginity, if that's the right word. It was something that on the one hand I really wanted to get rid of, like it was this burden to be a virgin. But on the other hand I really didn't want to. I knew there were things that I wanted to do with my life, so I didn't want to get pregnant as a teenager. I had this big thing about Rick Springfield, so I would say that I was saving myself for Rick Springfield as this excuse for why I didn't have a boyfriend and why I wasn't having sex; really, why nobody wanted to have sex with me. It was this overarching narrative that I constructed. I let that go after a while, and then virginity was something I wanted to lose by my first year of college, just really feeling burdened by being a virgin because it seemed like nobody else was a virgin at all. I don't know if that was true or not, but you just felt that way. And it was before this whole Victorian virginity ring thing that was going on. I don't think I lost my virginity until I was twenty-two.

My junior year I hooked up with this guy and we were going to have intercourse but he couldn't get in; the door was locked. Not the door to my dorm, the door to my body. Then he asked me if I was a virgin, and he didn't want to have sex with me since I was a virgin. I guess he didn't want to be the one to do that. I don't know what was going on in his head, but knowing him—(he's still someone I keep in contact with, and there was this periodic hookup thing after that)—I don't think it was an aversion to virgins, but more just him feeling like he didn't want that responsibility, like I would have these romantic notions of him for the rest of my life as the first, or maybe hate him because he was the first. The first time we got together sexually, I remember him observing that he'd never slept with a black girl before. I remember thinking, What the hell does that mean? Is it somehow different, or what you expected? I didn't ask any questions about it. But I remember being bothered by it for a while afterward.

It seemed like after I wasn't a virgin anymore, it was okay to have sex with me. Because he came to visit me here. Two or three years ago we ended up having sex anyway. And it was good; it's just not something I would do now. It wasn't something I regretted after he left, but I was like, it's time to grow up; that was from the past.

It's funny but I can't clearly remember when I lost my virginity. I can't remember for sure, not because I've slept with so many, but I can't remember a sequence of events. For some reason my senior year, I was suddenly hot property. I think it was this guy who was a friend of my roommate's. He was a nice guy, and he really liked me, but there was something that didn't click for me. But we ended up having intercourse, and, well, we started to once and I felt like I had to confess that I was a virgin, so I told him and he said that he knew. And I was like, "Well, how did you know?" And he said, "Well, you tense up, your thighs are really tight." He had this whole schema worked out, not that I think he was very arrogant, but there was something. I feel like it was something that was weighing on my mind so much that I should be able to remember. Like it's such an important event that I should be able to be really sure about it. But for some reason I just can't be positive if he was the one.

We had gone out. I had met him before, and then I think weeks later my roommate said, "So-and-so thinks you're foxy." And I remember saying, "Foxy, what kind of word is foxy? Where'd you get foxy from?" So I said, "Well, hook me up with him." He was nice, you know—nothing else was going on. So we ended up going out to see some fake reggae band and dancing and having a good time, and we ended up getting really drunk and going back to my house. And we did our deliberating whether or not he was going to sleep over. Yeah, tedious. Got naked and I don't even know if a condom was involved here, actually. I could walk, I don't think I was at the point of passing out drunk. My speech was probably slurred, just laughing a lot, but definitely drunk. We fooled around and kissed and felt each other up. And yeah, I remember we started to have sex, he got on top and then I felt like I had to confess, so I told him that I was a virgin, and he said he knew. It's all messed up, the sequence, because I ended up seeing him again like two or three times after that. But I know that I had sex with him; I just don't know if it was this time or later on. I don't remember any sort of blood or hymen being broken or anything like that.

I remember thinking, Now this is weird. There is another person inside of me somewhere. I still think that now. It's bizarre. But once he explained the whole "Your thighs are tense," I remember trying to relax and chill out. He said things like "I think you're really beautiful." Which nobody had ever said to me before. But even though he was pretty much a stranger to me, I for some reason trusted him; but I don't know if that had anything to do with whether or not we used a condom. I think that was just stupidity.

I decided that I didn't want to see him anymore because he was acting like we were in this relationship, and I hardly ever saw him. He wanted something I just didn't want to give him, and now the tables are turning on me. We slept together three or four times and I went to a party with him, came back drunk, and then said we needed to break it off. But then called him again when I was drunk, very late at night. That's not something I'm proud of. And it's just not worth it, to do that. If you have to be drunk to sleep with somebody, you're pretty much not attracted to them, so there's really no point doing it. But I felt like I had not had a boyfriend, and was wrapped up in all these ideals of having a boyfriend, and not feeling attractive, and feeling like when I was with this person, at least somebody liked me. But then I decided that I really didn't need my self-esteem to sink any lower, and also compounding it by using this person. So I felt like there had to be something that I was missing. I don't remember anything about contraception. I didn't even really worry about it. Stupid, just dumb.

I remember, actually, that my period was late one of the times. I got really stressed out and worried that I was pregnant, and I wasn't. I just considered myself very lucky. I don't think I had an HIV test until I moved to Seattle, which was a few months after that. I decided I'd been having unprotected sex, and I needed to check it out. Anyway, this guy, he wanted a relationship but I didn't feel like we had a lot in common. I think there was a class issue there. He was a friend of my roommate's and he lived in the next town over. I can't even remember what he did for a living, but I guess he was working class. I just didn't feel like I could talk to him about much of anything. He would come over and we would chat about this person we had in common, maybe go out, and I remember being very uncomfortable until we started drinking because we didn't have anything to talk about and it was very awkward. Then I remember another time he made a really homophobic comment in front of a friend of mine. He said something about somebody being a fruit. I wound up responding, "A papaya? What do you mean, a fruit? What does that mean?" I felt, This isn't something I want to deal with. I don't feel like challenging him on this. I think at that point some of our differences were starting to come out. I remember him wondering what I was getting so revved up about. At the same time I can't figure out if I was looking for excuses not to go out with him, just because I wasn't attracted to him.

Then came the dry season. Feast or famine. I moved to Seattle. I did try to go out and I ended up doing a lot of stuff by myself, like going to clubs. And I met this really nice guy, but nothing ever happened with it. Knew someone who worked at a store near where I worked, and we went to a movie once, or a concert, and he was a world music deejay. I don't know what his ethnic background was. He might have been half black or half something else. He was this beautiful brown-skinned man. But nothing really came of it. It just didn't seem like he wanted to be pursued. In the past I've sort of pushed and pushed and pushed, until they had to be like, "Look, I don't want to hurt your feelings, but I want to be just friends." And I didn't want to have to relive that experience over and over again.

The one black guy I liked in high school, I tried to talk to him a lot and to sit next to him on the bus when we went on field trips. I remember one field trip in particular, I was sitting next to him and basically just came out and asked him, "Is it possible that we could go out?" or "Do you like me?" And he was like, "No. I like you as a friend," but nothing was going to happen. Then it turned out he had just started dating this other woman. Not that it had anything to do with it. I would go hang out with boys and get to a point where I would see if they were interested in me. I always felt like I was being the pursuer. Part of it was that most of them were white, so I felt like it's not something that would have occurred to them if I didn't bring it up or pursue them.

It just made me more and more depressed about myself. I used to think, Why am I so ugly, why don't they like me, what is wrong with me that I always seem to like white guys? Because I would see black men on campus, and I'd think, He's fine, he's cute, but never really do anything about it because we weren't in the same circles. It's a big campus. I tried to deny that I liked white men for a while, and went to the black student union meetings, and on a study abroad to Haiti. We were all black except for one person who was my roommate. But I just never felt black men found me attractive. Toward the end of college, and even to now, I don't feel black men find me attractive; or the ones that do, or the ones that say something, it's more like harassment, or they're old enough to be my father. And that doesn't appeal to me.

I've been seeing someone for a year now. This guy, he goes to school with me and he's a working-class white guy from Kentucky. It was one of those things where I was pursuing again, but not in my old patterns. I don't feel like I hounded people, but was just very persistent. This time I just thought he was cute, and if he wanted to go out and do something, fine, and if he didn't, whatever. It didn't matter much to me. Months before we started going out, I had a friend in town and was talking about taking her to this other city and I just mentioned it to him in passing; and he was like, "Oh, if you want to go, give me a call." And I just went and didn't call him. Hadn't even thought about it, and afterwards I found out that he was really hurt that I didn't call.

Finally I just had to ask. I said, "Is there something going on between us?" and I was incredibly shocked when he said, "I was wondering the same thing." That just floored me because I knew that he meant he was interested too, but I'd never gotten past that point before, so I didn't have any script. I was just like—okay. So he kissed me, and we talked a little bit more. Ended up making out, ended up in bed. Didn't have sex. We didn't have sex, like intercourse, for three or four months. We did lots of other things, things I didn't do before. Like with that working-class guy I mentioned before, he gave me oral sex, but I wouldn't go down on him. I just was not going to go there. It just did not seem like anything I ever wanted to do. Ever. It seemed at the time like nothing I would ever want to do, with him or in life. But that changed, and my current boyfriend and I have oral sex. It's something that I like, which I hadn't expected, ever. And also me giving him a hand job, or him fingering me. Trying out different positions if we can figure them out. So that was predominantly what was going on the first three or four months.

But, he's not a person who's into commitment. I don't know what the big deal is. I just know that this is not a relationship that's going to last after one of us leaves the city. This will probably be pretty soon because I'm applying for grants to get out of here. Part of it is that I'm in this relationship where he's not forthcoming. It's very important to me for him to tell me that he loves me, and he hasn't done that. I don't know why it's so important for me. I think the first time I said it to him, he had this reaction that was just like, Oh, God. And me being very sort of hurt by that. He's just a very closed-off person. I think since we've been going out, he's opened up a lot, but really only with me and not with other people. So my friends are like, "Why are you going out with him? He doesn't give you the attention you deserve. He's boring." But I don't find that. I find him really funny, and intelligent, and we get along well, and we have pretty good sex.

Race doesn't come up because we don't hold hands in public or kiss in public. I was trying to figure it out. Is it because he doesn't want this pressure of being in an interracial relationship and letting people out there know? Or is it just that he doesn't like those sorts of displays of affection? He told me he just doesn't like those sorts of displays of affection. But I think that race might to some degree be an issue, because I asked these really obtuse questions. I said something like, "So do your parents know you're seeing me?" I didn't say, "Do your parents know you're seeing a black woman?" or "What would it be like if I went to Kentucky with you?" He never came out and told them, but he assumes they know since I've met his sister. She came to visit and I met her, and he always talks about, Rita and I did this, or Rita and I went here. We went for a little vacation, and so he talked about that with them. I know I am the first black woman he's been involved with because he's only dated one other person seriously, who was white. This is part of the problem: it's a relationship that I know is not healthy for me, and if I feel uncomfortable asking him these questions, then it's not a relationship I should be in. But I've been alone for so long that I just have a really hard time letting it go. And right now I'll be thinking but can't make my mouth do the talking. I'm meeting him for lunch, boy is he in trouble. . . . It's a question I've wanted to ask but just haven't felt comfortable asking, and I think it goes along with this whole other list of questions that I've wanted to ask.

When I see him, it's great, and we have sex like once a week. I see him on Saturday nights and occasionally on other times during the week. Just last week I broached the idea of, maybe we could get together two nights a week—sort of ease him into it. And he said stuff that made me think he was giving me a line.

I feel like I've been lucky so far, just in that the men that I've been with, there hasn't been a problem with them being satisfied and being like, Okay, it's over, who cares about you. If that happened, I would be pretty disturbed about it. That would be someone I wouldn't want to see again, if he was only concerned about his orgasm. Like rolling over and going to sleep. But with the boyfriend I have now, we both have an orgasm and then roll over and go to sleep. They've been very attentive. There are things I could learn to do better, like I could learn how to give a better hand job, or learn how to give a better blow job, but that goes back to my whole learning from books thing.

I'm very lucky, I've never been raped or anything like that. It's a constant fear I walk around with as a woman, but it's not something that I've encountered. And in a way that played into my sexual relationship now. Because I have all these intellectualizations about rape and that kind of violence; but in my own sexual relations, I like to bite and to scratch him and sort of get rough sometimes. At first I was having guilt about that— just feeling like this is not how sex should be; it should be gentle, and not rough. But it's something that I enjoy, and it's consensual. We tried handcuffs. Whips don't appeal to me, or golden showers or any of that stuff. We haven't tried anal sex; I don't think I want to. It's just painful. I'm sure it doesn't have to be. I guess it's pretty much what people call vanilla sex. But in my mind, my fantasies, the whole restraint thing, like the handcuffs, I think of that as different from the Velcro restraints and things, where you have bedposts and you can't move, and the person is teasing you. There's something that I find really exciting about being teased, and for me to hold off, like, How long can I not touch this person when they're doing this?

Sometimes we'll play—actually, it's stupid, but we started playing strip Uno. It was this teasing thing, like we're sitting in front of each other in partial states of undress. It was a game of how long can we keep playing this game before we have sex.

I go back and forth on kids. Lately it's been that I don't want to have children. On one level, I really do feel like the world is a bad place, and there are things I don't want to have to explain to a child. If someone calls my child a nigger, I don't want to have to comfort them, or combat that negative influence. But on the other hand I feel it's a challenge that I would like to take up. If I have to make a decision it takes me forever because I don't want to make the wrong decision. So I wouldn't want to have a child and feel I was constantly monitoring what they watch on TV and trying to help them along. I don't know, I can't decide if it's selfish, or if I just don't want to bring a child into this world and have them be hurt. Because I don't think that's something I would be able to stand. I have a friend who has a four-year-old son who I'm very close to, and if his feelings get hurt, I just get completely devastated; and I don't want to have to go through that. I keep wishing there was a computer program where I could code in my stuff and code in whoever my partner's stuff is, and see what our child would look like, and then have this picture to put on the refrigerator. That's my child.

On the other hand, I feel this obligation to adopt. I feel there's already a child here who needs help. I could do that and not feel I brought another child into this world who would have to deal with all of this. I would adopt a black girl. My father just doesn't get it. Because I'm the only child, my father asks what would happen to the family name. But if I adopt, the child will have the family name.

I don't know if my dad ever really counted on me dating white guys. He saw that most of my friends were white; my best friend from the tenth grade on was a white guy, and I think after that he asked me, "How's your boyfriend?" "He's not my boyfriend. What are you talking about?" With my current boyfriend, he asked me what nationality he was. And I said, "He's American." Just being smart. But I finally sent them a picture of him, and my mom said, "Yes, he looks like he's a nice-looking young man," which is the standard reply. But race doesn't come up. Because I really think that my mother would be happy if I never got married. She's always saying, "Get your education," and, "If I had it to do over, I wouldn't have gotten married so young."

It's hard to know what people see first. Is someone treating me a certain way because I'm black or because I'm a woman? Usually I feel it's because I'm black. I've gotten very militant about daily interactions with people, not putting up with certain behaviors. Like being in a store, and the store clerk ignores me, then telling them, "Did you not see me standing here? Did you ignore me because I'm black?" and, "I won't be shopping here again." Like that. I think they need to know. I had one encounter in New York where I was in an office-supply store with some friends, and we'd come over from work on our lunch break, so I was wearing a skirt and was sort of dressed up. All the other employees in the store are wearing red smocks that say "Office Depot." And this woman comes up and asks me if I know where something is. I just looked at her and said, "Just because I'm black doesn't mean I work here." She got completely flustered and said, "I didn't mean . . ." And then she just walked away. I was like, Yeah, you did mean that. And I'm going to tell you about yourself. At the same time I'm very proud to be a black woman. If I had any control over it, I wouldn't come back as a white man. But I don't know if I would want to come back as a white woman or not. That's a hard one, just 'cause I feel like there might be an advantage in dating situations. But if I came back as a white woman, it would be just my karma to be only attracted to black men.

I think I've gotten a lot more careful in picking white men. There are progressive white men—and by "progressive" I mean ones who are working on their racism, and working on all of their different -isms and things. And not going out with someone who I felt was dating me because it looked good, or it made him look good in certain circles or whatever. But it's this really hard thing to balance, and sort of hypocritical because I remove my current boyfriend from that pack of white men, and all the time say things to him like, "White men are so stupid," or "What's wrong with y'all?" But also feeling like I'm doing this sort of abstraction, like if there was an overhead projector, there'd be this white man title, and it stands for a certain power and certain oppressive element in society, whereas I have straight white men who are friends and recognize they have some of those things going on too. I think it's been a shift; it's very different from college where I was very, "If you say anything homophobic, I will never talk to you again." Or racist. You know, being very rigid. And I think I'm becoming, I don't know if it's less vigilant, or just more relaxed and accepting of people.

I have to be specific because I have black gay male friends who have accepted me for being a feminist and holding certain ideals, which is very important to me. I don't feel I've encountered a straight black man who would date me and accept that. It's like with the whole club scene thing: I think that there are progressive black men, but they have their own issues and they're dating white women, or they're dating women who are Latina, or they're dating Asian women. They're dating everybody but black women.

I have internalized some sexism, always thinking about losing weight, and I've been on this lipstick train all of a sudden, where in the last couple years I've been amassing huge quantities of lipstick. You know, appearance things; at the same time having this attitude about white women—I call white women "trixies" a lot, but it's usually very specific. White women in sororities, and my own stereotypes of who white women are. One time somebody asked me who trixies were, and I said, "Well, they're little white girls." And it being this jealousy thing, but on the other hand being repulsed. I would never want to be in a sorority or acting like I see some white girls do.

I go back and forth when I think about the future, if it's a white man or a black man, not really caring which but feeling like it has to be someone who isn't afraid to tell me they love me, who is attentive, who isn't afraid to share when he's having some sort of problems, or feeling pain. It would be good to find somebody who wanted a family because I feel like my family was defective in so many ways, and I've really come to distrust the whole institution of families; but on the other hand, it's really something I secretly want. And I go back and forth on marriage—it's patriarchal; gay men and lesbians can't get married; it's only for the tax break. But on the other hand, it would be really nice to feel secure and to know that there's somebody there. At the same time, having been single so long, I've gotten to be really independent; so that's something I want to hold on to, even within a relationship. I guess it would be some sort of long-term relationship. Being with someone who I was still having fun with, not going to a restaurant and both of us sitting there reading newspapers and ignoring each other. I guess just feeling that in the future we would be helping each other along and not feeling that the other person was holding back from anything, and really just not regretting being in the relationship, which is what I feel like now. I wish I'd never started it so that we wouldn't have to break up.

# Linda Rae

WHEN A GIRL CHILD, a female child, is born, she's born either into a family where there is a mother and a father, or it's the mother. I'm speaking from the African American point of view. The mother and most likely the grandparent is there. I just think about my own childhood and being raised. My father was in the service so he would travel a lot, and my mother was a nurse and she worked a lot. My grandfather died, so my grandmother came to live with us. So there was five children; I was the middle child, the oldest girl. Therefore I took all the chores that my mother would ordinarily be doing while she was working trying to make the money. My father was away, and he was pretty promiscuous because I have a sister my same age who looks just like me; the only difference is that she's a darker complexion than me, but we look like twins and we have different mothers. So I think about how it was for me—we were sort of like a middle-class black family in a small town in Georgia in the 1950s. Little town—blink and you're through it. Our values were: you go to church, family comes first, you keep yourself clean, you don't wear wrinkled clothes, your clothes are ironed—because I did the ironing so I know they was ironed.

We never talked about sex. That was one of the things that never was talked about, even though my mother was a nurse. If it was talked about, it was talked about in a negative view, like if you had sex, if you kissed, you would get pregnant. Babies came from the cabbage patch, and your "thing" was nasty. You was taught these negative things, I never even was told about my period. I fell down on my bike one day, and I thought I had broke my "thing," and I was embarrassed and ashamed to go and tell my mother that I broke my "thing." Like I did something bad. And blood was coming out, and my grandmother, oh, she went and got a big sheet and tore the sheet in these little squares and folded them up and told me to put them between my legs, and that would happen once every month, and I would have pains, and that was it. I never knew what it was that I was having. It actually influenced me not wanting to ride a bike. It totally went out of my head; I don't know how to ride a bike anymore.

My mother never really got a chance to tell me anything. My grandmother was the dominant one in my family. I was the oldest child. I was always told I was never going to be anything, that I was different because my skin was lighter than the rest of my brothers and sisters. I didn't know that I had a separate father from them. I didn't know this; none of this stuff was told. So therefore, they were hiding their own sexuality. My mother was promiscuous and had this child out of wedlock, and I didn't know this. All I knew was that my father was away at the service, and he would come home and bring me things, and then he would leave again. But I never knew that my mother was not married to this man.

My grandmother was an abuser; she abused my mother as well as me. I didn't know that she was abusing my mother until I got grown, but she abused me. I mean she used to beat me like an animal. With a whip, and boards, and those hickory sticks. Down South it's like, spare the rod, spoil the child. And she used to take all those hickory sticks and whup 'em together and beat me. I mean she beat me to the point of submission. I used to have whips all over my body, and I was real, real light-skinned, so she used to take me and dunk me in the creek so that the scars wouldn't stay, so that my mother wouldn't see it because I was so light there was no way you couldn't see it. And the thing about it in the neighborhood, people knew about it.

I kept having this recurring dream about this blood coming out of me. There was this woman living down the street, who was sort of like the hooker type of woman in the neighborhood, for lack of a better way to say it. She used to let me come in her house while she was putting her makeup on; and she would take a bath, and she would put those water bottles that you take the douche with, she would put it up inside of her. She had me so brainwashed that when she said, "When you put this up in here, it washes all the trash out of your body," I was visualizing all the cans and bottles and papers and stuff; and she would say, "Look, you see it coming out?" when she did it, and I believed. I was around eight years old, a couple of years in school.

I used to sneak out the back because at the end of the evening, the old folks used to sit on the front porch, and the kids would be in the back playing. So I'd just sneak down and go across the way to this lady's house. I can remember the first sexual experience because it was the year before I went to school, around five years old. I started the first grade, and my brothers started making me have oral sex with them. At first I thought it was a funny type of thing, and then whenever I'd see the white sticky stuff come out, that was like, uuuuh. It was terrible, and I would cry and cry and cry and they threatened me not to tell. Adults would ask me why. They thought I was mentally disturbed because I would cry and cry and cry and they didn't know why I was crying, and I was scared to tell. My brothers would threaten to kill me. My youngest brother, he was two years older than me, and the other was two years older than him. It went on until I was about eleven or twelve. It all happened the same time, because my grandmother was beating me so profusely; it was just too much. And I decided to fight back. One day she hit me, and just the rage came into my body. I had an apple in my hand, and I threw that apple as hard as I could up against the wall, and it looked like applesauce—that's how much force I put into it. And I beat her until I couldn't—they had to pull me off of her. I was a scrawny little thing, too, but it really took a lot to pull me off of her.

My brothers, they'd be sitting on the porch, and they wanted money. They used to take me next door to this little dirty old man over there, and he would jerk off on the wall, and he would give them money. I would just stand there and he would fondle my, whatever little titties I had, or play with my vagina, or I would sit on his lap. And to me at that time, his dick was this big, like fifty inches long because I was so little. I remember the smell of alcohol, that strange urine smell . . . So you have to understand that everything that was pertaining to sex to me was dirty, and wrong, and sneaky. And after I beat my grandmother up, I still never really told them about my brothers making me have sex with them.

I finally just got a chance to tell my mom about some of these things since I've been in recovery. Those are the things that kept me sick, those are the things that kept me using drugs. By the time I was fourteen, I was in a reform school. And when I went to a reform school, I'd still never talk about it because the trauma was so much there, I just stopped talking. I didn't utter a word. I would just sit and look and stare and draw pictures. I used to draw and paint and all that.

This was a reform school for what they called "bad girls," yeah. It was a farm, initially a farm, and everybody had chores; but they put me in isolation because I wouldn't talk. So they kept having these different doctors coming to see me, and counselors, and there was one counselor that I really did trust. I knew that people drank spirits, but I didn't really know what alcoholism was. And this one counselor used to come and get me every night, 'cause she said I was special. She'd let me watch TV, she would give me candy, and she would always put on these little outfits. She'd be drinking and she would act weird, but I really didn't relate it to alcoholism because I didn't have a point of reference. I guess after I started talking to her, I trusted her; and then she got drunk one night and she raped me. So my first encounter of having a sexual orgasm was doing it with a woman, repeatedly. At first it was frightening, but then eventually it became pleasurable because I just submitted to her; so that was my whole, my whole outlook on that. I knew it was wrong, but it didn't feel bad. I was again threatened not to talk about it, so I didn't.

They found out about it because she was an alcoholic. She had me tied to a bed and fell asleep drunk. They heard me screaming, and then they came and all the shit hit the fan. Of course, suddenly I was well, now I could leave, and I could go home because I was cured. It was a big cover-up. Big bureaucratic bullshit where people can't deal with sexual issues. They couldn't deal with this issue because they didn't have the capacity to understand how this could happen, how the bad girl made her do this. I'm tied to the thing, I'm still a scrawny little thing, you know. I think during all of this stuff, all I could really hear was my grandmother telling me I was never going to be anything, I was never going to amount to anything, that I was bad, and that bad things happened to me because I was bad. The only thing that I could never understand was what I did that was so bad. My uncles used to try to—they molested me—used to try to have sex with me. I went to stay with my aunt when I got out of reform school because I was not going back to stay with my grandmother because I'm sure I was going to kill her the next time. I was plotting how I was going to dig a hole and bury her alive. That's how much I hated her. So I went to stay with my aunt, and her husband would chase me around the house all the time, and my cousins would molest me.

And everybody in the whole damn town was related to me, so it wasn't like I was going to find a boyfriend. But after watching enough TV I figured I could get me a husband, and get me a little house with the picket fence, and a couple little babies and a dog, and a car in the garage. And everything would be fine. I found a man. He was much older than me. About eight years older than me. I was about fifteen years old, I think; I was fifteen and he was twenty-two or twenty-three years old. He was in the service. And I got pregnant. First time I had sexual penetration, I got pregnant. I hated it; it was terrible. The blood and all of that, it was terrible. It was nothing like what the counselor had done to me; it was entirely different. So it was like, Something's wrong with this picture. What am I missing here? I didn't even know I was pregnant. I was like three months pregnant before I even knew it. I was having morning sickness, and my auntie figured it out; and then they found out that I was pregnant, and they sent me to another reform school for pregnant girls. So there was a time that he didn't know that I was pregnant. He was in the service, and by the time that he found out, he thought that they had just shipped me away. Found out that I was pregnant, he had got married. I had just had the baby, and he found out about it and he called to the place where I was, and they wouldn't let me talk to him. I found out that my family perpetrated the whole thing. He wanted to adopt my child. You know, that was his kid and he wanted to adopt the child. I talked to his wife, and she said that I was too young and I wouldn't know what to do, that she could take care of everything. And I said, "I'm not giving my baby away." My family tried to get me to give my baby away because that was an embarrassment to this supposedly upper-middle-class black family. They were all sick as hell, every single one of them. Motherhood was an out for me; I felt like I was somebody's—this baby was so beautiful, and so wonderful, and so I couldn't give my baby away. Got pregnant when I was fifteen and had the baby at sixteen; we moved to Connecticut when I was sixteen going on seventeen, and I went to high school. His father died in 1970; my son was killed in 1970, and his father died two weeks after that.

The man that I was living with beat my son to death. It was the hardest thing I ever went through in my whole entire life. By the time I got out of high school and started going to college, up here in Bridgeport, I got involved in drugs and the street life. I had another son, and the guy that beat my first son to death was my second son's father's best friend. I started going out with his friend just because I wanted to make him angry, because he was fucking around with somebody. And I got pregnant by this guy. So I had my son, then my other little son, and then I was pregnant with a daughter. I got involved in the street life and started using drugs; and when I was out there in the street, he was beating them all along, but nobody ever told me that it was happening. None of my baby-sitters or anything— I came home one night, and my second son was really sick. His stomach was swollen, and I took him to the hospital and made it look like he had been taking some pills. And they pumped his stomach. But in essence what happened was that he had been beating him, and he kicked him in his stomach, and his bowels was perforated and they burst. And so when they pumped his stomach, they just pumped him—they forced it out of his system. He was three, almost four months old. And I was pregnant.

They locked me up, they locked him up; they said I had something to do with it. My whole life was just destroyed. I drank and drugged so much after my son's funeral, and DSS [Department of Social Services] took my other son away from me. In my head, I could hear my grandmother saying again, "You're never going to be anything, you're never going to amount to anything, you're bad," and that's the way I felt about myself. I drank and drugged from the time I woke up in the morning to the time I passed out at night. And I was carrying a child. I was six months pregnant.

You know, sex was a thing for me to do to make you love me. And all the men in my life, I used that. And nothing else in life was important to me but to have somebody to love me. And sex was the way to do that. I learned how to have the best sex; I knew all the ways that you could have sex, and I prided myself with doing it so well that how could a man cheat on me 'cause I'm giving him everything he wants. And sex—it's nothing, no end-all, cure-all of everything. And I spent a lot of my life doing that. Even in prostitution I would do that. I mean, here I was, an educated person. But I was always able to get over my trauma because I had secretly in my head this goal that I was going to have that little white house and the picket fence, and nothing was going to stand in the way of that. When I met drugs, drugs was like the way of blocking out the misery and my way of continuing to stay on my route to my goal to have this man that's gonna make me happy forever and ever and ever.

I had my daughter; I had her premature. And I'll let you know how little I knew about mourning, about the bond between a mother and the child. She died two weeks after she was born, but she was so full of drugs and alcohol that if she'd lived, she would have been a vegetable. I buried her, and I never cried. My way of transferring my emotions was that she was dead because her father killed my eldest son. So she should be dead. It's sick, I know it's sick, and believe me I've gone through therapy and worked through some of this stuff. But at that time it was real, it was just as real as the nose on my face. After that my whole life became a revenge thing about men. I was going to destroy marriages; I was going to destroy relationships; I would make a man believe that I loved him and then drop him like a hot potato, walk away from him and destroy him. That's what I set out to do, and I did it so easily.

The man who killed my son went to jail, but he only spent eighteen months in jail because they said they couldn't prove that the blow that the baby-sitter saw him hit my son with was the one that killed him. You know, just bullshit. The system. He was a man. In Connecticut, a man is God. Whether he's black or white, you understand, a man has the upper hand over women no matter what. And all his friends lied for him; they all knew what was going on. I didn't even know he was an IV drug user. I didn't know—I was so stupid and young and naive because I was so sheltered from the outside world, to drugs, in Georgia; but I was exposed to all this other stuff, just being a woman. I didn't even have a clue of what it was to be a woman. It was what I saw on TV or I saw at the neighbor's, the Beaver Cleaver's crap. That's what I saw, and that's what I thought it was. And having no idea how, no sexuality of my own, I always took on "the man's the leader of my life" to show me how I was supposed to act. I had no role models. I just did whatever I thought I could do, whatever made me feel good. So it was really quite natural for me to do drugs. Because when I did drugs, I wasn't that quiet person anymore; I can tell you I was arrogant, and I could do things, and it worked for a while.

The man I was living with, the man who killed my son, got me hooked on drugs; so prostitution was the way to get the drugs. I continued it, the prostitution. I've worked all my life. I've never missed a link in a job—there's no gap in my history of working. I was always a highly functioning addict. I could turn it on and turn it off. When you talk about how they think we should be prim and proper, and use the proper etiquette and proper manners—I knew how to do that real well. I knew how to hold on to a job real well. It was easy for me to mask my addiction, it was easy for me to mask my pain. It was easy for me to mask my sexuality until I realized in some later stages in prostitution there was time where we got paid to be with other women, or we would be getting high and we would be with the other women, but we didn't consider ourselves lesbians. We just considered ourselves having fun. It felt good—who wants somebody to stick a dick in 'em and come in 'em? I hate that to this day; I hate for a man to come in me. I don't like the feeling, and it just stinks, and it just wasn't my thing. It wasn't natural to me for somebody to be shooting all that stuff up in me. Why should I let 'em? So I learned how to have sex with men where—ride around, come on my chest, come on my back, come between my titties, come under my armpits, or shoot it against the wall, all kinds of stuff just to keep them from coming inside of me. And they loved it. They loved it. That was unbelievable.

I did finish nursing school in Bridgeport—I barely made it out of school, really barely. Right now, if somebody asked me to go do hands-on nursing, I would not be able to do it. Anyway, soon after my son was killed, I moved from Bridgeport because it was impossible for me to live there even after they found out that I didn't have anything to do with my son's death. My family turned their backs on me. It was like, I can't live like this. So I moved to New York, got me a job at a hospital. I worked on the nut unit in triage, where I ended up a couple years later. That was my first job, but I was always able to get a job. I could talk more shit than the radio.

I was just snorting cocaine and popping pills most of the time. Returning to alcohol because I got a hole in my nose from snorting so much cocaine. When I hit New York, I had hit the big leagues. Right away I was right on top—I had no idea. The first pimp that I met, I married. I didn't realize that he was the caliber of pimp that he was; he owned property, he was a businessman, he had everything. I had minks and diamonds. The fairy tale, the white house with the picket fence. I knew that he was a pimp, but it didn't matter to me. I had my little white house with the picket fence. And that was the beginning of me really learning about what it felt like to be loved, because I knew he loved me. But he was a sick person. He had four or five other women, all the time, and he was an addict. But he was a different kind of addict than I was used to. There was nothing conservative about this person. He used and used, and he was controlling. He controlled me, and he beat me all the time.

Out of all the sexual relationships I'd had with men, I felt loved and caressed when I made love to him. It wasn't like I was fucking him. He took time to find out what made me feel good, and I didn't have to fake the oohs and the aahs. My oohs and aahs were real. And he married me, and I thought this was the greatest thing under the sun. He gave me everything that I could possibly want. I had a child for him, and he helped me get my other son from DSS in Bridgeport. We had a home, we had a life. But again, you know that belief that if he didn't beat me, he didn't love me. I was raised with those ideas, so how could it be any different for me? Besides, I was really, really pretty. He wasn't that good-looking, and he was really, really jealous of everywhere I went. If I went to the meat market and came home with two nice T-bones, he would say that I fucked the guy in the meat market to get 'em, not believing I had to pay him for 'em. He was just that jealous. He used to have people follow me around.

Eventually, the same thing happened with him that happened with my grandmother. He beat me and beat me until I started taking karate lessons. That's another place I learned a lot about my own sexuality. Karate taught me that I had to have self-control, that I had power, the power to think through things, the power to make changes in my life, the power of decision making. I never thought I had that kind of power. And violence was the last resort; I didn't have to react to the person that was causing violence to me by another means of violence. Because I would be verbally abusive. "Kill me, if you're gonna beat me, kill me, kill me. I don't care! You're wrong, you're wrong." And that was wrong. Virtually it came down to that because he was an alcoholic also, and he used to come home, wake me up in my sleep, and beat me. I never got a good night's sleep. I look better now than I did when I was twenty-five. I was with that man for nine years and kept getting beaten and beaten. But I started fighting him back, and he started leaving me the fuck alone after a while. Because I learned how to fight good. Then he found out that I was taking these karate lessons and went down to the place and beat the guy up in the dojo at gunpoint. And I couldn't go back there anymore. But I kept in touch with my friends; I met a lot of friends. I had already been going there six months, so they knew.

Everything in my life has been a learning experience. Even my husband was the biggest challenge of my life, and I left him even though I didn't think I could be by myself. I always had a man; I'd never lived by myself. I took my kids. I planned it, plotted, saved the money, and got me an apartment in Manhattan, and moved to Manhattan, took my kids, and that blew him away because he thought I was so codependent on him that I couldn't do it. That was the beginning of the end because I didn't realize that I could do this on my own. I'm the one that worked; even when I was out there prostituting, I got the money first. So what do I need him for? It was like living this double life. But then I began to bond with my children and know what motherhood was, and how important it was, and that's when I began to mourn my two other children. Because I could see their faces in my two children. And I realized that the drugging and all this other stuff that I was doing was hurting them.

So when I got the apartment in Manhattan, he came back—he called me one night from the bar where I used to hang out and said he wanted to talk to me. Said, "I want to see the kids. I haven't seen the kids." So I got the kids, he got to see the kids, took them back to the baby-sitter. He said, "We're going to go out and have a few drinks." And so he got me high and said, "Bitch, did you think you was going to get away with getting away with my kids? I got the best years of your life." And he put me in the back seat—I was in the back seat already, actually—and the brother was driving, and he jumped in the back seat and he beat me from Manhattan to Brooklyn. I can remember coming over the Brooklyn Bridge: I could see the lights, and I was just praying to God that he would take my life because that's how badly he was beating me. And he beat me. I had on shorts, my body was—it was the summertime and I didn't really have a whole lot on, and he beat me, and he thought I was dead. I just passed out, blanked out. He threw me on the Brooklyn Bridge and left me for dead. His brother called the police, called 911 and told them where I was. This was three or four hours later. By the time they came to get me, I had over a hundred rat bites on my body. I mean, just imagine it. I had this recurring dream up until about three years ago. I was unconscious but my subconscious was awake, 'cause they said if I had been awake when that was happening, I would have had a heart attack. When the authorities came to find me, I ended up in Bellevue. I didn't know who I was. I had amnesia. His brother came to see me in the hospital—that's how I remembered.

That's when he told me that he'd already got the best years of my life. Fuck you. I don't need you. Don't nobody want you. So by that time, by

'78, I still had my kids. I was working a little half-ass job; but I was doing so much cocaine, I was just barely functional. My kids were just from baby-sitter to baby-sitter. And I know I was hurting them, I knew I was. So I got enough money to have a penthouse apartment with everything you could imagine. I put everything in the car that I could possibly put in the car, and I left New York. I went back to Georgia. We have a home down there, so I went back there to stay with my brother in the house. And I couldn't stay there, shit. Nurses only got paid about seven dollars an hour. No way—I would bring home about two hundred dollars a week. That was nothing! After I'm used to having thousands of dollars. When I went back down south, I imagined that I was going to go back to my roots, where I came from, and everything was going to be fine. My kids were so happy, and I was okay for a while. Instead, I think I fucked everybody from the east side, west side, north side, up side, you know, trying to fill up that black hole. It just didn't work; I was just running from myself. And I left my kids there. I had to go, I had to leave; I couldn't stay there.

Yes, this was the brother that had molested me. But my brother was married and had responsibilities by then. There was nothing inside of me to make me think that he would do that to them. Then there was nothing inside of me that would help me confront him with what he did to me. It took me, like I'm saying, just in the last six years since I've been in recovery, to work through some of that stuff.

My kids were there for a year, just a year. I came back to Connecticut and stayed with my mother. And got a job. I was doing good for a while. I got a job, a good job, sent for my kids, and then I met my second husband. Got married to him. He had money, he was older than me, and he would provide for me and my kids. I married him so I could have another white house with the picket fence. And my husband loved me so dearly. But I wasn't ready; I was an addict. I was an addict, and we moved to California, and that's when all hell broke loose. I learned about freebasing cocaine. Just like they say, you see the TV go down the drain, and the car and the house, everything. It was fast. It was fast. I was very depressed in California. I was married to an older man that I didn't love. And I was fooling around on him. I didn't feel good about that; I do have some morals and values somewhere stuck down inside of me. My kids were in gangs, and eventually my husband and I split up. I started back to prostitution. I ended up going to jail, and my husband had to take my kids.

You name it, I did it. Between prostitution and grand larceny, and larceny by trickery, and selling drugs, and boosting—you name it, I did it all. I just kept changing names because I was a master of disguise. I could put on a wig and look different every time you'd see me. When they finally caught up with me—I think it was God; I felt like in this whole process, God had to pick me up and walk me through some of this stuff because any normal human being would have lost their mind or committed suicide by now. But freebase cocaine brought me to my knees. After I got out of prison and my husband sent my kids back east, I came back to Boston, to Connecticut, to Bridgeport again, and started out and I was doing good for a while. But you can't just stop freebasing cocaine. I could slow down, but I could never stop. And then I started drinking much more.

Then I got me a little apartment, got me a nice job, the whole nine. I was always with some guy, and that's how I met my fiancé, the last guy that I was with. Before I came into treatment. He was an electronic engineer. He was cool. He helped me stay together. We got high, like drinking or snorting cocaine, but I didn't know that he was shooting drugs. This man gave me the best sex that I ever had in life; and on top of having the best sex, he was so considerate and so loving and so doting and so wonderful— him and my kids just blended. It was unbelievable—like those were his kids. The most perfect situation that I could see in my life, this was; I was asking God to help me be good so I could be with this man, so we could be happy forever. We were engaged to be married. A couple months before the wedding, he left town. I was devastated. I could not understand what happened. What did I do wrong? I was, again, internalizing it, and just went crazy. My kids were all getting grown; they were teenagers by now. My daughter got pregnant, had a kid. My son was going to jail, back and forth. It was just really, really bad and I was just using more and more and more drugs. Until I started selling it. I was selling large, large quantities of drugs, and the way I sold my drugs, you wouldn't believe. Most of my customers were men, and I used to keep the cocaine in my drawers—basically, so nobody would steal it from me. But I used to tell them, "The cocaine that I'm giving you is so good. The reason why it's so good is because it has the aroma of my pussy and that's why it's so good." And they just believed that. I used to have them lined up coming to buy my stuff. This was the bottom of my drugging days. What I didn't know was that my partner had AIDS. He never told me. And I've since found out that he was going to the shooting gallery, shooting drugs in places that I didn't know, I couldn't detect. Because he knew that I was a nurse, and I would know a needle puncture. I used to think that dope fiends were the worst kind of people on the earth—not realizing that I was a dope fiend. So I didn't go find out about being HIV-positive until I got in recovery. I got busted with a big lump sum of drugs.

They gave me the options: I could go to treatment or I could go to jail. Seven to fifteen years in jail? Yeah, I'll go to treatment. And all the time that I was in treatment, I just had no idea that I was ever not going to use again. I had it all planned. I was thirty days committed. I was gonna get high, had my people on the phone—come and get me when them thirty days were up. And the twenty-ninth day that I was in this treatment center, I got the message of desperation. This woman came in—what they call commitments coming in from Narcotics Anonymous. And this woman started telling my story. It wasn't my story, but it was her story and it sounded like mine. That was the message of desperation for me. It was the message to tell me I didn't have to live like that anymore, that I was somebody; and this was the first time that somebody told me that they loved me and I believed it. You know what I'm saying—the message that comes from another individual, comes from their heart, soul, and spirit. It just felt like it traveled across the room, and it hit me that I'm a sick individual. I am an addict, and I need some help. You're not using because you feel good; you're using because you don't feel good. There's a way for you to feel better about yourself. And I have not—from that day in 1991, January 15 of 1991—I have not used a mood- or mind-altering chemical. I haven't thought about using, even when I tested positive for HIV. I was fourteen months clean when I tested positive. And it was like, the message came to my head, "You're never going to be anything. This is a punishment from God." It came there, but it was a fleeting moment. I started to work here at AIDS Center, and I had only been working here two months before I found out I was HIV-positive.

See how God takes care of you? God took care of me; he put me in a place where I could get taken care of. Yes, because these people took care of me. I really learned about my own sexuality and sex and began to talk about it by working this field. They talk about the gay and lesbian community—I get my information from them. Because I know the struggle, I know what it is like trying to be yourself, and trying to love and lust at the same time, and knowing the difference between love and lust. I'm able to talk about me, my sexuality, my life, and with an open book because I don't want to hurt anymore.

I'm going back a lot of years. We've been talking about 1970 to 1990; 1994 was the first time I ever went back to my kids' grave. It was the first time I was able to cry, to get rid of that pain. It's still there; it's not like it's gone. But I look back on my whole life, and I say to myself, How did I become HIV-positive and go through all the things that I did? What was God thinking about, and how am I going to survive? The way that I survived was because I learned who I was. I learned that I don't have to let somebody use my body to love me, and I don't have to use my body to make somebody love me. That I have a message to give, and that message all starts from within. It's not about how good you can screw, or how good you can suck; it's about how well you can use your point of reference to make you a better person. I'm sorry that my point of reference had to be so strong and so harsh and so abusive, but I was able to get past that. And now I can feel my pain, and I don't feel like I need to go and have a bottle of Jack Daniel's or a snort of cocaine to make it go away. It's about having a good support system and knowing about my body.

I know what my body is feeling. And because I'm HIV-positive doesn't mean that I should be so grateful to have a man that I'm gonna let him screw me when I don't want to. If I don't want to have sex, I'm not having sex. "Well, I'm taking a chance having sex with you," they say sometimes. Motherfucker, that's your problem. I told you I was HIV-positive.

Now if you took a chance, it's 'cause you want some pussy. Bottom line. Don't try to lay no guilt trip on me, 'cause I have none. I'm taking care of me. You're not having sex with me without a condom. If the condom breaks, it's on you. You know? Simple as that. I'll feel bad for a while, but I'll have to get over it because it's just like we signed a contract that we're going to have sex with each other. I'll let you know what your risk is; I'll tell you what you need to do to protect yourself; I know what I need to do to protect myself. However, you haven't even been tested yourself, so why are you going to tell me that I'm putting you at risk?

My daughter's in the navy. She'd had enough—I mean, after she had the baby, and she got married, and her husband was in the army. They had this big formal wedding, and I knew where she was coming from: the white house with the picket fence. I know, it was my dream; I could see it in her. It was something that kind of transferred, or something going on. But I could see it in her, and the first time her husband did something wrong, she was ready to split up. He did something wrong, she couldn't forgive him. My daughter, she will not forgive or forget. She's just like that; she's one-sided. Because she was raised with me, she knows the difference between right and wrong. I never neglected to tell my kids about sex. I sit them down when they was little, showed them movies, talked about sex, gave them condoms, talked about STDs. I gave them sexuality, I told them what love was, I told them what to expect when you do certain things to someone, and how to have relationships. So they had a point of reference; it's not like they weren't prepared. Any mistakes they made, they knew that they wished they had of listened to me. But she's okay; she's in the service now. She has a son, my first grandbaby, my doll baby, sweetheart, punkin-poo. He's eight years old; he's the joy of my life. I have two other grand-children, but he's my favorite. Though I'll never tell them that. She stays in Maryland. She's getting out in June, then filing for divorce. He's an addict, and she can't deal with it. She says, "I was raised with an addict, and I'm not going to live with one."

I understand where she's coming from. I tell her though, "You're being judgmental," because people that are addicts, it's not their fault. My son, he lives here. And he's married, just got married. Has two kids. I have a grandbaby—a little granddaughter and a grandson. So he's totally well. Let's see, I'm in my seventh year of recovery, he's in his fifth year. He and I never talked about that part, but I'm sure he was doing everything under the sun. He was just like me. I knew that he drank too much; even in high school, he was just a little drunk.

I have finally told my mother about some of what I have been through. My mother's seventy-eight years old; she doesn't need this trauma. She's not a healthy woman, but I did talk to her about it and she cried. She never had a clue about any of this. And it hurt her so bad that I didn't tell her. But she had to understand. I think the reason she cried was because she went through the same thing. And she wasn't able to tell anybody. Her kids were the number one thing in her life. It wasn't about a man, it was about her kids. To this day she's like that. She would run over people with a bulldozer for her kids. That was her dedication; she loved her children. So I talked about it a couple times, and I let it go. She knew that I had a hard time, but she wanted me of all the kids to have everything. When I got into recovery, that was the best thing that could ever happen. I started going on TV and doing newspaper articles, traveling all over the world, and she just didn't know that it was because I was HIV-positive. So when I told her it was, it disheartened her. She didn't show it, but I know it. She wants to die before I do. She doesn't want to see me die. I told her, "Well, I'm not planning on dying anytime soon. I'm too busy. I don't have time to die. God's got things for me to do."

And you know, you have different views when you become a Christian. I think that when you start getting closer to God, the trauma starts to move away from you. When I say trauma, I mean things that used to make you so upset and bent out of shape. They move away. People move away from you because they can feel your spirit. Negative stuff—it just moves away from me. I can't tell you, there's been a lot of things that happened to me. In recovery, I've been able to just—it just runs off my back. I don't even get stressed out. That's why I think I've been living with this virus this long and never been sick because HIV ain't got shit on what I've already been through. I have a lot of wonderful people in my life, too. I really have some wonderful, wonderful people.

Since I've been in recovery I have a strong group of really great women friends around me, and that's probably what's been missing all my life, is women. I didn't have women in my life; it was always men, men, men, men. This is the first time in my life that I've ever been without somebody living with me. I've got a big, beautiful apartment and it's laid from the front door to the back door, got a brand-new car, got two fur coats; those are material things, but I bought them. And I don't go and sleep in nobody else's bed. My support system is full of spirituality. Not so much religious spirituality, but just individuals who have worked through issues and have something to offer, that don't open up their mouth to always be putting out negative stuff.

My twelve-steps sponsor, she told me, she said, "Linda Rae, when you look in the mirror, I don't want you to look at the skin, your hair, your body, I want you to look into your own eyes, and look into the pit of your soul, and you find the little girl that never got a chance to come out and play, and then you'll find your sexuality." I thought about it, and it took me for the longest time to figure out what she was talking about to me; and what she was telling me was, "Let the little girl that never got a chance to grow up come out and play." It was innocence. That's what it was, innocence. Before anything ever happened, there was an innocence, there was a peace, there was something that was untouched by anything. And I can be that woman today, I can start where I never finished, never got a chance to start. I can be that person, and I can be coy and I can be shy, and I can laugh nervously, and I can play little-girl games, and I can play hard to get. Things that people take for granted today. You can do that and still be who you are, and it keeps your spirit young. It keeps you ready, the woman side of you, ready for the trauma. But the little girl is always protected from that because she's the part that you use to make you feel good.

I'm forty-six now. I realize that sex is not that big of a celebration for me. I think now the intimacy around us is being able to have conversations. I love to be kissed, and I love to be touched, and I love to be held, and I love being helped out of the pity pot. Let me be on the pity pot for two and a half minutes, and then pull me out. I like to be able to tell somebody about what I feel when I'm feeling sad and miserable, and if I want to cry, I can cry and he won't say to me, "You're just being a punk." It's just my emotions; it's the way I feel. Because I cry a lot alone. Or I cry to my girl-friends.

I know that there's this part of me that is attracted to women, but not enough for me to want to live a lesbian lifestyle. It would only be a sexual thing, and I don't think that's fair to a person. Because I'm a very lovable person, and if they fell in love with me, then I would hurt them. I know that every now and then I would have to have—I'd get the fever for the fla-vor of a Pringle. It wouldn't be fair to them; so I won't do that. But I don't deny that part of my sexuality. I nourish that part of me, I celebrate that part of me, that I know how to be with a woman and feel sexually, men-tally, and emotionally fulfilled. But I get my best fulfillment from a man. Most times you have to teach a man how to make love to you.

You know, penetration is not really important. I remember, especially while tricking, being with men who fondle you and grab you and touch you hard, and rub your clit real hard, and I don't like that. Since I've been in recovery, I realize I don't like that, and I will say, "Don't do that. This is the way I want you to treat me, and if you continue to do that, you get kicked to the curb." I know how to set limits now with relationships. If it's not good when it comes to my physical body—this is the only one I'm gonna get. I feel now that this is my castle and it deserves to be treated with tender loving care. If you can't do that, then [*signals "You're out"*] and I don't have a problem telling somebody that, either. I think I would be do-ing the next woman an injustice if I don't tell him that he's too rough and I don't like that. I think a woman has to have enough courage to tell a man how she wants to be treated. And I do that. I also know how to make a man feel good. What I don't do and won't do is let a man make that be a prerequisite to us having sex each time. You get a little bit of something and that's it. It's not like I'm gonna have oral sex with you until you come. You can't unlearn how to give oral sex; it's just impossible. Once you know how, and you get into it, you know how to do it good, you do it good. But

I still don't like come in my mouth or in my pussy or anywhere else. That's still there. I think being HIV-positive scares me because I know there's a potential for transmission of some other STD. I don't have sex without condoms anyway. I can't do that to anybody, even though the chance of me giving the virus to someone is very slim. My immune system is very healthy. I don't know why, but it is. It's Jesus—I do know why.

I didn't know the difference between being African American and being white until I got older. So I don't think that my family influence, whether I was African American or not, had anything to do with it, because I came from a fucked-up family, period. My grandmother was a Blackfoot Indian; my grandfather must have been African American—at least he looked that way—but he might have been Indian. My mother was half, and my father was black, so it sort of was a mixture of stuff. God knows what's in my other brothers and sisters. I just know that I was always lighter than everyone else in my family. And I was treated differently because of that. So it made me have a complex that I wasn't white, I wasn't black, but I was something else. That's what we do; us as African Americans do that to each other all the time. You light-skinned, you're half white, you're yellow; you're given all kinds of different names. And naturally, if you're feeling like that, you make different decisions—the first guy that I actually literally went out with when I came down south was a white man. His mother and father had a fit. Since I've been HIV-positive, I have turned a couple shades darker. I don't know why; something happens with HIV and pigmentation.

Having sex with a white man was an entirely different thing. Well, let me tell you something. All of the tricks and white men that I've been with, some are perverted son-of-a-guns, I'm telling you. There's a guy walking around right now, a schoolteacher with my name carved on his chest. I carved my name on his chest with a hat pin, week after week after week, with the scabs on it—peel the scabs off and make it deeper and deeper and deeper. And I know that there's no way that was ever going to grow back into anything. After I carved my name, I put liquid heat on it. I've had white men that had me defecate in their mouth and urinate in their face, tie 'em up and whip 'em and call 'em dirty names and things like that. Now, I don't know any black people that do that. Ain't never met one.

And the thing about black women—a black woman is naturally sensuous and sexy. It's just our skin, you know, the way we love. That love translates itself into our bodies. And it all depends on how you feel about yourself. If you look at yourself and you don't feel sexy, if you think you're not appealing, then you won't be. I weigh two hundred pounds, but I find ways and means to make me not look like two hundred pounds. And I ain't trying to lose no weight. I don't have to; I'm HIV-positive, I'm forty-five years old, and I got twenty-eight-year-old boys running behind me. Honestly. I don't think there's anybody on this planet that don't know I'm HIV-positive. I've been on every major news station in this country. I've traveled to six other different countries. I've done everything; there's no way they don't know.

This disease is not going to stop me from living. And if I didn't get into recovery, if I didn't get with the women I got with, that showed me how to be a woman and showed me what my sexuality was and that I had one, I wouldn't know what sexuality meant.

I tell you what I think about today's black people. I think black women spend too much time talking about what happened to us instead of what to do about it. There's nothing wrong with you getting up off your ass and doing something about it. I make a difference in people's lives every day. I have HIV; I live with this disease. I've lived with addiction, I've lived through abuse, I've lived with sexual abuse. I've lived through things that they could never even imagine. That's a wealth of information. I need to get that information out. We have power in ways—our experiences are rich. If you was born to an upper-class black family, flaunt it, yes, you have the right to do that. Don't be ashamed—well, it depends on why you do that. Not if you're trying to make somebody else look bad, but because, yes, I have gone this far and there is no reason why Linda Rae from the other side of town cannot live the same way and have different experiences from me; but we all end up at the same road because we reach back and pull the other person forward. You don't just sit there and say, "Well, I got mine and you got yours to get." 'Cause you know that was the old saying. And historically that's true. We don't go back and help each other, we're so busy in the mix. We don't even need all that shit. I've lived in penthouses in New York, on Central Park; the people were that big, with a fur coat for every day of the week. My kids, little mink coats going to school in a limousine. That's one of the reasons I had the hardest time when we was living in poverty, because they were not accustomed to that. But they didn't realize what Mommy had to do to get them there. Now they know the difference, and it was a rich lesson for them. I have never been afraid to tell my kids about my shortcomings.

We are afraid of our children. The kids out there, they aren't doing nothing more or less than we did. It's just a different year, different substance, and different attitude. My mother would have beat the dog shit out of me if I was standing on the corner, finger popping, talking with my pants hanging off my behind. She'da beat the dog out of me. I would have beat my kids down if I caught them out there. I would say ninety percent of the parents that got kids out there who are either using drugs, have used drugs, or doing something illegal, or they're so caught up in their career that they can't see what their kids are doing because they have to go and go to work and do what they have to do to take care of those kids. So therefore there's a lack of supervision. And by the time the parents find out about it, the kid is already an addict.

The drugs that they have out there today is set to make you an addict the first time you use them. The euphoria is so great. It took me awhile to become an addict off the drugs that I was using. I do a group at this detoxification program with newly admitted addicts, and these kids only been using like two or three months. They look like they been beat up. Living in the streets, with STDs that smell like Lord knows what. How, in three months? It took me twenty-three years to get that bad.

Rap music? I think rap music is a bunch of bullshit. I hate it, I don't like it, I never did like it. I think it's a way of separation from one generation to the other. Somehow I like some of the little sayings that come out, you know, "dope" and all that stuff. I like that because my kids and I, we grew up together, so what they picked up, I picked up. But rap music has just gotten so bad, and so nasty and so way out there; you can hear the messages but it's the way they act when they doin' it, the bodily expressions, like I'm all cool, and I'm all that. Why can't you put on a three-piece suit and go up and rap? What's the difference? What are you trying to project? That you got to wear your pants hanging down off your butt to say that you're different? You look retarded to me.

I go to the high schools, and I look at these girls and they look like they're twenty-five, thirty years old, not teenage girls. And the kids live in my building; I've watched them grow up. The kids next door, the young girls they all come here; I'm one of those people scrape up everybody in the neighborhood, make them come to an AIDS training. And every time they got a problem, they come to me, which I love because that way I get a chance to connect with them. Their belief in sexuality is that the guy wants them to have sex because "If you love me . . ."—the message hasn't changed, the story hasn't changed. If you love me, you'll have sex with me. Then they talk about the condoms. I'm telling them about condoms, I'm saying, "Bring your boyfriend here." "Oh, no, I can't tell him." So you know what I do? I just go right to them when I see them together, and I say, "Look, I got a whole box full of condoms in the house if you need 'em." Because the girls won't talk to them about the condom. They feel like it's the boy's idea to use the condom, but you the one gotta protect yourself. So they're already thinking, contemplating sex at nine and ten years old. My God, it's everywhere for them to see it. I think that a child should begin to learn about sex as early as elementary school. Because they already know. You talk to one of them, they'll know. Instead of telling them that babies come from the cabbage patch.

When I'm talking to people/girls about sex, I take it back to the validation. How do you feel in the situation when somebody's touching your breasts, or touching your face? Or touching parts of your body where you don't necessarily like that touch? Most girls are told about sex, and they have that fear, if they're allowing that boy to do it. Think about what you are feeling. Do you feel hot, do you feel like you want to take your drawers off? No. Most likely not. The ones that do it are already having sex. But

I'm talking about before sex. How do you feel? Does it feel like you are ready to take on this woman challenge? Or are you still feeling like a little girl? If you feel like a little girl, then you need to protect the little girl. And you should be able to say no. You should be able to not succumb to peer pressure. This girl lived in my building—she's in college now—I remember her coming to me and talking to me about thinking about having sex. She told me how she felt about having the sex: she didn't want to have the sex, but she liked this boy so much that she wanted him so bad. And I said, "You're fifteen years old, and you probably won't even like this boy when you're eighteen. Because he's going to grow up, he's going to look different, he might get ugly. You might see somebody else you like better. And if he loves you, he'll wait for you." She went on and had sex with him anyway, and it was horrible and terrible—gave her a yeast infection. She didn't use a condom, and then he gave her an STD. She was so embarrassed. To this day, her mother doesn't even know about it. Her mother thinks she's still a virgin. And I had to go against my better judgment and take her without telling her mother to a clinic at the hospital so she could get treated.

I wanted to tell her mother, but I didn't want to break her confidence because she was just beginning to be empowered. I was bringing her to AIDS Action to be a peer educator, and I was taking her around with me and showing her a lot of stuff. I'll never forget her telling me how she felt about having sex with that guy. She said she could feel God looking at her, and she knew it was wrong, and she didn't enjoy it. And I told her, "The first time you have sex, you don't enjoy it anyway; you're gonna bleed, it's gonna hurt." Penetration. We teach teens if they're going to have sex for the first time how to make penetration happen before the penis goes in so it won't be so painful. All that stuff, and lubrication, so they'll be ready for that. Then we talk about the importance of getting married and consummating your marriage, and the chances are that you'll be with that person forever and ever and ever—which could be a myth, but you tell them, try to give them options.

I have a program with this ministry, and I'm dealing with how the church plays a role in all of this. I think the church has been judgmental for so long that the Christian population is going to be the hardest and probably the highest at risk for HIV than anybody. From their point of view, all of the people that have HIV are people who have sinned and they're going to hell anyway, so they might as well have AIDS. I'm working with this. I've been doing it for two and a half years, and it's been the hardest thing I ever do. But I'm not giving up. I'm getting into some churches and teaching them about the disease and talking to them about support. If they have to have sin, I just throw the Bible right back at them, saying that Jesus forgave people for their sins. Give 'em sin, but then say, "But these people have been forgiven. Let ye who have no fault cast the first stone." You got to give it back to them like that so they can understand it. This disease is real.

What makes them think that God's not watching all of them? This is a part of the master major plan. But God doesn't want this to continue. That's why I'm here trying to tell you that you have to help. You have to talk to your children; you can't turn them away. You can't preach abstinence to them all the time and not let them know that they have options. I'm not saying preach to them that they should use condoms, but let them know that they have options. You give somebody a condom, it doesn't mean that they're going to have sex. And, if you don't give them the condom and they have sex anyway and get AIDS, then what are you going to feel? We need to put some responsibility on the parents, put some responsibilities on these ministers because they don't even want to talk about it in the pulpit.

I have gospel concerts and trick 'em. I had a boat ride, put five hundred people from all different churches all over Philly, put 'em on the boat for a gospel boat cruise, food and everything, get them out in the middle of the water, stop the boat, and bam! HIV education. I had six HIV-positive speakers speak. What was they going to do? Jump off the boat? There were tears. I've never seen people crying so much. Because they never knew. They never understood; they'd never been around anybody who had the virus. And they began to have some knowledge. Then I had a gospel concert; then we had a black and white ball. They thought it was going to be dancing, everybody dressed up in either black or white, long gowns and everything, and then they came and we had a program. I had six HIV-positive people speak and then the pastor came up and gave a sermon. Had people in tears. It was like a healing service. People were turning their lives over to God, they was on the floor praying—it was amazing. I've done four events so far. I've been into eight churches now doing HIV education, and I've done some TV shows. I have people that call me to come and speak. The only problem is that they want me to come and speak, and I just can't do it. It's too much for me; I have a lot of responsibility and I just can't do everything. I used to try to, and I was making myself sick and I had no life. I was one stressed-out, mixed-up, overworked person. Now I work nine to five. I don't work weekends and holidays. Don't bother me. That's my way of taking care of me. I can never keep a boyfriend because they can't keep up with me. I'm either in Africa, or Paris, or Germany, or Florida—I'm everywhere. It's too much for men.

I'm so proud to be an African American woman; I know what that is because my title is the African American education programs manager. I was the African American education specialist. So it gave me more desire to learn about me and learn about my people, and me as a woman. I am the woman, the black woman, that went to the White House and spoke to the President. I am the black woman that told the most influential people in America to get up off their ass and do some work. Get some passion for HIV. I'm the woman who's been in a predominantly white male agency doing good things in my community. I'm the African American woman who has a son and a daughter that no matter what their mother has been through, they look at me and they love me and they empower me and they respect me. And I respect them right back. They know that I'm available for them. And I know that from my African American heritage is where I got my strength and my pride. It was transferred to me; I didn't just get this. It was transferred to me from my ancestors—somewhere along the line, that spirit came and jumped in me and I'm carrying that spirit on. So I'm really happy to be the vessel. I'm doing the best that I can.

# Joclyn

MY NAME IS Joclyn. I'm thirty-seven years old. I was born in Salt Lake City, Utah. I am the youngest sister of four, so I have three older sisters. No brothers—I've always wished I had an older brother. My parents separated when I was in sixth grade. They just recently got divorced. My mother is eighty-one years old, and my father is eighty-six years old. They'd been separated since I was in sixth grade, so they were separated for twenty-five years, which just blows me away. I was born in Salt Lake City, and we moved from there to Boston, Massachusetts, and then from Boston to New Jersey and then from New Jersey to Philadelphia. It was at the point when we moved from New Jersey to Philly when my parents went their own way. I'm married. Been married for seven years.

My father was a minister, but in addition to being a minister (he didn't ever have his own church), he had an executive position with the church. That's why we moved so much—because he kept getting transferred. My mother says he kept getting fired. I don't know the real story to that; I just know we kept moving. And my mother, before she retired, was vice president of a college. They're both retired now. My father's looking for a new wife. That's why he divorced my mother. He put an ad in the classifieds in a national newspaper and is looking for a woman. Yes he is.

The sister next to me, there's six years between me and the next sister, and then there's only a few years between her and the oldest. So, of course, I was supposedly an accident child. The sister next to me, she went off—I think maybe it was seventh grade—she got married when she was eighteen. I would have been about twelve. So after the sixth grade, I was really raised by myself, pretty much me and my mother because the other two sisters were older and out of the house.

Well, I've been trying to figure out what intimacy is myself. But I know what I would like for it to be. And that is to be in a relationship with a male or female, that you can talk to about anything and everything, and know that you're safe in saying that with that person. Know that the information that you pass on to that person—you won't be judged by whatever you say, you won't be ridiculed, you know you'll be accepted, and that person will hear what you're saying. And they'll share their feelings with you, they'll feel comfortable sharing whatever they are feeling with you, good, bad, or ugly. And just loving that person for who that person is, and loving that person totally. When I don't have that, that's when intimacy's being broken. Maybe that's a fantasy to have a relationship like that. It's not to say that you can't get mad at the person or that the person can't disagree with you or anything. It's not a perfect relationship. But I don't know that I can say that I've ever really experienced intimacy with a man or a woman, unfortunately. I think that in every relationship I've ever been in it's been conditional. Intimacy is that unconditional love, that unconditional acceptance, and I don't know anybody that's ever accepted me unconditionally or just wanted me in their life just because I'm a nice, warm, loving person. There's been some motive there. Some agenda, some expectations of me, something that I had to give in order to receive what it was that I needed. I like to think that my standards aren't unrealistic or asking too much. But I think that we all just have a lot of baggage, whether we know it or not.

And when you have this baggage, it's just hard for some people to give and hard for some people to receive. It just makes it very difficult to have that ideal relationship.

The person I've felt closest to was my aunt—she died. I feel as though I had that type of relationship with her. I said earlier I hadn't, but I really do feel as though I could tell her anything, I could talk to her about anything, and that she loved me unconditionally. And I guess maybe I've been searching for that relationship with someone else. Ever since she died, I have not been able to find that in any other relationship. But the one person I did experience that with would have been my aunt. She passed when I was a senior in college.

Before my recent group of friends, I probably had two, maybe three women that I considered close friends. As close as I can be. They accuse me of not being intimate or close with them, from changing clothes to you name it, you never call me, we don't ever get together. So I consider them as close as I can be, but most of my friends, two I'll say, have wanted more than I was able to really communicate.

I'm comfortable with my sexuality. I feel more comfortable around men than I do women. Like I won't disrobe in front of a woman, but I will without thinking in front of a man I'm intimate with. I feel very uncomfortable undressing around women, particularly because my mother shielded her body. I don't think I've ever seen my mother's body. She would not undress in front of me, so it made me feel like, Okay, we're supposed to hide our bodies and not undress around each other. My girlfriends always tease me about it because I'll always be in the closet or taking my bra off under my shirt, or something like that. They're like, "We have the same things." And I'm like, "But you can't see mine, sorry." I just don't want them to see my body. But my girlfriends make a big deal out of it, and they tease me because I'm like that.

I learned about sexuality from my sisters, my older sisters. I watched them get in all this trouble. I watched them get caught. I watched them get pregnant. I watched them have abortions. I watched them date boys, kiss boys, talk about boys; I listened to my older sisters talking about boys sometimes when they didn't know I was listening to them talking about boys. They were very sexually active, my sisters were. Probably because we were brought up in such a very strict household, my father being a minister and all. And he was just very anal, and very—just ridiculous. Just very rigid and distant. The only thing he was concerned about was us impressing the white people. It was very important. And I think it ended up giving us a poor self-image. Me, I'll talk for myself. Because white people were all that and a bag of chips. And black people were whatever; we weren't important. My sister still to this day tells this story—she's forty-something years old now: My father used to have these little meetings at the house, and he made these hoagie sandwiches, and my sister wanted a sandwich. And my father said, "No, these are for the white people." "You're not good enough to have one of these" is the message that she heard. He said, "These sandwiches are for my church members" or whoever he was having over. And she has always internalized that as being, "I wasn't good enough for the hoagie sandwich, but Joe White Boy over here was." He was just very distant, the disciplinarian. And grouchy as I don't know what. He counseled married couples and they were like, "Oh, Reverend Wilson, you're the best thing and we just love you and we just think you're great," and everything. And we were like, How is he able to do this to these people and come home and be the biggest bear in the world? After the sixth grade, I didn't have as much contact with him, thank God, no. But I had enough, though, to know that I did not want to be there, and I had seen what had happened to them. I had been punished and beaten by him for doing—being on the phone or just whatever. He's just grumpy. Angry, very angry.

I never have known my parents to sleep in the same bed. I thought that was significant to tell you. I never saw them hug or kiss or hold hands. I never saw them show affection. My father would give gifts, and my father would tell jokes. Very repulsive jokes that would gross my mother out about boogers and stuff like that, just nasty stuff. She just really hated that kind of talk. But I would never not sleep with my husband. I want to sleep with him, and I'm very touchy with him because of that; I want to be the

opposite. And he snores real bad too. But I'm going to sleep with you anyway! I just get him to turn over.

My mom gave me a book about my period. She wouldn't even talk to me
about that. The book tells you what it means to menstruate, why it happens, just a very—very easy to read pamphlet. It looked very worn, like
she'd passed it on to all of us. And she gave me another book. She gave me
a book about something else. She never talked to any of us about sex. She
would never say anything. She would always have these rules, "No boys at
home when I'm not here." And of course, that's when they would come
over and I would have sex. If it were too quiet down in the basement where
me and my boyfriend were, she'd come and rattle the door like she was
coming down. But she would never say, "I don't know what's going on
down there but I hope you know that having sex is not a good idea at your
age." She never made one mention either way or the other about sex. It was
just an understood kind of thing.

It was ninth-grade summer—I was going into the tenth grade when I
started having sex. I had been dating him since, or known him since, seventh grade. So we had been doing really everything but, you know; we had
really been doing some heavy petting. And I kept him off for three years; I
thought I was doing pretty good. There was kissing and petting and stuff.
I don't think we were doing oral sex. He was using his finger a lot. Yeah, I
think I was ready, I mean, he was probably having me climax with his
hands. I don't recall—I knew it felt very good, but I don't recall actually knowing at fourteen what an orgasm was. I knew it felt great and I
couldn't wait to get together with him so we could do this some more,
which was probably why I wanted to have sex—like if this is good, I wonder what that other thing is like.

It did not hurt; I did not experience pain to talk about. I remember it
feeling very good and I was feeling very euphoric afterward. He probably
came too fast, but I just remember thinking, Oh, this is great, I could do
this again. This is cool. Safe, comfortable. I got a call the next day. We had
been dating forever, since seventh grade, and this was tenth grade. We

stayed together all through high school. And he was shorter than I was, and that really bothered me a lot. He was muscular, but he was small, he was real petite, and I felt so big with him. And I wanted a big man; that's all I ever craved when I was with him. I always felt so big, and I guess I was probably the size I am now. Almost five foot eleven, tall and big. I'm not skinny. I'm a big woman. Even now I would not feel good with a man who was shorter than me, I feel big now, I do. I never felt real feminine; and with him, it wasn't never gonna be one of these, "I'm a pick you up, woman, and take you to bed." This man would just break his arms off trying to carry me. After that I dated big men, tall men.

I wasn't concerned about virginity, not even a little bit. And I knew that this guy really cared about me. I didn't protect myself. He was withdrawing before he ejaculated, so I was confident that I would be safe. My sisters told me about contraception after I told them we had sex. My oldest sister, who's ten years older than me, she took me to the family-planning clinic after I told her. I just thought I was being safe. I don't know that I even knew about condoms. Maybe he did. I think he knew about them, and I think he started using them before I was actually on the birth control pills. But I remember he would bust the condoms—he was very nicely endowed. I know the first time we were not protected. But I think after that we were like, "Hey, aren't we supposed to be doing something? Aren't we supposed to be using something?"

I think that boyfriend was really more like a father figure than a boyfriend. He wasn't terribly older than I was; he was maybe three or four years older than I was. And still the same grade, so that tells you something. But I don't know what happened to him, if he stayed back or what. But he was very, very mature. And very overprotective. Very protective. And really caring and loving. I mean, he was more like a father. He was so square, kind of. He wouldn't do bad things; it was like, "Maybe you shouldn't curse." Just like a father or something, I don't know. I think I was not as influenced by my father as my sisters because I wasn't dating— I didn't start dating until after I left, he left, or whoever left. So I just think I was wanting somebody to love me, and this guy loved me. And he cherished me. He would kiss the ground I walked on. And I was eating it up.

As my Catholic high school teacher said, "Girls give sex to get love. Boys give love to get sex." I was giving sex to get love; and he was giving it to me. So it was fine. The sex wasn't bad. I never had to have it. I don't know that I've ever been—yeah, I've been horny, but I don't masturbate. I don't do anything about it. I was separated from my husband for nine months, and I didn't masturbate. I just don't care.

You know what? I really think that my first orgasms were really when I—I guess I allowed myself. Well, this guy was just so wonderful; he was seven feet tall. It was a one-night stand? Two-night stand. He had to come back for some more of that. But he lifted me up, made me feel like I was this little person, and laid me down; and I had an orgasm with him. He just, he massaged my whole body and . . . he caressed my whole body, not massage, was caressing my body and just holding me and touching me in places I did not know had the potential to be stimulated. I don't do many self-exploring things. I don't masturbate, don't know how to masturbate. Masturbation to me is like tickling yourself. I can't tickle myself. You can't tickle yourself. This won't make me feel good. It's just never had any appeal to me. But this guy. It was probably the best sex I ever had, but he had no personality. I can't remember two words he spoke. He could be a mad killer for all I know. Just didn't know anything about him.

I think it was just the way he was touching me and caressing me, and it just made your whole body melt. We just had that rhythm. Some guys are clumsy, and they're like—they're lying down and they've got their hand on your hair, and they're pulling your hair out or something. And you feel like, Oh, God. They're saying, "Just tell me what to do." I don't want to tell you what to do. Just do it. You know, I don't have to give you a book. What do you want, a road map? But since then, I have not felt that way. And if I know what an orgasm is, that has to have been one. Probably multiple orgasms at one time. But that never happened again, not at least in the last seven years. I was just kind of being with a lot of people before I got married. I guess overall I've had sex with, I'd say, about twenty. And he was just one of those people.

I like foreplay if it's good foreplay. If it's not good foreplay, I'm like, "Let's get this over with." The kissing, the talking, I don't want somebody to just come in and jump my bones. I like to cuddle. I love back massages, and foot massages. I don't know whether my husband's just not good at giving me oral sex, or if I just don't like oral sex, but that does not turn me on at all. I don't know if it's 'cause I haven't had the right guy to give me oral sex. White men, I hear (I don't know this), are more attentive in foreplay and oral sex. But black men are more just wanting to, Let's do it. Let me get off. I haven't really had many sexual partners that were just interested in getting themselves off and not being concerned about me. Even though they may come before I'm even halfway there, they're still either apologetic or something. They're showing that, I'm sorry, I really care, we'll do this again soon.

I've thought about being in bed with two people with both of them making love to me. It would be nice being the center of attention. Just various things maybe, if not at the same time. Obviously that would be quite difficult. But working a different area. I know it would never be a reality. I don't think. Unless something happens. Why torture yourself, if it's something that's not going to be a reality? I think I'm a little prudish, just a little. I'm a little shy; I'm not going to pull out any whips and chains. I wouldn't feel comfortable if my spouse wanted to pull out whips and chains. I'm not into anal sex either. If my spouse were into anal sex, I would not feel comfortable with that. So I think I'm pretty boring when it comes to sex.

I'm regretting the relationship I'm in now. I'm getting all old now and dried up. I kind of wish I didn't marry him, hadn't married my husband. I got married because I was twenty-nine. I know that sounds stupid; it sounds stupid to me. I didn't want to be thirty and not married. Why did I get married? I had been through a long string. After that first relationship that I had, way back in seventh grade. I had gone through a string of really bad relationships. When I met my husband, he was the first that was dependable, had a job, had a car, had some ambition. And I was like, I'm not letting this little fish go. I just kind of jumped on it. Because I'd just had—either guys were cheating on you, they were not working, they were not sincere, they were—there was just something major wrong with all of them. And when I met my husband, he seemed to have every attribute that

I ever wanted and he seemed to be everything that I admired and was looking for in a man. Of course, those things come back to haunt you.

Well, the ambitiousness turned out to be just this drive that you would not believe. And a person that was not going to be satisfied with anything that he achieved or obtained, and projected all of his lack of self-worth onto me when I was having self-esteem issues myself and was not really strong enough to handle that projection. We've worked through all this supposedly, but there's still a lot of scars, wounds from the earlier part of our marriage. A lot of things were said that you kind of can't forget and that I guess we're both hanging on to. Just recently, the latest issue is that he wants a baby. And I'm not really feeling comfortable in the relationship to provide him with that.

I don't know about motherhood. If you ask my sister, she's like, "No, she wants to be alone, she wants to watch her soap operas, she wants to just go fly off to St. Thomas when she feels like it and hang out on the beach. And she has her little perfect house with her white carpet, and she is not mommy material." That's my sister's opinion of me. But if you ask me, I think part of me is scared of missing out on that experience. I'm thirty-seven; it's not like I have a real long time to decide. Then another part of me says, Well, maybe I want a child, but I don't want it with this jerk husband that I have. And then you say, Well, get divorced. You're thirty-seven; two years later you finally meet this man, and God, you're forty years old. By the time you guys get married, then your chance to have kids is gone. So, do I want to be a mother? I don't know. I don't know. I have a lot of issues about parenthood from my mother, in terms of her always telling us she didn't want us, she didn't want any kids. "I didn't want you, I didn't want any of you." She said, "You were all diaphragm babies." And I said, "Why didn't you just have an abortion?" She said, "They didn't have those back then." My mother was forty-four when she had me.

She was very emotionally abusive growing up. So I—she would kill me for saying this—but I feel she really messed us up. Messed me up, anyway; I won't speak for anybody else. You know, with the self-esteem: She called me stupid all the time, and, "God, I can't believe you passed the sixth grade. How in the world?" And, "You'll never get in any of those schools"—colleges. Just constantly . . . I don't know, but I just don't want to have a child and not be able to love her, or him, because I don't think that my mother has ever been able to love us. She has this much in her glass to give, you know, from where she came from. And she was very distant. She never wanted me to come in her bed; I'd be scared at night and I'd want to come in her bed because I thought the boogie man would come in my room. It was the first room when you came up the stairs, the very first room on the right. And one of my sisters was very hateful; she used to always tell me, "You're the first room, you're the first one he's gonna come get." So I used to be so scared at night, and she used to reward me if I did not come in her bed. You know, "You're a good girl. You did not come in my bed." And if I would come, she would just be mad at me the whole next day. Wouldn't speak to me. I know I wouldn't do those things to my kids, but I'm afraid that—what if I had kids, and I did not want them, like she didn't want us? And didn't have the capacity to love a child the way a child needs to be loved. And just love them manually. Like, You're crying, so I guess I'm supposed to hug you. Come here. You know, don't do me any favors. Children are so perceptive; they would pick up on it if I were that way. And I'm so scared of being my mother in every sense, from her marriage, to being separated for thirty years and divorcing when she's eighty-five, to being this emotionally distant, unloving mother.

Because of what I experienced, and because I've never wanted kids, I've never said, "I'm going to get married and have ten kids. I love kids." I've never felt that pull. Anything I say I feel, she says, "I felt the same way." And I hate it when she does that because I'm like, Oh, no! I don't want to be you. God, please help me! And every time something would happen in my marriage, she would say, "I know you don't want to hear this, but your father said the same thing." So I feel like I'm her clone, almost, in that if I feel the same way my mother felt when she was my age and about kids, that's the way I'm going to react. I love my little five-year-old nephew. I took him to the circus last night, and it's the scariest thing I've ever done. I love him to death, but I have never baby-sat for him. I'm scared to death to do that. I'm really scared of kids. I'm scared they're going to cry, I'm scared they're going to hate me. I'm scared they're going to hurt themselves in my care. I'm scared of kids, I really am. And then when they cry, it gets on my nerves. I feel like—you know, those commercials where the mother's slapping the kid around or something. I'm scared I would just lose it.

If I don't have them, I'm afraid that I will be sorry and feel that I've lost out on a really wonderful, beautiful experience. And if I do have them, I will be insane, crazy, ready to shoot myself, and they won't love me. I'm going to end up on Ricki Lake with this child, and she's trying to kill me. I don't know. I wonder what I would do with my life. What would my life be like later? The person I've told you about, that I was most intimate with in my entire life, my aunt that died, never had kids. She never got married. I really wish she were alive to talk to me because she seems to have lived a very fulfilled life. She traveled, she had us, she had me, I mean, I was like her kid. She was more like my mother than my mother was. She definitely loved me like a daughter. And I could do that with my nieces and nephews. But I don't feel that connection to them. I feel bad that I'm not this kind of aunt that my aunt was, to my nieces and nephews, but feeling harassed. And thinking, God, was I like this when I was this age? No way! I had to have been more considerate. It's scary. I survived the circus. I did my one little aunty deed for the year, for the whole century. It's terrible.

Every woman with children that I've ever talked to in my life has told me, "Don't have kids unless _you_ want kids and are willing to do it by yourself, because your husband is just not going to be the kind of support that you want, or you think, or you need him to be." That's black women; I don't know how white women feel, but the sisters I talked to have pretty much said they deal with the brunt of the responsibility. And I've told my husband, "If I do ever have children, I'm going to need more than fifty-fifty—more like sixty-forty. Exactly, that's right." And he said, "Well, I will have a nanny, I'll go get a nanny." And this last week, it was so pitiful: "I promise you, if you have a baby, you can come home and you'll be like, 'What baby?' " He wants one so bad. Isn't that terrible? It kind of just cuts [strikes] a chord with this dude, don't you think? It's pitiful.

Racism and sexism have impacted me as an individual, yes. In terms of sexuality, yeah, I think it has. The white-girl image is not obtainable for a black woman. Blondes you see every day. You know, Barbie doll, hello, we aren't. I work with Barbie every day. And blue eyes, blond hair, makeup just perfect. White, yeah. It's very hard not to live up to that image. But trying to duplicate the image—a lot of black women do, including myself, unfortunately, not being able necessarily to duplicate it. But my hair is straight. I wear makeup. I guess that's not a white thing necessarily, but . . . One of my sisters was a black power radical in the sixties, so that's another story. She's slightly sold out; she finally permed her hair. But gosh, yes, it has an impact on my life every day, all the time. When I walk into the briefing at my job, I'm the only black person at the briefing. As it is there's this expectation. I'm in charge. So they suck up to me. I don't know, there's that electricity, there's that—you know what I'm saying. You can feel that, Oh, you're black. I've got to fly with you for three days, a black girl. And I gotta listen to what you're going to tell me for three days. Yes, it has an impact on me because I feel that I have to be professional, I feel as though I have to be better than they are all the time, I feel like I have to prove that I'm not this bitch, black people or women are constantly proving themselves. Black men are constantly proving themselves. I have to be nicer to the customers than my white counterparts because if I were to say some of the things that the white girls say to the customers, I would be written up. I can't get away with things that they can get away with. But yes, it plays a big role.

I think white people now have put us into two categories. You got good niggers and bad niggers now. There are the articulate ones—you speak so well—and they're surprised. And we have the ones that are intimidating, that are loud and boisterous and aggressive and street. So I think we have two images, they don't know which one we are until we open our mouths. Or maybe a well-dressed, ignorant black women will walk in there, and they think you're an articulate one, and you say, "Gimme dat," and they're like, "Ooh." And they're like clutching their pearls. I think we're perceived two different ways.

In other words, black, white, ignorant, articulate—do I think that they think we all like to have sex and good sex? I think they think that we're the best thing. I think white men probably desire black women because they've heard that black women are animals in bed. I still think white men want us. I think they want it. Not all white men, but I think—what's that guy, Hugh Grant? He's got a supermodel at home, and she is what every black and white woman really has aspired to be. To have this image, this supermodel image. And he's got it and doesn't want it. Wants that black booty.

All of this makes me always want to prove them wrong. It makes me always want to set an example for my race, that we aren't like that—which I don't think is necessarily healthy. But that's what I think a lot of us do, what a lot of black women do—that's what I do. Every time I have an opportunity, I—and this is going to sound very strange—but I try to not act like what the white people perceive black people as. Which I guess means acting white. They think we're going to be street, they think we're going to be, "Yo, yo, yo" all the time. I'm not going to give them that, even though I'll be that way with my sisters. I'll be down with my sisters, but I'm not going to be down with you; and you're going to try to be down with me, but I'm going to say, "Excuse me?" "Oh, it's cool like that, Joclyn." "What are you talking about?" I don't like that; I don't even like to play that with them. It's my personal thing: don't go there with me. That's my home life. I'm here and I'm acting professional at work, and I don't want to educate you. I'm not going to educate you on my life. It pisses me off.

There's a lot of double standards. You ain't supposed to be seeing nobody else, but he can go out and be with two women and everybody, but you're supposed to just stay home and wait for him. I don't have that problem, but I know that many black women do. That I know of, anyway. And we're racist among ourselves even. You know, light skin, dark skin, that kind of thing. That has had an impact, that in itself. I get more flack about it from women, about being light versus dark, than I do from men.

I don't have any sexual attraction whatsoever to white men. I don't. Black men are hard enough. I can't imagine being in a relationship with a white man with all the other barriers that come up, and the issues just being in a black relationship are hard enough. Anyway, I prefer black men. I've seen some attractive olive-skinned, or whatever you want to call them, and I've been like, Oooh, he looks good. I've been attracted that way. Like, not bad for a white boy kind of thing. But maybe because my father worshiped them so much, I wouldn't be caught dead with one.

How am I going to achieve happiness and peace of mind? Oh, God, I think start being really honest with myself and stop lying to myself. Stop being afraid and move on and do the things I know I need to do. Stop doing things I know I don't need to do. It's like a diet: you know what to eat, and you know what not to eat; you know what's good for you; you know what's not good for you; you know what's going to put weight on you; you know if you don't exercise. I feel like I know all those things, but it's just, doing those things is what's hard for me right now. Getting off my lazy butt and doing those things. Taking that chance. Going to that gym and lifting those weights and feeling that pain that's associated with making all those decisions.

I would like to be divorced from my current husband and be with a guy that is just carefree, fun, loving, and just into me, and us have a very intimate relationship, maybe a little kid, and just be living, just being happy. That's all I really want. I want to be able to pay my bills, of course; that would make me happy. That's what I want right now. I think I'm very responsible, but I love to have fun. I do. I go to work, I do everything I'm supposed to do. I don't call in sick so I can have a free day, and whoopee let's have fun today. I don't do that. Just when I have the time off, I want to spend it as enjoyably as I can, and I just want somebody who's not so serious and stiff all the time at forty-five that they can't chill out. I don't know, it's probably not possible. It's probably not a realistic expectation. I don't know, I guess I want to believe that you can find that special person, that special mate, and that person that is just wonderful to you. I don't know many people that have that. I met one girl today, and she sounded like she had that, but you know how you find out stuff after you know people. They'll say, "Oh, he beats me." So I don't know anybody who has what they want.

# Amparo

*I* WAS BORN in New Jersey, but I was raised in Baltimore. I have my mother and my father, my brother and my sister. I'm the oldest child. How old am I? I'm twenty-four; that means my brother's probably going to be nineteen in December, and my sister's going to be seventeen in September. I'm twenty-four. I can't believe it. I just graduated from college in '93 with a dual major in sociology and philosophy. I'm very into the arts—my mom's an artist—and that's what I do right now. I have a part-time job so that I can work on my art. And I plan to go to grad school for sociology. I have to always say this: both my parents are black, even though one is Hispanic. People don't know that Hispanic can be black, too. My mom is Haitian and Cuban, but she was born and raised in Baltimore. My dad is African American. His mother's from St. Croix as well, so a lot of Caribbean influence. He was a lawyer—he was trained in law. He had his private practice, and now he works with the government. I guess I would say we're middle class and Catholic.

Church was a big deal. But it was a big deal in a hypocritical kind of way, in my opinion, because at one point it was very liberal in my house as far as what we thought about other religions. And we never read the Bible.

My mom's an artist; I guess whatever comes along with that kind of mentality or is supposed to, it was pretty much prevalent—very open-minded. But at the same time, on Sundays, we had to go to church. And things like Good Friday and Easter—I guess the average things. It was a big deal, but it wasn't. We went to Catholic schools, and that was important to them.

I don't know if there are any defining characteristics for when something seems intimate to me, but I guess I look for just little clues; I look for how well a person knows me, or if we're speaking the same language. I go more by how I feel than how I think, even though both of them are involved. We're going deep with this; that's a hard question. I guess I feel closest to my boyfriend now. We spend every breathing moment together. I don't really like that, but that's what ends up happening.

It's been a mind-opening kind of relationship because I had set ideas on how things should be. But this is completely different. I guess I'm going through that right now—trying to define what it is that I want from something because I remember my mom saying, "Okay, you can't get into anything too quick. You always have to think it out." So I end up being the kind of person who took that to the next level, and I think everything out. Just judging on that, from the beginning we got into this too fast just because we clicked. And I believe we had sex too fast even though it was a month afterward. Everything was too fast, and deep inside I'm uncomfortable with all those facts; yet, we have trouble being apart. So I don't really know what to make of it. I know we're close. Why are we close? Gosh, I have no idea. I guess it's intrigue. He's a very peaceful person and I really like that because I tend to be a little bit more fiery. He's just really calm. What draws me to him? This is exactly the kind of stuff that I'm thinking about and need to know if I'm going to continue. I had to challenge my definition with him because when I judge things like passion, love, intelligence, all those definitions have turned around to become something else. Three times over.

I didn't want to repeat what I did before. I had a four-year relationship with somebody and I pretty much lied to myself about it, and I ended up lying to him about how much I cared for him. But it lasted four years, and I was basically in that relationship for security; I think both of us were. I wasn't attracted to him. I had a weird sense of commitment. I didn't date at all in high school. I had one thing that maybe I could call a boyfriend. So I'm thinking, Well, I have a boyfriend, I have this commitment. And even when I wasn't happy, I was afraid to let him down. I knew he was that kind of person who would probably put me through a guilt trip, which he did, really bad. So I knew I didn't want that. I knew I didn't want a situation where I was lying to myself or the other person. I think what I try to do with my relationship now is keep talking and asking questions and always trying to get the truth straight and trying to be real. I think that was the quest because I didn't want what I had. Both of us try to do that. And it helps because I really believe that he has a good sense of me, even from the beginning. He knows when I'm not being straight up with him, and I know when he's not being straight up with me. So basically we try to communicate.

I am a heterosexual. I've had other experiences. I haven't slept with women. I had a threesome experience, and that was a male and a female. I would say I feel comfortable with my sexuality. I don't think it's just something that happens. I work at it; it's very important to me to be comfortable with my sexuality. How do I work at it? By asking myself questions all the time, and just trying to be honest with what I feel, like, "Okay, why do I feel this, or why do I feel that?" I just try to work through that. I wouldn't say I feel a hundred percent comfortable, but I don't know who does, really.

For my mom, being Haitian and Cuban, sex is just something you don't talk about. You only even half talk about the period; you don't talk about necessary stuff. But she's very liberal-minded, and it's weird because I knew she wanted to tell me stuff, I felt her wanting to tell me stuff, but she couldn't. She wanted me to have something different than what she had, so she tells the story that she sent me over to my aunt's house to learn about menstruation. My aunt has four kids, and she had no problem discussing it. I don't remember that. I don't think it ever happened.

Books, I guess. Definitely school. Catholic schools always have some little program where you talk about that; but of course you talk about it in the way that's prescribed. Also, neighborhood kids. They all said they did "it" but nobody knew what "it" was really, but you knew it was something. And you knew you were close. You knew you were doing something. It was vague, but everyone acted like they knew. This was an all-black neighborhood, but I didn't speak English yet. I went to kindergarten not knowing English. My father wasn't around in the beginning. I was with my mom and my grandmother . . . well, I'm not too sure if he's my father. I haven't found out yet. I found my baby book, and it didn't have his name in it.

When I was little, I found some pads from Kotex in a bathroom sink cabinet—my mom says I'm lying about this, but I'm not. I don't remember how old I was—I must have been five or six—and I said, "Mommy, what are these?" She looked at them and she said, "Oh, those are for fat ladies." My mom, she's overweight. So she said, "They're for fat ladies," and I didn't ask any more questions after that. She said it so matter-of-factly, like it was true, and I kind of felt stupid for not knowing why a fat lady would need them. So I'd look at the pad, I'd take it out, and I was like, Wow, why would a fat lady need that? And I remember thinking that it looks like something you would put in your underwear. Then I remember knowing about a period and menstruation for a long time, but I didn't know what happened during that time. So when I was around eight or so, I went to books to try to find out. I remember also talking to my friend across the street about it because we were the same age, but she got hers earlier. I think I had gotten to the point where I knew it was blood that came out, but I didn't know how or how often, or if it was constant, so I remember asking her specific questions like, "Well, does it come out all the time?" And she was telling me, "Sometimes you see little eggs." And I was like, "Whoa."

I had an interesting situation. I was participating in an "extreme choice" study in which they had a control group that got a placebo, and then they had another group that got the medicine, which was taken by injection. I didn't want to do this study, but apparently it was something that people were in line for because they had the medication on the market for precocious kids. What the medication actually did was to make you taller. They delayed your puberty so that you would have more time to grow, because once you hit puberty, you have a growth spurt and then you stop growing. The idea was to have more time to grow and then get off the medication; and then you just start your puberty. So that's what I was involved in. At first it was okay because I think I got some time off of school, and I got to stay in the hospital and it was really cool. But when it came down to them telling me it's an injection every day, like an insulin syringe that I took every day, I didn't want to do it. So they just pretty much made me do it. It was okay. They claim that I got a couple of inches taller out of it. But my puberty was delayed, and I was waiting for it when I was fourteen, thirteen when everybody else got it. I remember crying one time because I didn't have it and the girls at school were getting it, and they were bonding over that. So I was like, I've got nothing to talk about. I guess you feel like, Well, you got it and you're a woman now. I was upset over that.

By the time I was twelve or thirteen, I knew everything about menstruation. My mom and I talked some; she read my clues, I think. One time she initiated a whole conversation. But I could tell it was hard for her. I got my period when I went to college, at eighteen. I started the study when I was twelve, and they claim that I probably would have gotten it when I was thirteen. But I didn't get it until I was eighteen, because it's a four-year study, and it takes your body some time to readjust. So I actually got it my first week of school. It was just weird.

By that time I had gone through so many things with it that I guess I was happy. Happy or surprised, I don't know. I had almost gotten to the point where it was kind of cool that I didn't have it. And then it came. I knew I had been on this medication and it took my body some time to readjust. So I guess there was a little bit of worry. I wanted to be normal, you know. I grew about three to four inches taller than I was supposed to. They say I would have been between four-eight and four-ten. And I am five feet tall, now.

Around six or seven, I was experimenting with myself and I was like, Hey, what's that? It didn't feel good like good, but it just felt sensitive. You know how you just touch a sensitive spot? It was just like, Why does that feel like that? Then I did it again. It was just sensitive. I kept playing around with it; after a while, it felt good. I also experimented with a female when I was young. A girl from my neighborhood. I was maybe between seven and eight. We were touching each other, kissing each other in my house. Basically, curiosity. I was like, I don't want to touch it. But then when she went to touch mine, I was like, No, I don't want you to touch mine. I just really remember her being the only one who would want to do that. And I guess at that point I was just not close to other little boys. So it was just more comfortable, I guess. And she wanted to, so . . . It didn't continue. She might have moved away or something like that. I'd say I was about nine or ten when I started masturbating. It's always been regular. Maybe once every two weeks. Or once every month. I don't think I knew when I was nine that it was an orgasm. Hmm. I guess I just intuited it. At first I didn't even know what I was doing. I was like, Hey, what's this? It wasn't until sophomore year in college, when I first connected the fact that, Oh, well, I've come before, by myself. I just thought I hadn't come, ever. It was something separate.

My first vaginal orgasm was in intercourse. I think it was with my current boyfriend. Yeah, well, no. The first time was with someone I was seeing before him. And that was oral. But the first vaginal one was with this one. Now I know myself better, I know exactly what it is that I need. But the vaginal one, um, I don't know, it just felt good. I want to say more comfortable or—it just felt different, a different kind of come, I guess. I can't even say which one I would prefer. I don't know, I prefer the intimacy associated with coming vaginally. It feels different, too. It is softer. I want to say it's not as intense.

I had sex for the first time in my sophomore year in college. I think I would have done it in high school had this other guy wanted to. He wanted to, but I guess we just really plain didn't find the opportunity to. But I would have with him even though I was a virgin. It's not like I was saving myself for anybody. No, I was in a sense. I just wasn't very social, so I never put myself in a situation where somebody was around; I didn't date. So nobody was around that I could do it with, basically. And the other thing is that, I went to an all-girls Catholic high school, and it was white. So when they had dances, the white guys from the brother school would come. I wasn't attracted to any of them. And they probably weren't attracted to me at that point. They never asked me out.

I was with my boyfriend the whole year before we did it. It's so funny because I was all open in my mentality, but it was just that I wasn't attracted to him, and I didn't want to be with him, really. It was just security. So all of a sudden my mentality changed, and I would tell him, "Oh, I want to wait." I remember even saying that I have a lot of messed-up stuff in my head about sex, and I just want it to be right. I guess it was half true. What part of it was true? I didn't think about any specific thing, I just thought about it being dirty. I had very mixed ideas; like I said, it comes back to the religion for me, the religion and the culture. So sex is something that's dirty. Not something you shouldn't do, but I guess something you should do when you're married. But even then, I can remember thinking, it would still seem dirty if I was married.

I finally decided to have sex because enough time went by. I just decided that I wanted to do it, and I guess I was comfortable with it. I wanted it to be a whole day; I wanted him to plan something for me. So we went out to dinner, etc., and then that night we tried it, but I was like, "That thing's too big." I had seen it before, but it hadn't been inside of me. I was like, "No way. That thing is not going inside of me." We ended up doing it the next day. The next day we were successful. It was good because even though I didn't care about him like I wanted to believe, we were good friends; so it was just a friendly thing. He was laughing at me the whole time, like, "Look at your face, ha, ha." In a way I'm glad that was my first experience because it didn't feel great, but it was emotionally comfortable. Physically it was just, What are people raving about? I mean, What is the big deal? It's not anything. It must take time or something, I was thinking. We did, and eventually it got better. But I never came.

The sex got bad later, emotionally bad because I really just wanted to be out of it, and I didn't care about him anymore. I wasn't attracted to him. So it just got to be dirty. Not dirty, but just something I didn't want to do.

A lot of times I remember not wanting to do it and just doing it anyway, not necessarily because he expected it, even though that was one of the reasons, but because I just didn't want to talk about it. I knew if I were to say something like, "Well, I don't want to do it," it would open up all kinds of things. We were friends, but we always talked about stuff outside. We didn't talk about our relationship. So I knew if I said, "I don't want to have sex now," it would be something just completely out of the ordinary, and I would have to talk about it, and I didn't want to have to do that.

I went away. I was in a study abroad in Brazil for a while, and whoo, I started exploring my sexuality, boy. That was a crazy year. I had sex with my second person; I had sex with a male and a female. Well, I didn't really have sex; we just fooled around. And I messed around with this guy that looks like my boyfriend from high school—that was the only reason why. I think I had a little orgasm with one of those people. But it wasn't dynamic, it was just short. I can't remember how.

I told my boyfriend before I left that I was going over there to get away. Deep inside I knew I didn't want to be with him. I always wanted to go to Brazil, but I knew part of it was getting away from him, which is weird. I don't know why I was playing these games with myself. At that point I'd just rather not confront the situation. I told him before I left, "I want to date other people. I'm going to be over there for a year." And he was like, "Well, it's not to have sex, is it? Or to do it with anybody else?" And I said, "No, no, I just want to go out with different people." He asked me like that, and he knew how I answered. So he knew. And then it was strange because he put a real deep guilt trip on me over that, or I was putting it on myself, or both. But I remember he told all his friends so they had the impression, Poor him, she went over there and had sex with other people. So all of a sudden when I came back, it was like, Oh, poor him and not poor me. These were real close friends, so it didn't affect my relationship with my friends, but it definitely affected my head. I felt mad guilty. Even though we did have an understanding before.

I broke up with him right when I got back. Over the phone. It was terrible. It was during the summer, so when we got back down to school, it was my first senior year. I had two senior years. I remember writing something about how I missed him. I don't know if I meant it; it was weird. I guess I did miss him to a certain extent. I guess I missed the security, just him being upset with me and not speaking to me. But he was never one to really show his feelings that much, so he would never be mean to me or anything like that. But I could tell he was just upset. When I broke up with him, I felt liberated. Just real liberated. Then when I got back to school, I just got back together with him. I don't know why, but it lasted another year. And then he graduated first; we came in together and he graduated first.

He had a teaching scholarship, and he was going to San Francisco. I just stopped it right there because he was making all these plans. San Francisco is far away; he was going to be there for two years. And I didn't feel about him like I was supposed to. It was a couple days before he left—and we were both very much in denial—but I came to him and said, "This is not working out." He knew my feelings had changed; he knew I didn't do anything while we were having sex. It's like deep inside he knew, too. He had to have. So when I came to him and said, "All this is weird and it's not working out," he wanted to say, "What are you talking about?" I said, "You know what I'm talking about." So that was it. San Francisco wasn't far enough for me. It was a lot of guilt. I just didn't want to see him again, really. We always talked, even while he was in San Francisco. But they were weird conversations. It was never completely discussed. I still want to discuss it; it lasted too long and too big a portion of both of our lives not to discuss it.

The guy and the girl thing in Brazil, I want to say it was just being drunk, but I think it would have happened even if we weren't. First of all, a lot of people who were in Brazil and who do exchanges to Brazil are like, No one knows me here. I can do whatever I want and go home. So everyone was on that mentality, and everyone had this really trendy "I'm bisexual" thing. Everyone was doing their thing, experimenting, whatever thing you were on. So that, number one, made it possible. And I guess the guy and I had been attracted to each other. I think he's the first white guy I was ever like, Wow. But we never did anything about it. He liked this other girl, the girl. She was a virgin before, and then they were basically together. She was Brazilian, but she was raised in Mexico.

Let me tell you, it's hard to say how race matters only because of all that comes into play. At one point I thought about the fact that I was the only black one in the group. In the threesome. At another time I thought, Okay, these are two exotic women with a white man. But his mother's French; that doesn't make him less white, but it just adds another kind of cultural thing on it. And he's Jewish. All these things came into play, but the other dynamic to it was the fact that we were all American. We were all foreigners in another country, so the things that unite you are language, culture—you find out what really unites people, and race is not the strongest thing. Not necessarily.

But that wasn't the first white man. The first one was, I think, the third person I'd had sex with. I don't like to say never again because I've done a lot of stuff I said I'd never do, but I really don't feel comfortable with a white man. And aside from that situation, there have been two white men, and it just didn't feel good. It felt like we were using each other: I was using him for sex, and I knew he had a thing for exotic women and black women. So it felt like I was being used. It was weird because, when you think of it on a logical level, we were both doing the same thing. I mean I'm sure there's probably a certain amount of exoticism in my head for him because I'd just never done it with a white man.

With the other one, I knew it was just stuff that was in my own head that I didn't feel comfortable with. Just the fact that he was white. But it's too much stuff to think about. When I have sex, I don't want to have to think about this extraneous stuff. I just want to have it be somebody I'm comfortable with so we can move on. And this is the same thing with an interracial relationship. It's cool, if you want to deal with that. I don't want to deal with that. I really don't because I have enough to deal with. It's just the thing of simplicity. But I don't regret it. I don't regret it at all because I got a chance to find out what that was, and I got a chance to really find out that you can have sex with your friends. I had sex with people that I would never have a relationship with and it was cool because we were friends. I didn't think that really could happen. I always thought that you would have some little inkling of something where you want to be together. But sometimes we were basically bored and just wanting to have sex.

I don't think I see race like everybody else. It's interesting when you try to cross those lines, because how you're raised makes a difference on what you experience. I went to Haiti two summers ago, and I had an experience with a lighter Haitian, not black. I went to his house late at night just to do that, and I left. I couldn't do it. I just couldn't do it. I guess he had the same exoticism kind of vibe to him, even though he wasn't white in the same way as American white. I think the exoticism factor exists with black men too. I think my dad has that for my mom. We talk about that openly. It's just obvious. She's like, "You just married me 'cause I'm just a little Hispanic and I had long hair," and he's like, "Yep, that's true." I think my boyfriend has that for me, too. But it just doesn't matter with him because everything else is in place. I don't know. Like I told you, I can't define anything with my boyfriend now; it's hard for me to place anything. So it's sort of thrown all my ideas and feelings out of whack. But it gives me an opportunity to really think about what I'm doing. Because nothing makes sense.

I just don't like walking down the street in my neighborhood sometimes. Sometimes it's okay what they say; you know, I'm flattered by it. But just men and catcalls, I don't want to always have to live with that. I mean, leave me alone. And then it affects me in terms of my clothes, because I would like to wear stuff that's more sexy, for me; I like looking at myself in the mirror, looking like that. But I don't want to do that because I don't want the attention. I don't know anyone like those stereotypes of Hispanic women—like Chiquita Banana and all that. Maybe I look like that to somebody else, but I don't feel like that. And I think black women, from what I've observed, try to step away from sexuality because we are viewed as too sexual. I play tricks with myself. The initial feeling is to step away from it, but I always try to combat that feeling. So then maybe I'm more overt with my sexuality. Like I said, I work on it. I don't know if it's good even to be too overt with it, but for me that's better than stepping away from it.

I wish I hadn't had sex in Brazil with the person that looked like my high school boyfriend. He was another white Jewish man. The boyfriend from high school, he was black, but he was very light-skinned; and so this guy looked just like him. And it was terrible, it was very terrible. At least with the other white man, we were friends, like I said. I felt objectified and used and dirty and all that stuff, but we were friends. He respected me as a person. I know that. This guy, I don't think he even respected me as a person. You know, I deal with that: I didn't really respect him as a person. It was terrible. Not only was the sex bad—even if the sex had been good it would have been better—but I didn't get anything out of it, nothing at all. He didn't know what he was doing; he was having sex for the second time in his life, and he was just hyperexcited. And I know for a fact what was in his head because when I left Brazil, they were telling me that he was talking about me, saying, "Oh yeah, I did her and she's easy." And I hate that. I don't even want to have to think like that. Because it was me, too; I was using him, too. I don't respect him as a person, especially not now.

I would like to be as open as possible in life and sex. I'd like to be open with the right person. Because there's just been something beyond that I haven't felt, or that I've felt glimpses of. I'd like to be able to feel that it's something completely good that I'm doing. Because I don't always feel that way. But I'd like to be able to feel that it's good: sex, the energy, the power, the drive, everything associated with it. For me it's just life—that's where it starts. There are always going to be problems; I'm learning that from my relationship now. I had an image of a perfect relationship, at least at some point. But now I'm learning, No, you've got to keep working at it, and there's always new problems. And I get frustrated. My boyfriend, I'm jealous of him in a way because for him life is just okay, cool. I mean, he has problems, but I'm the crazy one.

I wish everyone was like that. I wish I was like that, just open to it.

But, at the same time, there's got to be caution because it is something that is very powerful. And I think that was probably the message behind that whole Catholic thing before people started messing it up. It's just something to be careful with. It can be good; you just have to be careful, that's all. But it's not bad.

# Cocoa

*I* NEVER REALLY have focused on saying out what I really believe; I've kept it kind of inside. Sometimes I find myself as a person struggling to stand up for my identity, without letting someone else find out who I am and what I believe in. Someone may be very strong about being feminist. I may not be or feel like I'm that type of person, but I feel they have the right to be who they are. Sometimes it feels like they're trying to force me to be who they want me to be, and it's not always good. Because I have a totally different viewpoint for myself, but I don't always feel comfortable speaking out for myself.

I'm thirty-seven years old. I'm divorced; I was married for thirteen years. I have no kids. Both my parents live together—they're still living. I have three brothers, two sisters, so six of us. Everyone's still alive. Right now I'm a Christian, and I'm into the Baptist denomination. I've been a Christian for a long time, but I've always liked it from a different aspect. It's not just a set of rules, but building a close relationship with God, and building a close relationship with God is different than following a religion. A lot of people don't seem to understand that. Let's see, like I said, I was married for thirteen years. I got married when I was twenty-one. I don't think I really was ready to get married at that time, but because I felt I was being pressured into it, I just went ahead and did it.

My parents were both from Chicago—not from Chicago, they were raised in the South. My mom is from Mississippi, my father from Tennessee and they met up in Chicago. Then we moved because my father got a job at Ford, so it's like a middle-class family in the city. We were born in the city, but no real bad things happened, just normal things. My dad drank sometimes; he's an alcoholic. But he wasn't an alcoholic all the time, so I can't say he was just drunk every weekend. Holidays mostly, and then he would go on this binge for two weeks. I think that had a lot to do with my perception of things.

My mom actually worked as a nurse's aid. She didn't always go to church, but she was always there for us, and she tried to make it as best as possible with what she knew. I think my mom didn't really deal with a lot of communicating about anything, because I think she was afraid. She didn't really talk to us; she didn't let us know if any problems were going on. I think she sheltered us from a lot of things. So that kind of sheltered our viewpoint of the world. She was afraid of a lot of things, and I remember one statement: I was thirteen; I said I wanted to be a stewardess, and her comment at that time was, "Why would you want to be a prostitute?" And I thought that was weird; why would she think a stewardess would be a prostitute? But then stuff would fall apart and when I wanted to go to school for the arts, to travel, she didn't want me to go that route. She wanted me to just go with everyone else. And, like I said, in that wanting to please other people, I went ahead and did that, even though that's not what I wanted to do. I really wanted to go away to school for travel and then eventually move out to California and be in the arts.

Intimacy to me is actually being able to share feelings and comments with someone and not worry about them running away from you. If someone had to come to you and tell you something that would be very, very important, or their fears, or what they wanted, they would be able to share with you and know that even though you may not understand it at that time, that you won't run away—and that's what I call intimacy. You can open up and you can say whatever it is that's on your heart, without really worrying about that person judging you or thinking bad things about you because this is how you're feeling. I don't think I've received that, not even with my parents. I couldn't tell anything to my family about anything, even to this day. When I remember boys, my mother never asked me any questions about it. She just said, Do you want to come home? But she didn't discuss what was wrong. And I just thought that was weird.

I think I've been taught, if you ask a question and someone doesn't answer it, then you're not supposed to be asking that question—something's wrong with your question. But sometimes you're just trying to get to know a person a little bit better, and things that people call very personal, or things you really want to know about that person—you're not taught to ask those questions. Just keep it on the surface. And I don't live my life like that. I have a roommate, and her name is Lisa. I really care a lot about Lisa; I can just share anything with her and she's not judgmental about any of it. She listens, and that's good; she hears you and she's a very good friend. So she's taught me a lot: that you can share, that people will understand how you feel, and they'll be there.

I didn't learn anything about sexuality from my family. I learned it from looking around and trying to say, This can't possibly be what sex is or what sexuality is. I think I did understand what it was. If you're a sexy person, you can be a sexy person without having sex. There's a charisma about people that people may be drawn to, and that doesn't mean that you're trying to be sexy. I think in my family, my mom was afraid of that. My mom didn't even feel comfortable enough talking about the natural flow of menstruation; she didn't explain it to us. She had a young lady next door talk to us. She began to tell us about the menstruation process, and I thought, Oh, okay. I really thought, This is weird. Why are you talking to us about the menstruation process? Maybe my mom should be the one talking to us about it. But she never said anything about it. And I realized at that point in time, that's why that young lady was talking to us. I think maybe my mother felt she couldn't talk to us. Like I said, she was really afraid of us getting pregnant. I don't know.

I can't remember if me and my sisters talked among ourselves about it.

We may have. My sister Serene, we were pretty close, and we talked and giggled about everything; and we just thought it was funny, I think. Because we weren't at that point. But when it did come, we knew about it. My sister started, then my other sister started, and then I started.

When I thought it was on, I mentioned it to my one sister. But actually what happened was I just hit myself on the bike and I was bleeding. When it actually came, I didn't know what to do. I told my mother finally when it did come, and she told me—back then they had the little belts and you had to go in and put the belt on. And I said, "Well, should I get a belt?" She said okay, and so I went and got it. The sanitary belt. I was trying to put this thing on; I kept trying to hook it together. How can this stop me from bleeding? I don't know how this could possibly stop me from bleeding. So I went and got her, and I said, "I can't do this." And she said, "What do you mean, you can't do it?" "I can't do it." So I went back into the bathroom, and she said, "Well, where's the pad?" And I said, "Pad?" She said, "You didn't get the pad?" I said, "No, I didn't know I was supposed to." So she didn't actually tell me that I needed to go get the sanitary napkins and put the sanitary napkins on with the belt. I didn't know any of those details. It had never happened to me before.

She's just very uncomfortable with talking about it. Even now, she's very, very supportive with me being on my own, but she never talks about the intimate details that you sometimes want to be able to share with your mom and say, "These are the problems I'm going through." As she's been getting older, I think that she's shared with an older lady, but she never told us about the problems. Which is good I guess, and bad, because we never got an opportunity to see her at her weak moments, and what she was struggling through. And that she actually survived it. Which might be a bit different.

I think I tried to talk about her life one time, and she shut it down. So I realized I'd better not say anything about that; I don't think she's ready to discuss that. I was with my ex-husband one time, I don't remember the question that I asked, but he noticed also. And I said, "Did you notice how quickly she cut me off?" And he said, "Yeah." And I said, "I won't approach that subject." I can't even remember what it was. I think it was about learning a little bit more about our family. I think it's about separating from people, because my mom didn't feel comfortable with her family, with the drinking, her sisters—which is good. Sometimes you have to pull people out of an environment. But we were pulled out so much that we really didn't know anything about the other part of the family. She didn't talk about the family, connect with anyone; these were my aunts and I never talked to them as a child. They came over sometimes. But I don't talk to them now; I don't feel close to them. I just know that they're my aunts. And I don't think it should be that way.

For some reason I think my parents thought I was faster than the other two, and maybe I was. I was more eager to get out, I wanted adventure, I wanted to do something with my life. And I enjoyed boys, I enjoyed boys as friends, I enjoyed talking to them. I remember one time I was sitting on a man's lap, as a little girl would sit down on someone's friend, not sexual or anything like that. My dad came in and yelled, "Get off his lap!" I was like, Oh, okay. I'm not sure how old he was; I think it was just an older man. But it wasn't like I was sitting on his lap and he was fondling me or anything. I was just a young kid, affectionate, giving someone, a friend, a hug. Maybe he was twenty or something like that. I was probably six or seven. So I said okay, and I got up. I didn't understand what he was trying to say.

My mom was just so frightened, and she would actually tell my dad. I remember—I think I was eight or seven—and I was kissing a little boy in the hallway, and the neighbor across the street saw us. And she told my mom, and my mom was so upset—she was just highly upset with me for kissing a boy. It was fun at that age, and he was like my little boyfriend at seven. It was just a little kiss kiss—I thought, well, maybe I'll just kiss this little boy. But she was highly upset, and not saying, "Cocoa, don't kiss little boys." She just said, "I'm going to tell your dad," and I think that's wrong.

My dad surprised me because my dad actually was laughing. But when he called me, I was really afraid. He said, "You know, your mother said you were kissing a little boy." I wasn't even in the house; I was in the yard, and he was on the balcony. I said, "Yeah." And he said, "Don't kiss any other boys." I said, "Okay." And that was it. So he was not as paranoid, I think, as she was. And I remember another time when I was thirteen, just getting into a high school, and I wasn't able to receive company until I was fifteen. But no one ever told me that, so I was just looking at friends as friends. A friend across the street invited someone to come over to talk to me, to meet me. And I was sitting on the steps talking to this young guy, just like my friend, and I had my sister and everyone else up on the porch. All of a sudden, my dad came rushing out the door and yelling and saying that I couldn't see company—"Cocoa, you're not allowed to receive company. You have to tell that young man to go home"—totally embarrassing me. That just showed me he didn't trust me, and I didn't understand why.

I didn't have a rule until he said, "Oh, well, you can't." I had to pin them down: "Well, when can I receive company?" And he said, "When you're fifteen." I said, "Okay." And I remember with Coleman, when I did turn fifteen and I asked him to go on a date, my father said, "You could not wait." And I said, "You said at fifteen I could go out." "You couldn't wait. You couldn't wait. You're fifteen. Now you want to ask me if you can go out on a date." "Yeah, that's what you said, 'When you're fifteen, you can go out on a date.'" And his remark was, "You didn't waste any time."

I felt that they did not trust me. And they didn't know who I was, because even though I was their daughter, it's like they didn't know me as Cocoa, the person. Yeah, I'm just a normal teenager who explores certain things, but you should know that you taught me enough values, that I wouldn't always give in to peer pressure. You didn't know where my head was because you didn't take the time to sit down and really talk to me about how I was feeling or what I was thinking. In my mind, I was not going to get pregnant in high school because at the time, number one, I wanted to finish my education. And number two, it was just too much of a hassle, it was too much pressure, just too much going on to get pregnant. But even at that point then I did not want to just have sex, just to be having it, because it was more important to me than just casual sex. I've talked with a lot of boys because I've had a lot of boys, men, who were friends. And I would listen to them and what they would say about girls once they, you know, had sex with them, and how they felt about that whole situation. And there was no way guys were going to talk about me like that. But they felt free enough to talk around me because I was a friend. They were not dating me. So I actually saw and felt the double standard there.

And, with my parents, we had separate rules from our brothers. I don't think my brothers—my one brother, he's one young man—a lot of pressure was not put on him even as far as achieving in school, like the girls. We knew we had to bring home good grades. It was a girl's thing; I don't know why. It's sad on both parts because I didn't think it was causing him to try harder or to do anything. He just took out the trash, while we were responsible for cleaning the house. We would do his dishes, we had to do all the housework, and we had to be in at a certain time. It was different treatment. I don't know if he had any sexual rules about receiving company or anything. I don't think my dad paid any attention to him, because he left the home a lot of times. He would go out and play sports. But I don't think they ever asked him what he was doing.

I don't know how I learned about sex. How did I really learn about sex? You learn about it from your friends. One time they did have a sexual education class at school; I think we were in the sixth grade, and we had to get permission from our parents. They talked about where babies came from, and I think that was it. But as far as really exploring sexuality and understanding what it was about, no. My sisters and I didn't talk about sex. No, it was a funny relationship with my sisters. We had kind of a hierarchy. My oldest sister, who's just two years older, we really didn't talk about it; our lives were just so separate. We looked at her as the special one because she was treated different than we were. She never really got a whipping—she only got one whipping in her whole life, and that was like a tap-tap on the leg. But with us, it was an all-out beating. I don't know why. She was the first female baby, but we had an older brother that had died. But no one told us anything about him. My mother has never said anything about this dead baby, to this day. My dad was drunk one time and he told us. But he told us never to tell our mother that we knew. And we never said anything. And my other sister had no interest whatsoever in sex or boys; she was just more interested in her books. Me, it was like, I want to have fun, I want to go out and talk with my friends.

For me virginity was something I wanted to keep. And then for high school, I knew when I wanted to have sex, which was when I was eighteen. I wanted to experiment after I got out of high school, when I felt that I would really want to make my own decisions. So I knew that at that time, I was going to do it. I chose to keep my virginity on my own. And I remember that I was talking to a young man, and we made a bet—and it sounds kind of crazy—but he said, "I bet you'll get pregnant in high school," and I looked at him and said, "I bet you I won't." And I didn't. Even to this day we laugh about it, that he made a bet with me: "You didn't think I could keep it, but I could." I had physical contact, but I was not going to have sex. I didn't believe in boyfriends. I saw boyfriends as controlling at that point in time, telling me how to live my life. And I didn't want that, I didn't want it. I guess I saw so much of the double standard going on, and I just didn't want to get involved with someone because it seemed once you got involved, you kind of changed. I talked with my friends, and saw the changes they were going through with the boyfriends they had, and I thought, No way. So I just hung out with them.

It was a lot of fun. There was this one guy I fooled around with. Not to the point of taking all your clothes off, but rubbing up against each other, rolling on each other, actually fonding his penis. With his hands in your panties, but never taking your panties all the way off. Pretty much just that. Never took my clothes all the way off. Even one point in time where you got close to having sex, but it was, "No way, take it out. No, no, I told you I didn't want to have sex, so don't try to jerk your penis inside of me. Get up." And I didn't appreciate a lot of that. I had this feeling, right? I had orgasms, manually. I did have that; I didn't know what it was. It was through manual sex, and it was fine because I was still stimulated, and I just didn't want to go on. And I was like, Hey, maybe that was an orgasm. I felt that, yes. You reached a peak, and the peak felt good to you; but since I wasn't having intercourse, I didn't really know what that was. Then I actually had intercourse, and the orgasm came or the sexual peak came. I didn't really know what that was because it was really a difference for me than the other one. It came and then I was relaxed and I didn't want to have sex anymore at that point in time. So when it happened again, I didn't want to get to that point because I felt like once I got to that point, I didn't want to have sex anymore. I didn't know how to ask somebody, What is that? We'd get together almost every day for a while, but we didn't have sex; we'd just hang out. Because I enjoyed him as a friend. We got along, we talked a lot. But then it started cutting back to maybe once a week, to the point where I was just not interested in him anymore.

I felt that he was not loyal because I knew he had another—well, he had a girlfriend, and then he had a child. I asked him about it and he told me. And that meant, hmm, you had a child, you're not telling me the truth. And then this other girl I knew became very angry with me. So I was asking him, "Why does she not like me? Why is she angry with me if you're not still talking to her, if you're not involved with her in some other way?" And it was true. He was still involved with her, but then also, she was pregnant. I said, "No, I'm not going to get involved with you, with this young lady here and she's pregnant. You need to think about how you're going to react with her son." So we didn't talk at that point. But after we got older, maybe juniors or seniors, I would talk with him or go out with him because he was not involved with her at that time. But I didn't find him honest because he wouldn't tell me the truth. I was looking for honesty. If you are not ready to have a one-on-one relationship, then tell me, but don't pretend one thing and then do something else.

I think he told other people about what we did. And that angered me because he actually told one person that we had had sex, when we had not had intercourse. And he told his friends on the football team, and they started coming up to me like they wanted to talk to me, like they wanted to go out with me. That really made me angry. Because I felt, Don't be coming up to me all of a sudden. Why do they want to talk with me? My friend then told me that he had said he had intercourse with me. And I said, "Well, he's lying. He has not had intercourse with me." And I explained and told her what had happened, and she said, "Well, you know him." I said, "I know him now." That made me angry.

For a while I went to a community college, for three years. But my dream was to go away, to move to California. And I met another young man that I knew in high school, I knew him already, but we started dating after. His name was Benson—he's actually my ex-husband. He was fine. He had dreams and he wanted to do certain things. He seemed to be an okay guy, wanting some things out of life. Seemed to be all right, treated me nice. So we went out a long time, for two years, and he kept asking me if I wanted to get married, but I really did not want to get married at that point in time; I didn't know the reason why. I could tell him why I shouldn't get married, I just—I didn't know what else to do, I guess.

I wanted to become my own person. I wanted to start standing up for what Cocoa believed in. I wanted to achieve some things in my life. I wanted to work, number one. I wanted to find out who I was and what I really believed in. And I felt that the only way I could do that finally was to move away or get away from my environment and all of what people would say. Because I realized I was different. I tried to explain certain things to my family, and they would look at me like, I don't understand what you're talking about. And that's okay, but I still believed, life has something else to offer, and you can know a lot more than what I'm finding out here, and the only way I can do that is to get out. But once I started dating Benson, I think I put that on the back burner. I was having fun, or a social life. And I thought even at that point in time I did care for Benson, did love him, that perhaps we could do it together. Even though you're married, if a person believes in you and you believe in them, you should get to chase the dreams. That's how I looked at it.

He was supportive, he was very, very, very supportive of my dreams. He did not want what I wanted, and I didn't find out until later, but that was okay. He was afraid of losing me. But in the end, he really lost me because when you're afraid of things, you lose what you're really afraid of instead of learning to grow with that person. It's like you're trying to hold on. And that's what happened. It would have been better for him to say, "I'm not sure about that. I don't think I want to do that."

I went after Benson; I wanted him—I wanted him with sex lust. I wanted to experiment with sex, so I did. I didn't go with him immediately; I waited awhile, maybe six . . . three months. And then I finally decided. But it was in my mind already that I was going to have sex. I was eighteen, and I decided that I'd go and get on the pill so I would not get pregnant. I heard people talking about a pill. I didn't do any active reading, I just happened to know there was a family clinic in our neighborhood. I just decided at that point in time, I don't want to get pregnant; I know there's some things out there. So I went to the clinic, by myself, didn't tell anyone. I was just going to go to the clinic and get checked out.

I remember going to this family clinic in a lower-class neighborhood. I made my appointment, I came in, I sat there till it was like three o'clock on a Friday. The appointment was at one. And at three they had not seen me yet, so I went in there and I talked to them, "Well, I've been here since one o'clock. No one has seen me, and it's getting near four," and they would get mad because it was closing time. So the doctor came in—I'm not sure what she was but she was not black or white, and she was mad because I was near the end of her time. She said, "I don't know why you are always running late. You should learn to be on time." And I told her, "I was on time. I was here; I was just out there waiting." So she said, "Just lay back." So she gave me the tests. She was giving me the Pap smear, and she just took the thing and just stuck it up inside of me, just pushed it in, and I went, "Oh!" And she looked at me and said, "You've never had sex, you've never had a Pap smear before." And I said no. I was practically in tears. And she said, "I'm sorry, I'm sorry." I already made an appointment at one o'clock, I came here to get some pills, I was paying for it, but she treated me like I was not paying for it, and that really—it just made me angry. And I thought, I'm never going to a clinic again because of how they treat you. Here she is, she had no compassion, nothing. She didn't know anything about me. She just made a judgment call—that I'm sexually active already—so all she's doing is just coming in and taking a normal Pap smear test without taking out the time to talk to me and tell me about what is going on.

I got the pills, but they weren't the right kind. But I never told my mom about any of it. They started hurting my legs, so they'd been saying if you have problems, come back immediately. And I did. I went back to them, but then I found my own private doctor, even at eighteen. I had a job, and I decided, No, I'm not going to go through this. So I would get regular checkups; and then I would begin to start reading and talking with some of the doctors about how it feels, how it's too dry, and they would tell me, "You're not being stimulated enough." And I thought, Okay, I didn't know about those kinds of things.

The first time, we made a decision we were going to do it one night, go to a hotel; we had no other place to go. He was living at home, I was living at home. And we went to this little beat-down hotel where the bed was nasty and dirty, and he could not enter me the first time. He could not do it; I was too tense, and I don't know why I was so tense, but intercourse didn't happen the first time. We had to try at least three times before it actually slipped in. I think it was because I was so tense at the final moment that I could not relax. After it happened, it was like, Is this all it is? Is this what people are making a fuss about? Gosh, I waited all this time for this? That's how I felt. Oh, well, then I would talk to my friend, this person who was my friend, and she told me when she did it and I told her when I did it. And we both thought it wasn't anything. It hurt, but it'll get better; and after we kept it up, it got better. It felt good. But then it's like, you go through your whole life, and this is what you're waiting on. This is how it feels.

I don't think we really talked about orgasm. All we'd talk about was whether or not it was exciting. A lot of times it was like, "Yeah, it felt good," or "No, it didn't feel good." I don't know if she knew that much herself. And I don't know what I was looking for. I think I was looking for fireworks to go off, and to feel wonderful, and to smoke a cigarette afterward—and I don't even smoke. But the whole myth—this wasn't it at all. So I was still searching.

I thought, I'm not being satisfied here; we need to figure out another way. He would listen because I would say I don't feel good about just jumping in bed, I want it to be romantic, I want us to make love, too, not just have sex—and that's how it felt. He was willing to try what I would suggest or I'd ask him, "How do you feel about this? Let's try it this way, or let's try a romantic dinner, or try music, or try this," and he was good at that. So I would start reading, trying to figure out, How can you put spice into your love life? And I would try those things, and those things—they were not working. I began to think there was something else wrong, besides the physical part. I started to think there was something wrong on the inside of me, why I wasn't I truly enjoying it, and I began to search. This was after I got married. I began to really look inside myself and say, Well, now, this man is trying very, very hard to please me, and even though he does it, I'm still not satisfied. Something is wrong with me, not him. And I began to search then, actually go on a soul search to find out, what is it that I'm missing and what is it that I'm looking for? Because it's not here.

I did have an affair when I got here. I was having so many problems late in the marriage—this was like the tenth or the eleventh year. And that affair was a mistake. I thought it was something and it wasn't. I thought I was falling in love, and it was not like that. We were having problems in our marriage at that time, and we weren't talking. And when we would talk, we would have an argument. So for some reason we weren't being friends, and I couldn't understand it. My husband had an affair, and he didn't tell me, and I didn't know about it even though I would ask him. Then I slept with someone. But when he found out about my affair, he was very, very angry with me. But he never told me he'd had one. I suspected he had one. Finally we did separate and we talked about some things, and I met the young lady—she told me. He worked with her, and I didn't meet her before then, but after I separated, I met her—well, I saw her come to the house. After awhile I just said, "You know"—because I was ready to get out of the marriage—"I want you to have a good life. And don't think I'm coming back." The woman, I met her, and she seemed to be an okay young lady, but he was not dealing with a lot of issues still. It finally got to a point where she just wanted to leave him, and so he asked me to talk to her, and I did. I sat down and I said, "I believe Benson really does love you, and I think you'd be good for him." And they connected that I was saying that, I think, because I wanted to get away, and I didn't want him to feel so hurt by me. So she began to talk to me about a lot of things, that they did have an affair while we were married. And I asked him, and he still did not answer. He said, "No, no, not while we were married." If he would only tell me the truth. All I want is for people to tell me the truth.

I don't know why they lie. I think it's about ownership or possessive-

ness. I don't know. I guess that they feel that you're their queen and you be-
long to them, and no one else has the right to touch you. I think that's why
they get so angry. But they don't see it the same way. They don't see their
sleeping with someone else as actually hurting you at the same time. But if
they get caught, I think they've been taught never to say that they've done
it. Just keep saying no, no, because you can't prove it as long as they deny it.
But that only hurts more. If you'd finally tell the truth, maybe we could
work through it, but if you don't tell the truth, that person can't trust you.

After some soul searching, I found out that I had really low self-
esteem. Number one, I was very afraid of making mistakes. Because I
thought that when you made a mistake, people didn't understand. So you
try to put yourself on this pedestal and be this perfect little person that has
no bad thoughts. And that's not true. Perfect little person—little girl—to
me was, you didn't think about sex, you didn't curse, you didn't do things
like that. That's what a little perfect girl was. I think I was trying to be a
little perfect girl for a long time, even though I had all those desires and
ambitions, things I wanted to do. But yet, what I wanted to do, other people didn't want me to do, so how could I be two people?

I think it had a lot to do with my dad's drinking. I found out about
codependency. You'd say, "Well, will you drink again?" and he'd say, "No, I
won't drink again." But then he turns around and drinks again, and no one
talks about it. They just act as if it did not happen. And everyone's very bitter, and very upset, and disturbed. You don't know if he's going to come
home or not—you just have uncertainties. So it begins to build on you. You
don't feel you're worthy because of the cheapness, and you're just ashamed
of how your dad is—you don't want people to see that your dad drinks.
He's just a human being, but he was going through a lot at that point in
time. And he couldn't talk to anyone. He couldn't talk to his family. He
couldn't share that. And I think if we were allowed to talk about how we
felt, it might have made a big difference.

I'm working through it a lot, and a lot of times, actually, it makes me
work on my relationship through Jesus Christ and with God. I always believed in God, and it's like He's never been the one to say, "You've got to do
this in order for me to like you." It's like, "Just come to me the way that you

are. You know, I love you exactly the way that you are. Let's just find out what it is that you're really feeling, how you feel, and why you feel the way that you're feeling." And so you just start to trace back why you feel the way that you feel. And I think my whole issue was trying to be something that I'm not. I enjoy sex, I enjoy being near men, I enjoy men. But I enjoy relationships at the same time, and I want people to enjoy me. Sometimes sex may be good, sometimes it may be bad, but at least let's sit down and understand what it's all about, what's going on with me, and how I can share me with you, because I want to share myself with you, I want to give you love. But if you're not honest, I'm not honest, I can't give you love.

I'm actually in the process of writing a play about women and their relationship with God to finally admit what's going on with them, because I went through a lot. I even got to the point where I wanted to kill myself. I wanted to die because I didn't understand why I couldn't be the way people wanted me to be. Even though I smiled, I was ready to die. I was searching the Bible for suicide, and I thought, What is the matter with me because I cannot pull this thing together? I wondered, How did I end up like this? I wanted to talk to someone, I wanted to be able to explain things and be open about a lot of things. But I really began to search. Why do I think this way? Is it because people constantly tell me this, or is it that I really believe this? That's the soul searching. You just have to be who you are. When something's self-destructing, eventually you'll see it once you begin to notice your pattern. Why are you going back into that pattern of behavior? Finally I got to a point, in my thirties: I don't want to live my whole life like this. That's why I decided to stand up for what I believe. You have to give a person the chance to go through growing up, and I wasn't given that chance.

I don't remember masturbating when I was growing up. I tried it once or twice after I got divorced. It was fine. I thought, If I can bring myself to orgasm, why can't men do that? I don't do it now. I bought this book about the sexual woman. I wanted to begin to experiment with sex again, figure out how I can please myself. How could I be pleased by a man if I really didn't know what I wanted, what turned me on? And how would I know what felt good to me unless I really tried some of the things to see what felt good to me? So that was my process of beginning to understand more about sex. Because if you don't know who you are, before people want to touch you, then how can you really enjoy the sexual experience or the lovemaking experience? What is oral sex to you, why don't you like it, what is it? I like giving oral sex. I don't necessarily like getting it. I guess I like the feel of it. I like the way it makes the man feel, and there's more control. Compared to receiving it—I guess maybe I just don't like the taste afterwards when you're kissing. I want to brush my teeth and everything afterwards. I don't think I want to kiss after that; I just don't like the taste. But I still want to feel close to that person, so that's why I don't actually let him give me oral sex. I guess it's a mind thing. Like I said, I'm beginning to learn to accept a lot more, my own body. I'm more receptive, and I think I'm getting to that point that it's okay.

So I have had orgasms from manual stimulation, not vaginal ones. I began to become really concerned about that. Why can't I really reach an orgasm in the vagina, during sex? I've actually had a couple of men since I was divorced. And one was very, very good, very great, and when we went to do it, I asked him, "You seem to know how to stimulate a woman. How did you learn to do this?" I wanted to know. He said that he learned to listen to women and give them what they wanted, and to give to them and not take.

Altogether, I've had three partners, Benson and two other guys; all of them are black. I'm not interested in sleeping with a white man, I don't know why. I just haven't been attracted to white men. Maybe it's just a mental block. When I was in high school, one of my teachers was interested in me, and I didn't know he was pursuing me. He had taken me out to dinner for a graduation present. I just thought it was a graduation present, but it really wasn't. It was a date. And I didn't know that. He treated me very nice. Then we were laying on the lawn looking at the stars, and I was thinking, Why are we doing this? And then when we were going home, he tried to kiss me and I realized. He was very nice to me, but I didn't look at him that way. I just looked at him as my teacher. After the date, when he tried to kiss me, I thought, Wait a minute, this is not what I went out with you for. I really thought it was a graduation present, not that you had any interest in me whatsoever. So I never saw him again and really didn't talk about it after that. That was the extent of white men, not just coming up to me, but noticing some of them. I worked in this store one time, and this one guy picked me up and kissed me when he was leaving. We were just walking into the back room, and he was leaving, so he just grabbed me and kissed me. I didn't even think about harassment or anything at that time. He worked with me. He was just a young white guy. To myself I was like, I don't know you; I don't even think about you in that sense.

I wouldn't say anything when men would cross the line. I'd just look at them and try to move and think of it as another thing that I deal with. Just listening to them say, "Oh, you're cute, you're pretty," then it's like, Yeah, okay. I remember, I was taking driving lessons one time, and the driving teacher told me he thought I was pretty. He was showing me how to parallel park or to park, and he was on the passenger side, and he bent over and kissed me. And I looked at him, and he said, "See, you did a great job." And I just looked at him really weird. I don't know why it didn't make me angry. I remember in high school, this one young man was going to try and rape me in the hall in school. But the teacher came at that point in time, and I never said anything. I never told my mother, I never told anyone. I didn't know him at all. He was just in the school—I'm not even sure if he was a student. But I guess maybe because you're taught silence your whole life, not to talk about things, that you don't think about your life as actually in danger. That's how I thought. I didn't tell a teacher. I didn't say anything and I should have said something. But I didn't say anything.

I don't think I've had any fantasies since I've been young. I think I've always had these dreams, how I visualize my life: we're boyfriend and girlfriend, we make love, we have all this wonderful fun time, we decide to get married, and that's the end of my life. I could never go past a happy time once you get married. We could have a wonderful time, do all kinds of things, make love, all times of the day . . . Or you go through and you don't have any underwear, and you make it in an elevator, you make it in the basement, you make it on the table . . . you know.

I actually did it in a building once, an office. I was stripped totally nude. Late at night. It was a shock to him—it was the one guy who listened. I'm actually open to having a good time sexually, and it doesn't bother me. But if you act as though something's wrong, then it shuts me down. It shut me down one time because I was having oral sex with Benson, and he said, "Oh, don't do that." That was really our first getting together, and he told me not to do that. I thought I was doing something wrong. So I never had it with him again, even though he was trying to get me to do it, because of his disapproval of it the very first time. I would try, but I couldn't do it because of that.

I don't have sexual fantasies. I've had someone eat jelly or ice cream [off of me], but I actually did it; I didn't fantasize about it. I would read something and say, Hmm. I would go to a bookstore and I would pull out books from the sexual section or psychology and start to read, and I would get positions, and I would ask people questions. I would say, "Well, let's try this, because I don't know."

When I'm experimenting, I do actually like the guy. I mean, it's not like it's some stranger. I would tell them that I'm not bored but that I want to learn more about sex. They say all right. I just wanted to try something different, I wanted to learn to have an orgasm, and more than one orgasm at one time. I wanted to learn to come more than once, come twice, three times. And I learned. And for some reason I would like to look at men, open my eyes to find out what is it that I'm doing to you, and I'd want to watch. At one point someone wanted to videotape me, and I said, "No, we can't tape this." Nothing on record, you know. You just have to keep it up in your head. Not that you wouldn't want to watch it one time, but no, videotaping is too dangerous to me these days.

I've never been pregnant. At one point in my marriage, I wanted to get pregnant. I didn't know what was wrong, but I found out I have a little polyp blocking my uterus right now—which they can remove, but I didn't know that at that time. They told us just keep trying. I thought it was something mental. We didn't go to the point of taking the tests because they were so expensive.

Right now I think I would not want to get pregnant. I don't think I could take care of a baby right now. It's not like it's the end of the world for me. Because of where I'm at in my life, I'm okay. I'm not even sexually active to the point where I'm having vaginal intercourse. I'm trying to really review what I want out of life, and talk with the person more, and get to know him one-on-one. What do you want from life and what do I want from life? More of a relationship where I can talk with this person, so that if something happened, and that person could eventually not have sex, how would I feel about this person? I'm trying to review it.

I've always wanted to adopt if I did not have children. And so it doesn't bother me. I still want to have kids and I still want to adopt. Whether I have them physically or whether I adopt a child, I'm passionate about children and I want to have one. I've never really thought of myself being pregnant my whole life, but I've always thought about raising a child. But not the actual pregnancy.

Sexually, I guess I have regrets. Actually, having another man while being married. That's the only regret that I have. If I had experimented with not just my husband and other men, I would be fine. But that's the only act I really do regret, simply because of how it came about. It came about because of being unhappy in the marriage situation and not because of really loving that person.

I think the sexual double standard is a big part of sexism. What a good girl is, what she should be doing, what she shouldn't be doing, instead of exploring anything, learning about the person. Sex does not make you a bad person. So I think that plays a big part. And being a woman, what you always get: being smart but not expecting you to use your brains. When you do things, you're not expected to think through processes. You're expected to do whatever the man tells you to do. And I don't agree with that. It makes you feel like you're not a person, that you're not important, and you don't have any worth.

I understand there is racism in America, but I think I've experienced it in my own culture more so than outside my culture because of the dark skin/light skin thing. It's so crazy; I never understood it. It has affected my self-esteem a lot of times. My being dark-skinned has made me think I'm not pretty or that I have to do things for guys to like me, or for people to like me. I think that's just so stupid. I've actually had people think, She's ugly because she's too dark. I've heard it. Or, they'll say, "You're pretty for a dark-skinned lady." It was mostly from men and the desire thing.

I've lived with that my whole life, and it's just frustrating, aggravating, to the point I did try to change my look. I got my skin lightened, and everyone had a perm to make their hair longer and red, and I thought light skin with brownish-red hair would be very pretty. And that's what I tried to do to myself. At fifteen. It messed up this part of my skin, and I didn't realize what was going on because I thought it was working. My mom looked at me and said, "What have you done to yourself?" I didn't know what she was talking about. Then I realized what I was trying to do, but I never talked to her about it. Finally I just got the cocoa butter for my skin and just started accepting me the way that I was. I have short hair, dark skin, that's all I can do. I can't make boys accept me or like me. And I think I was living in a bubble for a long time, till I finally realized, I can't do this anymore. Everything started coming down on me at one time. Because I had pressure from so many areas and from so many people that I just couldn't deal with who I was. And now I'm finally getting to the point where, this is me.

I think I was getting to the point where I was getting frustrated with men because you feel a need to perform: you need to be a certain way in order for me to like you. That has a lot to do with sexism, I think, because if I'm not acting a certain way, maybe you won't go out with me, or maybe you won't like me. When I talk to men, I ask them, Why is it that when you do something that I don't approve of, you think that I'm bitching or nagging, or that you can't get anything right, when I'm expressing my viewpoints to you? I'm telling you things that bother me. Why do you feel that I'm not being a good woman or something at that point in time? When you do something, you don't want me to come to you or confront you with that. Or if I do something, you won't confront me or tell me. I feel that I need to speak what I believe, and you may not agree with it, and that's fine, but I still should be allowed to say it.

I think racism and sexism affected my sexuality in a sense because they did not allow me to really become the person I was supposed to be. Because I was trying to be something else. Even with racism, I'm supposed to have long hair, light skin, and be gorgeous; and with sexism, if you're a nice girl, you don't dress a certain way, you don't go to certain places, you don't do certain things. And now it's like, I'm Cocoa, and there's certain things I like and certain things that are nice-looking to me, certain things that are not. I dress many ways. I'm thin. If I want to look very, very pretty, I like a dress that's really pretty, that's nicely shaped, that's cut in the back. But that doesn't mean a person's trying to be a whore or to get a man. She just happens to like that dress. I think we tend to look at different kinds of dresses, really short or low-cut, and assume that that person's being whorish and she's trying to get a man. Sometimes certain things look really nice on a person. If it fits their body and they're not trying to flaunt it, it's not a given that that's what they're trying to do.

I don't think that society understands black women's sexuality or that they represent it well because, again, when I look at it and society, when they think that black women are very pretty, they hardly ever go to the dark-skinned woman as being pretty and sexy. They go to a light-skinned woman with long hair and say this is pretty, and when they see the dark-skinned lady, they say this is the nurturing type. And that's not representing all women. Or if they show a dark-skinned woman in a sexual light, she's poor, she's loud talking, she's not intelligent, she's not smart. They show the light-skinned one as very intelligent. I see that a lot and it makes me angry. I know it has an impact on my little niece, and I see her do certain things. She watches BET and MTV, and certain things that she thinks are sexy, she plays those same roles. It has had an impact on me, but it doesn't impact me anymore because now I can see it and stop it for myself. I think you just have to constantly work through it. It's not like all of a sudden you just unpack it all and you recognize it and say, "I recognize this is what's happening." You just keep working through it.

two | GUARDED HEART

$A$LTHOUGH SOME LEVEL of guardedness is a necessary form of self-protection, too high a level interferes with intimate give and take. The women in this section are at a highly defensive moment in their lives in matters of sexual intimacy. They express a longing to give freely, yet find themselves unable to do so, giving instead in bits and pieces. Guardedness, an overwhelming need to protect oneself, seeps from every page of these stories. These women are only too aware of the pain that may come from abandon, from letting go.

Some fear being stigmatized by the many sexual labels that adhere to women and the stereotypes that all too often define women's sexual expression. Audrey says, "I think if guys knew how many men I slept with, they would think less of me. They'd say, 'Oh, you're kind of slutty, huh?' . . . I guess you expect guys to be promiscuous and it's okay for them. It's just not okay for us." Aracely shares similar concerns: "I think women have been kept from expressing themselves freely, and I think that's a problem. . . . I want to be able to claim my own sexual identity. I don't want somebody saying, 'You're oversexed.' Or 'You're not sexed enough.' "

Other women want to avoid making bad sexual choices and prevent betrayal, mistreatment, and abuse. Pam identifies herself as a lesbian and says she "felt right with it [as early as] high school." But she also felt that "it might not be popular with other people, that people might think bad of [her]." She defines herself as "self-protective" and is "always looking for the way somebody's trying to use [her] sexually." Years of incest rape at the hands of several older brothers have contributed to Soupi's less obvious guardedness. She prefers the term "making love" to "sex" but admits that in the past she has "played with a lot of men's minds. I've played with men's minds because men think they can control women. . . . I show them they can be controlled."

Carliese believes she has difficulty expressing how she feels because of a childhood spent with a strict military father who was also an alcoholic: "It affected my ability to express how I feel. Very, very much so." This caution was reinforced by a husband who stole her money and ran off with a coworker. Not surprisingly, for her "being in a relationship with a man is real hard. It's real hard for me to peel myself, expose myself, like a onion." She manages, though, to keep her eye on the possibilities: "I think there's some good guys out there. They're just real hard to find."

# Soupi

*I*M TWENTY-SEVEN years old and I'm a Libra. I am from a little town in Mississippi with a population of about ten thousand people. The black population was less than a thousand. I am getting my master's degree here in Arizona and I also work three different jobs. I teach basketball, I am a work-study student, and I work at the children's fund in town. I would say I work somewhere between seventy to ninety hours a week. I don't get paid a lick, but that's okay—I don't do it for money. I do it to keep busy. I have to be honest: the only reason I've cut down on my hours is because now I have a man in my life. When I didn't have a man in my life, I worked all the time. I'm just the type of person that has to stay busy.

My hometown is a redneck town, and I hope someone just runs up there and knocks on the door and says, "Hey, I heard you all are a bunch of racist pricks," because they are. A handful of whites helped me to succeed because I didn't have the family support that I needed when I was young. And now that I'm older, I'm realizing it, but when I was young, I couldn't identify it. There's eleven of us. My mom had three children, but she married my dad when I was almost two—he's not my real father. My birth father is a totally different story. When my mom married my dad, she was six months pregnant, but not by him. But you know, he fell in love. He fell in love with her and they became friends. And then we got all of his kids that still needed to be raised. We weren't one big, happy family, though, but we're a big, happy family now.

They actually raised nine of us together. The others were already grown—the two oldest girls moved here because they wanted to be close to Daddy. And when we were raised there were three girls and six boys in the house. The two girls were the oldest, and they brought their kids because they had kids my age. So we were raised like a little tribe. We lived in a two-bedroom house with a back porch and one bath, and they put screens up. I'm talking, I'm from a poor family in the country. You got ghettos in the country. They got these screens, and then they put plastic on the outside of the screens to keep the rain from coming through. And then they put bunk beds back there on that porch and made it a room for the six boys. So there was three beds. They had three beds and the three girls shared one king-size bed.

My baby sister and I, we fought, but that's because we're so close in age. My older sister, she's eight years older than me. And we each slept on one side of her, so there was really no fighting. She was mature enough, plus she basically kept the house in order because Mom and Dad both worked. My mom ran my uncle's grocery store, but she was listed on the income taxes as not working. And my dad worked at a brick company for the longest of time. He worked at the brickyard the whole time I was a child. Both of my parents are African Americans. My mom is from my hometown, but her family's originally from Texas. And my dad is from Arkansas.

God has always been an important key. My mom, she used to make the rest of them go to church, but I loved going. She made us go to church until we became teenagers, and then we had a choice. She felt that it was her job to expose us to religion, but in the end it was only our choice whether we were going to believe or not. But we grew up in the church most definitely. Nondenominational. We're Christians. It's all based on truth. Perception's truth. So the way you perceive the Bible is what matters. It was about reading the whole Bible and letting one part tell you how to read another so you understand. And then you know the truth. The Bible is prose and poem. It's God's way. God communicates to us the same way blacks communicate to each other. And if you've noticed, blacks really never get around to saying yes and no straight on. There's a way to tell you yes and there's a way to tell you no, and depending on whether we want it to be a good yes, or a bad yes, or a good no or a bad no, you say it differently. We've really based our communication on what we've read in the Bible because we were raised in the church. So, that's how the Bible communicates to me.

Coming from a big family, I was also an outsider. See, I'm the first one to go all the way through college, without kids, without being married. So I spent a lot of time alone, but I can talk to a person easily, even though I am really shy. But when my shyness starts to show, then there's something intimate there. It's lost when I don't care if I hurt that person's feelings or not. I know I am in an intimate situation if it's uncomfortable and I'm pleased to be where I am, but I'm still uncomfortable. When their feelings are no longer important to me, that person is no longer important to me. But I really try to be considerate to others. I always try in all situations to put other people first. And most of the time you gonna start out on my good side. But when you get to my bad side, you're there.

I trust everyone, and if I get betrayed, it's probably because I set myself up for it. I don't really point fingers at anybody, and I don't really care if I can count on somebody else because what it boils down to is, can I count on me? If you can help me, great; if you can't, I'm going to find a way to get it done. And if I need to talk to somebody, I'ma pray.

In my life, I've been closest to my Uncle Bobby. He's been more like my grandfather than my uncle, though. He was an orphan who ran away from home. My grandmother, with her brothers and sisters, had been working on this railroad in Texas, and she raised him just like she raised the rest of her brothers and sisters and herself from the age of nine. He was such a wonderful man, but nobody ever knew the story. I think I know his story, because I was the only person he talked to. He talked to me all the time, and he used to tell me that I have a wise soul. He'd say, "You don't understand what I'm saying today, but you will one day." He used to just sit on the front porch and talk to me. I've never been that close to anyone else in my life. And when he died, that really felt like betrayal. That was when God and I had to get on the same page. I was like, "Okay, God, hold up. I have accepted that love is not in the picture for me. I accept that I have a family where there's no love there. I have accepted that I'm going to be used by friends, and that there's really no such thing as a friend. I've accepted all these things, but the one true friend, and the one human being I know truly loves me for who I am, you took him. How could you take him?" And then it took some praying—I didn't give up on God, I was just angry. And that's how I dealt with it.

As hard as that was, I'd been through some stuff that was way worse than that, so that was easy compared to what I'd already been through. Out of six brothers, I was sexually abused by four of them. I was sexually abused from the age of about four through twelve. For eight years I was my brothers' toy. As one got on, then I was passed down to the next one. The others were my stepbrothers, but one was my biological brother. My mom had two girls and a boy. I can remember the very first time so vividly. We were in the barn, and he said, "Come on, we'll teach you how to play dick and pussy." Those were his words—"Teach you how to play dick and pussy." I was four. See, this is the kid that never played with anybody, and she was just glad that somebody wanted to play with her. And he said he wanted to play. So we go to the barn in the backyard, we go up to the top loft, and next thing I know he's taking off my clothes, I'm screaming, it's hurting, there's blood everywhere, he takes an old oil rag, wipes the blood off, and then tells me, "Don't tell Mama because if you do, she's going to beat you."

At first, it happened a lot. An awful lot. I'd say probably about once a week, once every two weeks—at least in my mind. I really can't say now after all those years. It just seemed overwhelming. And in my older years, it would happen during the summer months when we didn't have school and they were left in charge of us because Mom and Dad had to go to work. I loved school because when I was at school, I was nowhere near my family. At school, no one there had any care, didn't care anything about this shell that you see. They care about this [*points to her temple*]. To this day I can't stand being called beautiful. I can't stand being called pretty; I don't like compliments. To this day. Because it has nothing to do with who I am. This that you see, this can't tell you one thing about who I am. It cannot tell you one thing.

Daddy wasn't strict. Daddy I realize now he's a strong man, but back then, to me, he was a coward and a weakling. He made the money to make sure we ate. He slaved. I felt pity for my dad. I felt sorry for him. I love him and I think I know now that he's strong. It takes a strong man to put up with that bullshit my momma put him through. As a kid, it seemed like my mom controlled that man. Why tell him what happened to me, 'cause if he tell her, she gonna beat me. Mom, always gonna be Mom, and I didn't want to deal with Mom. And being afraid of my mother, I never said a word. My mom found out when I was twenty-four years old. At first she said was I was lying. Then she told me, "Well, if it was true, you need to confront them about it. And when you do confront them, then I'll believe you. But I still love you." And then my mom also told me how when she was a kid she was sexually abused by her father. When I was a kid she always used to ask me, "Is Nathan touching you?" That's my dad. "Are any of the grown men touching you?" She never asked the right question. I feared no one the way I feared my mother. She was the strongest woman I'd ever seen in my life.

Other people were afraid of her, too. Grown men afraid of her, grown women afraid of her. I don't know if you know what a bulldevil is, but my mom took a bulldevil once and beat a woman with it. A bulldevil is kind of like a cactus; it's got these little poisonous needles throughout it. She pulled it up and beat this woman so bad that this woman was in the hospital because she'd been exposed to so much of the poison from the thing.

The woman started the fight, though. My mother never started fights. But people would get it in their head that they were gonna test her, just to be tough. You know how it is, the gangsta attitude, the ghetto attitude. The only difference between the ghetto in the city and the ghetto in the country—and I tell people this all the time—is that in the ghetto in the country, rather than stealing, we go fishing. In the city, I believe they steal because they need. They need to eat, they're hungry, they're cold. In the country nature provides everything we need. We can go fishing for food; we can go chop down trees for heat. We can grow our own foods. And we wore hand-me-downs. You can turn a blanket into anything.

My mom was an activist in my community. She did everything to make sure black folks got what they deserved. See, all the black folks live on one side of the tracks. So there were black people in my life. At school it was the white kids. She fought. She didn't care what she lost, she didn't care what the family lost, she didn't care—if it was a wrong, she was going to right it. And that's the reason why a lot of people were jealous of her. "If you don't like what I'm doing, take me off; I'm on the hilltop, knock me off." That's what kind of attitude she had: "Move me. You don't like what I'm doing, you make me stop." White, black, she didn't care.

Why didn't I tell my Uncle Bobby about my brothers? I ask myself that a thousand times. I think he knew something was wrong with me, but he felt like if I wanted him to know, I would have told him. And I'm making excuses for him. I mean, this man loved me. And I didn't want him to think of me bad. I felt guilty about what was going on because I wouldn't stop it; I was afraid to stop it, and I kept justifying it. I kept saying, "I have to stop this, I can't stop it because . . ." When I was finally old enough to understand what was going on, I thought that if I stopped it, they're just going to go to my younger sister. I felt like I was stronger by protecting my sister and letting them do to me what they were doing to me because I was protecting my sister.

A lot of the times, as I got older, the only way they could keep me doing it is by saying that they were going to rape my little sister. They'd say, "Well, if you don't do it, I'm a make her do it." So I did it to protect her. The last time that it happened to me, my brother and I had a knock-down-drag-out fight. This was with the next-to-youngest brother. The very last time it happened, I was twelve and he was sixteen. At the end I told him, "If you ever touch me, I'll kill you. I'll take your life. If you touch my baby sister, I'll take your life. Better not ever touch her." No, she never even knew it was going on with me. And if it did happen to her, she hasn't told me. My brothers never bothered my other sisters. Me and my sisters talk about it on occasion now. When I get depressed, then me and my sisters talk about it, but my baby sister still don't believe me. When it happened with the youngest brother I kind of felt like I enjoyed it with him because there was a closeness—it was more of an affectionate thing when I was with him. And it's sick thinking of a kid being in that mind-set, and I've had to deal with that, too. But you know, I was a kid, I had no idea what was going on—just trying to deal with it. As an adult, first I had to deal with the embarrassment, the pain, the hurt, and blaming myself. And I went through all of those stages.

I've never confronted them. Because, see, I was labeled a slut because my mom didn't want me to go to college. I was supposed to do just like everybody else, stay in town and work. But now all of a sudden, I'm a hero to my family, even though in my family I'm in a different class than everyone else, so I'm rich without no money. How can I have money? They think because I'm educated, I have money. So, everybody loves Soupi and everybody does what they can for me. They help me when I need help, but I don't ask them for it. But they're so willing and giving. My brothers on the other hand, they get really quiet when they get around me, and I can see the fear in their eyes. And it's like, "I love you whenever you need. You know, you're my sister." I think it is getting more sincere as they're dealing with their own guilt and their own ghosts. I don't think I need to say anything to them. I mean, they know I know. I really truly believe that they know that I know. They know I remember. My oldest brother was sixteen years old when I was four years old and they did it to me. They were all in puberty when they were doing this. So how can they not know what they were doing when I can clearly remember what was happening at four? Surely they know what they were doing.

Luckily, I didn't start menstruating till I was seventeen. I was blessed. I had God with me, I'm telling you. There's no way anyone could've went through what I went through without having faith. In junior high, I started being exposed to lesbians, lesbian coaches. What happened was, here I am, unsure of myself. All these other girls are talking about sex and how much they love it, and they don't know what's going on in my life. And I'm sitting there going, They can't be having sex. I thought this was sex—what I had actually experienced, that's sex. What they're talking about can't be sex.

There was a girl who used to say, "We did this, and then he touched me," etc. In my mind I'm going, "That couldn't have happened to you. There's no way in the world that could have happened to you. It's just not possible because I've already experienced that." I let them tell their stories, and when it came time to tell a story, I would say, "I don't know. I'm a virgin." I stuck to that story a long time. In my heart, I was a virgin until my first love. But that's down the line.

Everybody, including my mom, thought I was weird. She used to tell me, "Don't grow up to be gay. Oh, you're going to be gay." Then everybody said, "She's going to be gay because she's a tomboy." I played with the same boys that raped me all the time—football, basketball—because I loved sports. And I didn't have to talk to them to play sports with them—there was no talking, there's no talking in sports. There's exercise, action. You know, I just wanted to play. So being so athletic, everybody said, "She's gonna be gay, she's gonna be gay." Little stocky, cocky little girl. I was short forever, but I have, as you can see, a lot of muscular tone in my body.

In middle school, the kids were teasing me about being gay, and one of my coaches took me back in her office and she said, "If you choose to be gay it's okay, it's no one's business but your own." She just had this way of looking at me and touching me that made me wish she didn't touch me. She'd always pat everybody else on the shoulder and pat me on the butt, and I hated that! And when I asked her about it, then she started patting everybody on the butt; and then I spoke to her and said, "Don't touch me. Whatever you do, don't ever touch me again."

There was a black girl and a black guy that were coming out at the same time during my junior-high year. Everybody knew the guy was gonna be gay and everybody knew this girl was going to be gay. But everybody thought I was like this girl because of my physical features and my athleticism. But on the other hand, I had school, and I always had church. So school and church kept me from letting everybody convince me what I was. I think the other two kids in my school became gay because everybody told them they were. They didn't have to be. It's a choice. I think there's an attraction for all human beings to some point. I've felt attraction to women, but not sexual attraction. There was, "Okay, yes, she's beautiful," but there was not that feeling like I wanted to do her. I never wanted to do a woman, I just wanted to be this woman. She's a good woman, she's a beautiful woman, somebody needs to protect her. And I've always been very protective of anybody that I felt could be abused.

The one guy that was coming out, he and I were really good friends— really good friends—and I wouldn't let anybody mess with him, either. When anybody else would talk about him, rather than confronting them I would just grab his hand and say, "Let's go play." See, I learned at an early age, earlier than a lot of other people, fighting isn't best. My Uncle Bobby probably told me. "Just walk away and go play. We can still have fun. Let them be angry. They're the ones mad, they're the ones wanna hit you. You don't have to act like that."

I was exposed to lesbians all the way through college. I have to admit that during my college years, I actually was starting to believe that maybe I was gay. My team had a lot of lesbians. Then there was this lesbian coach, well, I didn't know if she was gay or not, but she prided herself in being a virgin yet, and still you never saw her talking to guys. She was always looking in girls' faces. And to me that was kind of suspicious. About three or four of my teammates were gay. But the lesbians always talked to me. I guess it's because I've never really cared about what your sexual preference is; I will talk to you if you want to talk to me. There was this one girl—she and I became really, really good friends. We were like best friends for a while. She would always tell me about her boyfriends, and I'd be like, "Oh, that's cool. She'd say, "Well, how can I solve this problem with Tim?" And I'd suggest she do this or that. Then, three months later she tells me, Tim, Tom—whatever his name was—is actually Margaret. Okay. And I said, "You're telling me this now because . . ." And she said, "Well, because I'm very attracted to you. And I think you're attracted to me." And I couldn't argue that point. I was attracted to her, I did enjoy being with her. I did enjoy talking to her, I did enjoy hanging out with her; that was true. But did that mean I was gay? I wasn't, you know. And she was saying, "I have this desire to be with you." But I said, "Well, you know, I don't think that's what I want to do."

And then after thinking about it for about three days—and this is the first time I've ever admitted this to anyone—I called her up and I said, "You know, I think I want to be with you, too." After she told me she was attracted to me, we weren't talking on the phone anymore. She wouldn't hang out with me, and I just wanted that companionship back. And if that meant sleeping with her to have my friend, then I would have slept with her. So, when I called her, she told me I wasn't gay. She said, "Soupi, don't even worry about it. You're not even gay. You're not gay." I asked her how she knew. She said, "Because I know. You're not gay, and I was trying to convince you that you were." She was really honest with me. She told me, "I was playing on that weakness and on our friendship, and you don't deserve it. You've been a really good friend to me, and I shouldn't do this to you." I tried to stay friends with her, but we stopped talking. It was her choice—she walked away. I don't know why she walked away. I mean, she was a good friend. I was a good friend to her because I put a lot into my friendships.

I have to say all of my experiences of dealing with whether I was gay or not were always with white women, and they were always blonde, and they were always blue-eyed, and that really scared me. I was really thinking, Maybe I am gay, because maybe I have this attraction for blond, blue-eyed women. And they all had short hair. I was like, Oh, God, something's wrong with me. I prayed about it—God, I don't want to be gay. But see, one day I just realized that if I don't wanna be gay, then I'm not gay.

I had no boyfriends in high school, none. And the reason, I found out, is because my brothers had threatened to kick all their asses. I only found that out after I came back a couple years after being in college. This one guy who I knew from high school seemed suddenly interested in me. I asked him, "You didn't even want to talk to me. Now all of a sudden, I'm just the bomb, right?" And he said, "Yo, it wasn't even like that. When you were in high school, your brothers threatened to kick our asses if we messed with you." And then there's this part of me that's saying, No the fuck they didn't. That's going on in my mind every time I see my brothers.

I say, I'm good enough for you to fuck, but not for them? Everybody else gets to have sex, everybody else has boyfriends. I can't get a boyfriend; therefore all my teammates think I'm gay. All my teammates are hiding behind their lockers when they're getting undressed in the locker room, and I'm putting my head down thinking, I'm not gay. I don't know why they think I'm looking at them. And it's not fair; it's not fair for everybody to want to make me gay. I'm not gay. I don't give a damn what they look like. They don't mean anything to me, you know?

I was always by myself in high school. At lunchtime, I had lunch in the gym; then I shot ball. At home, when I got home, it was time to study. Once I finished studying, I went to the park and shot basketball. I wanted basketball to take me away from the hell that I lived in. I hated Woodlawn, I hated everything about Woodlawn, and I hated the people in Woodlawn. Family never meant anything to me until I got older. I didn't care about family, I didn't care about Woodlawn, I just hated Woodlawn. I didn't care that people wanted me to be gay, that guys didn't want to sleep with me. How does it feel to see the ugliest girl in the school get a boyfriend. She got a date for the prom. My brother paid a guy to take me to my junior prom. And my senior prom, I went with these other four girls. Here I am, one of the top students in our school nobody ever associated themselves with us. Nobody cared.

This is a white town. The one black teacher I had—I had him for health—he used to always rub my hand, and it made me feel so uncomfortable, and everybody was like, "Why does it make you feel uncomfortable?" I couldn't tell them that it was because of my brothers. I was like, "Look, I don't want him to touch me. Go tell him, keep his hands off me." And I told the principal, "Just tell him to keep his hands off of me." But he lost his job, and then I felt guilty. But then I found out later that I wasn't the only girl who complained about him touching her.

When I got out of high school, I worked to save money and went to a local college. And I walked onto the basketball team. I was the third woman in the history of the school to walk on because they've always been ranked in nationals. And the fact that I even thought that I could walk on that team a lot of people thought was ridiculous. But I knew what I could do. I told the coach, "Man, I can play basketball and you don't have one girl that can guard me one-on-one." And he didn't; one-on-one I couldn't be beat. When it came to playing team, I sat on the bench because I didn't like this team stuff; it wasn't working for me. I want the rock; I want to be able to shoot the rock when I want to shoot the rock. I want to be able to dribble the rock because I was the point guard during junior high because I was short. Then all of a sudden, I had this growth spurt and shot up to six-one, but I still had this point-guard mentality. I was the best player on my high school team, so I ran point even though I was the tallest. But he wanted to make a post player out of me, and I didn't want to be a post player; I wanted to be a guard. I didn't like my back turned to anybody; I like to face things. I'm one of those people who faces issues. I don't like to run from anything.

I lived in the dorms because my mom kicked me out. When I told her I wanted to go to college, she said, "You're not going to college. You'll take your black ass and get a forty-hour job and pay some of these damn bills. Quit trippin'." "No," I said, "I'm going to college. Either I'm joining the military or I'm going to—" "Ain't no daughter of mine joining the military, you'll be gay—must be gay if you're going." Either Uncle Sam would accept me, or college would accept me. And the one that came in first, that's the one I'd be doing. I got real strong after the abuse stopped. That's why I didn't care about being alone. Yeah, it hurt my feelings; but it didn't matter because all of a sudden, I realized my destiny was in my hands, and nobody else had any control over it. I was never going to disrespect my mother the way my brothers and sisters did. She had all the problems, the schooling problems, the fighting back, all of that. The last time my mother whupped me was when I was seventeen years old. I mean, I laid over, and let her beat me with a switch. But when I turned eighteen, she was going to whup me again, and I was like, "Oh no, I'm eighteen years old, and according to the law, I don't have to do anything you tell me to." She said, "You can get out of my house." I said, "I can do that." I left, and she asked me back. Between the time I graduated from high school and started college she kicked me out about five times. Three of them at gunpoint.

She couldn't do to me what she did to everybody else. When she said,

"I'll take your life," I said, "Then do it. Stop talking and do it. It may have worked with everybody else, but it isn't working with me anymore. Do it." Growing up, she whupped my ass about everything. I got whuppings for other brothers and sisters. When we were young, if one person messed up, all nine of us got a whupping. And then somebody moved out—there was eight of us, then it was six of us, then it was five of us getting a whupping. You got a B in school, you got a whupping. "You're an A student. I don't expect anything but A's from you." I got a whupping for everything. Everything. I was afraid to open my mouth.

After she stopped trippin' and realized I was going to stay in college, she said, Okay, this girl's going to do what she wants to do, let me go wash her clothes. Okay, I'll make you some dinner. Eat a good meal. There was a little mothering. I actually started seeing my mother as a mom when I got into college. When I was in high school and elementary school, it was all about, take care of yourself. If you can't do it for yourself, ain't nobody else going to do it for you. Take care of yourself. That's what it was about.

My mother put me on birth control in high school. Never asked me was I having sex, she just decided I was old enough to be on the pill. She took me to the family doctor and he gave them to me. And she made me take those pills. Believe me, I got whuppings on days when I forgot to take that pill. One time I got hit in the face, then still got a whupping, and got grounded just because I forgot to take my birth control pills. This is for somebody who's not even menstruating, and isn't gonna have sex, and I have to take this damn pill every day. I don't know if my mother knew that you have to be menstruating to be pregnant. I hated taking that pill. My mom thought I was the most secretive person in the world. I was secretive, but I wasn't having sex. My mother wouldn't talk to me, well, because I didn't talk to her. But all she had to do was ask. If she asked, I'd tell her. She never showed me that she cared.

I've been sick all my life; I was born sick. They didn't sign my birth certificate until October 16, and I was born on the twenty-ninth of September. But they wouldn't sign my birth certificate till then because they thought I was going to die. I was born sick, and I stayed sick the first two years of my life. I didn't start talking until I was three; I didn't have any hair on my head until I was two and a half years old. And then I was sick, and rebellious. And the doctor told my mom that I was going to be deaf and dumb—these were doctors—because when they'd talk to me, I wouldn't respond.

I didn't like people. I just didn't like 'em. And I still think to this day that I don't like people. 'Cause I'm dumb. I admit that I'm dumb. But the fact that I know that I'm dumb means I can do something about it. But other people won't admit that they're dumb. You know, I had pneumonia twice, by the time I was two. And the doctors didn't know. They were just basing it on the fact that I was sick. My mom was on medication the entire time she was carrying me. My mom told me that she did everything she could to try to make herself have a miscarriage while she was carrying me. So she was taking outside drugs and doing everything to get rid of me. She didn't want to have me; she couldn't stand my father. And she didn't want to have his child, but she didn't have the money for an abortion. I think she could have got the money for an abortion. I just think a part of her was fighting inside.

My older brother is eight years older than me. She had an abortion sometime after him. And then she had me, eight years later. And then another one, a year and ten months later. So I asked her once, "Why such a gap between me and my brother?" And she admitted she had an abortion between me and my older brother. And I said, "Well, if you had an abortion once, why didn't you just have it twice if you didn't want me? Get rid of me." And she used to tell me as a kid all the time, "I wish I had had an abortion." I said, "I wish you had too; then neither one of us would be going through what we're going through, would we?" Every time she tried to hurt my feelings, I'd hurt her feelings back. My mom bent over asshole backward for all of my brothers. She'd take food off the table to send money to my brother, the one that got the full academic scholarship to Rice University.

That's the ironic thing about it. The one brother I looked up to most because he was brilliant was the one that I fought off of me when I was twelve. But he was my hero, and he was the best athlete at my high school and one of the smartest, one of the top ten in class. And all I ever wanted to do was be half as good as he was in school, half as smart as he was. I was always competing with what he had already done. And when I got whatever he made, I wanted to do better that year. I just wanted to be better than him. At the same time, he had brain surgery his senior year and still finished in the top ten of his class. He had a tumor on his brain. They said that it had happened in the eighth grade. He played football and he took a really bad hit, which made him stop playing football. He never played football again, but they said that it traveled and it took that long to get to his brain. Brilliant, I mean this man is brilliant. My mom would just take money away from us to send to him, and he's down there doing coke lines and drinking. He flunked out eventually.

When I got my first period, I bled for a day. I knew it was coming; I had already read up about it. And I was hurting really bad. I had been at home sick, throwing up and vomiting for two days, and my mom thought I had the flu. And then all of a sudden we found out I was bleeding, and she started saying, "Oh, she's a woman now, she's a woman." And I was like, "Whatever, Mom. You don't have to tell everybody. It's not something to announce." I'd been to the doctor trying to find out why it hadn't come yet because my baby sister started when she was thirteen, and here I am not starting till seventeen. She's got boyfriends, and this and that, she's already out doing the wild thing, and I'm just like school and books, basketball and books, that's it. So I knew it would eventually come, and when I got it, it was no big deal. My mom had the doctor talk to me about it. The doctor was the one who educated me on the pill. So when I finally got my period, she took me to the doctor to find out why I only bled for a day, and he said that I was just going to have an irregular cycle.

My mom never told me anything about sex. I think she would have rather I had never been exposed to sex because of the way she felt about it. I really think my mom thinks that sex is a tool that men use to control women. The way I see it, it's the other way around—it's something we use to control them. When I stopped the abuse, all of a sudden I was stronger, and they couldn't do anything to me. When I wanted to have a man in my life, all I had to do was sleep with him. When I didn't want him in my life, I stopped having sex with him and next thing you know, two weeks later he's gone. I'm tired of him, so I won't sleep with him anymore. So, that's how I would control them. And I knew that if I was having sex with him, he would stay in my life because, I have to admit, I'm good in bed. I know I can rock any man's world. I've never had a complaint. I know how to do what he don't know how to do. Especially because my first love was eleven years older than me, so he taught me a lot of things. So, when I finally started dating guys my age, I already knew what they didn't know. And after what I would do to them, they would be like, "Whoo!" and "Whoa!"

My first love was my baseball coach at the Y. I fell in love with him. I thought, This is the guy that I would really choose to be with, because he cared. He'd always ask me how I was doing. When I was sad—I could be laughing and smiling in a crowd, but my eyes would show that I wasn't there—he could look at my eyes and tell. He'd take me aside and ask me what was all this fake show back there, what's going on, are there problems at home, problems at school, are you having problems with basketball, etc. He cared about the little things in my life. I had this attraction to him and I just really wanted to be with him physically.

He didn't want to be with me. It took me a year and a half to finally get him to sleep with me, when I was about to turn eighteen. I had told him I wanted him to sleep with me on my eighteenth birthday. And he was like, "I'm not going to do it with you at all." And finally, it just happened three months before my birthday. We hung out all the time at his house. He lived with his mom, but his mom was gone because it was Thanksgiving weekend. We were hanging out and listening to music, and I used to always give him back massages. And then he was giving me my back massage, and all of a sudden it just happened. You know, nature took its course. Oh, it was great. And to this day I still use the same analogy. It was like having chocolate cake, chocolate ice cream, and chocolate pudding all wrapped up in one event. It was great because with all the other girls the first time it hurt, it hurt so bad. But it didn't hurt for me. For one thing, he knew what he was doing. And number two, there had been five years since I'd had sex, but I knew all I had to do was relax. The fact that I was concentrating on relaxing and that he knew what he was doing combined to-gether made it a great experience. It was beautiful; it was wonderful.

We spoke recently and he told me we had sex a lot. I thought we had only slept together three times. So I guess I only slept with him three times when it really mattered to me. Even though he told me we used to have it all the time, I only remember three times. I guess I was there, but it proba-bly felt too much like what it used to feel like before. It didn't hurt. It got to a point with my brothers where it didn't hurt. So, I knew how to be somewhere I wasn't. Or think about something else, or create a mental block, or I would just totally shut down while it was going on.

We just hung out as friends. Only a few people knew. The reason that we didn't stay together was that he ended up marrying the girl he cheated on me with. But he was only sleeping with her because he slept with every-body. He had two kids by her. He says, "You know, I was in love with you then and I didn't want to admit it. And when I realized how bad I hurt you when you found out about her, I realized I never wanted to hurt another female like that again, so I decided I wasn't going to break up with any more females. They were going to have to break up with me." He wouldn't break up with her. She got pregnant, so he married her because he felt like it was the right thing to do. And now they're just roommates with kids. When I saw him recently, he was so excited to see me. I saw him over Christmas break for the first time, and as a matter of fact, it was ten years to that date, I had told him at that exact same location, "I'm in love with you." And he said, "You don't know what love is." I said, "Man, trust me. I know what love is, I'm in love with you." He said, "No." I said, "Man, I'll come back ten years from now, and I'll tell you, at the age of sixteen, I was in love with you." And never even thought about it again. And then ten years later I told him, "I was in love with you when I was sixteen."

After I left my mother's house, I did not get back on the pill. I hated taking the pill, and I had this rebellious attitude. In college I felt I had to sleep with guys because I did not want to be thought of as gay. I had four abortions in two years. I only kept one boyfriend at a time, but of course I got the same "Oh, it ain't mine" story. Okay, whatever. I got the money; I hustled up the money for the abortions. I tried the condoms; twice I got pregnant without a condom; twice I got pregnant with a condom. Well, the first two times it was with a condom. So the last two times, I was like, Fuck a condom, man. The condom ain't doin' nothing for me. I gotta thank God for that because I've never had a disease. I've never had a sexually transmitted disease.

Getting pregnant was stupid. I didn't want to be pregnant in the first place. Getting rid of the pregnancy was really simple. My mom had told me so much that she regretted having me that I realized that there was no way in the world that I was going to bring a child into this world that I would regret having. The older I get, the more I think I act like my mom. And I hate that. But there's this respect and love I have for her now that's so overwhelming that I'm glad I'm like my mother. But I didn't think that then. I didn't want to do to a child what my mom had did to me. I didn't want to tell a child, You weren't wanted. I didn't want to tell a child, Every time I look at you I see your sneaky-ass daddy.

I didn't want to wind up doing what my mom did. My mom left my biological father because he got her and another woman pregnant at almost the exact same time. I have a biological brother that's a month older than me. My biological brother's mother told him. My mom didn't tell me. My mom believed in this idea of love—and don't get me wrong, I believe in love—if I don't believe in anything else, I believe in love. She didn't want my father to choose to be with her just because she was pregnant. She knew he had another woman. She wanted him to be with her because she was in love with him and he was in love with her. And that wasn't the case. He told me that he felt he should do the right thing and be with the woman that was pregnant. And I said, "Well my mom was pregnant." He said she didn't tell him. He didn't love her. And there's nothing you can tell me that will make me believe that he loved my mom because in reality, even if the other woman was pregnant, he would have went with my mom.

My dad was about an hour and a half away. But I only saw him when I was seven, sixteen, and again when I was twenty-one. I invited him to my high school graduation. He did not come, he did not respond. When I was sixteen I cussed him out and told him I didn't need him in my life. When I was seven, he bought me this beautiful pink dress that I later found out my Uncle Bobby had actually made. And he bought me this bike that I found out my mom had actually bought. And they just let him say that he gave it to me. And when I found that out, I told him he was a sorry-ass man. "How you gonna tell a seven-year-old child that you gave her all this stuff? Did you really think the truth wouldn't eventually be told to me? You're a sorry man—I don't need you in my life." I don't know why God did this to me, but I remember the conversations so vividly. Every time August twenty-second rolled around, he would call and say, "I'm thinking about you." I said, "For what?" "Because that's your birthday." I said, "No it ain't." He said, "Yes, it is." "My birthday is the twenty-ninth of September, man, get real." I said, "Look, that's your other child's birthday, not mine. We're not twins; we weren't born on the same day. I was born a month later, asshole." Since I've been in college, he tries to stay in touch with me. And there's a part of me that's saying to be nice, be nice, he wants to try. Just to say "Hey" every now and then. So call him and say, "Hey, how you doin'?" I've never gotten a birthday card from him; I've never gotten a birthday present from him. Don't want one.

I have this fear, every time I'm sexually involved with a guy, that after I have sex, I feel like I must be pregnant. So, then it don't matter to me: He can come in me as much as he wants because hell, I think I'm pregnant already. And even with the abortions, I think I just got taken, three out of those four times, for a lot of money. Every time they did the thing, they could never find anything. And I'm like, you know what, these people took my money, just went in there, flushed me out clean.

After each one they told me not to do anything till two weeks later, but each day, each of the first three times, I went back and I played basketball, because that was my release valve. I just wanted to play basketball. I never passed out; I didn't bleed. There's this mental part of me that was just like, Fuck it. I wanted to die. I didn't care anyway. I've had this strong urge, this love of death, been wanting to die for a long time. Not now. But there was this part of me that was just like, Fuck it. I'm halfway there. Just travel the rest of the way, and die. When am I gonna do something that's gonna look like I accidentally died? Because I didn't want to commit suicide. With

God, I want to go to heaven. How am I going to trick God into killing me? And that was basically what I was doing, trying to trick God into killing me in any way possible.

The being pregnant part was just stupid. I mean, the first time was accident. Second time was stupid. Third time it was very stupid. The fourth time I'm just a fool. They were all a long time ago. As a matter of fact, after the last one, the doctor was really honest. He was like, "Look, I can't keep doing this." The first times the doctors had the same look, but they didn't verbally say anything. You'd just see the look in their eyes. But the last time the doctor was like, "I don't see anything." He wanted to do a pregnancy test and I said no, that I just wanted to do it, get it done with. I said, "Can't we just go through and perform this?" He said he doesn't see anything, only this clot of blood, but there was no fetus. And the last time I was supposedly eleven weeks. I said I had the money and I would give it to him; just do it. I have the money here. Just do it. I just did not want to be a mother.

All the fathers, each one of them, wanted the child. I asked, "Well, do you love me?" They wanted to know, "What does that have to do with it?" "Look, man, I'm not trying to bring no child into this world if it's not going to be loved, or that is not going to see two parents that love each other." My parents fought a lot when I was a kid, and I don't want a kid to see that. I mean fistfights. I saw my mom hit my daddy in the face with a wine bottle and knock all his front teeth out. My mom was a very violent woman, very violent, very violent with me. She'll take her problems to her grave with her. But my point is to not get the problems that she has, and I guess that's one of the reasons I face all of my problems, because I know my mother won't face her problems. She'll create a problem over here, a big one, to avoid another one. She's just got problems everywhere, and she's so sad and so melancholy.

I've been in love three times. I have been, and I currently am in my third one, and I think this is the right one. The first love was of course the baseball coach. The second love turned out to be gay. Boy was that a strike, a blow to the ego. After the fourth abortion, I decided, I'm not having sex anymore. I'm not sleeping with guys anymore. If I cannot be involved with a guy without having sex, then fine, we won't be involved. That's when I stopped dating black men and started dating white men and Hispanic men, because they can be in a relationship without being sexually involved. I had this perception that all black men only wanted to be involved in relationships where sex was involved. Every time I tried to have this kind of camaraderie with a black man, if there was no sex, there was no companionship. With the Hispanic guys and the one white guy, it was more like a real relationship to me because they cared about me beyond sex.

One of the Hispanic guys I was in love with, Juan, told me he thought he was bisexual, after we got close. He said he was never with a man, but that he had urges. We were best friends, so we could tell each other anything. Just last August, when I was having surgery on my knee, it all came out. Everybody swore that I was going to marry him since that is the only reason my mom could imagine me staying in school to get my master's degree. It would really have to be because of a man. Women in my family think a man has to be involved for you to stay put. But that's not why I stayed. I had been talking about him for the last two and a half years. Of course I'm talking about him—I'm in love with this guy. And he knew how I felt about him, but he was constantly telling me he was not in love with me, and that he doesn't love me like that. He was so honest the entire time, and I just would not believe him until finally he calls me on the phone while I'm at the hospital and asks how I am feeling. I wanted to know, "Why aren't you here?" Then I find out that he's been seeing this guy for the last month before I even went in for surgery. And he thinks he's in love. And then he's admitting that he's not bi but gay. It was the perfect relationship for me because there was no sex involved. That's what I've always wanted, a man who'd be there for me and I didn't have to sleep with him.

I've recently started dating this guy I've known here for the past five years, but I'd never looked at him as a boyfriend before. He took me to Tucson, then we went to the Grand Canyon. We go out to eat, we hang out at bookstores, we laugh. It's a good relationship. But I'm smart enough to know it's not that he's just my friend. He admitted that he is attracted to me, but he can't tell whether the attraction is because he's horny or because he feels for me. He said he doesn't want to be with me unless he knows he feels for me. And I respect him for saying that to me. But I came right out and told him, "I ain't had sex in four years. I'ma be honest with you, I just wanna fuck the hell out of you. You know, we can still be friends and be sexually involved." And he said, "No, I don't wanna be like that. I don't want it to be just sex." I asked him if he was a virgin. He said, "No, but I like sex to mean something to me." This is weird to my ears, coming from a guy.

At the Christmas holidays, we go our separate ways, and we agree to call each other when I come back from the break. But when I get back, I go to work and there's this other man who is at my job, shooting basketball, the most bodacious hunk—arms, oh, my God, I loved his arms. And we shot ball together. Then we hung out together and he went and heard me sing the national anthem at the basketball game. He didn't believe I could sing until he came to the game to hear me. I also told him I could shoot basketball, that I was a better shooter than him. He didn't believe that either, until I outshot him. Proved that to him. So he's found that if I tell him I can do something, I really mean it. I will admit what I can do and what I can't do. I'm not one of those people that's gonna bullshit you.

He's twenty-two years old, and we've been dating for almost two months now. I got him whupped already. That's why he keeps talking about family. One day he'll say, "Let's do it, let's just go get married" and the next day he's like, "No, first we got to make sure we got a relationship with God." And I'm the one going, "As much as I love you and as much as I know I can grow to be in love with you (because there's a difference), I'm going to wait because I think this is the right thing. We've prayed about it. And I've got to give God the glory because God brought this man in my life when I didn't want to be involved with men. I said, No, I'm through with men. I've got one semester left, I'm going to concentrate on my thesis, I don't need a man in my life. God didn't have that in His plan.

For the first time in a long time I am really enjoying the sex. Not just because I haven't been involved with a guy in four years—that's not it. It's because it feels like it did when I slept with my first love. That's why I know that I can grow to be in love with him—because I can feel the difference. I mean, it's not like I'm making love to him, although I have. Three times I've made love to him, and other times it's been sex. But it was still good sex. The difference between having sex and making love is the point to where I just want to cry while I'm in the mood, while I'm doing it. I feel like crying because it feels so good, and I'm so glad that this man is holding me and this man is inside of me, and that I'm going to be in him. This is the way that if I could freeze time, I'd wanna be frozen.

I've had orgasms through intercourse, well, maybe once—no, twice. No, well, the real one, it has to be the once—there was a half one where I came right after he did. I mean, because it was so good. But the other time it was during. And it was unbelievable. That was probably the first time I've come during sex. Usually I come after the man. I mean like after he comes, after he's had his orgasm and he's put his sperm all over my chest or in whatever, while he's soft, I'll make him rub himself on me until I come. I've never come while a man is hard; I can't come until he's come in me. But I did the last time. I think we actually came at the same time.

I didn't get into oral sex until I hit the age of twenty-five. That's where Juan the gay guy and I were involved—we were involved with oral sex. We had this mutual agreement: we were just friends, we were best friends, but we both realized our bodies have a need, so we would just help each other come. And we did. But I don't think that had anything to do with how we felt about each other. I don't masturbate. I've never used my hands to help me do anything, and I've never put anything fake on me. There's too many men to do that. You can get a man to help you do that.

I have to admit, I've played with a lot of men's minds. I've played with men's minds because men think they can control women. But they like that, and I like to show them that they can be controlled—ooh, especially a man that don't think he can be controlled. That's the perfect man. Then when I come out victorious, I've proved to him I'm the one controlling this relationship. But then I hate that side of me because that's exactly how my mom does my dad. That is so my mother: "I'm the one in control, and I'm letting you know I'm the one in control." But now my mom's acting like a kid. She had a hysterectomy when she was forty-three, and ever since then she's been a totally different woman. She's been completely weak mentally. She has no confidence in herself. She's not a fighter anymore. She loves this Nintendo game and that's all she does.

When I first found out that I was a writer—see, I write, I draw, I sing, I do everything. My very first short story that I wrote was my sexual fantasy. It's called "Passion Cove." It was about me and this Italian guy, his name was Carlo and we went up to this stone and log cabin. And there's this nice fairy-white room. We're having a glass of wine, and we're sitting in front of the fireplace, and there's this big glass window, and we're drinking and having our little lovely time. Then we go for a walk, and there are beautiful rolling hills, with grass so tall it comes up to midthigh. And we're walking and we walk so far off that we look back and we can't see the cabin. When we get under a tree we stop, and we're just going to rest, you know, and he rubs my feet and he licks my toes. And then he plays with my ankles. Then he works his way up. After he rubs it with his hands, he rubs it with his tongue. And he works his way up from my toe all the way up. He don't miss a spot on my body. All the way to the top. Then we finally start having intercourse. We're in this grass that's so high, if somebody walked by us, they wouldn't see us. They could probably hear us or smell us, but they wouldn't see us. And then the clouds start rolling in, and we don't notice. We don't notice. Next thing you know, there's this downpour of rain, and we don't stop. We keep right on at it. And then right when he's on the down stroke, he gets struck in the butt with lightning, and I have the best orgasm I've ever had in my life.

He doesn't die, he's just shocked—the sex protects both of us because it's this aura. And I have this ultimate orgasm, and then we walk back to the cabin and then we do it again on the white rug. But there was just nothing as good as right there, having sex in grass this high. And when he hits that down, and he goes down and up, right when he hits that up and he pulls against that part that actually makes it feel so good. The electricity—ooh! I wrote that story when I was sixteen, and I still have that story. I still think today that's my wildest fantasy—making love in the rain in the tall grass.

Now, in the relationship I am in, we're having sex and I can realize that sex is important to him, but it's not important in the relationship. It's just the physical thing, which is good because both of us agreed it's just physical, it's just something our body wants to do. It has nothing to do with how we feel about each other. And we've talked about it like that. Just because I'm having sex with you does not mean I love you. Just because I'm not having sex with you does not mean I don't love you. It has nothing to do with how I emotionally feel about you. And I guess that's good for me; that's the one good thing that came out of being molested—I realize that sex has nothing to do with how I feel about a man.

A lot of women will tell you there's a difference between sex and making love, and some of my friends have told me that either way, it's all the same act. But that's bullshit. There has to be something special going on mentally, romantically, between both of you. There has to be this kind of kindred spirit going on—this aura—between both of you, which is what makes it "making love." That aura's going to stay present the whole time. Just saying "Let's have sex" is not making love.

# Audrey

*I*'M THIRTY; I'm single; I don't have any children. All my mother's side of the family is Dominican, and my dad's side of the family's black. I'm originally from the Caribbean; that's where I grew up, and I left there to go to college. I've been in the States ever since. I was raised by my grandmother. My parents had me when they were very young. They never married, so my grandmother was my primary caretaker. Don't have a very close relationship with either of my parents. Okay friends with my mother; we talk, but not that mother-daughter relationship. Have very, very little contact with my father. So my grandmother is definitely my primary emotional support in my life. My parents were around; they tried. But, like I said, they were pretty young, so I don't think they were really ready or knew how to raise children at that point in their lives. When they had me, my dad was eighteen and my mom was nineteen. When they were in the first semester of college, they were around, and I had to go visit my dad on the weekends. But after a while, it just seemed like their relationship disintegrated. I haven't seen him in about fifteen years. I still see my mom quite a bit. When I need any type of advice or anything, I usually go to my grandmother. I'm still very close to her. Now that I'm older it's kind of hard because she still tends to treat me like I'm twelve, and sometimes I don't get what I want from her. I don't hear what I want to hear, because I guess I go into conversations wanting to hear something, and if I don't hear it, then I hold it against her—that type of behavior. But if I'm okay with her, then everything is okay.

Well, interestingly enough, I went to Catholic school, but it wasn't important for me to go to church on Sundays. Religion wasn't very important in my family. It is to me now, I guess. I feel very grounded, and I have a very close personal relationship with God, a personal relationship. I go to church, but I think I know what I believe in, and I feel God in my life every day.

I guess to feel I can be intimate with someone when I can trust them completely. When I feel that they have my best interest at heart and I have theirs, then I feel that intimacy will follow. It is very hard to trust people when you don't know if people have your best interest at heart, but I think that's the basis for trust. It is hard to trust. I've trusted people before and then realized that they weren't deserving of my trust. You think, Okay, I'll never give too soon too much, and then you're like, I did it again, and this person proved to me that people can't really be trusted. I try to go by what they say and do. I think I have a very good instinct about people. I may not necessarily listen to it all the time, but I think I know when people are not being honest and when people are not trustworthy. Sometimes I ignore my gut. I guess I don't trust myself to make the right decisions in life. I'm like, Maybe you're just jaded, maybe you just don't trust people. You always want to think, Well, maybe this is the one time that I'm wrong.

I learned about sex from my friends, and from school, and from reading. My grandmother and mother didn't really teach me anything about it, and I think, Was that really the way to handle it? I couldn't necessarily have learned it the right way, and I was looking for things where I shouldn't have been looking for things. Looking for acceptance and other positive feelings from situations I shouldn't have been in when I was younger. I just felt that whatever my friends were doing, it was cool, so I wanted to do it too. So I definitely didn't start out with a good background on how relationships were supposed to be, and how you treat people, and how you should be treated.

I thought that if I asked my grandmother she would get mad at me. If she wasn't talking about it, then maybe it was taboo. It wasn't that way only with sex. She was just telling me the other day that she's so amazed that I can cook and do these things because she never really taught me. She said, "You've turned out so well and so independent, and I really never taught you these things." She's never said why but in my mind, she wanted to baby me and do everything for me, and she thought that was the right way.

I started thinking about it in junior high, around thirteen, when I turned a teenager. I started liking boys, and I started wondering and just asking. And all my girlfriends liked boys at that time. We were just curious, real curious, so we would read or ask older sisters. The teachers were mostly nuns—they weren't talking about sexuality. Actually, it was a sin to have sex before marriage. That's what we heard. And that would make us more curious, and we would sneak around and try to figure it out and get magazines like *Cosmo* and older magazines.

When it came to getting my period, I can't believe I can remember this—but that weekend I was visiting my dad, because I had to go every other weekend, and I kind of thought I was getting it, but I wasn't really sure. I just told my dad I had to go home. I think we had such a strained relationship anyway, so they were like, She just doesn't want to be here; just take her home. But I couldn't tell them. It was so embarrassing and I didn't know what was happening. So I just went home. I told my grandmother when I got home. I said, "Well, I bathed, and this is what's happening." And she said, "Yeah, don't worry, it's perfectly normal. I'll just go buy you some sanitary napkins. It's no big deal."

My dad was living with his mother on an island in the Caribbean really close to the island my mother lives on. It's a short plane ride away, not even twenty minutes. And my grandmother, his mother, she was really nice and she accepted me, but I never felt that he really did. Even when I was there, he would put my care into his mother's hands. And I just don't remember him doing anything to make me feel good, or saying anything. I don't remember it. I don't know if I've blocked it out; I just don't remember it at all. I've talked about this a lot to a friend, and I thought that it might be an issue for me that I never really had a father figure, but we've decided that you can't miss what you never had. It wasn't really ever a relationship there. I don't think he had an impact on my life.

I was very promiscuous when I was younger. I thought that if a guy had sex with you, he liked you. And I was sexually active pretty young, like fourteen. And definitely was not ready, did not know anything about it, just thought that sex is the way people show that they love you and care about you. So if a guy slept with me, then he cared about me. That's not the case at all. By now I have figured it out.

Where I grew up is such a small space that wherever you go, everybody's there. You go to happening places and everybody's there. My first sexual experience was with a twenty-year-old, and I was fourteen. And now that I look back, I'm thinking, I was a kid, I knew nothing. We started seeing each other on the sly. I met him when I was thirteen, he was nineteen, and my grandmother never would have gone for that. So I would sneak out and see him at the bowling alley or whatever. And then when I was fourteen, he brought up the subject of sex. He would say, "It's time, you know, it's time for you to go ahead and do this." And I was like, "Well, I don't know anything about it." And he said, "That's okay. I'll teach you. I'll take care of it." I feel like he took advantage of me because I was fourteen, and I mean I wasn't a very worldly fourteen, I was a very naive fourteen. When I think about that I get really angry; I think it wasn't very fair of him.

It took a while for him to convince me. He said, "Do this, start using tampons, that'll help," and really ignorant stuff that now I know was stupid, but then I didn't really know. When we had sex, it was quick, and it was painful, and it was like nothing that I really wanted to do again. He said, "I really love you, and I care about you, and that's what people who care about you do." But he had a girlfriend. I just didn't know any better, really.

I'm still angry about it. I just felt that he should have said, "Let's wait till you're seventeen or eighteen. Maybe you'll know a little bit more then." But I was just so impressionable. I believed that he would care about me if I had sex with him, and I just wanted a boyfriend. I read about contraception. My girlfriends and me, we knew from TV and magazines that you could get pregnant.

We were off and on for maybe four years till I left to go to college. I left when I was seventeen. But he would have girlfriends, and I would know, but I would still go out with him because he was so cute. I just thought he was the cutest guy in the world, and I would go meet him here and there, even though I knew that he had other girlfriends. I would see him out with other girls, and he'd call me the next week. But then I found a boyfriend in high school. I would still go out and see him, even though I had a great boyfriend, since I guess I really liked him, crazy about him.

The sex didn't get better. I never really enjoyed it. I never had an orgasm or anything; I didn't even know that you were supposed to. I just thought that sex was what you did when you cared about somebody. My boyfriend in high school was totally against having premarital sex. We never did it. He was like, "We have to wait. I'm going to marry you. We have to wait." He was really a nice guy, really, really cared about me. But I wanted something else; I wanted him to have the *umph*, and he didn't have it. He was too nice. He just let me get away with murder. So I'd just go back to this other guy because that was kind of dangerous. He was exciting, and my boyfriend was so nice, and he didn't want to have sex. And he put me on this pedestal, and I felt like, Why has he put me on this pedestal? I wanted to have sex with him. He just wouldn't. And then he'd find out I'd slept with this guy, and he'd get mad at me, but then he'd take me back, stuff I shouldn't even have been going through at such a young age. I was like fourteen, fifteen.

I always felt very unattractive growing up. My parents never told me I was pretty. And when I got to college, all these guys were paying attention to me, and it was amazing. I was like, Wow, I never knew guys would like me like this. I was so naive, so naive, and I thought that they liked me and I was really popular. And I was just sleeping around big time—well, not big time. I kind of felt like that first guy treated me bad, and I had everything under control. But I really didn't. I would meet guys and we'd have a good time over Christmas holiday or summer. We'd have a little fling and then go back to college and go back to whatever was going on at college. And the guys in college, they were looking for the same thing I was looking for—they were just looking to have a good time. They didn't want a serious girlfriend. So for the first two years in college, you'd get lonely, go find somebody, have a real meaningless relationship, and then go on to the next. I guess I was looking for somebody to care about me. But they wouldn't stay around long. I would just jump into it really quickly. I wouldn't even know them very well.

Then I met my boyfriend that I dated all through college. I was nineteen, so I'd been in college two years, and I dated him for seven years. And they were very interesting seven years. Very, very unhealthy relationship. I've finally figured out how unhealthy it was. But I loved him, so I wanted to stay in it. It was just not a good situation. I enjoyed sex with him; it was great. But so many bad things happened that after a while, I couldn't even enjoy that. I was like, "Don't touch me." There was so much missing emotion, just so much, and I never realized that when something is missing emotionally, even if you do have good sex, that too can go because there's no—your emotional needs are not being met.

He was physically abusive. He cheated on me. He lied to me. In the beginning, it was only occasionally, but it got to be worse as the years went by. Finally one day I decided, "If you ever touch me again, I'll kill you." And then it stopped. But by then I was so beat down, there was nothing left in the relationship; but it was easier to stay because I was scared of what else was out there. When we broke up, he told me he was breaking up with me because I was selfish, you know, everything was about me. And this was someone I did everything for. I let him stay at my house, when he didn't have money I gave him money, I let him drive my car. And he turned around and said I was selfish and that's why he was leaving me. I had a really hard time with him leaving me, too, because I felt that I did something wrong. I wasn't good enough, the sex wasn't good enough, whatever. It was a very, very bad time in my life.

Actually, the first time, I asked him to leave. He wanted to get married, and I just knew that *that* wasn't the right thing. Then a couple weeks later, he was dating someone else. And that was very hard because she was a white lady, and I felt personally insulted because I didn't necessarily think she was a great white person. She was a high school dropout and all these other things and I felt that it was a reflection on me that he would prefer to be with someone who wasn't quite up to my par. Does that make sense? Something wasn't right with me. I took it very, very personally. And I was fighting tooth and nail to get him back. I don't know why because he wasn't even worth having back. Then I had sex with him, whenever he would come over, thinking that eventually he would go, "Oh, the sex is so great. I want to come back." But he wanted to be with someone else and I just could not accept that.

I started dating someone else, someone that he knew. God, I've made so many silly choices in my life. I just wanted to hurt him. But I ended up hurting myself and a really nice guy, because this guy I started dating was a really wonderful person. He didn't deserve that. I liked him a lot; I just didn't love him. He wanted to get married. I knew that the feelings I had for him were not what you should have when you go into marriage.

He married someone else. He was angry with me, but he took care of me. At a time when I needed to be taken care of, he really took care of me, and I appreciate that. I don't know if I ever told him, but I do. And that's another situation where in the beginning we had great sex, but when I realized that the feelings weren't there, the sex wasn't very good for me anymore. At that point in my life I was just trying to treat people the way I thought guys treat girls. I felt like, Oh, well, they don't care about me; they just want to have sex. So that's the way I'm going to do it, too. I didn't want to get hurt, and I thought that was a good way not to get hurt. I mean, it wasn't like I was getting anything out of the sex, and I've asked myself, Why did I even bother? I think of guys that I slept with and I think, Why? Why did you even do it? I can't believe it! I guess the only thing I got out of it is, it made me feel like I was pretty, and worthy, and people wanted to be with me.

From my college years to now, I slept with about thirty to forty guys, I would say. My best friend in college was really loose too, and we've always had this love-hate relationship. I felt that, Oh, she's sleeping with so-and-so, so she must be prettier than me, so I need to make sure I had been with more guys than her. It was like a contest, and now I think how stupid it was. But that was part of it, too, one of the reasons why I was being so promiscuous. I felt that she was winning, and that meant that she was prettier and nicer. And guys liked her better. When I think about it now, it's sick. Well, I guess not hearing that I was pretty growing up, I felt that if guys wanted to sleep with me, then they would think I was pretty and like me. I would always equate those two things: Well, I must be very pretty because they do want to sleep with me.

I don't really enjoy sex if emotion is missing. With my last boyfriend we started out having a great sex life, and then it got not so great, after a while, after all the problems. I think I may have kept him around because of the sex. I thought, Well, if that's the only thing you can do, then that's the only thing you can do, so I'm going to enjoy it. I would take control of the situation—I'd make sure I got satisfaction out of it, and not only him. So if he didn't want to, I would nag until I got it. But if I go into a relationship knowing that this person is not going to be in my life for very long, for whatever reason, be it my reasons or his reasons, I won't enjoy it. Like my boyfriend that I just broke up with, I knew he was there and I really cared about him, and when I felt that he cared about me, I was able to let go and enjoy it.

I hardly ever meet men while I work. But being a person who travels all the time as part of my job has been hard for some guys I've dated. I mean, they have to be very secure—like my last boyfriend had no problem with it, but a lot of guys seem to think, Oh, you must have guys all over the place. So the guy has to be very secure to know that I can be gone, I can go to the end of the world, but I'll come back to you. Some guys seem to like the fact that you're gone because it seems to me that when I'm gone on overnight trips, they feel like that's their time, and they can do whatever they want, being good or bad.

I think most men cheat and that's what I couldn't make my last boyfriend understand that this is what I'm accustomed to. It's not that I'm trying to accuse you of stuff. I don't know anything different. I have the feeling he thinks that if he has cheated on me, he did because I pushed him to it by accusing him of it. But that's where we are on different pages. I know it starts with me, but I think he should have done whatever it took to make me feel more comfortable in the relationship, and I don't think he really wanted to do that.

I think my first orgasm was with my boyfriend my first semester in college. I didn't necessarily like him a whole lot, but he was just nice to hang out with. And I remember it was the first time I was able to relax. I don't know if I just wanted to think that I got one, because I knew I hadn't had one and I was wanting one so bad that I kind of talked myself through the process. I can't really remember. But I do remember feeling really good. I was like, Wow, so this is what everybody's talking about. It was a release.

I'd go into sex thinking that, well, I know the first time isn't going to be very good; I won't be able to relax. But maybe a couple times after that it'll be better. And I remember the first time with my college boyfriend wasn't that great, but the second time was amazing. I'd never felt that before. I dated guys for two or three months and never had an orgasm. I would just go through the motions. But then when I slept with the college boyfriend I just wanted to be with him. I thought, Okay, this is what it's like to be a woman. This is what is supposed to happen when you have sex. But I wasn't really willing to explore different things, like oral sex. I was pretty conservative.

I remember being curious about myself, and I touched myself and that was fine. After my first orgasm with that guy, then I knew. Then I probably started to touch myself and know that I can make myself feel good. It wasn't the same feeling as with someone else. It's not something to do by yourself all the time.

I was very free with my last boyfriend. We experimented quite a bit, and we had a great sex life. I could just let myself go. I could be myself and could tell him anything or share anything with him, and he wouldn't think I was perverted or nasty. I would satisfy him, but I really didn't need to because he just was great and we had a close relationship in that way. I would just think about him tying me up or stuff like that. I'd kind of get a kick out of that, or him doing whatever he wanted to me. We'd just talk about them. He was the first guy I shared them with because with my other boyfriend, the sex started getting really awful and the only way I could enjoy it was thinking I was with some other guy or I was in a movie or something to get me going, because I really didn't want to be with him having sex. But I was too scared to go out there and see what else was out there too. So I felt trapped, which is really sick because I was only twenty-six, and I had my whole life ahead of me. But that would be the only way I could enjoy myself, the only time I felt fine to enjoy sex with him.

When I look at myself in the mirror, I see a black woman. I don't see a Hispanic woman, I see a black woman. That's where I feel comfortable, and that's who I feel accepts me. I think I'm a little too dark and my hair's a little too wavy to fit into the Latino community. And I think black people accept me better. I never really questioned my heritage and my background until I got to college because being from the Caribbean growing up, everybody is mixed with everything else. When I got to college, it was a big deal, and everybody would ask me, "So what are you?" And guys seemed to like me because of that too, because I was different, mixed with something other than black so that was really weird. I just never have thought of myself as Dominican—which is weird to me because I grew up with my Dominican grandmother and had very little to do with the black part of my family, but that's where I feel comfortable.

I date exclusively black guys. They're so different and colorful, and the way they walk, and they can give you a line a mile long and it may sound bad, but they're just so colorful. And they're strong, they're so strong. I don't necessarily pretend to understand their struggle half of the time. Like my ex-boyfriend would say, "Well, I just had a hard day at work." And I would think it was just a hard day at work; I wouldn't think if he was a black man and the only black man in his department. I don't necessarily understand it all the time, I guess because when I'm at work, I don't think people look at me differently because I'm black—but I'm not in corporate America. I do understand that. But I just thought he was so talented and so smart that they'd look past his color, that it had nothing to do with his color. But I think he thought that they would talk to him a certain way or be unnecessarily mean to him because he was a black guy and they felt they could talk to him that way.

Well, I know that when my ex-boyfriend started dating that white woman, that really bothered me a lot and really made me feel insignificant for some reason. I felt that he was just dating her because she was white. And that was really, really hard for me. I feel that a lot of men seem to want a trophy on their arm, and that usually translates into a white woman. I really have problems with that. I will not date a man if I know he dates white women. That's my biggest problem as far as image. I feel that they, black men, look at us and say, "Well, this is not what I consider the ideal of beauty." They think we just want them for their money, and we're loud, and we're just not very smart. And they think that white women are smart and pretty.

But I think I have it easier than women who are darker than me, and I think it's a sad thing. I think that if they don't date white women, they will date as light as they can. My last boyfriend, the first thing he asked me when he met me was if I was white, or what was I. So I think he is—and his family is, too—color-conscious.

I often wonder, when a guy meets me and he wants to go out with me, is he going to take the time to get to know me, or do I just meet his criteria of light skin? One guy I met, he told me, "I do a lot of functions. You'd be perfect. I'd love you to come to these functions." I didn't really think about it, but later I realized he didn't care about me, he just wanted me to go to these functions with him because he really couldn't go by himself. And I'd look nice with him and would talk okay once I got there. But he never asked me anything about me, at all.

I've never gotten pregnant. I'm not telling anybody that, but my last boyfriend and I were trying to get pregnant. It's just hard for me to get pregnant. I'd have to go through treatment, so I'm sure that has something to do with it. I wasn't always really good about contraceptives; I just don't think I could get pregnant like that.

In college I didn't really hear much about—I guess AIDS wasn't on the scene then. When it was on the scene, I tried to be pretty good about using contraceptives; I always did. I mean I always used good judgment. My last boyfriend, I thought we were monogamous (I know I was), but we weren't using contraceptives, and that was fine. But then when I thought maybe he was cheating, I realized that I couldn't be with him because I didn't know. I didn't know if he was out there or not, and there's always that possibility that he could sleep with some woman and bring something back to me. When I found out that he was talking to this girl that he wasn't supposed to be talking to, I thought, Look, just forget it. It may not be anything. But then that's what came into my mind: if he is seeing her, he slept with her— there is that chance. And I didn't want to risk that.

The second or third time we had sex, we used a condom and it broke, and I just knew I was pregnant and had a really hard time with that. And he was just really wonderful. He was just really, *really* there for me. And we'd only been dating for two or three months at that time. We talked about it and decided that if I was pregnant, it would be fine; we would take care of it. But I wasn't. I thought he'd be a great father. So if it happened, I knew he'd be there for me. And I do want to have children more so than I want to get married, although I would love to do both. But if I had a choice, I would rather be a mother than be a wife.

I really want to be a mother. I don't have a family foundation, and I'd like to have a family, my own family, and I'd like to be closer to my kids than my mom was to me. Don't get me wrong, I'd love to have a house and a yard and a husband and everything, but I guess I'm at a point where I think it may not happen. And I just want to have something that I do right. Does that make sense? I don't think my career is anything to brag about. I haven't done anything really spectacular that I could say, Wow. I think it's just average, but kids would be something I did. I've got that maternal thing going.

If I had to choose between being a mother and being married, then I would say I want to be a mother. I want better for my children than I had myself. I want my children to have a house that they can bring their friends to, and be proud of their parents. But I guess I'm thinking that it may not happen. I'm preparing myself for that. I'm thirty, and this city is full of beautiful women who've done ten times what I've done. And there's not that many great guys out there.

I feel like I'll probably never be married. It would be somebody very special that would have to come into my life to make me see that all men are not like that. The probability of that happening is real small, I think. And I can't compromise my integrity and say, "Okay, well, this is the way men are," so I'm pretty much trying to tell myself I may be alone. For me, trust definitely is the key to marriage. And love, too. I want to be in love with my husband, and I want him to be in love with me. I don't want to be married just so I can say I'm married.

I meet guys that I want to date, but they're always dating someone else or running a game. There's just not a lot of guys out there who are looking for relationships and are really honest and good. There's always something. I know that people will treat me the way I allow them to treat me, but I also know that if somebody's being mean to you or cheating on you, it's not about you, it's about them. I do understand that. But it is easy to just say, Oh, I must not be pretty enough, or he must want somebody better than me. I guess that's my insecurities coming out. Once you've been hurt before, a few times, you just expect it to happen over and over and over again.

I definitely have sexual regrets. I would have not jumped into sexual relationships so quickly, because I thought that was a problem. I had no self-esteem; I felt really bad about being promiscuous when I thought about it. And, I thought that if my mom—my grandma—knew, she would be very disappointed in my behavior. But yet, I kind of felt like that was what I deserved. I mean, that's what happened to girls like me.

And I would only have sex with people who I knew for a fact cared about me, genuinely cared about me as a person. That means fewer partners. It probably would have been three, because I can only think of three people who genuinely cared about me in my life. So it would have been almost none.

But I probably wouldn't have learned as much about my sexuality. It took me a long time to learn about myself sexually. I would have been very inhibited because it took me forever to learn. I would say that this last relationship I just had has been the most uninhibited I've ever had, and I'm thirty years old. At the same time, I think I would have had a better sense of self, felt better about myself, because I'm not proud of what I've done—I'm not. I wish that I had thought more about myself at that point in my life. When I think about it now, I just think that they didn't even deserve me. I deserve so much better. I can't believe that I felt so needy that I felt I had to do that. I feel sad for myself. I'm not totally healthy yet anyway, but I just feel sad that I felt that was the only way I could get attention, and affection. They weren't worthy of me; they were not. Thinking about it, it's not a good feeling.

I don't really think things are equal. Even though black women are very strong and we're very independent, it seems like men don't look at it that way. I don't want to say all men, but they kind of look at us to be there for their needs and to take care of their children and to work to pay for their house. And I don't necessarily think they want us to be too strong—I don't think they like that. "You're too independent," that is one of their complaints. Maybe it makes them feel a little insecure about themselves. You know, I think they might look at it as they can't be above the white man, or white people, so the only thing left: they can be above black women. Everybody always wants to feel better than somebody else—that's how I look at things.

I think if guys knew how many men I slept with, they would think less of me. They'd say, "Oh, you're kind of slutty, huh?" But in reverse, it wouldn't be like that. If he slept with thirty or forty women, he wouldn't be "slutty." I guess you expect guys to be promiscuous and it's okay for them; it's just not okay for us. That's the way society is: it's okay for guys to cheat on you—you're almost expected to accept it—and if they have other women, that's just the way boys are. It doesn't mean anything because it's a sexual act for them. So I don't tell new guys I had sex as early as I did or how many. My ex-boyfriend asked me how many people I had slept with. I said, "Well, how many people have you slept with?" And he didn't want to tell me. I said, "Can you count it on one hand?" He said, "No, more than that." I said, "Two hands?" He said, "Yeah." When he asked about me, I said, "Well, you can count it on one hand."

It's not fair: I have to guard my past because I don't want people to think bad of me, which you will because girls are supposed to be nice and sweet and there when men want us. But men, they can do anything and it's fine. People say, "It's just the way they are." And it's not right: they can cheat on you and have sex and it's nothing.

# Pam

*I*'M TWENTY-TWO, from New York, single. I was raised with both parents. They're separated, but they live together. My dad works to place juvenile offenders into community-based programs. And my mom's a nurse. I have two siblings, a brother and a sister; I'm the youngest. I grew up most of my life without my sister; I didn't meet her until she was fifteen and I was six. She lived with us for five years—not very long. What else? I'm agnostic. Well, my dad is Christian, was raised Baptist. I guess he's still Baptist. I've thought my mom was atheist, but I'm not sure; I've never asked her. My mom is African Latina, from Central America. My dad is African American. When I was younger, in elementary school, I went to a mostly black public school, but then we moved to a mixed neighborhood and I went to a magnet school that was mostly white. I graduated last May from college. Now I do fund-raising for this nonprofit law office.

Intimacy is a certain level of trust, the ability to disclose things that mean a lot to me. Trust. And feel like I could rely on somebody, be able to talk to them, and feel unjudged and supported. You get intimacy by sharing stuff that means a lot to you and seeing how they treat it. See if they listen well. If I feel like, well, if I feel like someone's not listening to me, if they break my confidence in them, if they dismiss what I say, then intimacy dissolves.

I am very close to my brother. He's a good guy. He's not simply a good guy. I think I just needed a good friend—my family situation was screwy, and also I was sort of an oddball in school, so I didn't find it easy to make friends. I was a fat kid, and I was a smart kid. And I was a quiet kid. My parents don't really get along, and my mother has developed into an alcoholic, plus some other things, my mom's history that she's dealing with. The house was basically tense. Full of anger that's unspoken. So he was around, and we shared circumstances.

I identify as a lesbian. I'm comfortable with that identity, but I am not as comfortable with my sexuality as I want to be. I learned about sexuality in elementary school. Some of my first sexual experiences were in violence, not like rape, but I just have a sensitivity to being mistreated sexually. Some of my first sexual experiences I associate with being harassed. So my first idea of sexuality was harassment. My first pleasant sexual thoughts were that I had a crush on a friend of mine when I was around fourteen, fifteen, sixteen. I was just in love. It was wonderful and beautiful and great, that kind of thing. I made her my very good friend and wanted her to be my best friend. She was my only friend, actually. I spent a lot of time with her and called her all the time. She was my friend, but it wasn't equal. Actually, I felt sort of used. I felt like she used me for attention she didn't get from her boyfriend. Like even though I hadn't said I had a crush on her, a person acts a certain way when they're in love. And so I paid her all sorts of attention and it seemed like she would only call me when her boyfriend was ignoring her. She's still a nice person.

I felt all right with being a lesbian when I was in high school. I felt that it might not be popular with other people, that people might think bad of me, but I thought that people would be wrong, though, that they would be wrong with being a lesbian. My parents never said anything bad about gay people, so that was good. They're generally just sort of open-minded; they're kind of loving and they're kind of liberal. And another thing was, I spent a lot of time by myself, so group norms didn't really rub off on me. I just come to stuff on my own.

I told my parents that I was a lesbian at the end of my freshman year in college. And at first they didn't believe me; they thought I'd watched too many talk shows. That first summer was kind of rocky. They didn't talk to me as much and sometimes there were outbursts about, "How could you do this to us?" But since then, they're more accepting, more supportive. They're asking me about whether or not I have a girlfriend, and all my political stuff they support.

Even though I didn't think that anybody was attracted to me, I always had crushes on women, like that girl I was in love with in junior high school, and some other women I had crushes on. But I was just buying time in high school, waiting to get out of New York. I was waiting to leave my parents' home. The conditions in my house had just become too much for me. My mom had become more and more of an alcoholic and my parents had violent arguments. Not fistfighting arguments, but yelling and slamming of doors and people stomping out. And then one time my mom passed out from drinking too much, and she had to be rushed to the hospital to have her stomach pumped. I wanted to get out of there.

Junior year in college, I found a girlfriend. Till then, I was single and celibate. Freshman year, boy, I was all into gay bars. Of course, I didn't talk to anybody or meet anybody—I was up against the wall. But still, I was there every weekend! Holding up walls at gay bars, paying my five dollars. Waste of time. I don't think anybody you meet in bars is anybody you'd want to hang out with. I didn't just want to have sex. I didn't believe in that. I thought I needed to be in love to sleep with somebody. Now, I'm starting to question it. Some people I just want to sleep with. But I'm still not letting myself do it. I haven't approached anybody.

I fell in love with this woman my junior year. We started dating, and we ended up sleeping with each other. Why did I fall for this woman? Well, she was really extroverted. Really noticeable, really a beacon. She's bald-headed, and there aren't that many bald-headed women at my college. Bald-headed, walks around in boots and stuff like that, and she just stands out from people. When I met her and started talking to her, she was outspoken and just a ball of energy. I was very attracted to all her energy. She dances down the block, at the subway stop, like she's in her own world. And she's a runner, so she goes running all the time. She's really disciplined, and that's really attractive. She's also very smart. And, I had heard she was a lesbian. We knew somebody in common, so she just introduced herself. "I know such and such, you know such and such, hi." I was like, "Yeah, hi, how you doin'?" And then she saw me on television. And she said, "You know, I saw you on television. That's real cool." I had been on a cable show here talking about being a lesbian.

I'm very shy, but I'm politically a lesbian. I've been an out lesbian on campus since I've been there and worked with the lesbian-bisexual alliance they had there, helped them get chartered. Some stuff I'll be outspoken about politically, rah rah rah. So I just kept seeing her on campus. She keeps talking to me, and it takes me a while to realize these things, she must really like me. Nobody else talks to me this much about absolutely nothing. And I decided I liked her. So we just started hanging out together, and going to movies, having dinner together. All this while she had a girlfriend. Then she broke up with her girlfriend, became very depressed about something else, which caused her to withdraw from school, and she went to California which is where she's from, and came back. So it was a new semester; she was enrolled in school and had supposedly come out of this depression, and she didn't have a girlfriend. And I was like, "You know what? You and I are gonna date." She was living on campus, and she used to come visit me all the time in my dorm. And one day we just started talking about something, about how much we liked each other. And I said, "I think I'm in love with you." And she said, "Oh, really?" And we started kissing.

I was really scared. I mean, I didn't want to mess up. And I was thinking, Maybe we need to just be friends. This might be the wrong thing. But at the same time, I really wanted to be with her. So I kept going. The first time we just kissed. After that time, most times it was kissing and fondling. What's that called—digital stimulation, mutual masturbation, that kind of thing. And I guess three weeks into it, we started having oral sex. Generally I didn't have sex to orgasm. I wouldn't orgasm when we would have sex. I guess I would call it making out more than sleeping together. More kissing and fondling more than clothes-off type stuff. I'm still pretty hands off. I don't read erotica and stuff like that.

We were together three months—this was last year, two years ago. But it ended. She's crazy. She is very abusive. She would go into really big rages where she would talk about how she didn't like me, and how we shouldn't have never been together, and how I'm a pain in her ass. So I broke up with her. We were together formally for three months, but I just stopped talking to her last year sometime. So for a long time, even though we weren't girlfriends, we were still something. I'm back to being celibate and single.

Race matters because I've had attractions for this white woman, but I decided I don't want to pursue it because she's white. I don't even want to deal with my racism on top of other things I have with relationships. I already think I have too many obstacles with being intimate with people, and racism would just be another layer. I have problems trusting people; that's why trust is so important to me. I have really deep problems as to who I can trust and depend on, and expecting people to pay attention to me. I think we're all racist. I haven't tried very hard to work on my racism toward white people. I think I have a thing for light-skinned women. I probably do, due to the fact that I think they're prettier because they're light. That's internalized racism. I think I'd be more angry if a white woman said something racist to me, just different power positions in society and she has the whole world on her side.

I've had really good sexual relations, I think. I expect my partners to be attentive and ask me what I want, and to try new things. I haven't done anything different—just the regular stuff. Overall, I think it comes back to the trust. So if I'm in love with somebody and they pass the test, then I could trust them to touch me.

I'd like to be more assertive in my sexuality, be more comfortable about being intimate. Like I said, I didn't have sex to orgasm very often. I think that was deliberate, though: I didn't want to come because that would be getting too close to someone. So I think I want to unlock that about myself. And trust people more and allow myself more pleasure.

I got caught touching myself once, but I was in third grade, fourth grade. My parents told me that I shouldn't do that. I guess I was in my bedroom, and my mom or dad came into my room suddenly—I probably had my hand down my pants. And they were like, "You shouldn't do that." I don't remember exactly what they said. I just remember that happening. I stopped doing it for a while. But when I got a little older, junior high school age, I started doing it again.

I did it mostly at night when I thought my parents were asleep. I definitely didn't orgasm. I thought if I orgasmed I'd be really loud, so I stopped. I thought, I shouldn't masturbate to orgasm because then my parents would know, because I might—I don't know, I don't remember thinking about anything. I don't think anybody told me about orgasms. I just thought I would be so excited that I would scream. I didn't even try it when I was home alone. Later, in college, I had an orgasm. It was weird. I was dating some woman, and she was asking me about masturbation. Like, "Do you masturbate?" And I said, "Yeah." She's like, "Have you ever come?" I was like, "Naw." She said, "Well, you should try it again until you come." So that summer I went home and masturbated until orgasm. It felt good.

Sometimes when I'm masturbating I have sexual fantasies. I have masturbated around fantasies about having sex in public, like on public transportation. The fantasy is that one woman sees me and some other woman against each other on the train. And she's getting off on it.

My mother told me about my menstruation, and she referred me to some books, too. She probably told me that I would start bleeding to get rid of eggs that I didn't use for that month. And that I would need maxipads, something like that. No, I don't remember either of them talking much about sex or sexuality. Sometimes they'd ask me if I had a boyfriend, or anybody I was interested in. And I would say no, and they would refer me to books if I had any questions.

I was molested by a next-door neighbor when I was in elementary school. He would tell me I look good and stuff like that, tell me I should wear skirts instead of pants because I looked better in skirts. Then one day he had me come over to his back yard in a skirt and had me touch his penis, and I was supposed to masturbate him. I don't remember if I did. I don't think I did, but I don't remember. My sister was looking for me, so she called out the window, and I was like, "I gotta go."

I guess I put on the skirt because I wanted attention. You know, no one else tells me I'm pretty, this guy does. I felt it was wrong. I felt it was a really bad thing for him to do. I felt really vulnerable, like really it's better not to be attractive, because this is what happens. So I started eating a lot. Because I used to be much heavier than this, so I think that's one of the reasons I started eating, to make myself unattractive. So people wouldn't look at me. Well, men. I didn't tell my parents because, well, I just, I didn't like to draw attention to myself, and I thought this would give me too much attention. They'd be wondering, Why were you there with this guy? I didn't want any scrutiny.

Also, when I was in elementary school, these two guys used to tell me that they were going to—I can't really remember. Do something sexually to me. But they would follow me home from school and say that "I'm going to, you're going to." They were teenagers, and I was seven, eight. I told my mom and dad. And I asked, "Could my brother walk me to school every day?" And she said, "Your brother can't be there to protect you all the time, so you have to find some other way to deal with this." So I said, "Okay," and I walked to school by myself. Nothing happened; they were just talking, they weren't going to do anything. I was pretty scared. Well, I mean, I was scared but I didn't register it at the time. I don't think I really have gotten over those experiences. Well, I have a little bit. Recently I've been on this big kick to reclaim my body, about how people always misconstrue, have fantasies in their mind about what they can do with my body. But this is my body, and I think I'm pretty, and it's all right for me to be sexy. So it's all right for me to dress in form-fitting clothes and not be afraid about what other people see when they see me.

In the eleventh grade, I dropped a lot of weight, deliberately. I didn't set out to lose weight—I wanted to be stronger, physically stronger, so I started working out. So I became muscular, and a by-product of that was to lose weight. I had started to diet but I decided there was some type of plot against women to make you be thinner, so I decided not to diet. I was working out to be strong, not to be skinny.

Naw, I don't want to have kids. I don't want to be responsible for kids. I don't what to be where the check stops and somebody has to answer to raising a kid. I don't want to do that. I don't trust myself to raise a kid. I plan to do research on high school– and middle school–aged kids, so that way I could connect with kids. Plus I plan to have cats. It's the same thing—they're dependent.

I kind of wish I had more partners because I'm twenty-two now, and most people have had more partners than I have. So I feel like I'm at a lack or a deficit when I come to a relationship. I don't have as much experience just dealing with people. But I don't see how I could have done it any other way.

Is there sexism in the black community?! [*Starts laughing.*] Yes! The general distrust of and hatred of women. This whole deal with guys molesting me and stuff is about how women aren't really people and how they're the road to their desire, how we're not really here. They just use women for whatever. Woman hatred. I think I'm always looking for the way somebody's trying to use me sexually. So I am self-protective. I think they happen together, like sexism and racism. I had a friend who was attacked by this guy because he thought she was so exotic and highly sexualized because she's dark-skinned. It was a black guy, who thought since she was dark-skinned, and I think she had a natural hairstyle, braids or something like that, she was exotic and really sexually inviting. So he attacked her.

I think I'm very sexist. I think I've had problems taking my girlfriend seriously when she would get mad at me. I was like, Oh, she's just being hysterical. She is more butch and more aggressive and assertive than I am. So even though I'm the more masculine-looking, she's more assertive. I've always felt that I'm very masculine-looking, and I was a tomboy when I was younger. Well, that's how I see myself. I just hung out with guys and read comic books.

# Diane

*I*'M MARRIED, thirty-two, two children, a girl and a boy, five and three. My father is a minister, my mother's a schoolteacher. I was born in Tennessee, but I was raised in Charleston, West Virginia. Came to Charlotte, North Carolina, when I was a teenager, so I've been here about eighteen years. I have one sister, a younger sister. She's married. She's expecting her first child in October. I was an art major in college, so I plan on trying to finish my last year and maybe go into art education, become a schoolteacher. I didn't finish my last year in college. I do manicures now. I grew up going to church. I was a Methodist and my husband was a Baptist, so now we're in a nondenominational church. My parents are other nationalities, but we consider ourselves African American. My father's father was a full-blooded Choctaw Indian. On my mother's side, they're considered Creole; they're from New Orleans.

I don't feel that as a child I really received intimacy. In a friendship, I look for someone that I can depend on, that I can lean on. Trust is a big factor. I want someone I just feel comfortable being with, whether it's male or female. There wasn't a lot of holding or nurturing when I was growing up. So

226 / GUARDED HEART

it's kind of hard now dealing with it. If someone gives me a hug to say hello, it makes me uncomfortable. It's hard to break that. I guess I can speak about my marriage right now: when I feel that I'm not being respected in the relationship, that hurts intimacy. Respect is important in friendship too. If that's not there, then it can't go to a second level.

The very first time I had sex I was fifteen. I was really not supposed to date until I was sixteen, but my parents allowed me to double-date with someone at that time. I was a sophomore, he was a senior. And we just started going out, and one thing led to another. My family really didn't talk about sex. My mother grew up Catholic, my father was a minister, so we really did not discuss that. My father opened up to me more than my mother did. They said, "If you feel like you're going to have feelings like that, discuss it with me first," which I never really felt comfortable doing. I remember as a child they brought books that had drawings of where babies came from and that sort of thing. I know that I had a health problem, a cyst on my ovaries, dealing with really heavy cramping in school. They put me on birth control pills to reduce the cramping and regulate my period. And that led into birth control for my sexuality with my boyfriend at that time. My mother had taken me to the doctor, and they put me on birth control pills. So the doctor and I discussed the birth control pills then.

I guess I was scared in a way. Sexuality was scary to me because I was molested once as a child. By my father's brother. Probably about ten years old. So dealing with sex and someone touching you is always scary. He did not have intercourse with me, but just the actual knowledge of him touching me and doing things to me—you know, his being my uncle—was very uncomfortable. That very first time that I had sexual intercourse was very painful. I'm not talking physically but emotionally. It's always been a problem for me, I guess, intimacy . . . I'm not just talking about the sexual act of it.

I think I started having sex for the closeness of a relationship, not really having a close-knit family. I grew up watching my family fight or my parents having problems in their marriage. And abuse. My mom and dad. Physical abuse. I've seen him hit her, you know, hit with a belt, stuff like that. I guess watching that, you reach out for any type of closeness you can get. I'm not saying that was right at that time—I feel I was too young to really deal with sexuality. That's why I really want to raise my children differently, especially with AIDS out there now.

Anyway, we had dated maybe eight months, almost a year. He was white, blond, and blue-eyed. His parents were divorced, and both of them were remarried. I was accepted by his mother and her husband, but once his real father found out that he was dating someone black, then he forbid him to see me, and he did not pay for his college education until the relationship was broken off. My parents liked him; his name was Jamie. Although I never really discussed my sexuality with my family, I think they probably knew something but didn't want to ask.

He never pressured me to have sex. He was a very gentle person, very nice, and he respected me. He didn't hide the relationship. We went out on dates, we did things together. So when he started dating a white girl right after we broke up, it hurt. I think that was just a cover-up or a front for his father's sake. He did talk to his friends and other people, and they told me that he did care about me and the relationship. It was really hard, being fifteen at that time, my first boyfriend, first everything. I waited awhile before I was sexually active again. I think I had the next close relationship when I was about eighteen and I came here to Charlotte when I was a senior maybe.

At that time, I didn't really think about virginity. If I could turn back the hands of time and do things differently, I would. I would have waited. But some people believe in waiting till you're married, and I know this may sound bad, but I don't. Before getting married I think it's good to date and experiment. And I feel that you should know the person that you're going to marry—that's a lifetime commitment—and see if you're compatible. I would have waited at least till my early twenties, or I should say at least till I was eighteen, nineteen, twenty. I would have waited instead of having sex at fifteen and a half. I think that was just too young to deal with the responsibility of sex, of taking the risk of getting pregnant. Just the whole nine yards.

I was quite sexually active in high school and college, but I had five serious relationships, including my husband. Of those five, three were black men and two white. Generally, I preferred white men over black men. I don't know if this has anything to do with the barriers and the difficulties that black men have to face in our society—I don't know if that's the reason why they're harder to deal with in relationships, in terms of anger or just everything they have to face. I could say that the white men I've dated have been more passionate, loving, giving. But my husband is black. Why? I don't know. I don't know. I can say it was difficult in the white relationships in terms of people looking at us, or what our children would go through. That pressure all around the black family relationship. Although people never really knew what I was. They thought I was Mexican or Spanish, with my hair and skin and everything. A lot of people asked me, "What are you? What's your nationality?" I knew what my children would go through because I know what I went through growing up. They still have questions, which is kind of ironic; my kids look like they're Spanish also.

My boyfriend before my husband was Middle Eastern. He was divorced and about six or seven years older than me. When we met he was separated. We lived together for three years, and I thought we were going to get married. At least I wanted to. I felt after living together three years, that was the next step. I did get pregnant in the relationship, and I had an abortion. It was a difficult decision to make, but I was not working, and I was afraid to bring a child into the world, not knowing if we were going to stay together. And I was afraid of becoming a single mother. Ben did not want to have children; he was very adamant about that. He was afraid of the responsibility, he was afraid of marriage, being that he was divorced. He had the divorce while we were together. We just went through a lot. He had an affair in our relationship that went on for four months. I was just afraid of where the relationship was going to go. Eventually it broke off. I started seeing my husband, and I broke the relationship off.

I don't know why I got pregnant; I was on the pill. I probably forgot a day. That's the only thing I can think of. It was quite a surprise for both of us. I think I found out first, and then I went to the doctor because I was really sick, and they did a pregnancy test and told me it was positive, and told me of my options. I was really upset. Abortion was an option. I brought

Benjamin back with me to the doctor's office, and we discussed that with the doctor. Then we made an appointment, and he and my sister went with me to have the abortion. My parents knew about it. I felt comfortable telling them about it. They were very supportive. I should say my mother was more upset than my father; she thinks about that child from time to time, that it was really her first grandchild. And my father offered to give me the money for the abortion if I needed it, and I told him that it was not his responsibility. Benjamin paid for it, and the relationship started to sour after that.

I think we did not see each other for maybe a month. I had moved out, bought a condominium, and was interviewing as a flight attendant at that time. I met my husband, Thomas, on an airplane. And we dated four weeks, got married—I was twenty-six. He works with the airlines, and there were only two seats left on the plane in first class, so we ended up sitting next to one another. We talked on the phone, exchanged phone numbers. He was based out west. His family lived in Charlotte, so he was here visiting. He would fly back and forth on the weekends or days off to visit. And one day I got a call from Benjamin, like nothing had happened, and I told him that I was seeing someone, and he had asked to marry me. Ben was just very distraught, and was stalking me, and I had to call my parents. I know it was around eight o'clock in the morning when my dad and mom came over and they were talking to him outside, and he said that he realized what he had lost and he really did still love me and would do everything he could. He wanted to marry me. But I told him it was too late, too much had happened. I felt really bad because I knew deep down inside that I still loved him, but I knew I was really thinking with my head instead of my heart, and I knew deep down inside that he was the right person to marry. There were some things that he was getting into that I was afraid of, because although he was very smart, college educated, but he was making some wrong decisions in his life, and I didn't want to be a part of it. That was one reason. Then also, he said he could not promise about children, and I knew I wanted to have a family. So that outweighed everything, and we broke the relationship off.

If I knew then what I know now, I would not have gotten married to

Thomas. There's a lot of things about my husband I didn't know in terms of his anger, his temper. There's good sides about him, but there's also bad sides that sometimes outweigh the good, that I'm having difficulty with, and that's why I'm in therapy now. I'm in group therapy. But he came from a very good family background, and his sense of family values, children, marriage, religion, all that was good on the surface. I knew that I wanted to marry someone that had a sense of God and religion, and family values, and he was more of a friend to me at that time, someone I could lean on and depend on. We could really talk and bond at that point in our lives, and I guess that was the attraction. It was not a physical or sexual attraction. We didn't sleep together before we got married. We wanted to wait. He's not the best lover that I've had. I felt sometimes he was selfish, or rushed things sexually. He was not passionate or giving, but I kept saying to myself, "He's a family man, he's responsible." And that in marriage, sex is not everything. Although sex is not everything, it's important. I'm finding that if you love one another, it's important for two people to show that, in intimacy and emotionally. It's difficult for me. I don't know if I can say I'm embarrassed to talk about sex because I am talking to you about it; but it's hard for me to tell someone I'm involved with what I want sexually, to say, "Well, you're not giving me this, but I want this," or "That doesn't feel good, that doesn't feel right, but I want this."

Sex with my husband is rushed. I know it's hard when you have children, but I feel that things need to be planned, time needs to be planned. If you love someone, you have to set aside time. It's a lot of work. So I just feel that if my husband really loves me and wants to show me that, he has to be willing to say, "Hey, I have a couple of hours, I have an evening set aside, I have a baby-sitter so we can have dinner together or an intimate moment together." It has to be a mutual bond; if it's just one person, the marriage just won't work. I feel I'm always the one in the marriage—complain when I'm not getting enough sex or that I'm by myself all of the time. My husband's a musician trying to get into the music industry, so that takes up a lot of his time. Between that and working, he's never home. But I've taken the initiative on my part to switch two of my off days twice a month. That's not a lot of time, but two days out of the month, so we can have time together. Just like yesterday. That was the plan, but I ended up spending that by myself with my son. So I just feel that he has to be willing on his end to show that, and then the sex and the intimacy, all of that will follow.

Having our children wasn't planned either. I know my husband wanted children, I wanted children, and I feel that we just made a lot of stupid decisions in the marriage, and should have waited to have my daughter. But we wanted to have a baby. I don't know if that was just someone to love us or to give love to—I can't answer for my husband. I can say for me, I wanted someone to love, I wanted someone to love me. That wasn't smart, but we had our daughter. I got pregnant six months after we married in April. In December I got pregnant, had my daughter in September. Nine months later I got pregnant again, with my son. They're eighteen months apart; he was born in March.

It does sound romantic, and when people hear it, they're like, "Wow!" But there's a lot behind that. We're going through a very difficult time, and the marriage has been difficult for seven years. But I think with our family structure, our upbringing and background and belief of religion and family, things that we want, I guess that's the reason we've tried to make it work. But going through therapy after therapy, going to church, its just been a lot.

I wish I had waited to have kids. But, my mother was telling me, "You're going to be an old maid before you get married. You're not going to have children." I heard that over and over again, because I was twenty-six. That's kind of late for a woman to get married. People are having babies in their thirties or forties. But I wish I had waited, and I probably would have made a smarter decision. I don't think Thomas and I would have married. After dating him, really getting to know him as a person—who's to say? Maybe we would have had a better or stronger foundation at that time so we could talk things through and not fight as much.

Having my daughter was a better experience for us as a couple than my son. My son really wasn't planned. It was just a weird feeling, having the baby inside of me, or seeing an elbow move across my stomach. My husband and I experienced really watching me develop and change physically as a woman. But the bond after having her is just something I could not describe. You know, this person was dependent on me. The closeness is just something I can't really describe. I stayed home with both my children, till they were about two or three, I was really afraid to let anyone take care of my children. I think that has something to do with the sexual abuse as a child, and that was pretty scary. But my children, no matter how angry they get me from time to time, they've enriched my life, too. And I would not take that back. I love them very much.

I don't think having children has changed me in terms of what I want sexually. Or how I feel physically. I had two C-sections with my children. But I can say I feel uncomfortable in terms of my body, physically. I don't feel as attractive sexually as I did before. I don't know if breastfeeding has something to do with it, but my breasts are not as firm as they were before. Or the weight gain—that's why I'm on a diet now. I was more petite at that time. I gained about sixty pounds; I've lost twenty. I think weight and the scar that I have from the C-sections, the stretch marks you get from pregnancy make me feel less attractive as a woman than I did before having my children. Society wants to have this thirty-four/twenty-four/thirty-six woman, and the "model" type. I haven't really felt attractive sexually, and maybe not as free or experimental. Sex just feels routine.

I can say having children has made me want to be more responsible in life, learning to think things through a little bit more than I did before I had children. And maybe that's the reason I wanted to go back to school and better myself as a person—to set examples for my children. Being a mother hasn't brought me more women friends. I think dealing with all the things in life, an alcoholic mother, the abuse in my parents' marriage, the fighting, made me isolate myself, as an escape. Whenever I get upset, or something's on my mind, I isolate, and it's been difficult to make friends under those circumstances.

Having more children—that depends on my relationship with my husband. I've always wanted to have a large family; I've always wanted to have more children. I don't know about my husband. I think probably because of where our relationship is and where our marriage is at this point, he has told me, "Be grateful you have a boy and a girl, and we have two children."

I would like to have another child. Of course, I'm getting up in age. I don't want to have a child past thirty-five because I did have health issues in my pregnancy. I'm almost thirty-three. So I'm a little afraid of that, being that I did have C-sections and had toxemia and difficulty with birth. They told me my pelvis was too small to pass the head through. I had a difficult labor with my daughter.

I'm sure I did masturbate as a child. That's why I try not to get upset with my daughter because I know that boys do it, little girls do it. I remember I was probably my daughter's age, maybe five, six. I remember there was another little girl and boy and me, and it was, "I'll show you mine if you show me yours," that kind of thing. We were just curious about our bodies. So I did masturbate before I had sex, when I was maybe thirteen, fourteen, or twelve. You know, just touching yourself. I would feel uncomfortable about it now but I know I experimented with that. I really did not experience an orgasm having sex when I was in my teens. I did have an orgasm masturbating as a teenager. It just felt like a rush. I know it felt good. I guess I was scared and excited. I didn't tell anyone about it. The first time I had an orgasm during sex, I was around eighteen or nineteen. I don't know if that was oral sex stimulation, foreplay, or position. I don't know if any of that had anything to do with it. It's hard to describe, but I guess it feels better to know that you can experience that with another person, especially if you orgasm at the same time. It's just a more powerful experience than by yourself or with oral sex.

I think society puts too much emphasis on race. I don't think there is a true race. I feel that people should have the choice to see, date, marry anyone that they want to if they love that person. I get very angry when it comes to racism. Having white people in my home, a lot of people of nationalities in my family, racism is very disturbing to me.

In terms of sexuality, that's really scary at this point with the diseases and things going on now. I feel we need to make better choices and know the person that we're with, and monogamy is the key. I believe the sexual rules should be firm and the same for both sexes. My husband and I had this discussion. I don't feel that we should solely just beat the idea of virginity in the ground for my daughter. I think we should have that same conversation with both of our children. My husband says about our son, "Oh well, I'm going to get him his first person when he's sixteen, or take him here, take him there." And that bothers me. I know he was saying it in a teasing way, but that bothers me because I feel that when he or she is ready to have sex, they need to make sure that they're ready and take precautions and all of that.

I hate to say this, but I've always wondered what it would be like to be with two men. That's something I know that I would not do, but just the thought of it . . . I imagine someone pleasing me—just really enjoying being pleased instead of pleasing myself or pleasing someone else. With two men, I would get more attention. I sometimes think of this while making love.

I guess I'd like a closer relationship with my husband, more of a friendship where we can really talk to one another, more of an intimate bond. That's important to me; I wish that was different. I know that would be the foundation for a better relationship with my children and the whole family unit. We don't have a house yet, so if we had a house, we would have a little more stability to live comfortably and give our children a little bit more.

Sexual images are really out there now. You have advertising now for condoms, you have commercials for condoms. I saw a commercial the other day for HIV testing. Children are going to see that. So I'm sure kids these days are going to ask questions. When I was growing up, that wasn't on television. We had the aerobics, women wanting to have the perfect body, but now, in my children's generation, you have more people actually talking about sex. And you actually have stores that sell condoms or sexual devices and things like that, which I don't think was as common when we were growing up. It's scary. And there's nothing I can do. I can't control the way that our society is. I can't shelter my children. I have to be as honest and open with my kids as I can, although my family wasn't like that with me, and maybe they will make smarter decisions in their lives like I did not do.

When I was a teenager, I think I went into sex for the wrong reasons, and that was to seek out closeness, to seek out love that I was not getting. And you don't have sex for those reasons. You have sex because that's someone you love and you want to bond with that person. That's someone that you want to share your life with. I was having sex for the wrong reason, and that was to receive love from someone else. I think a lot of women do that. Sex is like alcohol or drugs: some women, to escape, they take drugs, some women take alcohol to escape, and some women may be promiscuous and have sex with a lot of different men to escape. I guess men do the same things. But I think the price for women is different, especially if you get pregnant, because the woman has to go through the pregnancy, maybe adoption or deal with the abortion, and I know what that feels like. A man does not physically have to go through what a woman has to go through. It's a deeper pain. I feel that maybe I could have waited and had sex for the right reasons instead of for the reasons that I did. I know I feel bad. I didn't respect myself enough. I gave it too freely, and that's something that a woman or man should hold sacredly and choose their partner wisely.

# Aracely

I'M TWENTY-FOUR and I am in a social-work program in the Providence area. I'm a second-year student; I graduate in May. I'm interning at a coalition of human service providers and community residents. And I work at a store too. I'm a real person.

I lived predominantly with my mother, who is a white woman. I have a black Puerto Rican father. Culturally, though, I'm Puerto Rican. So I've kind of gone between the two. I'm bilingual, but I definitely use English better. I mean, I definitely know more English. But when I need to, I'll speak Spanish. My father was around up until I was about eight years old, and then he took off with his new woman. And even when he was there, it was kind of rocky anyway. So I'm not very close to him. Talk to him every once in a rare while. I think the last time I talked to him was Christmas, and that's 'cause we called him. He lives in Puerto Rico now. When my father was around, he worked. But I have vague recollections of it. I think it might have been under-the-table type stuff, just odd things, because I know my mother was receiving welfare, so I believe it had to be. And then when he left, I remember being on welfare for a while. I think my mother got a job as a housekeeper. But even when she was working, there was food stamps and stuff. It's all very blurry to me.

I was born in Nyack, New York. My mother was born there; my grandmother was born there. When I was little, though, I lived in Puerto Rico for a while. I was raised as a Catholic. I made my Communion, all of that. I went to Sunday school. My mother always had me going; my sister was too young at the time. I have a much younger brother—he's only seven now—but neither of them were made to go to church. I had a best friend who went all the time, and we went together, and then I stopped going when I was about in sixth grade. I stopped going because a cousin of mine died, and I refused after that to believe. I had a fit, basically, and I was just like, There's no God then. Since then, I've switched up a bit on that. There's something; I know there's something. But I choose not to believe in the God that's considered "He" and has a long beard and blond hair. I choose not to believe, and a part of that is culturally as much as it is just my own questioning of what's really out there. But before that, I was a good little Catholic girl. Then I said there can't be, because you don't just kill innocent children. And that was it. I was an interesting child: I just always had ideas and opinions. I was very stubborn.

I guess I identify as biracial, black Puerto Rican. It's always been difficult, always. Especially if you don't get any support from your family. Well, I really don't know in terms of my father's ideas. That's not something we've ever talked about. Ever. But my mother once said, "I raised you as a white person." And I looked at her and I said, "You what? Look at me." I was like, "No, I don't think so." And I thought, That's funny, because I never wanted to be white. She said, "You're not a person of color, you're my child." And I'm like, "But, Mom, I am. When I walk down the street, it's different than when you do." So I've always identified very strongly as a person of color. It's whether it's black, biracial, Puerto Rican, or what that the difficulty comes. It's never been a question of deciding. And I think part of that has to do with skin color: there's no way I could be white.

I definitely see myself having a biracial identity, so I know that just as much as my background came from Africa, it also came from Europe. I can't negate that part, to do that is to deny my mother and I feel that connection. But I do know that if there's something, like a parade, that is to celebrate the African side, and one to celebrate the Europe side, I'm not going to the Europe side; I'm going to the other side. When anybody asks me, I usually say, "I'm a black Puerto Rican who happens to have a white mother." That's what I do. Most people, they're used to being able to say, "I'm Puerto Rican," "I'm black," or "I'm white." And not everyone falls into that. I have a problem when people are oblivious to it, and they make little comments never realizing that I am all three.

I know a relationship is intimate because there's a certain level of trust. That feeling of being able to basically talk about any number of things—maybe not everything, but any number of things that are difficult. At least for me. Intellectually, there's something there too, sometimes. If we're talking about friendships, or relationships that are nonparental, of course, nonfamilial, there has to be some kind of stimulating thing going on there for it to be intimate for me. Then of course, if you're talking about relationships, well, then you have a certain amount of sexual intimacy, which has to be there.

Sexual activity to me is when it's just sexual activity. There's no strings attached, no connections. But then sexual intimacy for me is more like where there is sexual activity but there's more of a connection there. It doesn't necessarily mean you're in a traditional relationship where you're actually seeing each other. For some people, it could just be like, "Look, call you up . . . Yes, I want to . . . All right." And you two are friends also. That's intimate to me, too. If I don't want to talk to the person afterwards, that would be nonintimacy. Talking and communicating, sharing—those all have to be there for it to be sexual intimacy for me—and, of course, the physical part.

I think vulnerability is something you have to worry about in every relationship. You're always putting yourself out there, and if it's sexual, even more so, I think. You are exposing yourself to somebody else, and they choose to do with it how they want. Vulnerability is just when you feel really exposed, really open, and, to use a clinical social-worker word, uncontained. Just where you feel really exposed. If one of the persons does something that breaks the other's trust or confidence, that breaks intimacy. I don't even know if that's the correct word in English. *La confianza*. What if it's that they cheated on you, or you on them? Or even something physical—they hit you, you hit them, something like that? That could also break an intimacy, I think.

Who do I feel closest to in life? I haven't thought about that. It's hard because you're close to different people. Automatically, my girlfriend. My partner, actually. I would go to her right away. I couldn't imagine going to anybody else. This is not to say, though, that there aren't some times when I feel she doesn't understand. Like if I want to talk about being biracial, which is a real difficult thing sometimes. She's from Guatemala. So it's different. She tries to understand, but it's not quite there. And I'm left feeling like she really didn't get what I was saying. She really didn't. I might have to talk to somebody else who is also biracial. But that doesn't mean I'm closer to that person than to her.

I identify as bisexual, not heterosexual. Although we play sometimes, she's like, "I'm not the lesbian, you are," and I'm like, "Naw, I'm not the lesbian, you are. I'm straight, I don't know what you're talking about." Both of us identify as bisexual. I knew since I was in elementary school. All those little crushes, they were on girls and boys. I was like, This is interesting, this is strange: Why do I like Suzy? But it wasn't something that necessarily troubled me then. I didn't really know; I was little.

And those little-kid sexual experiences, they were with girls and boys. Then by middle school, though, that's when it started becoming an issue. All of a sudden, people were learning the words. I didn't even know the word "gay" until I was in seventh grade. I found it out because I was called gay, and I didn't know what it meant. But I figured it out real quick. And then I had a hard time because I was like, "No, I'm not." And I tried to do all the hiding things: I got myself a little boyfriend. Sixth through ninth grade, I had a boyfriend, but at the same time I was liking all these girls. And I realized that the boys didn't mean anything to me. So by ninth grade, then I just said, "Ahh, whatever," and I started mainly being interested in girls. I started dating a couple of women, actually, because they were a lot older than me, when I was in twelfth grade. Then when I went away to school, I got back in touch with that boy side. All of a sudden, I realized, Hey, wait a second, I am attracted to guys, I am. But it was hard because I did that the other way around, where a lot of people, they start out as bisexual and then they realize, I'm really gay, really lesbian. I had this huge, strong lesbian identity my first year in college. Then I was just like, Wait a second, why am I attracted to him? And I came to grips with that, was like, Wait a second, you know what? You are bisexual. But my primary interactions are with women. I'm not interested much in having a relationship with a man. But I am attracted to them.

A lot of people feel, "You've got to choose. No straddling the fence here." And that's hard. But I choose not to choose. The Puerto Rican side of the family knows nothing. And they must think I'm the most studious woman alive because I'm just waiting. I'm waiting to get my degree before finding a man. So I think as soon as I'm done, they must expect I'm going to get married. But it's not going to happen. Not in the sense that they're talking about.

My mother and I, we didn't talk about it when I was younger. I remember once she made a comment and said something like, "I hope you're not going to be like so-and-so. I hope you're not going to be gay." Because I was a tomboy all the way. And I remember saying, "No, no, I'm not going to be like that." But inside I was saying, I am like that, Mom. That was hard. I didn't talk with anyone about it until I was a sophomore in high school. I told someone who was a really close friend of mine, and who's Mormon at that. I don't know what I was thinking. I thought, that intimacy thing. She's a friend, and all that. And she was. For about two weeks she didn't talk to me, no contact whatsoever. She didn't outright ignore me or anything like that, we just stayed away from each other. And then she finally talked to me, and she was like, "I just needed time to think about it." She said, "Look, I love you as a friend. I don't understand it, and I don't like it, and it's wrong in the church, but I love you as a friend." And I was just like, "Okay."

It made me feel horrible. I didn't like it. "Well, I love you, but it's wrong." If you love me, there should be no "buts." You know? So from there I think our relationship started going down. It wasn't hostile in that we still talked every once in a while—we still do—but it obviously wasn't as close. So I was like, Okay, then I don't need her. I don't need that. And I moved on and talked with my best friend at that time who was a guy. And I finally came out to him because he kept trying to be with me, and I kept saying no. He was like, "What's wrong, what's wrong with me?" And said, "There's nothing wrong with you. Actually, it's on me. There's reasons." So finally I told him and he said, "Oh, okay."

My mother was very open in discussing sex. It was just heterosexual sex. I always knew who she was dating. I think I was definitely a child who has to sometimes take on roles that would be parental roles. I was my mother's confidante; I was my mother's friend almost in a sense, but it was very one-way because I couldn't share my things with her. And to this day, she'll call me up, "I got troubles with this and that." But now it's becoming more a two-way street.

I was the oldest child. I had to take care of myself and my sister. My mom was at work. And my mother needed someone to talk to sometimes 'cause things got hard, and I was there. I remember one time a conversation about some guy who was interested in her and she wasn't at all, and I just remember her saying something like, "Ah, I couldn't imagine having sex with him!" She would say these things, and I knew what they meant.

That conversation did stick out in my mind. I thought my mother was cool because she wasn't afraid to talk about that. I knew that if I wanted to talk about anything sexual, I could go to her and talk to her about it. I couldn't talk about the homosexual parts, say, but I could definitely talk about the heterosexual. But I didn't, actually, because I was the kind of child that never really asked questions. My mother is a very loud woman. So to get a word in edgewise is kind of hard, unless you specifically say, "Mom, I have something to ask." She's a great woman, but there are some things about her. She's very loud, and I'm not. That could be a personality thing; I may take more after someone in my family who's just very quiet. But it's interesting because I can be very loud if I want to, and I can be very opinionated. But with my mother, I would just quiet down and shut up because there was no room to really do that. She was just the boss—she knew yes and no and right and wrong. It was very obvious. And the things I really wanted to ask questions about, I knew those were not things I could talk about, and those two things were crushes on girls and being biracial. I knew the two topics that were most important to me I could not talk about. I already explained how I knew not to talk about being sexually attracted to women to my mom. And the other one—well, that one started coming out when I was a little bit older. But before that, when I was really young, it wasn't even a question. I just knew that Mommy looked this way, Daddy looked that way, I came out looking more like Daddy, and that was it. It wasn't an issue. It's only hard when society starts to say that it's wrong or that you have to choose. I was fine when I was younger, but then all of a sudden, little by little, people were saying things like, "What are you? You're this, you're that." And I'm thinking, No, I don't think so.

I learned by silences. I think children learn sometimes that there are certain things you shouldn't discuss or talk about because parents never bring it up. It was never brought up, so I knew that being biracial was going to be a tough one. And so was growing up predominantly with a white family because once my father was out of the picture, it was white all the way. So I'd go to attend any kind of function, and I was the darkest person there. That doesn't exactly make for feeling very safe or comfortable.

Oh, I remember my mother pulled me into my room. She said, "Come here, I want to talk to you." So we sat down. I remember she was sitting on my sister's bed, I was sitting on my bed. And she was, like, "I wanted to talk to you about the fact that you're going to become a young lady soon." And I'm just looking at her like, What are you talking about, Mom? I think that must have been when I was in sixth grade. I think it was right about then, I remember, that I started wearing a training bra, and all that kind of stuff, started to develop a little more. So she started talking about it, and she was like, "You're becoming a young lady, you know. Your body's changing. And when young girls become young women, they start to have their periods," she said. And I was like, "What's that?" She was the first person I'd heard that from. I didn't know what that was, I didn't know. And she said, "What's going to happen is, you're going to start to bleed." I was like, "I'm gonna start to bleed? I don't want to bleed!" But she was like, "I don't want you to get scared because it's nothing to be scared of. This is natural. And what I want you to do is I want you to come and I want you to tell me. And then I'm going to give you what you need to wear," and this and that. I was kind of scared, but you know that sense of a thrill also? Kind of like, Wow, I'm gonna become a young lady, and you're waiting for that moment to come. You're thinking, Is it going to happen now or tomorrow or what? And once it happened, I didn't want it to come back anymore, let me tell you.

And I remember her telling me, "This means you're going to have to be careful." I remember her saying something about sex. I don't remember it all that clearly; I think it might have been because I wasn't interested. I really think that might be why I've just blocked it out, because I didn't care. Now, if she'd been talking to me about girls, that would have been a different story. But she said something about sex, I think, and that this is when a young lady can become pregnant. But we didn't talk about how the whole sexual activity works. I already had some ideas because, hey, I watched TV, and school, you know.

But when I did get my period, though, in eighth grade—I remember it was in gym class—I was petrified. All that talking for nothing. She talked all about it and I was scared. It wasn't even that I was necessarily just scared; I was embarrassed. Who was I going to go to and tell them I got— that I was bleeding? So I just took care of it myself. And then I went home and I told my grandmother. I didn't tell my mother, I told my grandmother. We'd sleep over there, my sister and I sometimes. So I told her and she, I think, gave me money to go get stuff. Sanitary napkins. I can't remember exactly what happened after that, really. I don't know. I think my mother just bought me some more stuff, and I think I remember her smiling, like being all happy or excited. I think she gave me a hug. And I was just like, This isn't joyous.

And then to top it all off, I remember maybe a year later, when it was still a very new thing to me and I still didn't like it, she told me that my cousin became a young lady. I said, "What do you mean?" She's like, "She got her period too." I was like, "Why are you telling me this?" I was so embarrassed. And then it dawned on me—"Mom, did you tell my Aunt Stephie that I got my period?" And she said, "Of course!" I was like, "I can't believe you did that." That's when I realized that mothers talked to each other about their children. And I was so embarrassed.

Being a woman, sexuality is definitely very important because I know this society runs very much as a patriarchy, very much as male-identified, and I think it's time that women reclaimed their sexuality, personally. I think women have been kept from expressing themselves freely, and I think that's a problem. But as a woman of color, I think it's important, too, just because of the whole way that we are perceived. And I want to be able to claim my own sexual identity. I don't want somebody saying, "You're over-sexed," or "You're not sexed enough." It's like, whatever, I'm just me. I don't know, I guess I'm very aware of the stereotypes that are out there: the hot-blooded Latina, the oversexed black woman. I don't agree with that.

I'm always conscious of being a woman who is also a sexual being. And I'm always conscious of my sexuality in whatever setting I'm in, particularly if it's very male. I don't know exactly how to explain it, but it's something that's always there. Whenever you're in a setting and it's predominantly male, it always means that flirting stuff goes on, this back-and-forth type of thing. I'm aware of it. I notice it's different, though, if I'm in a very white setting. If I'm in a white setting, I feel very sexless—if that makes sense—like nonsexual. It is like my sexuality doesn't exist, like I don't exist in that way, that they would never consider dating or going out with me because I don't fit that stereotype of what's beautiful in the United States. That's how I feel. For instance, all throughout high school, aside from that little boyfriend I had from sixth to ninth grade, I didn't have any boyfriends. I wasn't interested in any white boys. To tell you the truth, there was one white boy that I absolutely thought was just beautiful. He turned even more fine as years went on. He did. All the girls liked him. And the woman he chose to be with at that time was a blonde-haired, blue-eyed woman like himself. I was very aware of that. I remember feeling that I had not a chance because of the fact that I was a person of color. I was not a white person, I was not a white woman. And I think that really affected me. I was like, I don't want to be interested in them. After him I was like, *psh*. Whatever. The only white guys I might find attractive now are the ones I find on TV that are models or something. But other than that, I stayed away from them.

# Carliese

*I* JUST TURNED FORTY in May, and that has been a big issue with me. I work at a hospital—I'm a technician on a cancer unit. I've been working there for ten and a half years, and I've been working in a hospital for twenty years. I'm separated, in my second marriage. I'm from a family of seven children, and I'm third from the oldest. I have two older brothers and then me, so I'm the oldest girl. I was brought up in a military family, very strict. One of the terms that me and my brother have come up with was it was like a concentration camp. I was born in Alabama, and we moved frequently when I was growing up. There was a lot of prejudice because of being the only black in the whole class, and a lot of times my family was the only black family in the whole school. We would just move right in the middle of a school year and I remember one time the principal getting on the speaker—he didn't think that we had gotten there yet—and I think back then he said "Negro," "A Negro family will be coming to school here, and I want everybody to treat them good and be cordial," or whatever the term was. So I remember that, and it was hard, it was very hard. It affected my life greatly. My father was in the military. He was an alcoholic. Growing up he was an alcoholic, and right now he's celebrated twenty years of sobriety. It affected my life tremendously. I'm at the point now where I'm trying to overcome that and it has been a struggle. It affected me the most as far as feelings. I've never been one to open up, never just able to open up. Being brought up in a military family, you were told what to do and you did it. There was no question about why or later. It was just "yes sir, no sir," point-blank. And if he asked you a question and you weren't able to answer it, you had to stand up there until you answered it, if it took a half an hour or an hour. It affected my ability to express how I feel. Very, very much so.

My mom is a twin. Her mother died when she was born. So she had her twin sister, and then an older sister who's ten years older than she is, and so that sister brought them up. And she had a grandmother that brought her up. My mother's very, very important to me. She's my life; I love her deeply. We're real close. I think I might be the apple of her eye, and I think it might be the conflict with the other siblings, whereas I think that we just have a lot in common. And I felt her struggles growing up, with my father. And I can relate.

I believe in God. I used to wonder what my calling was, and I know that now, working in that clinic for ten and a half years, just being right there. Right now I'm at the point where people say, "Carliese, how can you work on that floor? It must be depressing." It's not depressing because I don't see it like that. I see it as helping people, and I'm getting just as much from them as I'm giving.

We went to church. It was a regular Baptist church with the whooping and hollering, and really not understanding, but just the motions. My mother, she would cry in church, and I would always relate it to pain. I never related it to her being happy.

I think right now being in a relationship with a man is real hard. It's real hard for me to peel myself, expose myself, like layers of an onion. I don't think that I have as yet been able to do that totally. With my job, as far as patient relationships, it's real easy. Patients tend to connect with me, especially older people. I love them and they're real wise and I listen to them. They'll always tell you something that's going to be beneficial for your life, and I look at it like that. With men or friends, I worry about being hurt, being misinterpreted.

I was a virgin when I met my first husband. He was in the military. I guess I was probably about twenty, twenty-one years old. And when I met Marcus, he was getting ready to get out the military. He went back to his home, which was a few states away, and we communicated for a year and a half over the phone. I knew that I loved him before I even had any type of contact with him. And I think that he knew that I was really needy and emotional, and he played that role—being what I wanted to him to be, a supportive listener. When we got together after a year and a half, I had my own apartment, and he moved in with me, which was very, number one, against my morals. I allowed him to take advantage of me. He used me. I was working. He would keep my car and pretend like he was looking for work and he wasn't. He would do things like play cards and use drugs— marijuana back then—drink beer, and the circle of friends that he had was just the same type of people that he was, and I was not. I was not like that. I was a hard worker, and I enjoyed just being home in the evenings with him. And he was not that type of person.

When I first got out of high school, I went to Job Corps and I got a trade in nursing. Then I went back home, and my parents was going through divorce at that point. My father wanted me to come live with him, and my mom wanted me . . . automatically thought that I was going to come live with her. So I had to fight to get my own apartment, which was the best thing I could do because at that time—I think I had to have been like twenty, twenty-one, nineteen, something like that—I was making a car loan and taking care of an apartment on a minimum salary. It was hard, and I felt good about that. So when I allowed him to move in, I was just completely taken advantage of emotionally. I remember one night we went out to a club and I had two drinks, zombies, that was real powerful drinks. I had never been a drinker, but I had two zombies. So when we got home about nine o'clock that evening, I was real relaxed. And I woke up about two, three o'clock to use the bathroom, and he was gone. My car was gone, and this apartment that I was living in had a dead-lock bolt, and he had locked me into the apartment. I had to call my landlord to get out because I had to go to work the next day. I don't know why I didn't have the key. He had the key.

So when I went to work that day, I had to take the bus. And when I got home that evening, he was just passed out on the floor. Dropped, just seeping with alcohol. I had just got paid that Friday. Back then I think I was making like $170 or $180 every two weeks. Apparently, I did not trust him, so I had my money in my trunk of my car after I had paid my bills. Got my car keys from him and went to the trunk of my car, and my money was gone. But his leather coat was in the trunk. And I asked him where was my money, and he just said, "I don't know. Somebody must have stole it." But his leather jacket was still in there. So at that point I remember my father coming over, he said, "Carliese, either one or two things can happen with you. You're going to either bring yourself down to Marcus's level and go down, or you're just going to have to get out this relationship." And I was not ready at that time to get out; I was emotionally attached. I remember calling his mom and sharing with her what had happened because at that time I wanted him to go—even though I was emotionally attached. And he started crying, and I was not even married to him. He started crying, and I look back at it now—those tears was weakness for me, and I couldn't take it. So I let him stay. Ended up getting married anyway. I was involved with him for ten years. Ten years.

And something worse than that happened. We was working at the same hospital, the same hospital I'm working at now, and he and this woman that he was working with both clocked out one day. She drew twenty thousand dollars out her bank, and they just left the state. I kid you not. You may think this is not true, but I found the information out from two people standing in the hall talking. I found out that he had left. And to make it so bad, I had just started working at the hospital, and nobody knew my character; they didn't know what I was about. And they kept mentioning the twenty thousand, and they felt like I was a part of their scheme. The apartment we were living in was right across the street from the hospital. And while I was at work, somebody broke in the apartment, looking for the money. And the reason why I know they was looking real hard was because I put twenty dollars inside a sanitary napkin box. They found that twenty dollars, so that's how hard they were looking.

He left then. They stayed in Tennessee for six months, and she bought him a truck. He called me; I took him back. I took him back. I had always felt that he was my everything. You know, the sun rose and set on him. And even though I was miserable and I was going through pure hell, I'll never forget it when he came back and we had sex for the first time after that. I knew then that it was over. Because the emotional attachment was not there, and the physical attachment was real strong. I knew that it was over. But it took me, I think, about a year, to wean myself from him. I had to literally wean myself emotionally.

In my family, there was spoken rules and then unspoken rules, and you knew not to ask. Like, if you were talking to boys, you were considered fast. I had no connections with guys. My mom, she was real strict about that. She had a big yellow folder, something like that, yellow papers, and she would make rules. I was the first girl that had a menstrual cycle at twelve, and she would specifically write rules: what I would do, and not to accumulate sanitary pads—I had brown paper sacks that I would have to put them in—and to clean myself. She was real specific and detailed. She told me what to look for and how it would come, what I would see when I menstruated. This was before it happened, because she prepared me a couple years prior. I was scared; I wasn't ready for it. I didn't want that. I wished I was a boy, that I wouldn't have to deal with that.

I was attracted to boys, but I didn't feel like they thought me attractive. And we would switch schools so much. I stayed in the same place from tenth to twelfth grade, and I just was not connected with those people. I was just real particular. I had my eyes on one guy, but I didn't explore it, or write him letters. I saw that guy a few years later, and I told him that I'd had a crush on him in high school. At that point he was married. But he was real surprised.

I had sex for the first time with Marcus before we got married. It was not powerful because it was, wham, bam, thank you, ma'am. After, he got up and went to be with some guys. It hurt, it hurt, and I didn't enjoy it. It was just basically something I was doing for him. There was nothing there as far as my pleasure. We had sex within a month or so after he moved in with me. I know he didn't pressure me. I felt it was just the thing to do—you know, in order to keep him. It didn't really ever get any better.

This might just be my scenario of it—but he was so large. I didn't have anything to compare with, but he used to work at a place where they would kill hogs and they would have to take showers after each day so he said the guys were saying, "Man, you sure are big," or something like that. That's how I knew that he was big. It always hurt when I had sex with him. I would tell him to slow down, and he would draw back. But it still hurt. I don't know if he was touching something, my ovaries, or what.

I was never able to have children. Back in '92 I had to have a complete hysterectomy. I had a thyroid tumor that was eight pounds inside my stomach. I don't know if there's a connection since we had tried to have kids but couldn't. But I know now, because I've communicated with him, that he has two sons since we've been apart. I had got on birth control and I was gaining too much weight. Then I tried the foam and that didn't work for me. With the pills, I was gaining too much weight. I figured that if I had children, one child at least . . . But I felt like this man was dependent; there was too much emotion there. I was glad I didn't have them in a way. Looking back at it.

I had orgasms through the oral sex but not through intercourse. He was very generous with that. Too generous, because I was not really in tune to my physical side, and it was overwhelming. And I think he kind of liked that. The climax would get so that I could hardly stand it. So he would hold my arms, hold them down to keep me from pulling his head away. I enjoyed it, but then it was too overpowering. Because I didn't know how to express my feelings, but I wanted to say, "If you could slow it down, maybe I could enjoy it more." But I was never able to say that. That's the bottom line. I was just not tuned into my sexual needs, and even though we were in the bedroom I didn't have it in me to say it. I think he had that bit of control.

I've never been with a whole lot of guys—four in total. With two, everything was just connected there for me, and I enjoyed it. Very much so. It was like a relationship where that was the common bond. We would just get together and have sex and not worry about the outside problems. I enjoyed it and he enjoyed it. That type of thing. This was between my first and second marriage, and it wasn't really a long-term thing. Just a few months.

It was exactly ten years since the hospital incident, when I had another bad experience. And his name is Marcus, too. I've been married for about a year or so. I met him five years ago, and he was a drug addict. Back then I think it might have been marijuana, and now it's crack, crack cocaine. So the same scenario, and the pain, emotional pain was deep. And it's because of the choices that I made in those two years.

The last time I had sex with my second husband was May of last year. From that time to this time, I've had one sex relationship. My second husband had brought me one of those vibrators, so that's what I've been doing in between. This second husband, I learned a lot from him. The sex with him was great. He brought out a lot of feelings that I didn't know how to express.

I'm kind of sexually attracted to Latino men. My friend is half Latino. I met this guy at my job—we have a little construction going on, and he's a painter there. They paint on contract and then leave. I was very attracted to this guy, and I guess he must have felt that I was real needy because—it was right in between Thanksgiving and Christmas—he came to the house. We did some heavy petting, and I felt okay with that because I'm kind of new at that. But I didn't want to go all the way, though. I think my whole life has been real conditioned and very organized and systematic, and now I'm just trying to get more laid back. Open up. And not to hurt anybody or myself, because I know about AIDS and I take care of patients like that, but just explore. Safely. It's real important.

I think it would have to be a give-and-take thing. I think I would look at it more as what I needed and not specifically what they needed, open up and get my needs met. At this point I think that I have a guard up and I know that I need to stay away from men that have all these negative drug habits. Having conversation with them is fine, but not wanting to change their lives and go through that whole scenario. Because I know that I'm a pretty laid-back person. I like to work and take care of myself, enjoy life, enjoy home, enjoy relationships. It's important for me to have a one-on-one husband-and-wife type relationship, but I know that I just need to make sure that the relationship is right.

It is difficult because of the relationship that I've had with my father and the way he is. I'm not even communicating with him since last November. And that's been real hard because basically, we're a real close family and we talk. And part of my siblings are living right here in town, up the street. The last time we talked, my father hung up on me because I was open and honest with him, and he started to break down and cry when I was sharing with my feelings with him, and I pushed back, and I shouldn't have. Now those feelings are coming back up, and I need to talk. This last time, he was saying, "I've paid my dues." I think he has a lot of guilt.

One thing I never put up with was hitting. My first husband slapped me one time. I was taking him to the store or something and he slapped me. They always knew not to do that. I was like, Don't hit me, I won't hit you. I was always scared of hurt and pain, so I never put up with that, that's one thing I can say. After we got through arguing, I took him to the store and left him there. He thought I was going to wait on him, and I left him there, and I went and stayed with my mom for a couple days. I never had that problem again. He would throw things; the emotions would be there so heavy, it would be just like hitting. Like this second husband, he would do things like throw a cup of Kool-Aid at the TV or bang his fists on the walls or raise his voice. The emotional stress would be just as devastating as the physical. My body would go through the same changes as if I was hit, as far as the emotional part of it. But I never sustained blows.

Now my father, he tried to have sex with me—it was verbal a couple of times. Let me see, I think when I was thirteen years old. He was like drinking and he tried to have—ask me to come in bed when my mom— she had gone to the store. And when she came back, I told her about it,

and she said that he was drunk and he really didn't know what he was doing. Kind of brushed it off. And then the time after that he kind of put his
hand on my leg—like, I don't forgive that—and saying he would give me a
lump sum of money if I had sex with him. I told him no. I didn't want to
do that. I think that was right in between when he was getting a divorce
and before I left the house when I was nineteen years old. We were driving.
I was just scared and nervous, and it was raining, and I remember I had
plaid pants on, I could see the reflection of his hand on my leg in the wind-
shield . . . And it was raining, and I remember being nervous and scared.

It's like a life-and-death thing—the life inside of me. My siblings, they
say, "Well, Carliese, why don't you just leave well enough alone?" As far as
talking to my father. A lot of times it's best to not even say, just do. Some
of them say, "You don't need to talk to Daddy. You already talked to him
and you know what happened." I just need to deal with some issues. Out of
seven children, I was the only one that turned out left-handed, and my father forced me to be right-handed. Ultimately, I'm still left-handed. But I
can remember the things that he did, such as tying my hand up when I
would eat my meals. He would put a mitten on my hand. And I was real
shy. I enjoyed sucking my finger; I sucked my two little fingers, and he
would powder my hands, with the mittens. He made me eat a raw onion
one time, stuff like that. So there's a lot of pain.

I think that black men in general don't take responsibility or do what
they need to do. I think that they're in a fog, and I think that the trust factor is real important, and it's not there. The men I have been in relationships with trust me totally. They could put a dime on me as far as my
dependability and my word. But I can't trust them. Instead of dealing with
the issue, it's always that power play of "You can't prove it. It's your word
against mine." I just think that black men in general just don't want to get
a life. I think that we as a whole have been dealt a bad hand as far as what
happened to our forefathers, but I think you reach a point in life where you
have to grab it and go for it, and not just sit there and say, "Well, I'm just
gonna have this pity party and drink and get high all the time." I don't
think it should be like that.

I think men, they're kind of like dogs, to use the expression, because they know, especially with me, the vulnerability and the neediness. I think what I'm looking for is what I didn't receive from my father, and they know how to conquer that and kind of play with it. And then when it's time for them to get with me, they're just going to go ahead and take advantage because the emotional attachment is so great at that point. I think there's some good guys out there. I always attract the knuckleheads for some odd reason. I do. But I think there's some good guys out there. They're just real hard to find.

What I expect at this point? I would like to be in a relationship where men would just hold up their side of the bargain, and just be truthful and honest and just upfront and trustworthy. I know that I am, and I just need that. I think, because a couple of people have told me this, you want life to be so perfect, life is not perfect. And that's where I'm trying to be more open and not so predictable.

I don't think society has affected my sexuality. I don't look at it like that. I look at it like we're all individuals, and as long as it's connected with the man upstairs, God, I can do whatever I want to do. I don't look at it as society has blocked it. I feel like I've been short-changed as far as not being able to grab at or leave those type of men alone. That's why from forty on, I want to make some good choices. I think I deserve it. And it's hard to hear me say that. The brainwashing, being brought up in that type of alcoholic environment where you're just told too many negative things, it was just so hard to say that I deserve something good.

I've never been able to connect with black ladies because of the choices I've made, because of my upbringing, and not feeling that I was a part of it. Like this group of friends I have now, we've bonded real tight. It's the most beautiful thing in the world, but getting to that point was real hard. It was like, I don't want to be part of this, and I don't want to expose myself. I think it's because of issues of being hurt so badly by men. Because I've never been a gay or homosexual or nothing like that, but sometimes I think about it. Don't fantasize about it, but I've thought about the couple that

I've been real close to and I think, Now, if I could find a *man* like this, I would be all right. I'm not attracted to women sexually, but I do look at them like I would want their traits in a man.

In terms of images, I think that, especially in the movies, black women have to act a certain way and be a certain size and do certain things. I mean, the sexual part is really important. If they're not acting a certain way, they wouldn't be in the movie. Light-skinned, and real small size. And have that whitish look—they always have to have straight hair. Images of black women in the media culture don't look like regular black women. I think it's real hurtful because even when I went to this all-black school one time they would talk about me being dark-skinned. I was just not accepted. Even in my group of friends now, I am the darkest one. I'm quite sure they probably haven't noticed it, but I've noticed it.

I have been in situations where if I saw a light-skinned woman or a dark-skinned woman and we were sitting in a room waiting to be seen or something like that, I would probably pay more attention to the dark-skinned woman. It probably wouldn't be consciously, if I thought about it, but I would identify more with her. I feel like light-skinned women would say, "She's not pretty enough," or "Your skin is too dark." Like, in the waiting room, this female was there, and I started talking to her. But normally my first thought was, I don't think I'm going to talk to her because she probably don't want to talk to me. But once we started talking, it was fine. I think if she was dark, I probably would have just gone in and jumped in there.

I don't like real dark-skinned men. I've always been attracted to brown-skinned. Not light light, but I married both times and it was like that. I never was attracted to real dark-skinned guys. Black men seem to prefer light-skinned women. Like right now, if I went to a party and guys would be there, I would feel like this woman may be an airhead, but she may be a size six and brown-skinned and curly hair, and they would be more apt to ask her to dance than me. My heart may be like my heart is, but they wouldn't see that. And that would hurt. Just like when I used to go out to clubs. We would be with girls around the table, and the guys would come and ask the girls to dance. They wouldn't ask me, you know. They would ask her, and she would turn them down, and they would go around the table, and I would say no, too. But I would never be the first one they would ask. It's something you don't talk about, but you know it.

| *three* | ALWAYS SOMETHING LEFT TO LOVE |
|---------|-------------------------------|

*I*N THESE NARRATIVES the women keep their focus on what pleasures and possibilities tomorrow might bring. Many of these women demonstrate a well-developed capacity to think beyond the current moment and imagine a new possibility. Theirs are not optimistic dreams for a happy ending; they are experienced, sometimes determined kinds of hope. Recalling her most recent and most important boyfriend, Anondra says, "I'd just rather focus on the positive and remember all the good things that we had in our relationship. This is like the best experience I've ever had with a man, and if it's the best experience I've had with a man, I want to keep it."

Queenie pins her hope on gaining more knowledge and a sense of possibility. She feels that "if your environment feeds you a negative, limited sense of who you are, that impacts your relationships . . . It's about exposure, not about money. Take me to the park with a picnic candlelight dinner, take time to find not an expensive wine, but something nice—or it doesn't even have to be based on alcohol—find a cider and heat it over a fire. Exposure takes your mind out far enough to research those things."

Both Rhonda and Millie believe that hearing and sharing their own voices and the voices of other women, especially of black women, will keep them moving forward. Rhonda: "Hearing my voice is important to me. I need to hear my voice in order to continue to feed myself and give myself the strength to go forward. And I need to hear the voices of my other sisters. So, every opportunity I get, I sit down in sister-girl groups." Millie: "Hopefully, in the future, I'll have a lot more voice. . . . Every time you talk about yourself, you think other things about what you talked about. So it has had the impact of making me think again about what's going on in my life. That's good."

# Rhonda

*I*'M THIRTY-FIVE years old. I'm from Iowa originally. I came here to Washington, D.C., to go to law school. I wanted to get out of my home state, and I wanted to go where there were black people. I am deeply committed, with no children. In terms of my family, there is Mom, Dad, an older brother, Jay, an older sister, and a younger brother, Rodney. We're the two-family thing because there's five years between myself and my older sister. My mother was a paraprofessional, a teacher's aide in the public schools; my father had a bunch of jobs. He was a CPA at one time, and he worked for the NAACP, the auto industry, and then he got his MBA and started to work for the city. He retired—well, he was fired—from his position in city development. He's also a reservist, and he retired from the reserves as a major general. Both parents are black and from the South.

My mother thought Baptists stayed in church too long, so we became Lutheran when I was very young. She took her spiritual guardianship very seriously, and we were required to attend church whether we liked it or not, whether we believed or not, until we were eighteen, if we were going to live in her house.

---

As an activist, I am constantly battling, I'd have to say in particular white males, but black males as well, about who I am as a black female and what that means to me—what that perspective means to me, fighting what I consider to be dismissive behavior on their part. And I think a lot of it is about not enough being known about the silences that we've built around. Audre Lorde is one of my sheroes, and I don't believe that silence will save us. So it's my belief that the more we talk about it, the more we can get out. And if I can help my younger sisters, this is a very good thing. I work at the juvenile court, and daily I see sisters dying from the silence, and it's painful. So my belief is that the more of us talk about it, the better.

Intimacy is trust. It's the belief that I can share myself, good, bad, or indifferent, and that you may not like it, you may not approve of it, but you're not going to slam me for it, and you're going to accept what I have to say and keep it confidential, if that's part of the relationship. That we have a basis for communication. To get there, there's actually two stages for that. There was a time when I trusted no one. I had no clue what intimacy was, and if you told me what it was, I didn't care. Over time, I learned there's still two ways for that to happen. One is that I instinctively know that I can trust someone, and I'm very seldom wrong. I trust my gut instinct about a person. We may later have a falling-out, but I'm comfortable with that falling-out because I know that what has gone before will not be betrayed. The other is just sort of a comfort level, being around that person, talking to that person. Early on I used to do little things, say little things to see if it would come back to me. I would send out a fib. No truth. This is a test. If it came back to me, in any permutation, then I'd know that somebody had said something about it, and if you were the only one I told, then it was you. That would be that. But now I take a leap of faith, and I trust first, and I just hope that it is right. Another thing that breaks intimacy would be insensitivity to something that we had discussed. Example: I'm an incest survivor. So if I shared that with someone, and we're having a conversation and they are blasé or insensitive about a similar issue, knowing that we've had this communication, then I have that whole betrayal thing that kicks in as well. And then I'm pulling back. Either you weren't listening to me, or it didn't matter. Either way, it's a negative. I don't think that's something you forget about a person. And I guess, given that in the past that is something that I haven't shared easily, if I have said it then it was clearly important for me, and if we're building that kind of intimacy, then those are the kinds of things that you try to remember.

I feel closest in my life now to my current partner. I think we have the healthiest relationship I have by far had in my life. At times I'm astounded by it—I can't believe it, I have to check, you know. But we communicate freely; we have a great deal of trust.

I identify as a dyke. My first memory about it was recognizing that all of my associations where I felt comfortable were with girls, or women. I was thirteen or so, and my sister had Psych. 101 or something, and I wrote her and said, "Oh, my God, I'm queer." And she wrote back and said, "This is normal for adolescents. Go to a library, get out a book, read it. You'll feel better. It'll be all right." I heard her, but I didn't think it was true. And it wasn't, and I knew that. It was comfortable for a minute. And then I was concerned that because at the time I was still being abused that I just didn't want to have anything to do with men. That was my way of dealing with it. When I got to be about fifteen and I still wanted to have nothing to do with men and actually found nothing about them attractive at all, then I was pretty clear. So then it was just a question of how do I deal with this. I actually went to my older brother and older sister again. She was just like, "Well, you don't have to do anything about it right now. Just chill out." My older brother was like, "Just don't tell your mother." Well, I later found that he had his own issues, but that's another story. So I didn't tell my friends, but I think they all knew. We had never talked about it, although interestingly enough, the two women who became my best friends at that time both came out during college as well. We called ourselves the Three Musketeers. So I just picked this guy to be my boyfriend. We talked on the phone periodically. We never went out, never kissed. Everybody just assumed he was my boyfriend. I was a gym rat because I was a jock, so I spent all my time in the gym; and there were a bunch of us, but we were never naming it or claiming it. So at that point, I was nonsexual. I have thought a million times about why this guy agreed to be my fake boyfriend and I haven't a clue. He didn't have many friends; he was kind of a strange person. We didn't even have a lot of friendship and intimacy. Later he got married and had children. His sister tells me he's doing really well. I haven't a clue. I still think about him periodically.

I played basketball, softball, soccer, shot put and track, and volleyball. All dykes hang out in the gym. My high school was one of the largest in town. The year after I graduated, they integrated. When I went there, it was almost all white. The cover boyfriend and the other two Musketeers were black, so we had a small community in this almost all-white school. The Musketeers, we never came out to each other, and in fact they had covers as well.

My younger brother and I—the start date is vague, maybe he was eight and I was nine. We're eighteen months apart, so maybe I was ten. But the abuse was ongoing. And in my house it was about power. He and I now have a very close relationship. And he has never apologized. We have never directly discussed it, although I did talk about it with my parents and my older siblings. Because I was the smartest, and I was the sweetest or whatever, and it created difficulties because my dad was a workaholic. So power over my body was the only power my brother Jay had in the house for a very long time.

I think it probably started with playing doctor. And then at some point it was time to stop, and it didn't. At one point, he told me flat out, "They won't believe you." But by then I'd begun to act out. So they weren't going to believe me. And ultimately, when I told them as an adult, they didn't believe me. It went on until I was about thirteen or fourteen. I took a Louisville Slugger, wrote his name on the top, told him if he ever touched me, I'd kill him. And that was that. He was never actually penetrating me, which for a long time I was in denial that this was even relevant, that it was in any way important. Because there hadn't been any penetration, and my understanding of abuse was penetration.

I'd be asleep, and I'd wake up and he'd be on top of me in the bedroom. I'd be in the bathroom and he'd come in the bathroom. He'd wait till my mother was gone and then chase me around the house and physically overpower me, which, after a while, since his growth rate was faster than mine, it wasn't difficult. After a while, he had told his friends. Now, I don't know exactly what he told his friends. I know that one night, my brother and I and a guy I'd grown up with in the church, we were downstairs playing pool. We'd been kids together, so it was no big deal. My brother pressed up against me, and he had an erection, and he said, "Come on, come on. You know you want to do this." And I was like, "Get off me, or I'm gonna hit you with the cue stick." I wrote my sister about that as well, which is the only sort of corroborating evidence I had when I told my parents. We had a cousin, who's a deaf-mute, who's a very physically powerful individual. And when my parents would leave, my brother would enlist his aid because after a while, I got pretty good at moving around, and I would fight back. As a jock, I wasn't exactly a wimp or anything. And the two of them. At some point, though, my cousin realized that I was fighting back much harder than whatever my brother Jay had communicated. And he would back off.

I didn't think my mother would believe me, especially because I had gone from being the perfect child. To this day, she still tells stories about how sweet I was, and then all of a sudden something changed. She has no clue what, but I became this harridan. You know, obstinate, disrespectful, I did what I wanted. I didn't buy the family line that your friends will all go away, but your family will always be there for you; it just didn't ring true for me. They'd have events; I wouldn't want to participate. By the time I was fifteen, I was getting drunk pretty much every weekend outside of the house.

When I came out to my mother at about eighteen, she told me, "How could you possibly know?" I was on my way to a friend's house, and then I was going to go pick up another friend from work. And on my way to my friend's house, this guy pulls up next to me in a car, and he starts rapping. He's kind of cute, and I'm like, Oh, this is all right. And then, in the back of my mind I'm saying. You just don't know, you just don't know. So okay, cool, we went and had drinks at somebody's house. And we were trying to do it on the floor. I was on my period, and he couldn't penetrate. Later I found out that there's a muscle that contracts if you're totally resistant. He could not penetrate. I consider that, though, when I lost my virginity. Such that it is. I wasn't trying to resist. It wouldn't open. He could not get in. I went home and told my mother, "Now I've tried it, and I'm still sure that I'm a dyke." She didn't want to hear it. It's like I never said it. Now she's actually aware of it. I have continually assailed her with the reality.

I made the mistake of getting pregnant at one time. When I was using drugs, I had periods of blackout. I don't know how many men I've had sex with. I couldn't tell you. Well, I turned eighteen; I decided I wasn't going to college. And I had taken money they had given me to send off applications. My senior year I needed a quarter of a credit to graduate and almost didn't graduate. Because I didn't care. And so I said, "I'm not going to college right away. I'm totally not ready; this isn't going to work." I had a job, and I went to work at my job full-time and started hanging out. Well, my older brother was smoking pot. He said, "You know, this can be dangerous. First time you try it, call me." I turned eighteen. I called him that day and said, "Okay, I want to try pot." So I went to a party with some of his friends. I got high there. Next day I called his girlfriend and said, "Okay, I want an ounce of that." And I rolled drugs like other people smoked cigarettes. Course I was also smoking cigarettes.

I was just working. Yeah, I had bought myself a car and was living at home. I had as little contact as possible with my parents and did what I wanted to do. Paid no rent, so I felt like, This is the life of Riley. While I was working at a restaurant, I was sexually harassed. And when I declined, I was fired. That was fine. I called up this college that had recruited me heavily. She said I could still come, so in January I started college. The school was just twenty-five minutes from home. No long trip. But I lived in the dorm. I kept smoking weed, I discovered speed, and I was still drinking very heavily.

I made dean's list my first three semesters. So my parents were like, "Whatever you're doing is fine because you're producing." I continued to be asexual. I was no longer looking for foils, although I dated a guy who was also gay, who's also my best friend now. But we didn't know at the time. Well, he didn't know; I knew. We didn't know about each other. I hadn't had sex with any women yet, but the fantasies, the imaginings—all of that was real. I used to write. And I had read *Well of Loneliness* and thought, This ain't me, but, I used to write stories and I'd write fairly fantastic things. When I was twenty-one, I burned everything I had written previous to that because I found out somebody was reading it. I'm not really sure who, but it was real clear to me that somebody had been in it. At one point, my brother Jay had been in it, and then I didn't know who else he might have shown it to. I used to tell people that was where I wrote out my pathology. And the writing was full of lesbian relationships. So I felt like I knew; I'd just never experienced it. I fell in love, fell in and out of love a couple times in college, but never did anything about it.

When all my friends graduated, I transferred to Iowa State. That was sort of the beginning—the first time I tried cocaine, the first time I tried acid, mushrooms, and the rest of the cornucopia. I was on the verge of flunking out, so I quit. I said I was bored. And I went to Utah for about six months and lived with a guy that I had dated, who later came out to me as well. I worked, did drugs. Dated a couple of women but never did anything. Fell in love but never did anything. He and I had a major falling-out. I came home. By now the drugs were pretty serious. When I was in Utah, I had been stealing from my job to support the cocaine habit. And they weren't aware of it, but I was starting to feel paranoid about being caught. It was a series of things. I was assistant manager of a pizza restaurant. I go back home, I don't admit the drug stuff, I don't accept it, I keep doing the drugs, and then I start doing drugs with Jay. He and I were like party buddies from hell. I started stealing. I had a series of jobs. In and out, in and out.

I had a friend who had been a friend in high school, and I chose her to be my first one. We had a very close and intimate friendship, so why not? I didn't tell her she was my first until I got sober, and she wasn't talking to me. I'm not sure why she stopped talking to me, but I think it was because I told her about the incest. Anyway, my parents were out of town. I lit a fire in the fireplace, and I got wine, and I put a blanket out in front of the fireplace. I must have been about twenty-three, twenty-four. Might have even been almost twenty-five. I got high on marijuana. And I sort of acted out what I had been writing, what I thought you were supposed do, part of which came from porno tapes because I'd never been there. I had no clue.

I don't know if I could say what we actually did do. She was more aggressive than I was, and I think that she saw it as me not forcing her, and I saw that as sort of getting cold feet at the last minute. She undressed me and then I undressed her, and we were kissing and petting during that time. I kissed her body because I thought, This is what I want to do, because by now I'm sort of into it. She was white, so I was making adjustments in my head, because I still remember thinking, I wonder what would be different about a black woman. I think I masturbated her to orgasm, and that was the first orgasm she'd ever had, so now she's very happy. We get up, we go in the bedroom. And being significantly slender at that time, partly due to the cocaine, I think, we were able to meld our bodies together. Then both of us had an orgasm, and it was nice. Then we fell asleep and woke up. But I did not wake up in a relationship, and she did. For me it was fun. I was like, "Let's go pick up the kids" (she had young siblings) or whatever it was we would normally do. We were friends. But she felt different, and she didn't like the drugs, and it got worse.

This is where my memory gets a little faded 'cause I was doing a lot of drugs. After Meg, I tried to sleep with Sharon, a woman who had been my roommate in college. But I couldn't go through with it because in college, she was in love with me. I had another roommate, actually, that I had a real crush on, and at one point they fought over me. And I'm going, I don't understand any of this because I'm not doing anything with anybody.

Nineteen eighty-seven is gone almost completely. I had a cousin who was supplying me with drugs and a nurse who was supplying me with this hookup for drugs. My aunts and everyone would just send me money because they knew I wasn't working. People just sort of supported me. I came back home. The drugs got even worse.

Every day, all day, I was using something. But I was managing to do a job, friendships. I came home one day, I saw my brother's car in the driveway, I saw my sister and my younger brother in the garage, I saw my dad's car, and I was like, This ain't normal. What's going on? I go in the house.

They found out that while my mom was down taking care of my grand-mother, I would take my dad's MasterCard out of his wallet, go to the bank machine, get money, bring the card back, go get drugs. They did an inter-vention. My dad knew somebody, and so I got to skip the waiting list, and off I go to a rehabilitation center. I did my thirty days in Shadowbrook, I came out, I used the day I got out, and then I got into this halfway house.

I went to the halfway house, did the halfway house sober and clean for about five months, and that's where I met Monica, who was my next lover and also my first black woman lover. I refer to her as my nightmare from hell. I wasn't attracted to Monica; I was attracted to the fact that Monica was attracted to me. It was amazing. Now, she can't tell me the time of day. I got put out of the halfway house. Because it was okay for me to be a les-bian in theory for them, but when I became a lesbian in practice, they hadn't a clue. And it made them uncomfortable because it was an all-women's halfway house. So they put me out. I had met Monica in a black lesbian support group that they encouraged me to attend. But once we started dating, neither one of us kept going to the support group. So we were together. I left the halfway house. I went to stay with another woman who had been in the halfway house but who had gotten out, who was back to using. So in no time at all, I was back to using. And I wanted nothing to do with Monica, who was also using.

Monica came looking for me at this other friend's house and said she had a place, you know, come live with her, and I did because the other friend's house was a pigsty, and it was constant traffic. This keeping-house thing sounded really attractive. So I did that. We were both using. We did something we shouldn't have done, and she got picked up by her PO [pro-bation officer] and got put on probation. So the next morning, the police came in and took her away. Left her son there with me, the whole deal. So I take the son, I call my parents and say, "Come get me." We take the kid to her mother's house, and then I go home. The PO told my parents, "Did you know that Rhonda and Monica were lovers?" Well, no, they didn't. So that was drama.

Lord only knows why, my parents never turned me in for any of the things I did. I went on a severe using binge, and I did some more illegal things. I stole from my parents because they were easy. I felt safe stealing from my parents. I took their card, and I was gone for a period of days. I think I kept taking cash advances, as much as I could get during any twenty-four-hour period. Eventually, the card didn't work, which told me they knew about me, and those bank machines take pictures. So, I talked to my dad, and he said, "You're going back into treatment, and you're going to go talk to the guy at MasterCard because this is a federal offense. And we won't press charges, but it's really up to them. This is a federal offense." So I went down there, and we talked, and he said, "You go right into treatment." And I'm like, "Fine, I'll go right into treatment." So I went right into treatment, again. They put me out of treatment. I got out of treatment and slept with a man. I haven't a clue why. I think I was looking for a warm place to sleep because at that point I had nowhere to go. I didn't know him at all. The sex was boring, totally uninteresting. I got up the next morning and went about looking for a place to call home.

I called my parents and whined my way back home. That didn't last long. I met another woman, Wendy, through another friend of mine in the program. We baby-sat a friend's child, and when the baby was asleep, we had sex. She woke up in a relationship, and I was like, Okay, whatever. I guess when you're using you are feeling lonely; you find someone and you try to grab hold, whoever that might be. Wendy also had a son, and then Wendy was three months pregnant at that time. So I stayed with Wendy. We got an apartment together; we played house for about a year.

We broke up because I had to go have my own abortion. I met a guy while I was with Wendy, who had a lot of money and a lot of drugs. There was contraception with him because he was actually very serious about not having children, because he had a family that he was separated from because of his own cocaine use. So he had a condom. I don't know what happened. I got up that night knowing I was pregnant. And I was at work one day where I was a housekeeper at this hotel and got sick cleaning a bathtub and knew that I was pregnant. So when I had morning sickness, I didn't get a pregnancy test; I went right out and scheduled the abortion. They did an ultrasound to ascertain not whether I was pregnant, but how far along I was. So we sat there, they got it on the screen, and somebody called her out of the room. I sat there looking at the child I still call Baby Rhonda while she was out doing whatever it was she had to do. I was sad, but I knew there was just no way in hell that I could bring a child into this world because I knew I wasn't going to stop using. And having a child was not going to be enough reason, enough motivation. I made a pledge to the soul of that fetus and said, "When my life gets together, I will come back to you, but I can't do this right now." That was the hardest part. I was sober for about two weeks after that, and then I went back to using.

I did go into rehab again. I was living in the same building. I had another lover. When I was living with Wendy, I met the woman downstairs. Her name was Christine. I fell in love with Christine and was in love for the first time in my life. But I was with Wendy, and I had some strange sense that I wasn't cheating on her, even though I had slept with these men. This was different. So I eventually left Wendy; we had a battering relationship. Originally she was beating me, and after a while I got tired, and I was beating her. And I was physically stronger. Then I realized that this was insanity and I couldn't do this. So I left her. I went back to my parents, and I started staying with my parents. I was working at a plasma center, so I continued that job. Then one day I decided I was going to go visit Christine. It was six weeks before I went back with her. Christine and I were together for three years. It was good in the beginning because it was exciting, but we had big fights.

It got to a point where she was beating me up, and I couldn't take it anymore. I snapped. So I'm screaming out the window, out the apartment door, I'm trying to get out, "Somebody call the cops. This crazy woman won't let me out." And then I just lost it, and I started fighting back. Then in the middle of it, she stopped and she laughed and said, "You've been holding out on me." And then we went back to fighting. When the cops came, we both went to jail. We were in jail for seventeen hours, thirty-six minutes. We were taken to the ADA's [assistant district attorney's] office, who was a woman. Christine explains that it was a mild misunderstanding, that we really love each other. And she lets us go—you know, "But don't come back." We go home, I run the tub, she makes us dinner, we eat, we lay down and go to sleep. I still have the tag that they put on my arm and the bag they put my shoes in, and she did too for a long time, because that was sort of going to be our line that we wouldn't cross again. But she actually did hit me again.

I went into recovery during that relationship, which is ultimately what ended the relationship because Christine was also an alcoholic. Her mother committed suicide when she was very young, and her sister had been pregnant by her father. Christine insisted that her father had never touched her, but it just didn't make sense, given what she had told me, that that didn't occur. So she was pretty dysfunctional, too. We would get high together. So I went into treatment again. She didn't want anything to do with me. And then I called the last night that I was in treatment and I said, "Please, can I come home?" And she said, "Yes." She never came to visit me; she never called me while I was there. And I was there thirty days. So I went home. Meanwhile, I was on the waiting list for another halfway house—a different halfway house, one that had a really incredible record. And at this point I really wanted it. I was tired of it. I got high for the last time on January 13, 1991. I got sober on January 15, 1991. The drug that I still miss is marijuana. Even though cocaine ravaged my life, I think my primary drug is probably marijuana.

I went home. We started up like we'd never left. We'd have—there was no intimacy at first. We were just having sex because we were supposed to have sex. But the relationship really improved. When it was time to go to the halfway house she was mad because things were so good. But I really wanted it, and so I left.

I wasn't feeling the sex. I was doing it just because she wanted it. And by then I had learned what made her happy. Penetration was very important to Christine. To this day, she has this thing she does with her thumb—I think it's double-jointed—she can make it vibrate. And this was supposed to have been pleasing to lovers she had had in the past. I never told her that I didn't like it. So I faked it; I faked it a lot. We'd do oral sex, but Christine had a real hard time coming to orgasm. So I would be doing this like twenty-five to thirty minutes. My neck would be sore, my shoulders would be sore, and then she'd start screaming at me because she'd say my heart wasn't in it. It's like, No, my heart's not in it, but I'm going to try to convince her that it is. That just went on for a long time. And she was cheating on me. I didn't know that then, but I know that now. I started to think she was faking orgasms because it was way too contrived; the timing was just too perfect all the time. And I just felt like, Well, I'm faking, so it shouldn't be so far-fetched that she'd be faking. Christine would have me masturbate in front of her, and I was afraid to do that because I thought, You're gonna know I'm faking. But she wasn't paying that much attention. But we were comfortable with each other.

For a while they let me out for visits. So sex actually was good for a while because it was a major event. When I got out, I'd come home and have sex. And then she was cheating on me, and I found out. So I was like, "To hell with you. I'm done with you." She talked me back into it. I went, I had a big fight with the woman who was my counselor, who told me, "Let go of Christine or get out of here." I told her, "I'm packing my bags." So I packed my bags and went home. And that's when I got high on the thirteenth of January. We were together about six weeks. I went out and used the rent; that was that. But she was really good to me when I came back. It was like this was all she wanted; she was happy now. I never had to clean the house; I never had to lift a finger. She was very warm, very pleasant. Because I always used to say, "The problem is, you always touch me when you want sex. You never touch me just to touch me." So then she'd start just hugging me, or rubbing her hands over my head, things like that.

So I thought, I've been sober now for about three months. I can do this. And then one day I was going to pay the rent and turned off on skid row. She had a fit. I hustled up the money for the rent, in part from my parents. Her ex-lover sent her a matching amount. She told me, "You're going back into the halfway house." And I said, "Well, you know what they said." She was like, "You're going back. I want you to get better." So we got high that night, and the next day I went back. Then I was under restriction: I couldn't see her; I couldn't talk to her, although I called her all the time. But they knew, and I would tell that I was calling. So over time it got less and less. Because at three o'clock in the morning, we'd be screaming at each other on the telephone because I knew she was cheating. So then I sort of gave in to the program, said, Fine. There was a woman in the halfway house about this time who had just come in and was black and was very, very sexy. Just oozing sensuality. She was attracted to me, told somebody the day she walked in that she was going to have me, whatever that meant. I was like, Okay, cool, fine. But not while I'm here because I already know: I'm the lesbian, so if something happens, it's my fault. And I know this, so we're not going to do this until I get out. But we would skinny-dip, and we weren't supposed to be skinny-dipping. All sort of borderline behavior in terms of healthy or unhealthy, as far as counselors were concerned. It was fun.

The best sex I ever had, up until Karla, who's my current partner, was masturbation. So I really didn't need a lover. I learned about it in the bathtub when I was seven or eight. By ten, I had my period. My mother came upstairs with a pair of my panties and said, "I told you to tell me when this happened." And I was like, "I'll wipe myself better." And she's like, "No, this isn't the end." And I said, "Well, what is it?" And that's how I found out about menstruation. She said we needed to go get the belt and we needed to go get the pads, and, "Dad, your baby's a big girl now." And I was just like, "Wait a minute, what is this?" She explained that every woman gets it, that it happens once a month, that I may or may not get these cramp things with it. Of course, when I got cramps, I began to understand. And that I should wash particularly well because it would have an odor.

After I found out what sex was from my classmates, I came home and said, "So, if I do this, I'll get pregnant?" And she said, "Do what?" "So if some guy takes his dick and sticks it in my pussy, I'll get pregnant?" And her response to that was, "Why are you talking like that?" The issue was not what I'd asked, but how I'd asked it. I finally got to see a movie at church, with the pictures and the animation, the whole deal, little sperm swimming to the egg. And that's how I found out about sex. It was part of Confirmation at about twelve, fifteen. I never directly found out about sex from my mother or father. The only way that I even knew that she and my father were having sex was one day I found a box of condoms. But it wasn't a conversation we ever had. And if they were going to have sex, inevitably they found a reason for us to leave the house. So when I came back and I was grown, my dad slipped me a twenty, and it wasn't too hard for me to figure out that it was time for me to go and come back very late. I had to leave the whole house. I didn't care.

For most of my life I thought that sex is how you connected with certain people; that how could you be in a relationship if you weren't having sex? I was supposed to like it. It made sense to me that I should. I enjoyed sex with Meg, but I didn't want to have anything to do with a relationship. In part, I think I started to connect good sex with a lack of a relationship. Sex and intimacy had nothing to do with each other. Now one hundred percent good sex equals intimacy. I think that has a lot to do with it. The ability to say, "I don't like that." Or, "Harder," and "Can we try this?" Karla and I got into experimenting with S&M. And that takes a lot of communication. We switch. She's a much better top, and I think I'm born a bottom. I'm the butch bottom. I'm not as good at being a top, and she's not as into being topped as she is into being the top. I think we're sort of settling into roles. We are commuting now; she lives in New York. The commuting gets pretty expensive. But the anticipation's fabulous. And we've talked about being a little worried about what happens when we're waking up next to each other every week.

I've been with Karla for a year and a month now. We met at a conference, and we just hit it off. My lover at that time was at home, but it was a relationship I was trying to get out of. We were all just hanging out in a group, and when we were leaving the hotel, she kissed me. She tells me, "That was a very profound kiss, Rhonda. I don't know where all of this came from." For whatever reason, it started the domino effect. I went to a mutual friend and said, "Tell me all about her." She went home and told her, "Rhonda's going to call you." I called her; we started having conversations; we talked on the phone probably an average of six hours a night, every night, until the first time I went to Philadelphia to see her. I'm there. I'm present in my body—feeling every sensation in a way that I had not been present in my body, that I consciously remember, because I'm sure I blanked it out with Christine.

The drugs was how I endured sex. I would go away, and my body would do whatever it was it wanted, it chose. I think it had to do with the party line about this great family thing that turned out to be, as far as I was concerned, a crock of shit. I wasn't safe in my house, so then I began to feel safe nowhere. My response to that was, Then no one is to be trusted.

But now things are different with Karla. We're planning motherhood, too. I told her about the abortion, about Baby Rhonda, and that I have to go back for her. She was very supportive. The one thing that would break us up is if I felt that she in any way became a threat to my survival. Because I told her, "As much as I love you—and I do, I love you more all the time— I love me better. My sobriety is it, because without it I have nothing. And I don't care what else I do, no matter what happens, that's just it." Definitely, we talked about what happened—she doesn't even drink. It's an amazing thing. She gets mad at me because I say, "If we entertain, we should serve wine. It's not a big deal." And she's like, "No, they can drink later, they can drink before." Very protective.

I believe that if a child is old enough to ask something, they're old enough to hear an answer. That answer becomes more complicated, more complex as life goes on. But if you can ask it, if you can articulate the question, then you deserve an answer. I want to provide the kind of information I didn't get, absolutely. Because it's just not fair. Why get them caught up in the subterfuge, the masks and wall and the mirrors?

How to become mothers—that's the only real argument we have. Because I'm like, "I'm not going to any sperm bank." I don't know—they tell me that this was the guy, and this is what his characteristics were, but I don't know that. His mother may have been schizophrenic. I don't know anything about that. I'm much more interested in finding a man that I feel a connection to, that I think is a good individual, and laying down. She says, "You are absolutely not laying down with anybody but me." So this is the problem. She doesn't want to know who he is; she doesn't want me to know who he is. Whether or not he actually penetrates me, if I know him, then there's this thing. She also wants to have a child, but she's cool with the whole sperm bank idea.

I think the S&M thing can go a lot farther. And we're taking it slowly, because certain things make me really uncomfortable, and I feel myself sort of leaving, and we stop. But I find as we do them more often, however we get to them, that happens less often. So that seems to me to be the road to pushing that boundary. And I'm into pushing it because I'm real tired of feeling like I'm bound to the missionary position, so to speak. I like being bound. I find lots of room for myself there. I like being told what to do. I enjoy that; I enjoy being punished when I don't do what I'm told to do. And I don't do what I'm told to do a lot. In fact, she gets mad at me. She's like, "You're not playing fair. You're supposed to obey, hello." "I'm getting what I want out of it, okay?" So I get a kick out of that. I'm not comfortable being bound, but I enjoy the process of getting bound. So my fantasy is a space where it's not just she and I. I don't know if she'll ever get there. So that may always just have to be my fantasy, or maybe a fantasy that we can play out, she and I, in some way. And maybe explore being a top a little more, but I think I need to understand being the bottom before I can be a good top.

For most of my life, I was Rhonda, I was militant, I was all these things because it had to be my way. I've told bosses that, I've told professors that. I still tell professors that. I don't think rigid, but definitely controlling. I gave up rigid. You see, as part of my sobriety, I understand that complete control is a complete fallacy. No such thing exists, and I know that. One of the reasons that I stopped doing drugs as well is that crack was coming on the scene, and it was getting crazy. I realized that I didn't have it in me to be as vicious and brutal as the culture required. I couldn't shoot anybody, I couldn't beat anybody up over something really stupid. I was much more inclined to share than to steal from people—things like that. I just didn't have what it took in that culture to be that way. And I had been in that position a couple times and had been unable to perform. So it was like, I'm going to die here.

Who Rhonda is today is a direct result of having taken that path. It's unfortunate, some of the things I've done; I regret some of the things I've seen. But I don't regret having gone down that path because I think I've learned things that I would never have learned otherwise. I was not set up to learn. My life was planned, from the moment I took my first IQ test. I was supposed to go to undergrad and get a business degree; I was supposed to go to law school and get a law degree. Then because at that time every major corporation wanted a black woman so they could double-dip for affirmative action programs, I would have made the big bucks. I hated it, I thought that was utterly ridiculous. I am so much more than my brain. The only thing that received any sort of validation in my house was my brain.

My mother was not going to deal with the fact that I was a lesbian. She was not going to deal with that. My father, interestingly enough, gave me the keys to his car. He said, "Be careful where you park my car." Because he knew where I was going. I was going to the gay bars. How he knew it beats me. So he was cool. He's been the coolest one every time. But there have been some closets. Me and my mother had one of the worst fights we ever had when I said I was going to come out to her family. When I came out to her, she was like, "What have I done to you?" When I told her about what happened with my brother Jay, she said, "You're lying. You're flat-out lying." After I got sober, I told her again, and we talked about it. And I was sort of able to set things in a context for her. Like, I gained weight at twelve. I blew up. A therapist once told me that was about creating a comfort space, which makes perfect sense to me. But it was also about getting powerful and being able then to get a bat and whup his ass. Explaining why I never wanted to be home with Jay alone. Me and my father almost had a physical altercation because he was going to go golfing with Jay, and leave Michael, who was the deaf-mute cousin, home with me. And I was like, no, hell no. So being able to then tell her, "Do you remember these incidents?" And then have my sister say, "You know, I remember that letter you wrote me, when Jay came up behind you in the basement." So my mother's response to me, to then believing me, was silence.

Karla is black, Latina, and Portuguese. She's from Cuba, which is why I always get slammed for saying African American, because she's like, "No, I'm a black American. I'm black, but I'm not African American." For me, the race of the father of the child is important. I have difficulties with interracial couples. There was a time when I didn't care. I guess as I got sober and began to see the world more completely, I began to care a great deal, although my brother Jay is married to a white woman. And they have children, and I love my nieces and nephew. But I don't want to deal with that dynamic, I guess. Which is really strange because if it's a light-skinned black man, I'll likely have a light-skinned child because my mother is really light-skinned; my dad was more brown-skinned. I think as I get older, my poles separate even further. I can see individual people and identify them and deal with that, but there's also this group called "white" to which I have great animosity and hostility.

My dad taught me that a long time ago. Oh, you can hang out with them, you can play with them; in fact, you want to because you want to know them. You want to know how they think, how they act, how they respond in any given situation. Never trust them. Ever. This was a big problem when he moved me out to a white neighborhood and there were no black people I could be friends with. I think it's more my mother's doing than his. My mother's kind of bourgeois.

Because of the color spectrum in our house, there were things you couldn't say in the house. Jay is my color, and then my sister and younger brother are closer to my mom's color. Calling my sister or younger brother yellow banana, or calling us tarbaby—that was not going to happen. It did come up, though, because my mother's family was pretty much her color. So when we were around them, Jay and I, who are darker, were treated differently than my other brother and sister. And it wasn't all that camouflaged.

Race really matters. I broke up with a woman that I really, really cared a lot about because she was white. I talked to her about it. I told her what the deal was. I said, "I hope you can accept it. Understand I really care about you. I think you're a dynamic woman." And I don't even let Karla trash her, because Karla's got more racial issues than I do. Because as a human being she was just fabulous. She was just white, which wasn't really her fault. Racism is one of the reasons I don't sleep with white people. Because it's like, How can you possibly sleep with me in a world where I am perceived as inherently your inferior? How can I sleep with you and feel like we're doing this as equals? I can't; it's not possible. No matter how much analysis you've done, and how race-cognizant you are, I can't do that. When I had sex with white women, I was aware of color differences, and I have never let a white woman top me, in any context. It's just not acceptable. I would never do S&M play with a white woman.

With Karla, I am her butch bottom in and out of bed. I take the garbage out, I carry things for her, I do the laundry. And I enjoy it; it makes me happy. I don't have a problem in that space, and if I don't have one, I'm not letting anyone else put one there. People tease me. She can look across the room and say [*makes beckoning gesture*], and here I come. I get dogged. And I don't give a damn what anybody thinks about that. Because she makes me happy, I make her happy, we're happy, and how we're happy is what's important. I think part of that is not having the sexism aspect. Because the dykes are laughing, but in their minds they're thinking, Damn, how did Rhonda learn to jump like that? Because my friends have told me that I have never been like that with anyone else. Not voluntarily. So they want to know what it is, what's the mojo.

In terms of society, I really think it hasn't changed very much. I think we're still either Aunt Jemima, Sapphire, or the industrial workhorse, and nowhere in between. People are very uncomfortable with my out lesbianism when I'm in a position of organizing. When I'm doing something and I'll say something that so clearly makes me a dyke, everybody's uncomfortable because that has no place here in a political context. Like Barbara Jordan had no sex life, if you listened to America. This hasn't changed. If you're powerful, you can't have sex. If you're a mother, you can't have sex. Now, if you're a whore, you can have all the sex you want, but that's all you can do is have sex. You have no validity anywhere else. And I think that's still the case. It has not changed.

It's increasingly important as I begin to realize that my experience as a black woman has been greatly colored by my lesbianism, my dykeness, and that I can't separate the two. At this point, I won't allow anyone to ask me to. Very adamant about that. I think it's an ongoing battle. I had a big argument with somebody about white pants. Just as an example I said, "Excuse me, who told you you couldn't wear white pants before Memorial Day? It's ninety degrees in Atlanta in April. Why I got to wait till May?" "It's just a fashion faux pas." By whose standards? Who told you that? Bottom line being, when they were deciding you couldn't wear white before Memorial Day, your ass was enslaved. So how you gonna let them tell you what you have to wear? So now I make it a point of wearing my white pants whenever it gets warm because it's just one of the more obvious ways I have of saying, "Hell no." That's another reason I don't deal well with white women—because I don't know what they see when they look at me. And I'm not trying to figure that out; I'm not trying to plumb their psyche. If I can't know, I don't want to go there.

I can be a woman of extremes, great extremes. And I tell Karla all the time: I go to one side, I go to the other, and then I'll work my way back to the middle. It's like walking into law school with a big pink triangle on my first day of school. Not only are you looking at a black woman, but you are looking at a black woman who's a dyke, who's going to tell you she's a dyke at every turn. And is going to tell you in case you forget and invisibilize me that I'm also a black woman. Hearing my voice is important to me. I need to hear my voice in order to continue to feed myself and give myself the strength to go forward. And I need to hear the voices of my other sisters. So every opportunity I get, I sit down in sister-girl groups. I don't care what we talk about, I need to hear your voices.

Increasingly, though, we are reaching out more and more to each other. I was in the law school talking to a white woman, and a young sister—I call them "the children," sort of traditional-age law students—walked by, and I was in a conversation, and she just reached out and touched me and kept going. That's not a common occurrence in the law school. That's not how we're taught as lawyers to communicate with each other. And I had to turn around and see who it was because I wanted to make note, because that was just an uncommon thing, and it felt wonderful.

# Anondra

*I*M TWENTY-ONE and will be twenty-two next month. My parents are both from Georgia. My mom is the third out of sixteen children. My dad had nine siblings, but he was the only son to my grandmother. When my grandfather (his father) passed away in 1993, my father found out that he had all these brothers and sisters and a half uncle who's nine years old. My grandfather was busy! My parents were high school sweethearts; they met in the eighth grade, and they dated all through high school and in college. My mom finally turned up pregnant with me and kind of pushed the process along; and so they got married, and they've been married for twenty-three years. I have a seventeen-year-old sister; that's my heart. We are really, really close. We don't argue or fight. We are so into each other. She is like my own child. I don't see my sister for a day and I'm just so depressed. When I moved away from Philly to go to school it was so hard for me, even though I was only forty-five minutes away. I feel like I missed out on her high school experience.

My grandmother lived here, down the street in the senior citizens' building. She was sick—she had diabetes, asthma, and everything. In my freshman year in college, my grandmother died. I took that really hard. My grades suffered, and that was really a bad situation for me. It was only that one semester, and then I realized that my grandmother wouldn't want me to go through this.

I was in the Baptist church all my life. I was really the only one, ever since I was young, that went to church in my family. My family would never, ever go to church. But I used to sing in the choir, and one day I was asked to join the choir. I really wanted my family to come see me sing in the choir.

Intimacy is when you feel comfortable. No matter what the situation is or no matter what you look like, how you're feeling, what's going on in your life, you're able to just sit down and communicate with the next person. I'll talk about my boyfriend. I felt that our relationship was the best thing in the world because we were so comfortable with each other, and no matter what, I could cry in front of him, and any old thing that was on my mind I could tell him. He would always know when something was wrong with me. That's how comfortable we were with each other. It was really nice. And when you feel secure around a person, to know that it's somebody that's always going to be there for you, no matter what you're feeling. That's what makes it intimate.

I feel that my sister and I have an ultimate, intimate relationship. My sister and I, we don't really hug each other a lot, but when we do, it's just the best hug. I try to keep our relationship together by letting her know that I am here for her, that I am her sister, no matter what, and when all else in this world has failed you, I will be here. No matter what. I love you and you're part of me and that's just how it is.

My boyfriend Rashid and I split, and even though we have the best relationship, it was really, really heavy. Right now he's applying to law school. He's a senior in college, and he goes to school full-time and he works full-time, and he's doing an internship for school. And there was just no room for our relationship. Rashid is a really focused individual. He's only twenty-one, and I can honestly say that he has accomplished more independently as a twenty-one-year-old male than I have, about to be twenty-two. This is someone who came from really far away to come to school here, got an apartment, pays for school on his own, does everything on his own, and works full-time. So the question is, then, Well, is he going back to law school in Arizona, or is he going somewhere else? If he goes back to Arizona, then where does that leave our relationship—if there is going to be a relationship at all? Those are things we had to deal with but he didn't want to talk about them. He was just thinking, We'll deal with it when we get there. So I just had to realize that even though I wanted for us to be together, he had to deal with it. He had to go through it and make the best decisions for him. That's how I have to try to deal with it even though it hurt me that we split.

I feel that intimacy is broken when someone lies to me. I don't like to be lied to. Sometimes people will say, "Well, I had to lie. I was trying to protect you." I just don't feel like lying to someone you care about is protecting them, regardless of what the lie is. I think that honesty is always the best policy. And this is something that I learned from experience: if you tell a lie, it's going to come back and haunt you. I feel like if someone was to lie to me, then I might feel that the intimate bond between us might have been broken. I'm not saying that it can't be fixed or resolved, but I think it would damage the bond to be lied to.

I had a lot of bad sexual experiences where I felt that the performance was unsatisfactory. And afterward I wouldn't feel good. It was like, Where is the pleasure in this? What is so good about sex? My first experience was awful—it was just bad. I think it was because I was not educated about sex. It was just something that happened to you. And everybody's doing it— then let's do it. I was seventeen and I had gotten into things before, but it wasn't all the way. I was seventeen with my first sexual experience and I hated it. I remember afterward that I felt so dirty. I was with my boyfriend, and we had been together for a year. He was my boyfriend all through high school, and I just felt, Okay, now I'm ready for this; we've been together for a while. And we did, and I felt just so dirty and I felt so nasty. The act was dirty. It didn't do anything for me. It wasn't anything pleasurable about it. It was painful. It was long and tedious, and I wasn't too comfortable with what I was doing. If I had been, I would have felt like I would have been able to speak up: Okay, I don't like that, or, Let's try this. But I really didn't participate in it; I was just there. Afterward I just felt like I didn't want to do that again in my life. I was thinking, Why am I doing this? I'm not ready for this. I could get AIDS.

All kinds of things were going through my head. I don't think that he knew I was a virgin until that time. It had never come up. He thought that I felt that it wasn't time, and I'd be ready when I thought it was our time and it would happen. He never pressured me. I mean, little jokes every now and then, but seriously, he never pressured me.

We dated for four years. We never had oral sex. Not in either direction. He brought it up, and he felt like, if I'm going to do it, so should you. And I was like, "If that's what you want to do, if you want to do it to me, that's fine. But I'm letting you know straight out that I'm not down for that." The whole act was gross to me at that time. I just couldn't even imagine.

We got comfortable with each other. I swear we had sex like three times a day because we went to school together. Once we started having sex, our whole relationship was basically based on sex. We just talked about this the other day. We're still friends. He has a wife and two kids now.

I asked my friend Tia, What exactly is an orgasm? I was like, How do you know when you have an orgasm? And she started telling me, and I was like, that's never happened to me. I was eighteen when it happened and I remember it vividly. It was my senior year. He was a junior and he went with us on a class trip to Puerto Rico. So we went to Puerto Rico and I turned eighteen then. I was the only one whose boyfriend went. We spent the whole day together, and that night, we went to our rooms, and then we went to have sex, and everything was really, really nice. And then it happened. And it was like, Wow! I remember I cried for a long time just because I was overwhelmed because it felt good, and because I was like, God, finally! Up until then, I started to think, Gee, is something wrong with me? Why can't I reach this point? He was equally happy because he felt like finally he had ultimately satisfied me.

Virginity to me was something I just had that eventually I would get rid of. When people say, "You should wait till you get married," I'm so glad I did not wait. I mean, can you imagine? I'm just thinking about my first sexual experience. I wouldn't want to experience the physical pain on my wedding night. I would want to already have gone through that initial thing and just be relaxed. I don't see how anyone can enjoy that on their wedding night if they never had sex before. So I didn't feel like I needed to keep it or needed to rush to get rid of it, either. A lot of my friends had sex sooner than I did. There was a lot of pressure in the high school. During a break period, we would have sex talks; everybody would talk about their sexual experiences. Then we had sex fests, like over spring break one time. It was to see who had the most sex over the week. I mean, there was a lot of pressure to have sex in high school.

I didn't care. It didn't bother me at all. I sat in on the talks and I listened and I didn't really care. I was happy with what my boyfriend and I were doing. I wanted us to have sex when I felt it was time to have sex. What anyone else said to me, regardless of their sexual experiences, held no relevance to me. One big thing in our school was blow jobs. I went to school with a lot of white girls. You know white girls—they did that, and they used to do it to guys anywhere. Guys—black and white—were going between classes. But, of course, guys were studs, and girls, if you had sex with all those people, you were a whore. A slut. I didn't have to deal with that—not that I would have cared what they thought of me—because I didn't have sex. And nobody ever knew my sexual experience.

I haven't had sex with any white guys. My mother works with this young man, and he is in love with me. He wants to take me out and everything. I'm not a prejudiced person, but I just feel like I love black men. I just love being with them, and I can't see myself being satisfied sexually, mentally, or any kind of way with someone other than a black person. That's just how I feel. I see a white guy and think, He's really cute, he's nice-looking. But when it comes to sex and stuff, I can't see it happening. My mother is right; she says, "I never have to worry about you coming home with a white man."

I don't think my mom had a conversation with me about sex, not because she didn't want to, but because she was uncomfortable with the whole situation. She said, "I didn't know you were having sex," and I said, "Because you never asked." She said, "Had I asked, would you have told me?" And I was like, "I don't know." She said I probably would have denied it, and I was like "I might have, but you never gave me the chance." She said, "Well, you're taking birth control pills, so is your sex life that active where you need to take birth control pills?" She asked if I used anything else besides birth control pills, and I said, "Yes, I use condoms all the time." Which is true. She said, "How many are you having sex with?" I said, "One." I remember my father was in the same room and never once did he look at me in my face. And he never said anything to me about it afterward.

I was so angry for the longest time, and I felt that she should have come to me without my dad being around 'cause I was already in an awkward position, you know? Now he says to me that he knows that I'm responsible enough because I was seventeen years old, I was making my own doctor's appointments, going to get my gyno exam, etc. My mom never addressed the issue of me going to get a g.y.n. exam or anything. After she found all of this out, she was like, Now we talk about sex. We don't get all into it, but we talk about it. She made a joke to me the other day. She asked me a question, and my answer was very moody. And she said, "What—do you need some?" And I was like, "Did you just say that to me? Did you just ask me that?" But she was laughing and was joking along to ease the tension. I don't want to know. I've never asked her about her own sex life. I'm sure if I asked her that she would tell me—I just don't want to know. I get queasy if I even think that my parents are having sex. I am mortified.

Every now and then I wear a skirt, or dress, every now and then. Even to this day, my mother says, "If I had your shape and figure, I would be wearing my little skirts and my little tops." But I do tend to dress provocative, when I go to clubs. I like to dress, but I dress nicely, and I like to show off my figure because it makes me feel good about myself. When I look good, my whole attitude about myself is much more positive. I feel like I can accomplish anything. I can take over the world if my physical appearance is well and my mind. I'm all set. I feel like can I walk into a club and just take on anybody I want to. And I like to feel that way. It's not because I'm conceited or anything; it's just because there's a lot of pressures for women to look good. You have to look good. And one thing I can honestly say about myself is that I don't do it to pick up a man. I do it because I want to look good. I want to feel good about myself.

I did an internship for a radio station, and the DJs there were very perverted. I just felt like somebody was looking at me, and in a way that I was uncomfortable with. And people would come up to me, and they were like touching. They would always want to hug you, play with your hair, and and I just didn't think that was appropriate. I made sure I didn't have any cleavage showing, or I didn't even wear a skirt.

My best friend became pregnant, and she was concerned about her mother and said, "My mother is going to kill me." This was our junior year in college. She was considering an abortion. I told my mother about it, and she told me that if I ever got pregnant, she in no way even wanted me to consider having an abortion because she got pregnant with me when she was young, and what if she had gotten rid of me? It just made me feel like, Wow! Now I know if I ever get pregnant, an abortion would never even cross my mind. I'm not against abortion. I'm pro-choice because, for whatever reason, you do what you have to do because you are the one that has to deal with it. I know for me that I just love babies, and regardless what my situation was, I would work just to make things work because I would feel that connected.

My friend, she had her baby. She had called here one day looking for me, and my mother was saying, "I want you really to consider, you'll always be thinking about that. When it comes to the time you were supposed to be due, you are going to be thinking about that. Later on in life when you have other kids, you're going to be thinking about that one that you got rid of."

I imagine that with my daughter, I would let her know it was okay for her to talk to me about sex and her relationships. My mom never really took my relationships seriously. She never really thought that maybe this is somebody that really makes my daughter happy. Let me find out a little bit about this person, someone who my daughter is spending all this time with. What is it about him that you like? What is it that you don't like?

What do you guys do when you're together? What do you do for fun? So I think for my kids I want to make sure that they knew that they could talk to me about anything because I think it's important for kids to know that.

I would talk to my daughter about self-respect as number one and how you present yourself as the way you're going to be treated. I would teach my son to respect black women because you have a mother and you have a sister and you have a grandmother. Would you want someone to disrespect your sister? Or your mother? You have to look at it that way.

I have had pretty good experiences with men, but I don't think that for the most part black men respect black women the way we are supposed to be respected. Rap music for example, I can't stand listening to it because the whore thing, bitch that—it's always about sleeping around. Women who have too much sex, they always portray them as whores, bitches. It's just unbelievable to me how we're disrespected. And I'm thinking, Why don't you write about a sister that you really like being with? One that makes you feel like more of a man because you felt like you had a good relationship with her? Why must you write about only that particular group of women that make you feel like a stud, that you have no respect for?

I think they need to know, too, that it's important that they respect us. A lot of young black males nowadays, they aren't being taught to respect black women. When I was younger, you were taught to respect your elders. That was a definite. You were taught that. So now I would never disrespect a person because that was something that was instilled in me: you will not disrespect your elders, regardless of the situation. So it's just if you want someone to know someone, you teach them that and you instill it into them and then they'll know.

Men in general have more advantages and more privileges. Black men might have a little more than black women. Of course, they are men, and also to go along with that they are black; but yes, I guess they do. Women and especially black women are always going to have to fight for that one little extra. For every extra a black woman gets, a black man has two extra. It seems like we are never, ever going to be on top. We're always one level below. And every time we accomplish one situation, there is another one that makes us fall down. It's like that game, Tetris: you're trying to stack up everything, but as soon as you get one complete row, another thing comes down and doesn't fall into place, and you go down.

Men can "respect" you and still be sexist, too. That's like a racist, a prejudiced person: they might respect you as a person, but they still might have their own little crazy ideas in their head. I deal with that all the time. Oh, sure, I go to school with eight hundred white people. I'm sure there's some who don't like me simply because I'm black, but they would never come to me directly to show it. I know for myself that if I was with a person who respected me but was sexist, I don't think that I could deal with a relationship. I'm going to need strong support as a woman, especially being a black woman, and if he's sexist already, then he's not going to be there to support me for what I need.

Whenever anyone asks me about the future I never say, "I want to be married. I want to have two kids who are successful." Me, I just want to be happy. Whatever it is I'm doing, plain and simple. If I don't ever marry in my life, if I never have any kids in my life, it won't matter, and it won't make me feel less than a woman. And fifteen years from now, who knows what I'm going to be? If I'm going to be married, I want to be married to a person who respects me as a woman and as his wife and as his partner. He's not going to cheat on me, and he's going to love me for me and not try to change me. If I have to be a mother, I want to have children who respect me as their mother but know that I am also their friend and they can confide in me no matter what. If I'm going to be a career woman, I want to have a job that I'm going to be happy to go to every day and I'm not going to hate it when that alarm clock goes off.

Society's love of white women doesn't impact me at all. The way I see it, there will always be something that someone else has that I want. I'm lighter-skinned, I'm thin—there's not much to me, and I don't base my life on how I live or how I look, even though I know that's a real situation. There are some dudes that would rather I have bigger hips or bigger thighs or something like that. But I can't feel any less of myself because he does.

I really, really wish that my mother and I were closer. I'm not saying that my mother and I aren't close, but I really wish that my relationship with my mother was better than anybody's. My mother always says, "Trying to talk to you guys is like trying to pull teeth." But sometimes it's like, You didn't care before, so now why do you care? I might be a little bit angry with her. I remember one time I was going through something and I was crying and I said to her, "Why can't you not be my mother for a little while and just be my friend?" And she said to me, "Because I'm not your friend. I'm your mother." With black mothers, everything is, "I am your mother and that is that and there is no room for anything else." It's as if what you're feeling doesn't count. "I am your mother and what I say goes and that's that. End of discussion." And I think that is so wrong. I feel like you brought me here; take the time to get to know me as who I am. Even with little things—I'll say, "Oh, God, I have a really strong craving for this." And she'll go, "I didn't know you liked that." And I'm like, "Well, you never asked."

When I went away to college, it got much better. My mom would call me every day, three times a day, and we would have so much to talk about. If I was here, we would say two words, "Hi" and "Good night." But when I went away to school, she called me every day.

My father didn't talk to me about sex or anything like that. My father and I have a good relationship. I'm more comfortable with my dad than I am with my mom. I'm a daddy's girl. When I was in high school, my mom took it down. I wrote a poem, this whole poem about my father and how no matter what I was in the world, where I was going to be, how old I got, I was always going to be my father's little girl. I wrote this in high school, and I typed it up really nicely, and my mother framed it. That's like my father's inspiration. He just loved it. I'm really close to my father. I feel like I can talk to my dad about anything—well, almost anything. I wouldn't talk about sex with him just—is that something you're supposed to talk to your father about? I know my father knows that I have sex. If I spent a night home, instead of with Rashid, he'd be like, "What are you doing here? You're not going home tonight?" Or something like that. But he never says anything to me. He doesn't seem to have a problem. Not at all. If he does, he doesn't express it to me.

So I had to call home and I'm like, "Daddy, I can't get my car out. Can you come bring me a shovel?" And my father, he brings me a shovel, and he comes upstairs. My mother and father came upstairs and they each sat down and had coffee. I mean it was just like—it was basically like I lived with him. Really it was. He just didn't have a problem with it. And one time my dad asked me, "How does Rashid treat you, aside from what I see?" My parents didn't really see Rashid too much because he had his own apartment. I kept me and Rashid from my parents for maybe a couple of months. I remember I was in my godsister's wedding this summer, and that's when they met him for the first time, after months of us dating. My mother always downed my relationship with guys and I thought, Wow, my mother is going to jinx me. I am going to wait a while before I bring him home. And I did. I was in this wedding, so I knew he was going to have to interact with my parents. So he agreed to it. He was fine with it. My dad said he was really impressed with him. He did the whole opening and closing the door and taking off your coat, but also my dad saw that we mentally clicked, which was important.

Sex with the love is on a whole other level. It's not just physical. It's emotional. It's mental. It's sensual. Whereas casual sex is just satisfying your need. I can honestly say that I have been in a relationship where I have had real sex, real love, and real intimacy, and real feelings. And that to me was the ultimate. It was the best feeling in the whole world. It feels like it is just you and him and no one else, and everything that goes on around you doesn't matter. I feel like if you are ever lucky enough to find a person that satisfies you that much, you should respect that person enough and yourself and that relationship where you won't let anybody else in to break it.

Guys are scared of commitment. Like this whole thing when me and Rashid split up, with us splitting, I know another thing that came across my mind was, Things are getting too serious. He's getting scared. That was just the easy way out. He is just trying to back out. I know now that is really not what it is. I really feel like, in him, I found my ultimate soul mate. I really do. I don't know. I guess because I had never, ever been treated in that way by a man before in my life. I was treated like a queen. For the whole duration of our relationship, he did all the cooking. He did all the cleaning. All the shopping. I didn't do anything. I didn't have to do anything. We were in touch; we were intellectually connected. We could have stimulating conversations about a lot of things. And I learned a lot from him. One day, he just came out of the blue and was like, "I'm so glad that I met you. You're such a nice person." I think we were watching a movie or something, and he paused the movie just to tell me that. I thought that was so neat. Just little things in him.

When we broke up, oh, my God. You should have seen me. I was a wreck. I was crying the whole way to school. I couldn't listen to my radio. Every day I came from school and I stayed in my room all day long. I think I might have seen my mother once, my family once. I couldn't eat, I wasn't sleeping, nothing. I wouldn't go out, and I'm a club head. I'm faithfully at a club. Thursday nights I'm there. I wouldn't because I was scared I was gonna run into him. I would sit and look at my phone just like that. I'd have the phone right there. I'm doing better now because I have great support. Some of my friends are angry with him, but I'm not. I have to respect him because I know he is an independent person, and he's making the decisions that he has to make to make his life for him to be content, which is really what life is all about.

I'd just rather focus on the positive and remember all the good things that we had in our relationship. I didn't think I was gonna make it. If I were to show you my journal, it would be page after page after page about Rashid, and how I coped through this day, and how I didn't sleep this night, and how many Kleenex I went through. But there really weren't any negatives, and I don't want to, after splitting, decide to start saying that he might have been cheating on me, or he might have been doing this, he might have been doing that. If that was the case, I don't want to remember it that way. This is like the best experience I've ever had with a man, and if it's the only best experience I've had with a man, I want to keep it.

How I define myself as a black woman is, I've overcome the odds—I wasn't supposed to make it this far. I wasn't supposed to get a high school diploma, I wasn't supposed to not have kids at an early age, I wasn't supposed to complete one degree and be finishing up another one. I feel that I am satisfied with myself and the choices I made in life and the consequences I've had to deal with. And to me, I feel that makes me a strong black woman. I've always been taught to feel that my views are important and I'm not inferior to anyone else. And that's just simple. I don't feel like I have to have kids; I don't feel like I have to get married to label myself as a black woman. Those are the nice things to be able to have in life. But if you never get them, it doesn't make you less of a woman, as long as you are able to deal with yourself and live contentedly and make it in this world when you're really not expected to make it.

Obstacles are put in our way. No matter whatever we do, there is someone who is always trying to knock us down. You deal with it; you go on and you learn from your experience that you know not to do that again. Something else comes your way, and it's the same thing: you get over it and you get back up and you deal with something else. Life is going to be a lot of those things thrown in your way. You just have to have the mentality to deal with it—that this is a part of life, and this is what I have to do to get through it.

# Millie

*I* TURNED TWENTY-ONE on Tuesday! I'm a senior in college, and I am going to be a student for a long time to come. I grew up in a small town not too far from Baltimore. My mom is there; she directs a mediation center. She does conflict-resolution training for divorce, parent-child custody, and stuff like that. My dad works for emergency medical services. My parents are divorced. My mom is bisexual. She's been with my other mother for about seven or eight years. There are four of us; I'm the oldest. My sister is nineteen, and then there's the next set of kids. They are thirteen and ten years old. They're all living with my mom. Well, they share both parents.

My parents broke up when I was fifteen. I was a junior when my mom moved out. But they had been breaking up and separating for two or three years. When I say that she's been with my other mother for seven years, it's because that's how long she's been in my life. They've been friends for a long time, before they were together as a couple. And her kids are the same age as all of us. Her son is a year and three days older than me; her daughter is a few months older than my sister. And her son is a few months older than my brother. So we all kind of considered each other cousins. We spent weekends together. And we grew up together, too, from when I was about twelve, I guess.

Both my parents were born in suburbs outside of Washington, D.C. My dad has roots in the rural South. My mom's family has been in the D.C. area for a long time. Her family extraction is French Creole, and there's lots of her family in and around the same area. My mom is a nonpracticing Muslim. And my dad is a nonpracticing Baptist. My mom raised us with a lot of emphasis on our individuality, and she really tried to refrain from indoctrinating us with anything. But she especially didn't want to raise us with a religion. She wanted us to be free to make our own spiritual choices. She became a Muslim but let it go.

It sounds trite almost to say that intimacy is basically closeness, but I think that's it. Closeness. I think that you're intimate with someone when you can be silent with them. Because I think we hide behind speech and chattering. I do. And when I feel comfortable enough with someone to say nothing, then that's a real signal of intimacy for me. And listening—when a man is a good listener, that's just automatically great for me. Don't tell anyone! But yeah, that's it. Listening, honesty, and sharing. Because I'm a good listener, too. Trust, because in order to have the exchange, they have to be trusted. Betrayal of trust is a major break in intimacy. This can happen in a number of ways. Like if you're sharing with someone and then they laugh at you, that's a betrayal of the trust that you expected when you wanted to share. I'm trying to think of my intimate or ex-intimate. I don't have many ex-intimates. Two very intimate spaces for me now are my significant-other sort of thing, boyfriend-type guy, and the other is my email circle. I am in this e-mail exchange, this circle of women. There's about fifteen of us, and we're quite intimate. We're spread around the country, but we do a whole lot of sharing in these completely honest and open and truth-bearing ways that it's like church in there. And it's really healing, it's really helpful, it keeps me whole, like for real.

One of my good friends and I had a pretty intimate long-distance relationship, and I think the distance helps us to be as sharing as we are. It certainly helps me; I tend to develop intimacy better over long distances. We weren't that close before she went away. And now our friendship has been entirely a corresponding friendship. So we e-mail. And she cc'd me something that she had sent through the e-mail friendship. So I replied, and it got sent to everyone. Some electronic thing happened, and I was in this group. The group keeps changing. I correspond every day, but different women have different styles and patterns. There's the core people who write all these messages, and then there's people who come in and people who write about different things. But our patterns are fascinating to me, and it's a lot of fun.

I identify as a heterosexual. I have had experiences with women, but I think I'm heterosexual. I am comfortable with my sexuality, but it's just really, really recently that I started thinking about my sexuality as a part of me that develops and changes and isn't just always a part of me, you know? I think my first notions of my sexuality were really passive. I would notice how other people reacted to me, like when you're in junior high and boys are liking you, and you're like, Why are they liking me? Or, Why are they not? And that first started to happen around school. So I think it came first from outside, from other people, witnessing other people's reactions. I think I liked it when people would like me, guys would like me. But I don't think I looked at it as, This is my beginning as a sexual person. I don't think I even looked at it as being mine. It was just like they liked me.

This changed recently when I began to be comfortable with people liking me, which took a long, long time. I was a really awkward, gangly little kid. And so when people started liking me, I didn't trust it. I was like, What is wrong with you? It took years for me to be able to accept anyone else responding to me in this way. It just was weird to me because I had for a long time not been noticed and not accepted. I was always a nerd; I was always the one who liked reading groups or the math group and the after-school program. And that didn't go over too well in the social scene, and some people tended to just not take too much notice of me—like, Oh, that's the really smart girl. And as I grew and changed and started to look different, and people started paying different kinds of attention to me, it kind of scared me. It made we wary—although on one hand I did like it.

But the expression of my wariness was that I refrained from reciprocating. I would just not have boyfriends. Guys would want to go out with me, and I'd just say, "No, that's okay. We can be friends, but I don't want to be your girlfriend." And that generally was my frame-up until tenth grade. That's what I would say. Guys would say to each other, "Don't even try to go out with Millie because she'll say no." Because I would. I was just weird.

I did like some guys, sometimes; they would be cute to me. But that didn't translate in my head to sexual interest in them. I'd just think they were cute. I had physical feelings. I think we all do. I think I've always been a sensual person, just antisocial. I'm sensual in my own space—like masturbation was an early thing for me. So that was probably ongoing throughout my adolescence. But that wasn't the only expression of my sensuality. It was always making things, just doing other creative stuff like I'd always play in my hair because I like to, because I like the way my hair feels and I like the way it feels to have my hand in my hair, so I always do that. And when I sit, I sit with my hand on my belly, like when I'm at home and I be reading, I have my hand on my belly. My general postures are self-touching postures. I like to touch myself. That's interesting.

I guess I started masturbating around eleven years old. I already knew what it was because my mom's very frank. She told me when I was young, but it still was really embarrassing for her to tell me, and I was embarrassed to hear it. She would tell me about masturbation, and say, "It's all right to touch yourself. That's really fine." And I was like, Uhh, don't tell me that. I guess I masturbated pretty regularly before I ever menstruated. It was how I had my first orgasm. I don't think I conceptualized orgasms as different from masturbation. It was part and parcel of masturbation. And as far as what she told me—just in the space that she'd say where it was okay—definitely shaped it, and so it wasn't a big deal to me either. It was just something I did. I went to sleep easy afterward. Sometimes I masturbated, sometimes I'd write in my journals and then go to sleep. It wasn't a big deal. But I didn't talk about it with my friends; it was a private thing.

When she was pregnant with my brother is when the whole reproductive stuff came out. Like this is how babies are literally made. I was eight when he was born. We got to see her get pregnant and then we got to see the baby. I was eleven or twelve when I first started menstruating. And my mom really wanted me to be comfortable with my body changes, and she would urge me to look at myself and to watch how my body was changing. We had a very permissive house; it wasn't the kind of house where you knock on the door of the bathroom, and if someone's in there, you don't go in. It's not like we were strangers to our bodies and to each other's bodies. So there was that kind of exchange and honesty about our physical selves among each other, between each of us and my mom.

She told me that menstruation was a cycle that my body would go through and that it was my body's cleaning itself out, but that it wasn't dirty and that it was a glorious thing. She gave me some warnings, like, "You might get cramps, and if you do, then tell me, and I can give you some medicine." And, "This is how you wear pads and tampons. I want you to wear pads for a while, but then you can practice with tampons." After I got my period, then I used pads for years, and then I used tampons. But she always had both of them in the house.

Maybe she knew I was a little nerd and was really not going to have sex, but she tied menstruation to sex by saying that it was because my egg hadn't been fertilized, that was why I was menstruating, and then when I started to have sex, that's how I would get pregnant too. My mom and I didn't talk about it. I got that coming from other sources, people like my friends, my guy friends who'd be really enthralled by the idea that I was a virgin. I was like, "Uhh, it's not a big deal." I don't know why they were into it. I think that they're intrigued with the idea of virgins because then they can hunt them and devirginize them. I think men in general are enthralled with the idea of virginity, patriarchy in general. They learn that pretty early, I think, to be enthused about a woman's virginity. But that wasn't something that I got from my mother, and I'm glad of that. She never gave us the impression that sex was a casual thing that you should just do all the time for no good reason, but neither did she put this heavy emphasis on your virginity, and I'm really glad of that. When I came to college, my roommate was a very religious Jehovah's Witness. What she knew about herself was that she's a virgin and her virginity is a gift she's going to give her husband. And I'm just like, "You reduced your value to your hymen? That's really sad." That was never baggage that I had to carry, and I'm really glad of that.

My mom wanted me to make an informed choice to have sex. She didn't want me to just have sex because it was convenient or because I was curious or because of pressure. She wanted me to be able to know why I was doing it. She wanted me to be able to value the intimacy of it; she wanted me to be able to feel safe within the space that sex creates. And she would speak about it in these terms, too. But I didn't have that kind of space, so sex for me wasn't really a question. I did feel kind of hunted because of the suddenness with which guys were interested in me. I felt kind of attacked by them, and I think I closed myself off, like, I don't want a boyfriend; leave me alone. For a space of time, maybe four years, all my friends were guys who were trying to be my boyfriend, and I wouldn't let 'em. So they were like, "Okay, I'll just be your friend." That's who all my friends were. But I wasn't interested in having a boyfriend.

My best friend was my sister, growing up. We were the weird family, there were not many families who were vegetarians. We were always the only ones growing up. There were not many black children who read at home and who didn't watch TV at home; we were the only ones. There were not very many black children who didn't have perms; we were the only ones. That's very important. And so when I did get a perm, and there's a real interesting correlation. One of my dad's sisters, who we all love, she would always be like, "When are you going to perm this child's hair?" My mom got tired of resisting when I was like twelve or thirteen. I didn't have a preference. I was just like, Okay, whatever. So that's when I got my perm, and that's when it started. It was weird because I'd gone through all of elementary and most of junior high, and then I get this perm and people are like, "Whoo, Millie's kind of cute." That was a whole level of weirdness too. And then, too, my whole history of being the weird vegetarian nerd girl, then suddenly that was all right. So that was kind of weird too. But it was clear that it started when I got my perm. I kept it throughout high school. Our hair wasn't a political thing for us when we were growing up. It's not a political thing for our mom, and we got a whole lot of our worldview from her. My dad worked three days and then was off for a few days. And he was working in a town really far away. So he was gone for three days working, and then he'd come back and sleep the first day, and then the rest of the days he'd be in the yard fixing cars. My dad isn't really a part of my childhood memories. He wasn't in the house a lot. He didn't interact with us very much. He used to make us toys and stilts, and he was real cool, take us on trips, take us to jazz festivals, and Harlem Week and stuff. But on a day-to-day, shape-your-worldview type of plane, that was my mom. And this is a thing we just talked about in group e-mail last week. About our hair. My mom has straight hair, and I think that for her, it wasn't the same kind of political issue to not have chemical alteration of your hair that it is for me. I have chemical alteration of my hair. And she was always like, "Your hair is beautiful in its natural state. Why change it? That's self-hatred." But at the end of the day, when I say she just got tired of protesting, it was like it wasn't her fight to fight.

I've had sex with one guy, the guy I lost my virginity to. He's the only person I've had sex with; he's not the only person I've been physically intimate with. I have fooled around with guys before him. With one, really. With one. I was sixteen. Like I said, I kept up my little refrain, I don't want a boyfriend. And then there was this one particularly persuasive and persistent guy who went to a college near my high school. I was a junior in high school, and he was a freshman in college. He was on their basketball team, and I was a cheerleader at my high school. They used to practice at our high school, and that's how we met. And he said, "I want to be your boyfriend," and I said, "I don't want a boyfriend." And he said, "Okay, I'll just be your friend." That's what he told me every day for three months and wore down my resistance, and so he asked me out one day and I said yes. We were friends by then. There was that intimacy of knowing him. So he wasn't a stranger trying to be my boyfriend—he was my friend. We dated. We'd go eat places, and when they had parties at college, I'd go there. We'd talk on the phone a whole lot. We kissed, made out and stuff, but mostly clothed. It was toward the end of the semester that we finally did get together like that. And then he went home for the summer.

Then I went away for the summer program, and that's where I met

Kevin. Kevin is my boyfriend now. And I just fell all up in love with him, like, Oh, my gosh, he was the most incredible guy I'd ever met. He was so cool and he didn't attack me. So I was just like, Wow, you're so dope. He listened, he spoke. We talked; we had whole conversations, and it was really dope. He lived in Philadelphia, and again, for me, intimacy over distance is good. The thing that was so cool about my high school boyfriend, who was at that local college, was that he didn't go to the same school as me. No one at my school knew who he was. He went to the college and no one knew him; he didn't know any of my friends. It was real cool. I've always been real protective of my space. It was really dope.

We wrote letters every day. But generally speaking, I didn't miss him. The program we were in brought us around the state so we could see each other every couple of months or so. And then we wrote letters all the time. Our connection was really strong. During the three-week program, we spent all our time together. We were both on the committee that ran things at the program. We were both on that, so we had a really good working relationship. And we'd go for walks and then talk forever. He's a good listener, and he'd say really interesting things. We just really got along. And then he started professing his love for me, which helped things along, and I was like, "Oh, okay, I love you too. You're dope. Okay, cool." So that's also what did it. We didn't sleep together until a year later, after we came to colleges in the same town.

I only applied to two schools—I'm such a horrible procrastinator. One school wanted their deposit before they gave me financial aid. I didn't have eight hundred dollars in my pocket, so I came here. I got that letter and I was like, Whatever. Forget it. And then Kevin had two choices, too. And one of his schools was near the one I chose. I don't know how he decided or what prompted his final decision. The fact that we were both going to be near each other had something to do with it. But it wasn't here in college that we first slept together; it was during the second summer we worked together at the program where we met. Up until then, though, we had physical closeness a lot—when we'd be someplace speaking, we'd make out or kiss and all that stuff. We went pretty far, oral sex, etc.—everything but intercourse. And then it was the following summer that we did sleep together, during the same program, the summer before we went to college. It was in a hotel because we had traveled, and that's when we finally did have intercourse.

We went on a trip to an amusement park as part of the program. After we came back from the amusement park, it was really late, and so they had to drive to where we were going to get the hotel. We got to the hotel, and I don't know how we managed to be in the room together, we were supposed to have roommates. Someone got sent to someone else's room or something. I started making him wear condoms because we were getting so close, and we both agreed that it was best because we were doing lots of rubbing and grinding. It felt good; it didn't hurt. During that three-week program, it was like every day that we would have these near sexual experiences. Sexual experiences without intercourse. Having sex didn't really change things. We'd already been so intimate that it was just like, Oh, okay. After that, during sex I still had clitoral orgasms.

I didn't start having vaginal orgasms until a couple of months ago, actually. I read something about it. And I think that made me realize the difference. Well, it could be that I've always had them and I'm just now realizing the difference. I read a tantra book on vaginal orgasms and the G-spot. After I read that, I could recognize it. I was like, Okay, this is a different orgasm than that. I could tell the difference. But when I first started having sex, it wasn't like, Wow, this is a whole new type of orgasm.

We have a pretty open and adventurous kind of relationship with each other sexually. Positions, like all kinds, all over, everywhere, different parts of the house, different parts of the bed, different furniture, locations. We're comfortable initiating things like that, like if I want to move onto the floor, I'll just be like, "Come on, to the floor." And it's accepted. We have good communication, like with pushes and tugs. I've known him for three years. You get to know how to tell a person what to do.

Anal sex has happened, but that's not something that I have high tolerance for. Okay, that was fun. But it's not a regular thing, every eight months or so. At first I like it, and then after a while it becomes uncomfortable. He isn't specially focused on that; it's just another thing. Oral sex all the time, both ways. Honey, ice. What else? He likes to hold my hands above my head, or he likes it when I do that to him and just hold him down. So that's not really bondage. When I'm engaging in sex, I don't tend to fantasize about other sex. But I do have some fantasies, like two men or a man and a woman, or to have sex with not really a group, but maybe with two people.

I prefer African American men; I'm more attracted to them. I can't imagine intimacy with European American men. I can think non–African American because one of my very best friends is Dominican. There are ethnicities other than African American men that I'm not averse to the idea of intimacy with. I don't know. Well, there have been historical relationships between blacks and whites that really turned me off about white men. This history is very present to me. Just the idea of being in a relationship with a white man is just so uncomfortable to me.

My relationship with a woman happened when I was away in Paris last year. We were friends—we used to be over all the time. She was a performance artist, and she lived in Paris. I spent the night over at her house a couple of times. I didn't spend that much time in my room because I had a roommate, and I'm not really a roommate type of person. We didn't have that much in common. Then, too, I was in a show with my friend, so we'd have rehearsal and all that stuff. And at one point we were in bed, we were going to sleep, we were talking, and she asked if she could kiss me. And I was like, "Yeah, that'll be fun." And so we did. We kissed for a little while and played with each other a little bit, and then that was it. Mostly breasts and shoulders. It wasn't really a big deal. It wasn't my idea, it wasn't like I was particularly attracted to her. She's my friend, but if I had to imagine a woman I'd want to have sex with, it wasn't her. It felt different because it was motivated by curiosity; it wasn't particularly passionate for me. It was like, Wow, kissing a woman. The fact that I was realizing that I was kissing a woman made me not be a hundred percent in the moment of kissing her.

Kevin and I were on hiatus at that point. He was in Ghana. We've had all kinds of drama. Like when I say he's my boyfriend, I say that with a certain amount of reservation because we've been trying to break up for the last two years. But we were on hiatus at the time because we were both away: I was in Paris, and I was going to go to Ethiopia; he was in Ghana for the year. Plus we had been going through drama before we left town. We'd been going through drama the entire school year. I had another intimate relationship that he had real problems with. I fell in love with somebody else. I didn't have sex with him, but I did have intimacy with him. And that was a big problem.

I went home for Christmas, sophomore year, and spent a lot of time with this brother who I'd known from there but also knew from school. And we hadn't really kicked it because he was so much older than me. When I came as a freshman, he was a senior graduating. So that meant when I was a freshman in high school, he was a senior. We just spent a lot of time together; and we developed a really strong intimate bond, emotionally, and we fell in love. It happened. And I told Kevin. My mom says that was my mistake. I told Kevin because I wanted to be honest. I didn't think he had to feel threatened because I didn't not love him anymore, I didn't not want to be with him anymore, I didn't not want to hang out with him. I just also loved this other guy.

Needless to say, that didn't go over too well. We spent the whole spring semester working through that. I spent the semester apologizing and feeling like garbage because I had done such an awful, evil thing to Kevin, who's been nothing but good to me. And just beating myself up. And being beat up, very, very viciously, emotionally.

His thing was he hadn't fallen in love with anyone else, and so what hurt him the most was the intensity of my emotional bond with this other guy. I didn't want a relationship with this guy, and he didn't want a relationship with me. We were exploring each other and loving what we found. We were both philosophy majors and our whole exploration was based on the idea of freedom and being able to love without ties and attachments. So it was as much the idea of loving like that as the love itself. That was just the elation that we were flying on. And to pursue it to a relationship, that wasn't even a question. That wasn't what either of us wanted to do.

I was just glad I was leaving the country, really glad to be going because I didn't feel like I had power. I felt as though I could have broken up with him, if I'd done it before that Christmas. The move from writing letters long distance to being right across the street from each other in each other's face wasn't really all that comfortable for someone who's been protecting her space for seventeen years. This is my first relationship with anyone at all, so there was a lot of stuff that I didn't say. There's a lot of things that I recognize now that I was feeling but I didn't know how to give voice to. So, after that Christmas, I recognized a lot of ways in which I hadn't been happy, but I totally didn't feel okay saying, "Well, actually, now that I think about it, I wasn't happy anyway, and so I don't want to be with you." I felt like I had to fix what I had done wrong. I had to make it better again because he was really very hurt, and I because I love him a lot, and I didn't want him to be hurt. I wanted to fix it. But at the same time, I was miserable. I was under awful stress. I was making myself sick—to hate yourself is not a healthy way to spend your mental time at all. And, I went away, yes— oh, God, fresh air—and it was wonderful.

He came to Paris from Ghana for Christmas. He came to visit me in Ethiopia. When we had a week off for our program and me and my two friends went to Ghana and spent time there he showed us around. I decided in Ethiopia that I didn't want to be in a relationship with him anymore. And trying to do that through the mail didn't really work. I was trying to break up with him through letters, and you can't call from Ghana to Ethiopia. It was all kinds of drama. So it was just constant back and forth: "You want to do this? Why are you doing this now? We're about to graduate anyway—what's the point? We're about to leave . . ." Just all kinds of running around in emotional circles. It's been a long year. We came back and he spent the summer in the Northeast, and I was just kicking back. And when we got back here, it was like I fell back into the patterns that I'd been trying to get out of when I was talking about needing to break up because I don't want it to be like it used to be. But I fell back into those same patterns. He was pressuring me to stay together, and I wasn't really wanting to break up. I wanted to be his friend; I wanted for us to remain friends, to remain intimate. Which with the magic vision of hindsight, I see it was kind of stupid. Because he was like, "That makes no sense. We can't do that. If we're going to be intimate, we're going to be together." He didn't want for us to see other people and see each other. He wants to marry me, I think. And so for him, the idea of seeing other people is a waste of time.

A big part of what fueled my initial wanting to break up with him was his huge double standard. You've had sex with so-and-so, and so-and-so, and so-and-so, and so-and-so. Four women while we've been together. It's not fair. Why couldn't I have had sex with my Christmastime friend? You know? He finally admitted over this past Christmastime that he had emotional connections with some women, and he can understand. Because he spent a lot of—a lot of the abuse was on the grounds of questioning my loyalty to him, to the institution we were building as a relationship, and also my integrity as a person almost. Like, "How could you love two people at once? People don't do that. What's wrong with you?" But even this past Christmas he slept with someone else—this makes number five. Yet it has to be said that monogamy has been his soapbox and not mine. From the beginning, he's into relationships, and I'm not and I never have been. That's part of what scares me it's about protecting my space and not missing him when he's gone.

But I love Kevin, and I was sixteen when we met. And he was like, "Okay, I love you. This is how it happens when people love each other." I had never loved anyone before, so it was easy to believe. And my response to his sleeping with other people has never been comparable to his responses to mine. I've been like, "Okay, why didn't you tell me first? Is that what you want?" If that's what he wants, then we can do that; but he won't say that's what he wants because then that means I can do it, too. So right now, I haven't called him my boyfriend in a really long time, at least for eight months. I definitely do feel connected to him. I just wanna not feel bound to him. I'm trying to achieve autonomy. It scared me the extent to which my conception of myself is through him. I'm tired of being part of this couple. I'm dependent on him for a lot of emotional stuff. I've always been a very autonomous person. And it's kind of weird how suddenly that's not the case. Of course it wasn't sudden, of course it took four years, but it's weird how completely it's become the case.

I think he feels the same way. For him, it's a real big deal that I've had these intimacies with other people, with the Christmastime one and this other friend that's intimate. So I think he would like to have broken up with me after that first Christmas, but he feels dependent on me too, emotionally. We're both doing this kind of thing.

There's this other guy. Like when I said people are listening, that's who I was thinking of. That's the most intimate I've ever become with anyone. We spent a week together and we just really clicked, and we just would talk. It was right after that Christmas, and he helped me to go through some of what I was feeling. He came here for a week, and it was really quick. There was no physical intimacy. He went back to California—I didn't think I'd ever see him again. We wrote letters periodically, every month or so. And then I went away and we continued to write letters. I'll think of him and he'll call me. Just a really, really profound connection. And Kevin's always been like, "So what's up with you two?" And I'd say, "Stop it. We're friends. Get your mind out the gutter. We can be friends." Kevin always knew how important he was, but he was never quite comfortable with it. I didn't pretend like we were just buddies. It was a profound connection, and I didn't try and hide that. He had moved to Boston while I was away. And we saw each other. That's when it became physical, I guess because of the profound connection. I went to visit him and we were intimate, not sexually but almost. Not sexually because I know the limit that Kevin says, and I didn't feel like crossing that boundary and causing that drama. So I didn't. And I didn't for myself, too, because I didn't want to go there with him. Although that line is so stupid, the line between intimacy without intercourse and intimacy with intercourse.

I was molested one time, by the boy who lived next door to me. I was locked out of the house one night. My mom used to be home when I came home, but her car had broken down and she had to walk home with my little sister. And I was just utterly stunned, sitting on the porch crying. My sister must have been five. That means I was six or seven. He lived next door, just a neighbor. We didn't play with him or anything. He was older, like twelve or something. He came on the porch, and I was crying because

I was locked out and scared. And he was like, "Why are you crying? Shut up." Then he started talking. There were kites we'd made on the wall, and he was like, "Which kite is yours?" I pointed, and he said, "That's an ugly one." He was just being really evil to me. And then he came over to me and he took his penis out of his pants, and he said, "Touch it, or I'll put it in your mouth and make you suck it." And I'm already traumatized—one, because my mom isn't home, two, I'm locked out of the house, three, he told me my kite was ugly. I'm just crying, right, and then he made me touch his penis. And I was like, Ooooh, and I had to touch it because I didn't want to suck it. It was just very traumatic.

Then my mom came home soon after that because he was still on the porch with me. I was still crying. My mom was like, "Baby, are you okay? I'm so sorry." And I'm hugging her, and then she gave him a dollar and said, "Thank you for watching her." Because she thought he'd been on the porch watching me. So that was rough. But when I told her—I told her when we went inside—she called his mother, who didn't believe her. His mother did say, "That never would have been done. That's not true." He had two older sisters and an older brother, though—maybe the older brother was ten years older than him. And my mom called, and his mother said she didn't believe it. Then that evening, her and my father both went over there. This is what I found out a couple of years ago; I didn't know this then. All the siblings said, "We believe it," because another cousin of his had said a similar thing, or he molested her too. The mother still denied it, but the brother beat the guy up. So he got his anyway.

I've never been pregnant, but I have taken the morning-after pill. I don't think that really counts as being pregnant. I would have an abortion if I had to. About having children, I think it's not something I really want to do. I don't consider it one of my goals in life, that I'm not going to be complete until I do. Marriage and children aren't that high on my list of priorities. But maybe it's just something I don't want to do. I used to not like babies; you have brothers and sisters ten years younger, you get to see all the stuff that's not fun about having a baby. I have friends who are just like, "I can't wait to have a baby." I'm like, "Okay, whatever. You've never changed diapers, have you?" And invariably, they haven't. I used to be like, I'm never having kids; kids are awful. They run away, they bother you, they're just terrible things. I've outgrown that particular mindset, and now I can see it happening. But I can't really see choosing to be a single mother. That would mean a commitment to the idea of having a child. I think if I had a child it would be because I was in a relationship, or married, or wanting to build a family with this person.

I have a number of regrets, I think, surrounding my relationship with Kevin. I don't even know what they are; they've changed as my understanding of the relationship and my space in it has changed. It used to be I'd regret about that Christmas, like I shouldn't have done that. Now it's regret about my lack of voice after that Christmas. So it changes. But there's regrets tied to that situation, definitely.

Racism and sexism are connected for me. I think right now it's more of an academic connection than a felt connection just because I'm in such a black environment. And it's easy for it not to be real when you almost never see any whites, which is the case now. Racism is something that I'm aware of and understand as having an incredible impact on my life and on the world. But as far as my interpersonal relationships go, I don't interact with white people, or really with any nonblack people.

Sexism is more a factor in my day-to-day life. I'm a drummer. I play drum bass. I'm a dancer too. And that's a really rampantly sexist arena. I drum with an all-women's drumming circle. I just started in January. Before that I was just drumming with a student dance company. I auditioned to dance for it, but then it turned out we only had one drummer, and since I had a drum and could drum, I ended up drumming for that year. That was what put me into drumming instead of just drumming with my friends or by myself. Because we would perform, and just the responses I would get. The things people would say! Grown men would just say the stupidest things, like women shouldn't drum because you'll go sterile. Just complete, utter nonsense. All the arguments that men used to say about why women

shouldn't go to college—you'll go sterile, it'll make you more masculine—
they say the same exact things about why women shouldn't drum. It's because the drum is a male sphere and it's an insult to the ancestors, which is
entirely false. The *djembe* was invented by a woman. It's like people don't
know, but it is a male sphere in this country, and there's a lot of testos-
terone surrounding it, like who can drum harder, longer, faster.

It is very close to my heart, the way that black male sexism bothers me
and keeps me from being comfortable. All last semester I decided not to
drum. I decided when I came back here I was going to dance and not drum
unless I could drum with the all-sister group. So until they opened up their
rehearsals, I was not drumming at all. And that's crazy. Sexism in the black
community goes largely unaddressed. Everyone thinks feminism's such a
white thing. So women are scared to talk about it, and men will just jump
down your throat if you even say the "f" word or mention women and not
the black man's plight. It's crazy the amount of silence that's required.
And interpersonally, I think, the whole double standard within my primary
relationship is a completely patriarchal construction. Utterly. I don't even
have to explain it. Sometimes it makes me kind of overwhelmed. And
hopeless. Wow, what am I going to do? It's just so much bigger than I
am. And at other times, I'm able to put it in perspective, and it's like
everything's bigger than I am, and I can do my own little bit. At those
times, it's energizing.

In the larger society, images of black women's sexuality definitely have
an impact on my psyche. I'm taking a course on images of women in the
media, and that's enabled me to look at the ways it has impacted me. I tend
to shelter myself from things that aren't personal, that harm me personally.
I grew up not watching TV, and I continued that kind of protection. I don't
tend to watch a lot of television or even listen to the radio. So I do kind of
cut myself off to a certain extent.

Hopefully, in the future I'll have a lot more voice. I can't imagine being
in a space that I'm not gonna have more control over. I feel like if I were to
begin a relationship tomorrow and he lived across the street from me, I feel
like I'd be able to negotiate more space for myself than I've been able to

with Kevin. We've had three years of history, and then you're like, I need space. And I'm going to grad school for English literature. Possibly get my Ph.D. I don't, I don't know if that's my goal.

Talking here, it's made me think. Every time you talk about yourself, you think other things about what you talked about. So it has had the impact of making me think again about what's going on in my life. That's good.

# Gloria

*I*'M FORTY-EIGHT years old and living in Boston right now but I grew up in the South. I came here from Virginia when I was sixteen, so my teenage years were here. My dad was a professor, and we traveled from one college to the next, finally ending up here. The longest I stayed in any place was from five to thirteen years old in Virginia. I have a brother that I grew up with. And I have some other siblings. My parents were divorced when I was two, and I grew up with my father. It was very unusual back in the early 1950s for him to take two kids and raise us. My mother has other children with my stepfather. She's in Louisiana right now. When we were young, she was a singer. She decided that family wasn't what she could handle and she wanted to pursue her art, so she left. I think she was happy with that decision at the time. Now, I don't know because we're estranged. I haven't seen her since I was about twenty-five. I sought her out when I was twenty, to try to keep some contact with her. So I know where she is, but it's a very awkward relationship.

When I was twenty-five, he remarried. He remarried once when I was in the first or second grade. But that didn't last long—maybe two or three years. He had two more children from that marriage. They left with their mom and we never saw them again.

My father just retired last year, and he got a fellowship, so at seventy years old he's starting a three-year fellowship. I asked him, "What are you doing this for? Where are you going to go? What you gonna do now, you know?" But he just loves school, I guess. My father is studying theology now and he's ordained.

Both of my parents are African American. And we have Native American heritage that I'm researching right now. It was on my grandmother's side. But it wasn't a big part of our upbringing, except that some things she did were maybe Native American traditions, as I'm finding out now. We never knew before.

Growing up we went to church. My grandmother was always something in the Methodist church. By the time we got to Boston she was senile, so she couldn't do it anymore, and my dad wasn't pushing it. I went to church on my own as a teenager, but I kind of drifted around. And then, when I got married, I tried to raise my son in a church but it was Catholic. His father was Catholic.

I've always been very uninhibited as far as talking about sex, or sexuality, or my relationship with men. It doesn't bother me to talk about it. I've gone through some things that I think can help other people sometimes. And I can see when younger women are going through something, and if I think I can help them, I'll start talking about myself and what has happened to me. And then they'll say, "You know, that happened to me, too." So they don't feel that they're so alone. I did feel when I was a kid, or when I was in my early twenties, that I was alone. I didn't have a woman to talk to, and I wasn't talking to my dad about it. And so I wouldn't like for my daughter to go through that, or anyone else. You can feel like it's not something that you want to whine about. You think that people will wonder why you put up with something. It's embarrassment and shame, and so you keep it to yourself. And we shouldn't. I think, if you can talk about just about anything with someone, if there's someone you can talk to that won't judge you, no matter what you do, you shouldn't keep it to yourself.

I think intimacy is a feeling. I think it's how I feel about someone, how they feel about me. It is more than sex—it's them caring about what my needs are and what my feelings are and my feeling the same way about them. I've had one-night stands, and you're not intimate with that person. Intimacy is talking, it's finding out more about a person. And when it comes to a point where you want to know what their likes and dislikes are and you're concerned about if they're upset or if they're happy, then it gets to the intimate stage. You're really telling your innermost feelings and not feeling that this person's going to use it against you.

I've found, recently, that there's one person that I'm intimate with that I've never had sex with. And that's because I talk to him, and he listens and I listen to him. It's different from any relationship I've ever had. And it's not love; we're not in love with each other. But it's friendship, and friendship sometimes can be intimate.

A break in intimacy is when you can't trust someone anymore—if you were sharing and then it was all a lie. I've had friends that I thought were my best friends, girlfriends, and we shared the most intimate details, you know. You think you were friends for years, and then you find out later that you were their friend, but they were not yours. And then, it's broken. I think that has happened to me twice in my life. With men, you know, that happens. I've always thought to myself, Oh I couldn't trust him; I was stupid; I should have known better. But with women, it doesn't happen that much, I don't think. When you get that close to girlfriends and they stab you in the back, it hurts much worse, I think.

I remember one woman that I had known six or seven years, and I thought she was my friend. When they say you should listen to your first instinct, you really should. The first time we became associated, she sought me out. Usually that doesn't happen. People seek you out when they have business to transact. She sought me out, probably because I was a neighbor and I was opening a boutique. She didn't say, "I want to go into business," we just started talking and became friends. As I look back, everything that was between us was based on the fact that she needed me. If she was upset about a man, she could call me at three o'clock in the morning and come over. She would stay at my house sometimes, or lie on my sofa, and I would bring her tea or whatever because I just knew she needed that companionship. She was like my own kid. She's a little bit younger than me, around eight years younger, but I treat my friends like part of me because I don't have a big extended family. Whenever I would call her, she'd say, "Can I call you back?" And she'd never call back. But I didn't really think about it; I thought she got busy and I let it go.

I let everything go until a few years ago. We had been in business together. She would ask me some intimate questions like, when I started to date a man or slept with a man that she knew, she'd ask me, "Well how was it?" And we'd talk about it. I had dated a white man, and she wanted to know all about that, and she said she could never do it. I'm a clothing designer and entrepreneur and about two or three years ago she was working, and I was struggling. But she said she needed help because she had bought a whole lot of stuff and needed to sell some. I came to her house and offered to peddle it for her when I was selling my things. So I did that. Never thought a thing of it.

I had a half brother that had died of pneumonia. When he died, we found out he was HIV-positive, and she was with me when I went to the funeral home. A few months later, someone told me that they had a microwave that I gave to her—that she had brought it over to their house right after I gave it to her. She told them that said she didn't want it in her house because my brother had AIDS. This is a woman who I shared anything with. She could have said that to me, "We don't know about AIDS, so you keep it, let me learn a little more about it." Or if she didn't want to say that, then she could have said, "You know something, I don't really need it. Maybe you should give it to someone else who really needs it." You know? But to take it and give me the impression that she needed it, and give it to someone else and give that reason . . . ? When I found this out, it set me back a bit, but I thought, what's more important—my relationship with her, or something stupid that she did? And my relationship with her was more important; she was a friend of mine. She had been there with me when my brother was going through his illness, and she would go visit him and so I thought, I'm going to let that go.

She had asked me a whole lot of questions about a guy that I had been dating, and then one day she said to me that a week prior, she had met him at the reservoir to talk to him. He made a date with her like a week before, but she didn't say anything to me. Why didn't she come to me and say, "Look, this guy that you're dating, he wants to talk to me, by myself." What could he want? She drove over thirty minutes on the highway to meet him. She tells me a week later that he said he was interested in her. She says that she told him that she could never date him. Because she was my friend, and he and I didn't have a one-on-one, I let it go. But I knew what he was all about.

Around the same time, she told me that she was seeing this man, and I find out that the man had already moved in with her. She asked me all my intimate details, but she was keeping things from me, you know? In January, she told me she was going to marry him. But it was not public knowledge, so she did not want me to tell anybody. I went out looking for wedding dresses with her because she wanted me to make hers. We spent days looking. In March, she telephoned me in the middle of the night and she wanted to come over because she was very upset. He had said he was going to get coffee and left, but he doesn't drink coffee, and she felt he was going somewhere else. And so she didn't want to be home when he got there. So I said, "Come on over." I was in a four-year relationship—I was living with someone. She slept in my guest room. In April we did a fashion show; she was in that. In May, she was supposed to go with me to this fashion show in another city. She never showed. I called, but she didn't return my calls. And this is the person I talked to two or three times a day. We were waiting for her with a van and all the stuff for the show. We waited an hour, but she never called. I never heard from her again until July.

I thought, something is up. It is going to be that she's either pregnant or married by the time I hear from her. In July, I wrote her a letter saying, "I have called you and you won't respond. If there's something I've done, let me know." And she wrote me a letter back saying, "Just bear with me, I'm going through something right now." So I accepted her explanation, you know how you just want to accept it, and then finally she called me two weeks before the wedding—I had already found out the date from someone else. She had asked me to do her wedding gown before and then disappeared. She went ahead and planned the wedding; there was a shower already planned for her. She had just completely cut me out. So what eventually happened was, she told me the wedding was planned for July 25 and asked me to come. She knew that I was due to appear at a big show in Dallas. She knew that date two years before when I applied to get into that show. I had told her my every thought. "Look, I want to be in the show; I hope I get in; I got in." So, I tell her I can't come because I have the show on the same day and she knew that.

I really didn't want to ruin her wedding by telling her off, so I waited until about a month later, in August. I called her and I said, "You really didn't want me there." She said, "Oh, I did want you there, everybody was asking me about you." "You didn't want me there because you never told me." I said, "What is going on with you? We're not friends. I've been your friend, but you are not my friend. You cut me off. You didn't say what was happening." She said, "Well, I was going through a lot of things." I said, "Well, then, you should have said, 'I'm going through a lot of things; you may not hear from me for three months. I'll call you.'" You know, say something. I told her about all the things I had let go. She tried to explain. I said, "There's no explanation needed for that, I let it go. But I'm just bringing it up to show you that there's just so many things I didn't say anything about, but this I cannot let go because I don't know who you are."

After we spoke, I knew that if she called me, I would talk to her, but I would not call her. She was an acquaintance now. But the next morning she called me back. And she said, "You know something, I want to try to explain what happened. I really don't want to lose you as a friend because you've always been there for me." She confesses that the guy she was living with and married was an ex-boyfriend of another best friend. She had previously told this friend that she would never date him and that she had already married him in November and that the whole July wedding was a fake. What she didn't know is that all this would make me cut her off forever. So I said, "So in November, when I was struggling, trying to take care of my handicapped son, my teenage daughter, peddling your things trying to help you because I thought you needed money, you had a husband that was working, and you were working at a job that you've been in fifteen years? But you used me to do that? And in January, when I went with you to look for wedding dresses, you were already married? And in March, when you stayed at my house because he didn't come home, you were married? You could have killed me. That's how little I knew about you. Because I don't know who you are. You're a stranger. I had a stranger in my house."

Women usually don't have an ulterior motive. Men, they have a goal. Usually it is sex. And once they get that they are through unless they try to keep several women out there that they can go to if they want to. And they usually don't cut off a relationship; they just do you badly enough that you will eventually break it off for them. They want to keep one foot in the door so they can always come back. Most of the guys that I have had relationships with, I'm still friends with. I get to understand them. Like with that guy my friend went to meet—we're good friends, because I knew what he was all about. So now I don't have any unrealistic expectations of him. But this thing with Monica caught me off guard. Women are usually there because they want to be friends. And most the time, if women don't want to be friends, they're not.

Most of the time, men see women as sexual objects, but they can get over it, they can get past it. If you can establish that it is going to be a platonic relationship right at the beginning, it sometimes works. But sometimes they won't hear that; they take that more as a challenge. So it's usually left up to us as women to keep it that way and not ruin the friendship. And I've found the best way to do that is to use joking. I say, "Oh, get out of here." But if it becomes more aggressive, then you get serious and say, "Look, you're insulting me. You're hurting my feelings here." And they'll back off usually.

I met my son's father when I was in high school, in my senior year. I was sixteen, and we had just moved to New England. I met him at a Christmas party in December of '66, and then started to date him. He was the first person I'd dated. I had never really been out with a guy alone before. My dad started letting me go out with him when I was seventeen. After about six to seven months I became sexually active. Up to that point, I had done nothing sexually, not even kissing or anything. I was scared, for one thing, and I was shy. And so with him it took awhile, and we were around people all the time. We started having sex in the summer of 1967. I started college in the fall, got pregnant in January of 1968, and got married in July of 1968. I had my baby in October.

I married him in July because I got pregnant. I thought that was the right thing to do. It was for all the wrong reasons that I married him. I knew that I didn't love him. I realized when it was time to get married that I really wished I didn't have to. But I thought I had to. When I had to tell him that I was pregnant my father said, "You know, everybody's entitled to a mistake. Don't feel that you have to do this, that you have to be married." But I wanted to. I wanted to because I wanted my kid to have two parents. I didn't have that. So I thought that I'd try. I don't think abortions were accessible then, but I didn't think about it. By the time I found out I was pregnant, I must have been at least three months along.

We used condoms, sometimes. There were times that if you didn't have a condom you still did it and it was just not an issue. I didn't really understand the whole process. And the first time I had sex it was not because I wanted to. It was because I had been seeing him for a long time, I thought that I was supposed to, because he wanted to, that maybe I should just to appease him. He was nudging me about it, we were kissing and touching a lot for months, but never taking our clothes off or anything. But finally, he planned it. You know, a romantic evening, sort of. He had gotten a place and all that. I didn't know about that. But he told me I didn't have to if I didn't want to. But I wanted to. And it wasn't even in the passion of the moment because I had to think about it, and I made a conscious decision to go ahead with it. And I did want to do it, but I thought I was old. I thought at eighteen, all my girlfriends from thirteen had been saying that they had had intercourse. And I remember being in the bathroom and someone saying something about intercourse, and I said, "Intercourse?" They said, "You don't know what that is?" And I said, "Of course I know what it is." And I went and looked it up in the dictionary. I didn't even know what it was. And this was in the eighth grade. And I thought, everybody has had sex but me and I had not. But I don't remember having any physical urges so strong that would make me want to go through with it.

And even after I got married, I hated sex. It was just not something I liked. I mean, I had never really—maybe because I wasn't really turned on by him. And I didn't know what being turned on was. Sex was like a function to me at that time.

And I tell my daughter—she's eighteen, a freshman in college now—"Never do it unless you want to. When you get ready to have sex for the first time, make sure that you're prepared to have this man in your life for the rest of your life. Look at him and say, 'Could I have this man in my life for the rest of my life?' If you think, 'I wouldn't want him in my life for the rest of my life,' then be very careful with what you're doing." Because, she doesn't have contraceptives, she's not on birth control or anything, but she knows about condoms. She's much more aware than we were. Everybody is now.

I didn't get any information from my grandmother or father about sex—none. It was taboo to talk about anything like that. I wouldn't dare to talk to my grandmother. Before we left the South, Dad had left us with her for a while to go finish college, and so it was just me, my brother, and my grandma. My grandma went blind when I was nine, so it was primarily me doing all of the housework, me and my brother. But she was very self-sufficient; she could take care of us and tell us what to do.

My dad would tell me things, but not about sex. When I had to have my first bra, my father took me to a department store, and he went and he talked to the saleslady, and then she took me and picked out what I should have. He would tell me I shouldn't let anyone touch me that was uncomfortable. If anyone was touching me, I should let him know. But he was very uncomfortable talking about it—in light of me being a girl and living with him, he didn't know how to handle it, I guess. I think I got more information from my girlfriends and their moms than I did from my dad. And to tell you the truth, I could have probably talked to him about anything because being a professor he'd probably talked to kids about some of everything. But he didn't say, "Do you want to talk about sex?" or anything like that. He'd say, "Well, you know you can tell me anything."

At ten, I remember a girlfriend of mine getting her period. And her mother and her told me about it and so I knew what it was all about. That was the first time I'd heard about menstruation, from my friend's mom. And I didn't get mine early. And I think the first time I even spotted I was fourteen. I didn't tell my grandmother or anybody. I remember my aunt coming once, and I overheard her and my grandmother talking. She must have been asking my grandmother if I had my period because I was fifteen. And my grandmother said, "Well, if she has, I haven't seen anything. She hasn't said anything to me." But they didn't even come in and say, "Come here. Let's talk about it." I had a girlfriend next door. Her father was a professor, like mine, and we were living in campus housing. She had gotten her period and so me and her talked about it. She had a mom and a sister. I remember us getting a tampon and trying to put it up there and we couldn't get it up there. And she would be in the bathroom with the phone, and I'd be in my bathroom with the phone, and she'd say, "Did you get yours in?" We couldn't do that. But I never had a regular cycle until I had my son. I only had maybe two a year.

Things with my husband didn't go well. Plus it got worse, because he became abusive. So then I really did not want to be with him. The abuse started during my pregnancy, right after we were married. Before that, he would get mad at me on occasion and walk away in anger. But I had never seen him like that before. I had never been struck, yelled at—because I didn't have that in my home. With two parents, with a mom and dad, you probably would have heard some arguing or some yelling or something. But my dad and his mother never argued. At first I tried to fight back, because I couldn't believe it was happening. And then you get to feel that this is a person that's supposed to love you, and he's trying to kill you. That's what I thought. He's trying to kill me. Then I started feeling sorry for him because he would cry, and he would say that he didn't know what happened, that he needed me, that he had all these problems, emotional problems. So I'm here trying to help this man. I'm not going to leave him, so I'm trying to stick by him.

And I know better now—I know now that they all do that after they hit you. They cry. Or they promise they're never going to do it again. What woke me up to him—because I had run away—was that he knew how to break me down. What I didn't know is that he had broken me down long before he'd struck the first blow. When I was pregnant, and then when I had my son (who has cerebral palsy), he had started telling me early—I guess all guys feel this way—"You like the baby more than you like me. You're paying more attention to the baby." And sometimes they do feel that. And then you try to make them not feel that. You try to give them some time, or whatever. We didn't know during the pregnancy that my son was going to have a disability.

And he started to say other mean things. My father drank—he was an alcoholic. He was one of those quiet drunks. He was a professor during the day, and he'd come home. He would have his dinner, he would make dinner for us, and then he started to drink. And then he would go to his bed and he would sleep. So my husband started to bring that up: "Your father's a drunk." Just hurtful things, you know, things like "Why don't you like my mother? Just because you didn't have a mother, you don't know how to treat people." Then I had my son. Well, he was jealous of his son. The one hurtful thing I still remember is him saying, "I hope the baby dies."

So my son was born with cerebral palsy. And he was very nice during that time. He was hurt, as I was, and he was attentive to me and my son at first. We were both in college then. But I had to quit college, because we needed medical so this kid could have surgeries and whatever special treatment that he needed. But five weeks after my son's birth, I was out there looking for a job. And so my husband had to quit too, so we could both get medical for my son. That was when the beating started. He started to say he's West Indian, from Jamaica, and that he didn't come to this country for this, and he's got to quit college, and I can't even have a healthy son. All kinds of mean things, he said. He was just terrible. Years passed. My son was about five years old when I left my husband.

The abuse happened about once a month. Or sometimes more than once a month, and sometimes two or three months would pass. What I attribute my strength to is my upbringing with my father and grandmother. My father would tell me all the time how smart I was and how much he loved me—where this man is telling me how stupid I was and how I couldn't do anything right. Eventually I came to my senses. I think that the thing that made me leave him was that my son became very nervous and scared by any loud noises because we fought. I had left him several times but I always came back, and not because I needed him to take care of me, but because my dad was gone by then. My dad left right after I got married—he left. And so I had no family here. I did not tell my dad because I didn't want him to worry about me.

So, my husband went back to college and I helped him. And it was not because I cared about him, but I knew that we had to have careers because we were out there struggling. He was reading electric meters and I was working in a bank as a teller. So I went back to school at night for computers and that's when the beatings really got bad because he would say, "You think you're all that, but you're supposed to stand by your husband. I'm supposed to be the breadwinner." But neither one of us had went back to school, and I knew that I had to take care of my son. He blamed me for the job itself. But I went into night school. And then I got a job as a programmer, because I knew that was the wave of the future in '71. So I got a job and was doing well; and then he quit his job and decided to go back to college. And I supported him and my family.

All of this happened while I was leaving him. I had told him I was leaving, and he wanted to go back to school. I wasn't afraid of him anymore and I knew we couldn't be together. So he left, he went down there to school, and I told him, "When you're done, we won't be living together anymore." I guess he thought that because I was so supportive of him I was going to take him back. But I did not. He was dean's list, very smart, and got his degree in accounting. When he told me he was graduating and asked me to come, I said no. I paid the mortgage on the house for two months and I got myself an apartment. And I left him the house so we could settle up later. But I did that because I was going to divorce him and I did not want the house to go down because he couldn't pay. Also, I knew that the house had a lot of bad memories for me, and as long as I lived in it, he was going to be stopping by because he had an interest in it. So I moved out, and he came back in August of '75.

December of '75 I met this man through a blind date my girlfriend set up. I had no intentions of looking for anybody. I went to lunch with him, but I would never go out at night with him. After I got away from my husband, I did not want to be close to anyone else for a long time. It took me about a year of seeing this new man on and off before I started to get close to him. And I think the first time I got close to him it was because he was listening to me. I never talked very much, but my ex-husband was threatening me—threatening to snatch my son. And I began to cry and I couldn't control it. This was the first time I had cried in front of a stranger. And so we became friends. I eventually married him, and that's my daughter's father.

That relationship lasted for about seven years. He was just not a man that should have been married because he cheated the whole time. I was thirty, I was very independent. And nobody took care of me; I took care of myself. I wanted more kids but had been told I couldn't have more since I had an ectopic pregnancy. After five years of being with him, I got pregnant, and he had never had a kid. This man had never talked about marriage or kids—he thought he couldn't have any. When I found out I was pregnant, I wanted my kid, even though an abortion would have been a very easy and logical thing. And I tell you what, I knew what I wanted. I was keeping this kid. So I told him that; I told him that I was pregnant, and since we had never talked about kids, I would understand if he didn't want it. But he did, and he asked me to marry him, and I said, "No. I did that the first time, can't do that again." I said that we could set a date two years down the road. If we were still together, and we still wanted to, we could get married. And that's what we did—got married two years down the road, and for the first time we were living together. It wasn't working, and he left. But we're still friends. We didn't have a bad divorce. We sat down and wrote out an agreement. I had my own house. And he had a three-family that he was living in. When we got married he moved into my house and rented out his house. He still had the property, but just to be sure that nobody went after anybody else's stuff, we kind of wrote our own agreement. I keep my house, you keep your house; I keep my car; you keep your car; and stuff like that.

Yeah, both of them I was with for almost seven years. I was five years with the first husband, and then it took me two years to go through the divorce from him because they didn't have no-fault ones then. And then the second husband, I was with him for seven years total. But with him we talked, we joked, we laughed. He was never mean to me.

I was more open with him. He was from the same state as me. We knew some of the same people from schools; and it just was very different. We had fun together; we traveled together. He was good to my son, you know. When I saw him, I was happy to see him, and I knew that he was happy to see me. It was romantic. It was like a good friend when you see them and you hug them. And he would pick me up and swing me around like a kid or something. It was just happy. So it was different—it was very different.

I never had an orgasm when I was with my first husband. The first time that I did have an orgasm was when I got away from him, and I was with someone else. I was older, I was more mature, and I was with someone I really wanted to be with—and then I realized I had not known what it was about for all that time. You know, it was just, it was different because I seemed to be more conscious of what I was doing. I was very thirsty for knowledge after my first husband. And I thought I didn't like sex, and all that, but I didn't know anything. I started to read books. I had never seen—I'd never seen like an erotic film and didn't see it with him, either, during the seven years I was with my first husband. I didn't see one of those until after I was divorced from the second husband.

I started reading and reading, because I realized that I didn't know anything about sex. I didn't know what I was supposed to do. I thought everything I did was bad—like you shouldn't touch a guy this way or that. I was reading this book, and it said that men's nipples are sensitive. I never knew that. So then I wanted to try it. I think another reason we got very close was because I'd be reading a book, and I'd say, "Let me touch your nipples." And he'd joke and say, "You're not going to be using me as a guinea pig."

It made him feel good that I was someone who was trying to learn something. Looking back and knowing now that he was out there with all these women, I guess I made him feel like he was macho or something, that he was teaching me. For me, it was the kissing, it was the intimacy, it was being with him that made it better. The first time I had sex with him, you know he was gentle and loving and kind. Most of the times when I had sex with my first husband, it was from fear, or just out of obligation to keep him from fighting or yelling at me or something. And I hated it, and I would go into the shower and shower and shower—it felt like rape. And he would be mad about that. "Why is it you always shower right afterward?" "Because I hate you," I wanted to say. But I didn't feel that way about my second husband.

My first orgasm was manual stimulation from him. I had never been touched like that before, not that I could remember. And maybe I had been—maybe my first husband had touched me like that, but it didn't feel the same way. It was new for me. I wanted to have sex all the time. He was trying to get some sleep most of the time. I remember one time he worked second shift and he would get in at midnight, and I'd be waiting for him. And he'd make me so mad because he would fall asleep. It was snowing out one night, and I'm fondling him and kissing him and trying to get him to have sex with me, and he fell asleep. I first opened the windows and let him cool off. But he was still falling asleep, so I took the covers off the bed. Then he woke up and he was like, "What the hell is going on?" "Why don't you just go home, don't come over here. You know, what are you coming over here for?" I said. Now it's very different. If somebody said that to me, I would be very upset. Like, "That's all you want from me, sex?" What I wanted from him was sex.

I prefer the vaginal orgasms now and then. They feel physically different; when the muscles are contracting with him still inside of you it just feels different. I can feel that all over—more than when it's outside because it's like all the muscles contract. The nerves are very sensitive then. That's when I don't want him to move; I want to be held—and stay in that position for a bit. And the manual one, it's like it's over and you don't even know it. Even after I learned about orgasms, I still didn't masturbate.

That's something that I still have trouble with. I just never enjoyed that. I always thought, well, if I get to that point, I'd just rather be with somebody.

Like I said, my second husband should never have gotten married, because he cheated the whole time. For the first few years, he wasn't living with me. But it was my bed. We had never promised to be monogamous. I was monogamous because of my situation, where I was coming from, my age.

I was monogamous, but he wasn't. He was seeing other people. We never discussed it. It never occurred to me to ask him. I never thought about it. I didn't care one way or the other at first because it was just a relationship, but if he had brought it up, I think I would not have seen him because I was just getting out of that bad marriage. And then a girlfriend called me, a little after I started seeing him, and told me he was seeing a friend of mine, someone who would eat lunch with me at work during the day. And so that was my first sign. And I thought about it, and I thought, Well, why shouldn't he? You know, I didn't ask him for a monogamous relationship, and he didn't ask me. We're both free to do whatever we want. So I never mentioned it to him, and I didn't mention it to her, either. But I didn't eat lunch with her; she was not my friend, just an office worker. But she had opened it up because we were at my girlfriend's wedding together, the girlfriend who told me about this, and she was a friend of that girl. So she came up to me at the wedding and said, "Is that your boyfriend?" I said yes. She said, "Oh, he's mine too." It's funny how we blame the woman, more than the man, because we think women are smarter.

I didn't really know how far their relationship had gone until a couple of years down the road. He was having his tonsils out and I was in his hospital room, and the nurse came in and asked one of the two visitors to leave to make room for this woman who was waiting to visit. And I didn't know he was still seeing her. So I said to his cousin, "Why don't you leave? And I'll stay, and she can come up." And then, whooo, so she didn't come up. That was the time I found out how many people he was seeing. Women were coming to his room. I was there another time and another woman was in there.

I didn't like it. I didn't like it. I decided, what I'll do is I'll just go on my own. I started thinking, looking back. I started noticing a pattern. He would come over to my house usually on Sunday night because he knew I was available. Friday, Saturday, he was dating other people. Important nights. At first I didn't put much stock in it because I didn't know why. But after I knew why, I would not let him have that pattern. I didn't say anything to him. Usually he would call me all during the week. If he came on Thursday, then I wouldn't expect him on Friday. He had worked it out that way and he didn't know I had figured it out. So if I didn't hear from him by Wednesday, he couldn't reach me on Thursday. And Friday morning I would pack my car and leave from work and to go visit a girlfriend of mine. He started to call me all during the weekend, he could never reach me. He started thinking I was seeing someone in New York. But I just was not being available to him.

Finally one day he said, "Do you want to go to New York for the weekend?" I said, "Sure." So he said, "Okay, I'll pick you up." I got a sitter for my son. He came and picked me up, and we were on our way to New York, and he said, "Did you call your girlfriend?" I said, "No." He said, "Well, she doesn't know we're coming?" I said, "You said you were taking me to New York." What he wanted was to go see where I was going every weekend, who I was with. So then he wanted to become monogamous. But he didn't, he just wanted *me* to become monogamous. He wanted me to be his girlfriend, but he was still cheating.

Before I had my son I thought, Is this it? Is this the way the rest of my life is gonna be? Unhappy with someone and I don't even know what real happiness is. What changed for me, by having him, was that I became more mature; I wanted to live. I knew that nothing could happen to me; that's what made me leave, too. Nothing could happen to me that would leave my son out here alone, without someone like me to be as caring for him. Anybody else was not going to be as caring for him, even a sister or my brother or my father because my son was incontinent, wearing diapers because of urinary problems. He had leg braces and all kinds of things that someone else might get tired of. And I was afraid that he would end up in an institution. So I had to leave my first husband to get myself strong and to be there for my son and show him as much love as I could. Being with my son was the purest love I had ever had, a love that you never have to think about. And as my son grew, I always felt that whenever they can ask the question, they're ready to be told as much as they could handle. So when he started asking about sex, he asked me about boys and girls and why he's got a penis, and that kind of stuff, I told him. My daughter was very much wanted, and I had planned on having other kids and just never could. So she was like a godsend. It was very different with the two pregnancies because with my son here I was, a very young, inexperienced child of eighteen, as opposed to a thirty-year-old with a career, a house, just on my own, a very independent woman. I knew that I didn't need anybody's support except that I wanted my daughter to have her father's love, and I would not have kept her father from her. Taking care of my son on my own, almost, with his father being very little help, was very different from having her, a healthy baby, and making the conscious decision that every other time she cried, it was her father's turn to get up with her. He moved in just as I had her, and later moved back out to his house. When we were married, every Friday night was my night out; every Saturday night was his night out. And when we were divorced, every other weekend was his weekend, whether I had somewhere to go or not. So it was very different. After we divorced, I gave myself some time to be able to date other people. I never brought anybody around my children unless I thought that I was serious about that person. I didn't want them to meet my children because I didn't know what I wanted to do. I didn't want my children to be too vulnerable to this or that person, and then every time you break up with someone, you're pulling them away from that person.

I started talking to my daughter about sex very early. At twelve I said, "Cheryl, are you sexually active yet?" She's like, "Mom!" I said, "Well I don't know, I have to ask you." So she said, "No!" But she knew; she started asking questions when she was seven or eight, whereas my son is very quiet and asks nothing. But her, she caught me in the bathroom changing a tampon one day. And she said, "Mommy what happened? You cut yourself." So I said no and I started to tell her the story and how it worked. And then I said, "But this is only for me to tell you; you don't go to school and tell other kids. It's for their moms to tell them. And you don't tell Nikki"—her best friend—"let Nikki's mom tell her when she's ready." And then, I remember there was a child molestation case on the news, and it was something about oral sex, and so my son said— He was sixteen. He's very sheltered; he doesn't have many friends. He can't get out and walk and run and do everything because of his illness. So he is not as socially developed as other people in his age group. He was twenty-nine this week. And he's still a virgin. Sometimes I feel so bad for him because he has urinary problems. He just had a new urinary implant put in.

So when he asked about the news, I explained that the candy man over on Jackson Street was luring kids with candy and then forcing them to have oral sex. So again, my son said, "What's that?" And I said that he forced them to put his penis in their mouth. And my son was like, "What!" He couldn't believe that. Cheryl was about five years old. She didn't say anything at first, and then she said, "Well, I know what that is." And I said, "Know what what is?" And she said, "A penis." I said, "No you don't." She said, "Yes I do! It's what boys have." So I guess she'd gotten that from other people. But then later as she got older, she would ask me questions, "Mom, what is this, what is that?" She would never ask her dad or her stepmother, but she'll talk to me pretty easily about those things. So I try to keep the lines of communication open. Because I know eventually she's not going to be a virgin anymore. But that's her choice. I want it to be her choice.

But I haven't told her about orgasms or anything like that. I guess we haven't talked about sex enough. She doesn't want to talk about it. But what I have done is I approach her with that part of it by saying, "Let it be something you want to do because when you're a virgin, having sex the first time, it is not going to be that great unless it is something you want. It may not be that great; it wasn't great for me that first time. It hurt." I've asked her things like, "Have you tried to put a tampon up there?" She said, "Yeah." But she can't wear one. I said, "Well, a tampon is very small compared to a man's penis. Let sex be something that is a conscious choice; then you will be more relaxed. Then it will be something that you might enjoy—because if you don't enjoy it the first time, you're probably not going to want to do it the second time."

I think she probably knows more than she's letting me know that she knows. I know that she has done some heavy petting and kissing and that kind of thing because one day she had this thing on her neck, and I said, "Is that a hickey on your neck?" And she said, "Yeah." I said, "So that's what you and Lenny were doing. Did you have sex with him?" She said, "No, Ma, not yet." But she's not afraid to talk to me about it. I think I don't tell her about orgasms and all that because I don't want to get her too interested yet. There's fear that she might want to experience it if it's so wonderful. You can never tell what they're going to do.

One thing I just love about her is she dates but not like we dated when I was young. When I was young, you dated one boy. But that meant, sooner or later where was that relationship gonna go? But the kids now, they do a lot of group going-out. The first time my daughter went with a boy by herself was when she went to her prom. And that's not because I stopped her or her dad stopped her; before that she didn't want to go with him by herself. She wanted her girlfriends around her, and he wanted his boys, they all went out together. And then after the prom, they all had each car behind another's. They did things like that. She's my only hope. My son can't have kids, but I want grandkids, but I don't want to talk to her much about it because I don't want to put any pressure on her.

I had the two relationships over that long period of time. And then I had a couple of one-night stands, just because I wanted to, and didn't want to see them no more. I guess I was as bad as a man in that respect, because after my second divorce I thought, Well, all I really want from them is sex. I think I had about three one-night stands. I was in my late thirties, early forties. You feel like that's all you want. And then I stopped. I just stopped having sex. That's when I started my business. I thought, I don't want no man in my life. They're destructive. Your feelings get hurt, you let your business go and you're just concentrating on them. I let my daughter go live with her father and her stepmother from seven to seventeen. My son went to go live with my dad down south for a year. And I started working on my business in textiles, art designing. It was hard, but my daughter was right here in this same town, and I had her around. We still had the same schedule every other weekend. But my situation was so terrible at the time that I had to sell my house, I moved into a one-bedroom.

So I said, "That's it. No dates, because then you'll get distracted. You'll fall in love, and then you won't do your work. And there's no paycheck coming in, you have to work." So for three years I was celibate, from thirty-nine to forty-one. Then I met a guy, like an idiot, and I was with him for four years. I met him when I was forty-one or -two, and I was with him for about four years. And I've been away from him for six years.

I've always done textiles. When I was a kid, my grandmother taught me to sew. And she did all kinds of clothing and crafts. She lived off of everything she did. She didn't work. She made preserves, and sold them, and grew vegetables and made quilts, and that's just how she lived. Later on I had my sewing room, and I would sew at home at lunch time, and do a couple of stitches on whatever I was doing, and then go back to work. And then it just started taking over more time, and I quit my job in '87. But in '86, '85, I had a tumor in my stomach and found out that I could have died. So then I thought, I don't want to be in computers for the rest of my life. I want to do something I like. I love computers, and I still have mine and I still love it, but I want to do the artistic side. I want the second half of my life to be very different; I want it to be more enjoyable; I want to work at something I love. So I went part-time at my job. So I started working on my business. And then when I would go into work, if there was nothing to do, I would feel, like, Why am I here? I need to be home working. I have other work that needs to be done. And then I quit. I worked part-time for two years, to see if I could make it on a half salary, and then I planned the move. I planned my daughter's going to her dad, I didn't ask him, but they asked me. I didn't want her to go, and then I had the tumor. And I thought, What if something had happened to me and I couldn't take care of her like they could? They both were working and had built a new house. So then we switched roles. She came with me every other weekend.

I was very present, whereas they couldn't be. She lived with them, but I was the one who was more flexible. Because they had other kids. So everybody would call me if they missed the school bus, because I could go out and pick them up. So I sort of helped them out too, you know. And we had a good relationship, me as the ex-wife, and the new wife, we had a good relationship. We're still friends. She would call me if something was wrong with Cheryl, and she didn't know what. We would get together and talk about it.

Race doesn't really matter in picking men. It is the way that they treated me that mattered. The six or so men I have been with have been African American, white, and Hispanic. I knew who cannot be in my future—who's not going to last. The Hispanic guy I knew was not going to be in my future, but that wasn't because he was Hispanic. It was because of his age, because he was much younger than me. I was in my late thirties, and he was about ten years younger than me. And I had been married twice; he had not been married. I had children; he had no children. So I'm thinking, Unh-unh. He's gonna want kids, he's gonna want his family eventually, so we know from the beginning that this is not going nowhere.

I've been exposed to it all, I mean I've been exposed to really bad racism because I was one of the five kids bused to an all-white school in the South during the sixties, '63, stuff like that. But I never thought of it when I did become sexually active; it never had any effect on me. And as far as sexism, maybe a little bit. My first husband was very male dominant, thought a woman's place is this and that. I'm more opposed to that than anything else. If someone says to me, "Well, a woman is supposed to do this," then I know we're not going to make it—unless I can try to talk to him and try to let him see another point of view.

# Veronica

*I*'M TWENTY-TWO years old. I just graduated from a historically black college last May. I started working at an art gallery for and about young people. I was an art major, and I'm trying to go to Milan to study fashion. My father was in the military for twenty years. I moved several times during the course of growing up. When I was thirteen I stayed in one place for a while, in the Baltimore area. My mom taught school, so when we moved, she was able to find a job. It really was a good match. Both of my parents are from the North Carolina. My mom's family are farmers; they own a lot of land there. I was exposed to cows and animals. I became a vegetarian at nine, and I think that, having these relationships with farms, shucking corn and dealing with vegetables, was part of it, too. My father is six foot three, and I have a brother who's seven years older; he's six foot two. So I was tall early, and very brown-skinned. I was in a predominantly Caucasian environment, so I had started to have these self-esteem issues. And my mom was like, "Look, you're tall. It's a good thing." Self-pride is a thread that has carried me to where I am, so I think it's relevant. Now I'm the same height as most people, a little shorter probably, but at the time it was a big deal.

I'm the youngest daughter, and when my brother was thirteen and I was about six or seven, he started to show signs of schizophrenia. Not wanting to go to school, having strange depression, the whole nine. He kind of went in and out of that. At the time, no one was really aware what it was. He went to University of Michigan for a while and came back because he had a breakdown, basically, and that was when I was about thirteen or fourteen. So I think that's also shaped my ideas about other things, about mental health and about him and his resilience to keep trying and go forward after setbacks.

We went to church, a Christian church on the military bases. In certain places, we had more connection with the black churches where we went outside of the fort, especially this last place. I was baptized when I was seventeen or eighteen, when I was a senior in high school. So I have a relationship with one particular church, which is always helpful, because it's like your community base. I don't really go to church—actually, I did a painting about that—but I don't really go on Sundays partly because I didn't want to get up when I had to. I felt like it was something really personal. Also, I started to learn a little more about Buddhism, and I wanted to have a total package or understanding about religion. But I do feel more ties to Christianity, and I understand the links between that and Buddhism.

I guess intimacy is a connection that you feel which is not going to be universal for everyone else with that person. Something that speaks about an individual's giving of themselves in a way that's direct to you, and to your feelings. Intimacy is a connection that is really focused. It could be a passionate focus; it could be friendly intimacy or family. I mean, there's moments at Thanksgiving or something when you're like, Gosh, you know, if someone else were to come into this environment, we maybe wouldn't act this way. I guess the level of trust increases—I feel as though the person that I am intimate with has a level of trust about me, or has entrusted me with information, or feelings, that I feel are genuine. Kind of a genuineness, a being-in-touch-ness. And sometimes, sexual intimacy doesn't get you to that kind of intimacy. Sex kind of takes the form of recreation more than an actual expression of trust. I think it can play a part in it, but it also can be separate.

Loss of trust, feeling as though there's been disclosure, breaks intimacy. That's pretty important, the trust thing. Or if what I felt was intimate wasn't necessarily as serious to you, that kind of thing. I guess I feel like there's a female closeness and a male closeness because I feel like I relate differently in some ways. I think I feel close to my mother, right now, and my boyfriend. But then I don't know. I really feel that there's times that I just connect with certain people, and I like to keep that going. Right now I'm at a state where I have some friendships that have gotten to a really nice level after five years of being here. I feel comfortable about my sexuality, but it could be even more comfortable. A few of my friends have explored bisexuality and feel comfortable with that term for themselves. For me, it was like, No? No. I'm comfortable with that. But I love women; women are fly. I really admire them, and I really can see a beauty in them. Men on the whole, I see some rare ones that are attractive, but it's other criteria that attract me to men. Most of the men I think are interesting have feminine characteristics. They're either really sensitive people, they have long hair sometimes, dreaded hair like mine, or they giggle. Or they have a cool relationship with their moms.

I learned about sex when I was about nine, when I was going through puberty and my mom took me to a doctor because I was developing breasts. She was like, "She has Hershey-kiss size lumps on her chest"—this was the language—"What could it be?" And I was worried: Was it cancer? What? So the doctor checked me out, and they're like, "Okay, pubic hair. This is puberty." No, it can't be, I thought. I just had no idea. My mom was like, "No, she's bleeding." What does this mean? It was because I was having a period. Masturbation was an issue when I was nine. I had a desire to do it. But with myself or with a doll. I think children do it, maybe when they're even six months old. I had a desire to keep it secret, so I guess I did. I knew there was some type of stigma about it. I didn't know what. I don't know if I knew what that term "orgasm" was, but I masturbated until I felt like stopping. And I almost feel like orgasm is like that sometimes; it's a point where you just feel like, Okay, that's enough. It was also exploration. At night was a time when I explored myself and just knew what was going on. Between nine and ten years old, she gave me a book, which was gigantic, *Women's Health*, and there's chapters on birth control. It was something that I had for a while, but it was a resource. I was into encyclopedias and dictionaries; I really liked this type of book. We didn't talk about sex, about menstruation, what it was, not so much showing the little diagram of ovulation or anything like that, but more like where the bleeding is coming from, what to do and how to get the pads, what to do about cramps. Just really general. Then when I was twelve, they had the whole Annie show. I hated it. It was this film on menstruation, and Annie narrated it, the woman who played in it on Broadway. She was sixteen or seventeen. She did this menstruation one, and I was just like, Uhh! It started off talking about how you're so lucky you can have children, and this is a great thing. And they're like, "Yeah, it's really okay." And I was just like, No! Because it's painful. I had cramps, which at twelve I thought was unnecessary. I also didn't think it was fair that these things are painful, and men are just in gym class not having to worry about red dots on their shorts, and they can wear white anytime they want to. These were issues for me at twelve or thirteen. I tried to explain this to my boyfriend, and he's like, "Okay." And also the fact that I was really becoming aware of how sexist this society was—the imagery I kept seeing in teen magazines and this kind of aesthetic. I thought it was very negative. It made me smell; I resented that process.

At that time, too, I guess I had experiences with women, girls. There was an older girl. We would pretend that we were having sex. So at that time, I was kind of frightened, discovering things on my own. But no one else had a discussion about "birds and bees" and such with me. Especially not my father. I would say he's very uncomfortable talking honestly about sex or cursing or—I think when he was growing up in the South he couldn't walk outside of his box, where his house was. And he would tell us that constantly, that he had these limitations. I haven't felt comfortable communicating with him about sex. On the other hand, my brother and I both find my mom a refuge just to talk freely. She's more open. I mean, my talking with her about sexuality and virginity is really indirect. Like I would say, "I'm really not trying to have kids. I'm really not trying to have sex until I'm married," and she's like, "Okay."

I had the idea from hearing lectures, Christianity lectures, that sex was not holy, but it was also something that was sacred, and that marriage was the place for that to happen. Also the risk of pregnancy. And I wasn't really thought of as desirable by a lot of guys either, so I didn't have opportunities where I would have been in sexual situations. I was the one who danced, who went to homecoming by herself. I have pictures of my dress. I felt like a very independent person, and people didn't really know how to take that, guys especially. Most of them were Caucasian, so the black ones were saying that I was an Oreo or something else anyway, even if they thought I was attractive. And the white ones, their moms probably wouldn't really be down. I mean, it's cool to be friends, but I think anything else would have been an issue for some of them. So yeah, I was kind of a loner. I was the extroverted lonely person. I had a certain amount of friends who were very international-clique friends, and there were some men who were friendly in it; but in terms of having relationships, it didn't happen till I was a senior.

I went to Catholic schools, and I went to anything that was structured. My father probably was the person who was adamant about going to church and trying to have these type of ideals. And I needed that kind of structure for myself, and I created that with the guise of Christianity. I guess because of moving too. I felt like after the first time it was really painful to me; I was probably eight or nine or ten. It was painful to leave people and to start all over in these other places. Some places didn't have kids my age, so it was kind of lonely. I had to really find something that spoke to me, and it was Christianity. Senior year, I went to a Lenny Kravitz concert by myself and sat next to a Hungarian guy who's from Budapest. At that time, the war wasn't initiated. I'd just come back from Europe, so I was really into Rome and that whole idea. I gave him my number, and then we talked, and it became a relationship. He called me his girlfriend after the second week, and I was like, Whoa, cool. He was older. He was twenty-one and I was seventeen. So then that relationship began. I don't know if I stopped it from happening before. But it wasn't available, and as opposed to going crazy over it, I just put that fervor in other things. Secretary for the class, my art, whatever, something else. And it evolved into that. It was also his maturity: for someone to come from another country and really be trying to do this here—I just really admired it. And the accent, I thought it was sexy. To this day, when I hear Hungarian, or something that sounds like it, oooh. I think that they're really close to Greece, and really close to Africans. I really believe that Slavic people in general have some ties to Africa. It was a really good mesh, that culture and me. Also, someone who was telling me that I wasn't weird. He didn't have the same preconceived ideas that something was wrong with me for doing what I want. He thought what I was doing was more normal than what people in high school were doing. The way I dressed, the way I talked, my speech. What I read—I was reading Diop at the time—becoming really nationalist about Africans and wanting to go to a black school. I didn't really have a lot of black colloquialisms, so I was the Oreo. Black people felt that way, but then Caucasian people, at this time, had a wannabe hip-hoppy kind of thing. It was an overriding weirdness underlined by the fact that I was, to them, wannabe white. Also, there was this type of hierarchy that happens with public schools where you have advanced classes, and that stratifies people who aren't in that class, and that you're not ever going to have classes with. I was the only African there, female. My parents chose to spend their money on getting a BMW or Mercedes or whatever they wanted to do; that made it seem like we were upper class. So there was that.

My parents didn't really interact with my boyfriend except for one time when I think I snuck him over, and they found out, and they were mad because I snuck him over. But they didn't really react to him. If they answered the phone, they were courteous. It wasn't a real big deal about his age, race, or anything like that. Plus my brother adamantly wants to marry a white woman. Cindy Crawford–looking, blonde hair, blue eyes—that's what he wants. So they had already had to voice their opinion about that. And basically it was, "If you're in love and this is the relationship you want, then okay." And I guess, what else was there?

After four months, we attempted to have sex and it didn't work out. He made this convincing argument. "What are you afraid of? If you want to have sex, if you get pregnant or if something happens, I'm going to pay for this. I'm going to be there. So what's really stopping you? Just because you're deciding to be a virgin doesn't mean that I have to be a virgin, too." Like, "This is your decision, and I feel like I'm being punished for your decision." At the time, it was convincing. And we had escalated things sexually. Started with just French kissing, to being touched, to actually being fingered, which I think ended up breaking my hymen already. So I was prepared. I think that was part of his design, too, to get me to this point. We had decided, Okay, let's do this. And decided to have an intimate evening, took a bath together, that sort of thing. His brother who lived there and his sister-in-law were gone. And we lit the candles, the music— and then it didn't work out. I thought I was broken; it didn't fit. I didn't really understand things going inside. Nothing had really entered me, so maybe I didn't have a hole or something. It didn't feel like anything was going to happen. So I was like, "I don't think I can do this." It's kind of bizarre. It was painful, so I was like, "This isn't really working." So it just didn't happen. We didn't have sex. And then that was it. We'll try again sometime. And then we ended up breaking up two or three weeks after that.

He met an ex-girlfriend and decided he wanted to deal with her. He was also going through this thing with wanting to go to school, and there were some more things emotionally going on with him being here and not knowing what he wanted to do—whether he wanted to go back to Yugoslavia, how he was going to make money here. So I think, dealing with that and dealing with a seventeen-year-old, mature as I was, it wasn't really what he needed. I'm mature about this now, I can see what the reasoning was, but at the time it was devastating. Devastating. I was listening to Tracy Chapman music after he broke up with me and just crying. Stayed in my room, didn't eat, lost a lot of weight. But then I got some clothes that made me feel good, new shoes. I saw him a couple of months later and he was like, "Oh."

The only racial issue was, I was really into Egyptian civilization, and like I said, I was reading Diop. I was taking an African civilization course. So I would always tell him and his brother and sister-in-law about Egypt and how their culture was like African culture. We'd have these discussions, and I'd bring my books and show them pictures of the Sphinx, and I was just really trying to teach them. And that was kind of funny because they were like, "What? Why is this an issue for you people? You know, we have a war. What's the problem?" They really couldn't see why racism was still an issue for me. Every experience I've had with other cultures, they're like, "You're an American first. Why are you talking about Africa? You just have a different culture." I was young, so I was really adamant about this.

I didn't have orgasms with him. My freshman year I met someone. I had sex with him, and that's when orgasms and having pleasure out of being sexually active happened. He had more experience, basically. I still controlled what made it good for me. Position, pressure. Mostly being on the bottom. And just really close. Like if the person's really close to me, like friction, that usually can do it. I guess it's something on my clitoris; I think that's basically what it is. I mean, I would just do it right away. I think I developed wanting to have it be pleasurable for that person, to try to time it where everybody can enjoy it, not just me. And then there might have been times when I did want it to be quick—it had built up. Maybe there was sexual flirtation all day and then it builds up to sex and I just wanted to have it. I didn't necessarily want it to linger on. So it just depended.

We were off and on until sophomore year. He went back to St. Louis, where he was from. He had a child with somebody else. When he was here, she was pregnant, and so he was like, "I'm trying to stick with this woman." She was in St. Louis, and he was just going to school here. She was older. I thought that he was going to not deal with her, or that he'd at least tell her the truth. I just had this naive idea that he would leave her. We were friends at first—it was just friendly for two, three months. And then it became something else. But I couldn't really separate those things, and I don't think he could either.

We just didn't relate anymore, and I dated other people, but he was jealous. I didn't tolerate it. I pretty much forced him into calling her and telling her what was going on, and then she was kind of naive. She was kind of, "Oh, okay, we'll work through it." So I was like, Okay. That's good for you guys. I mean, he was attracted to what he was, someone who was just kind of easy. So I felt like maybe that was meant to be. And as I was getting older, I just didn't think it was healthy.

After that, I dated some more, had some bad experiences, like dated someone, got intimate with them, and they were like, "No, I don't really want this relationship." And it became a theme of people saying, "It's not you, it's me." Or, "You deserve better." My ex-boyfriend was like, "You deserve better. It's not really you, it's me. I have issues," that kind of thing. I think that when I was dating people, I really put a lot of energy into them, and I don't think sometimes they necessarily wanted that. They wanted it to be a friendship. They backed away from this seriousness that I had about it. Or they weren't ready to feel that kind of strong love or intense emotion. And I guess there's something off-balance about me wanting to give it to them so soon.

I think in my life I've had this urgency to do things quickly. And just to do it passionately, because of the moving maybe. When I've gone somewhere, I just create friends. Whatever I'm gonna do, I'm gonna do it. And also my model is my parents' relationship, that's been pretty steadfast, so I don't think on a short-term basis, like, Okay, I'm just gonna fool around. I'm trying to meet your parents, what's really going on, is this going forward, like I'm not trying to play. They usually last about four months, which is really bizarre, and I've tried to figure out why it's four months. Maybe there was something I was doing to push them away after four months because I wasn't used to sustaining anything.

I chose men for attractiveness. I'd come up to someone and be like, "You're really attractive. What's your name? What's going on?" I was really that kind of person. I just didn't feel like there was anything stopping me.

In high school, I would have done it if there had been something to look at. There really wasn't. And when I came here and things were interesting to me, I just saw women always being like, Wow, he's nice, but letting them go by without speaking. And I was like, Why?

Most of the times after I dated the guy from Yugoslavia, they were possibly from another country. Tried to deal with someone who was from Morocco. That was kind of funny. And I tried to date people who looked like my father—one of them kind of looked like him. I was into astrology, so I was trying to read their signs. I didn't ask them—it wasn't a pickup line. But I was trying to see whether it was going to work out. Usually just kind of attractive, kind of artsy, which was an issue, too, because I'm an artist and labeled that. So usually they were still in my same sphere. They were poets, photographers. I really devoted energy to them, trying to see what's really going on early and not really giving them time to show their personality. And then, sometimes it was mutual, more times it was them saying, "I'm not the one for you," or "You're odd." I heard a lot of that: "You're an odd person. You're different."

It wasn't that hard to hear, honestly. My mom instilled a sense of self in me. She would say, "These are good things about you. This is why you're a beautiful person." Models are tall—I wanted to be a model. She was beautiful, the way she handled herself, the way people responded to her. I learned a lot from both of them. My father, he's a really good person. And I know I'm a good person. That's never been an issue. I've never felt that I'm just this horrible person and weird. And then I went to Italy, where I just fell in love with that country, where people were just like, wow. I was sixteen and maybe it was because I was black, too. But at the time, it was just what I needed—that I went away and I felt comfortable. When I went to the Village in New York, no one said that I'm weird. If everyone here feels that I'm weird, I know that this isn't the only place in the world because I've had these other experiences.

I want my lovers to be sensitive to my moods, how I feel, not just negating what they think I feel and doing things for themselves. Also, I need to just have my space. I don't know if I had that before. Now I'm developing this need to just have my time to do what I want to do and be by myself if I want to. I've had fantasy thoughts of women, but not sexually. But I've thought, If I was a guy, I'd date her. I like the idea of being outside. I've been having a real desire just to be naked in the elements. I really want to go to Europe or Africa or somewhere that has a nude beach. I don't know if it's so much for the sex; it's just something empowering for me. I just think that rules. I like clothes, I want to design clothes, but I think it's normal to be naked. I want to feel the elements, the air, the sun; rain would be cool. Most definitely. Warm rain.

I've had anal sex once. It was kind of an experiment, I guess. And, I don't know, it was cool for a minute. But afterward, it was like my body had to adjust. Because I was really into my colon health, like taking colonics, that kind of stuff. So I was really sensitive to that area. Afterward I felt more uncomfortable about it, but during it, it wasn't bad. It was just a different type of pleasure. It was an intensity, it was something different.

I went to this sex shop here, with my friends, and they had rings that go on men's penises, that go on their scrotum, like up there. I've seen it in the Kama Sutra. They used to put them on the penis. I think it's supposed to make their orgasm more intense. I'd like to have my boyfriend try that, just to see what that would be like.

I'm not really an underwear fan, so I started this underwear thing, like sexy lingerie-type stuff. Not really interested in any of that black plastic clothes with the whip thing. That's really not cool. That's just some type of genetic memory of slavery starting to creep in on that one. No. For me, no. I think that's another set of values that I just don't have. But I understand what that is about in terms of pleasurable pain. I think it's like when you got a sore and it hurts right there, and you touch it again, right there. And you go back to it. I kind of understand where that comes from, but sexually I don't want that.

I've had fights, but not related to sex. Like the first boyfriend, I hit after a fight. I was violent to him. It's really bad, but I hit him after an argument, and he cried, and it was kind of, Whoa. This was in freshman year. That's when it really just had to end, when it really was destructive to my psyche. That's been the first and last experience with that. It's not cool; it shouldn't have reached that point. I don't have any experience with that in my home, in terms of even spankings. My parents haven't had that kind of relationship.

Last summer, I found out that I was pregnant with the person I'm with. My mom had a baby when she was twenty-one, my brother, and she wasn't married. They got married three years after my brother. So that's been an issue. My mom really knows where that's coming from. And when I was twenty-one, I was like, Man, I gotta get through this age to break the cycle. Then I turned twenty-two, and it happened, and I was like, Okay, well, deal with it. It was a contraceptive error. I'd had a contraceptive error before and I'd taken a pill, the morning-after, and didn't have to deal with that again. This is two years later. And then, well, I felt like the ovulation time was over and I misjudged. So it was just an error. We used a condom and a film—VCF film it was called.

I was feeling bad, throwing up, the whole thing. I had just started working, making a decent salary where I could have supported a child if I wanted to. It wasn't the end of the world; it could have worked. But I just felt like the person I was with was in school, and the money issue wasn't really tight, and it just wasn't the right time. I just didn't really want to make that sacrifice. I wasn't feeling sacrificial, and I think that would have been a bad situation for the child. I felt like I had control of the situation, like I could do something. I didn't have to just deal with a bad situation. So I decided to have an abortion, called my mom, told her what was going on; she came down for support. But I also felt like, Wow, this is kind of neat—neat in the sense of just feeling differently, and that I'm a vessel, just what happens. Like what happens to your body when you are pregnant. And I swear I saw pregnant women every day, every minute. Everybody's pregnant all of a sudden. But I went ahead and I had an abortion.

The place was really cool. It was this feminist women's center. They explained it completely, broke it down, offered emotional help, wanted you to go back, walked you to your car. It was just really cool. My boyfriend and a friend of mine who'd had an abortion went with me. I felt pretty drugged for the next two days and just went through that cycle of what happens afterward.

My mom was reliving her situation that maybe she would have made the same decision if she could have, of having the abortion. It was hard for her because of the environment at the time. To be pregnant and not married was a real issue. It was like, "Oh, really? You're not coming to church anymore. You're banished." So she really relived that pain of people turning on her because of it. And also her mom and her had a really tough time with that because her mom was just so disappointed, so hurt by it. And they didn't get back together until shortly before her mom died. So it was a big issue.

I was waiting to feel different as a woman, to see if I was going to break down or whether I wanted to have this child. And I didn't really feel like that. I felt like it was really the right decision, and I also felt more prepared for when it does happen. My boyfriend felt it was the right decision. He felt part of the decision; he didn't feel like I just did what I wanted to do. And it made him feel more pressure to get himself together so that when he wants to have a family, none of this will happen. We're talking more serious commitment now.

My goals as a woman are really evolving now because I've graduated, and I want to go back to school; I want to go abroad. So I don't know. I want to have my own business and be in a place where I have some control over my employment. And I really want to spend some time with my child, for like five years after I feel I have a real grasp on my business. And after getting this traveling bug out of my system, seeing what I want to be in the world. So I guess that's my feeling, later. Later.

I don't have any sexual regrets. I'm happy with where I am now sexually, so I think those things were necessary, in terms of being with someone that I didn't necessarily want to be with later. I haven't really had unprotected sex, or not on purpose. I've had accidents, but I've been pretty responsible. So, no, I don't regret anything.

Do I feel there is sexism in the black community? [*Laughs.*] Yes. It's similar to what Caucasian people say, "Well, you're a 'good nigger.'" It's kind of like, "Well, you're an 'okay woman,' but there's some 'bitches.' " It's like you always have to make these distinctions about what kind of women there are, but it isn't the same when you talk about men. Also, there's things that just are expected. You're just not supposed to do or talk about certain things because you're a woman.

A gender example is meals during Thanksgiving or Christmas: I notice in my family, women will be the ones cooking. When a woman comes to the house, she'll immediately go to the kitchen and be like, "Do you need any help?" The men will go sit down in the living room, watch the big-screen TV, talk, whatever. But there's never that type, "Do you need help?" from a man. It just doesn't happen. Uncles don't do that, that I know of. The women will go and have their community there, and the men will have their community somewhere else, and sometimes they'll come together in the same room. But still the conversation is, "My husband is talking to your husband," that kind of thing. And after the meal's done, the men are just sitting down, and women are, "Okay, let's get up and help."

I didn't get a basketball when I was thirteen or fourteen, like my brother did. When he was that age, my dad gave him a basketball and took him to the gym: "I'm gonna teach you, son." They had this relationship that I was jealous of. Like, what? I'm tall, I can play basketball. What's going on? Why didn't I get a basketball? And I asked for one. I said he was sexist, at twelve. I said, "This is sexist that you presumed I wouldn't want this, or didn't ask me, or didn't present this to me the same way that you presented it to my brother." And also the fact that my dad doesn't really know what's in the kitchen. I go there every other year now, and he's still like, "Do you know where such and such is?" And I'm like, "You live here. Why would I automatically know where a pot is when you don't?" It's just that kind of stuff that I've seen at home.

I think that patriarchy and sexism are connected to everything, and I think that that's a key component in racism, especially the way that we've come together in political groups. Like if you look at the Black Panther party and how that didn't come together, even an Afrocentric movement like Ron Karenga's, and his ideal about that. And yet we still do Kwanzaa, but we don't talk about what other things go on with his mythology. I do.

And when we talk about leadership, we are very gender-specific in terms of who can help us. I think when they say, "We need a strong black leader," I don't think they really mean women. I think even for women who were powerful, even for Coretta Scott King, even for Assata Shakur, it's like, "She's attractive in her Afro."

Personally, like with my weight, maybe it's devaluing how pretty I am because if I gain weight, if I lose weight, whether that's attractive is such an issue. That's pretty sexist. What is that really saying about my personality? I think about whether my boyfriend is thinner or bigger. I don't know if I look at him the same way. I would presume that he would look at me differently if I change weight, but I don't know if I really look at him differently if he gets bigger or smaller.

I wouldn't serve someone just on principle. Maybe that's kind of detrimental. Maybe I really need to assess what the problem is and whether this is an example of what I feel. And whether I do bash men, on a whole, in my speech, whether I do really have a negative feeling about men because I have a negative feeling about patriarchy.

I think that at times I question being open about sex. I question whether people compute that and use words like "promiscuous" that I think are linked to this idea that black women are jungle things, that we are sexual people, the way we dance, the way we move. And I wonder, personally, whether the things that make me feel sexy, certain clothes that I wear, when I'm showing certain parts of my body, whether that's because men will think that that's sexy, whether I'm doing that to cater to that audience, or whether that's really internally sexy to me. Or even maybe some of the things that I internalize from television. What is sexy in terms of how I make my face up? I look at the way we decided what's pretty—like grease used to be pretty in the seventies, to have greasy skin and that hue. It's not anymore. And the black outline and the gloss, and what was really going on with making your lips look smaller and now making them look bigger. What's changing and why? When I do these things that look like magazines, do I think it looks prettier? Why do I think that looks nicer now?

I try to sift through these images for people with my complexion and relate to them and think that they're attractive. I see the beauty, but I think I look for affirmation through it, and I realize that it's minimal. And I realize, too, that even in the industry, once they have someone who has that aesthetic, they don't want another model like that. We have Roshumba. Can we perm our hair now? Can we have a permed Roshumba? I remember when I was about fifteen, I wrote a letter to *YSB* [*Young Sisters and Brothers*] because they had a contest of being on the cover for your personal style, and I was like, Yeah, I'm about to win this. Then I flipped back and it was sponsored by Revlon, so you had to have a permed style to be in the contest because Revlon was sponsoring this. So I was like, What are you saying? I can't have a personal style, a natural style, some word with "natural" in it? It was a kind of angry letter. And I sent my picture, saying, "Guess what? My hair is braided. I'm not really trying to perm it for this. And it's an insult for you, as an 'African' young magazine, to insist upon something that is unnatural to be the standard of a natural beauty." I was really upset. But again, people were just like, "Oh, this is what you have to worry about? Isn't there something else you could be doing with your time?"

When I was in North Carolina, for example, and I was growing my hair out and it was short, I did it in kind of balls. Words like "pickaninny" were used. "Your hair was prettier when it was longer. Could you take your dreads out? And if you perm it, how long would it be?" Younger girls and also older people. Or, "Your hair's getting longer. It's looking pretty." I think that being brown-skinned also was a strike against me being pretty, that all these other elements could at least help me be somewhat pretty. But if my hair is shorter, then that's taking away already. The jokes would be, "You're so black that . . ." And I'm critical of the psychosis; I think it is a problem. I see it as a problem with identity and self-worth. Plus it's family, so if they don't see these things about me, even if I have personal feelings about being beautiful, it still hurts. It still takes away something from me. You know what I'm saying?

# Queenie

*I*'M FORTY-FOUR years old. I'm a native to the South. Right now I'm separated. This is my second marriage. I was married when I was twenty. I stayed in that relationship for two years, and then I was divorced for fifteen years and remarried again by the time I was thirty-eight years old. In that relationship, I had three stepchildren—I've never had any children of my own. My educational background: I finished two years of college. I worked for a mass communications company for over twenty-five years. Then I stopped that, started my own business, and then I stopped that to start a new one. I'm in the midst of writing the business plan for the new business, an event-planning facility. My parents moved here, but they were both from small towns in Alabama. She moved here when she was eighteen years old, which was a big thing back then. At some point in time, she met my dad. And then they got married, and a few years later they adopted me, and then they adopted my brother.

I don't know who my birth parents are and don't want to. I thought I did, but you would have had to meet my mother to understand that it was amazing to me that someone could adopt a child and love them as much as she loved me. If she had been my biological parent, I don't know how she could have loved me any more. And at one point, after she passed away, I thought I might want to know. But then I decided, I've got enough family problems with the family that I have, and I love them very much and they love me. So I didn't. But I forgave her because she had to make a decision, and the decision was to make sure that I had a good life. So she gave me up for adoption, and my guess is that she was young. I was not the oldest child, I was the third or fourth child, and at that point she could not financially handle another child, so she gave me up for adoption. The weird part for me, I think, is that I was raised or reared as the oldest in the birth order, so I have the birth-order tendencies of the oldest child.

Before I was born, my mom cleaned people's homes. And my father worked for the post office, but he worked on the railroad. Before they flew the mail, they'd hang it on poles in big sacks. The train would slow down, and you'd reach out with this pole and pull the sack of mail in, and the train would keep going, and you'd take it to wherever it was supposed to go to be sorted, and then the train brought it back. My father passed away when I was seven, and my brother was five, so my mom didn't work for two or three years. Then she went and worked in a school cafeteria for eighteen or twenty years. At the time of my father's death, we had just moved into a new house in an area that was being integrated, and we were the first or second African American family on the street. We moved into the house in August. My father got sick in November, went to the hospital, never came home, and died the next February. He died of cancer. Back at that time, they didn't realize the link between smoking and cancer—it was lung cancer. So he suffered a stroke, and then they discovered he had cancer and then he passed away. I think he was in his early forties. It's funny, because when I think about when I was young and they told me he died somewhere around forty-four to fifty-five-ish, that seemed so old to me, and I'm around that age now.

We grew up Presbyterian, which I found completely too quiet for me. We were very involved in church. My mother stopped going to church after my father died. She was very angry. What I'm realizing now is that she was very depressed and probably never, ever stopped grieving. Back then, in '59 or '60, when you were a widow with two small children, people were afraid you were after their husbands. So your relationships shifted very drastically, which is what happened to her. She felt very isolated, plus the fact that she was already depressed and didn't understand that. And, we weren't even thinking about therapists then. We stopped going to church as a family, and there was a huge gap as a young adult. Somewhere around twenty-five to twenty-six years old, I started feeling a need to be connected to a church again, so I started attending my uncle's church because it was United Methodist. It had enough of the order and protocol of the Presbyterian but a little more energy, you know, the gospel music. So I'm still a part of the United Methodist church now, hugely involved, probably more than I need to be.

I know that both of my mother's parents were African Americans, but my father was lighter in complexion than me—and I am very light—with really straight, like curly hair, but his features were also so sharp that it almost makes me believe that one if not both of his parents were not African American. I don't know about my biological parents. My bond is with my mother's family, and I don't know if it was because my parents didn't have much of a bond with his parents. They lived in the back of the woods in the county, and my father left home at an early age and became a merchant marine. At the time that he left home, he couldn't have done that as an African American. So he obviously was able to pass and do what he wanted to do as a merchant marine. I was thinking that this was part of the reason he was estranged from his family, although my mother never talked about it. Something was going on because we never went to see his family at all, none of them. I have never laid eyes on one of his family members. I asked the question of my aunt when my mother died. It never occurred to me to ask my mother earlier. Death raises a lot of questions that you just take for granted. After my mother passed away, they would not come, not his mother, not his father, no one came to the funeral.

Intimacy means affection and security to me, the ability to be mentally and emotionally naked with a person, to have that much trust. That's very important to me because it takes me a long time to work up to that point in any relationship. Friendship is big for me. Trust. I mean that blind trust, where you never think about it. You just absolutely trust the person. To get there, I feel I have to build on a friendship first. So you begin that with just talking and sharing because if you can share your deepest, darkest fears and hurts, then you trust me, trust me never to use those things against you, to never laugh at them, to never take them lightly. And then again, if you can trust a person that way and they trust you that way, then it goes from there.

With my second husband, when we started, we were really good at that. There were a lot of forces working against us. But we were very good friends. We were friends for many, many years before we even started to date. Then we dated for a time, took a break, and started dating again. But the friendship never died. When we talked to each other and we weren't dating, we would talk about relationships and our hurts, and the things that gave pause in the relationship.

I have a lot of extended family. I call extended family who you go with somewhere, everywhere, and yet there is no biological connection in any way. I have a sister—I call her my sister. She knows everything there is to know about me, and she loves me anyway. She's a good friend, but now in my heart, my soul, my mind, she's my sister. It almost makes me cry to say it, she's been the person who's been there for me, always. I've known her for over fifteen years, and she's one of my biggest cheerleaders. It's the purest and closest thing I've ever come to know as unconditional love. I mean, my mother's love had conditions on it—well, there were rules. And to a child those are conditions. Then you grow up and find out that they love you anyway.

In my entire life, I can remember one guy in high school who was homosexual, because he was dressed as a girl, and that's how we'd know. He'd come to school and show me pictures of when he dressed up as a girl, with makeup and heels, and he walked and talked it. But it's funny, when I thought of him as a homosexual, I never thought of the sexual act—I just thought of him acting effeminate. But in the time when I was divorced and having a really good time partying, the people, the circle of my friends I was moving in were people who were heterosexual, homosexual, and bisexual. So at that point, it was okay.

It's hard to say if I feel comfortable with my sexuality. I think I am more comfortable with it now than I have ever been because my mother was so concerned about sex before marriage when I was growing up. The number one sin as a girl that you could commit was sex before marriage. And then right next to that was if you were pregnant and you were not married, you should go to jail. So the things that were said to me to help me not have sex before I was married were so stern and so scary it took me a long time to be comfortable with it, and there are still some times now when there are things that I'm uncomfortable with. My mother was an older parent, so all my skirts were down to my calves, and most of my tops were up to my neck. They started talking to us about it at school when I was in seventh grade. Which is too funny, because I remember them splitting up the girls and the boys and doing a kind of "scared straight talk" with the girls, saying, "Keep your knees together." I mean, they didn't say those kind of things; they just kind of talked around it.

Now, I encountered sexuality from older men who were relatives, who were slightly overaggressive. It took me a long time to be able to say this out loud—I felt it had a lot to do with the fact that they knew I was an adopted child, therefore it was not like incest because I was not related.

There was no assault, but there was inappropriate touching, inappropriate kissing, you know, too tight, too long hugs, touching me in the wrong places when I was sitting on their laps. Those kinds of things. So I became real aware. It's funny, because as a child you don't really understand it. But when you look back on it, you had those feelings, but you didn't realize why, that sense that something was wrong with the space and the tone of voices and the way you were being held and caressed. Some of it was at family gatherings, some of it was at times when I was being babysat. See, my mom didn't go out a lot, and she didn't trust us to a lot of people, but there were times with a couple of people she did trust us with. Sometimes when I was taken from one place to the other because I was too young to drive. So I can remember in the car. And just when we were playing, there were old cousins who were doing things that were inappropriate, but I didn't know they were inappropriate.

Well, I tried to tell her once, and it was so devastating to her that she freaked, and I never tried to tell her again. She was so upset and she was so angry that what she said to me in essence was that I was saying it, not to get attention, but because I was angry about something else and that was my way of getting back. I can't remember the exact words, but I can remember her reaction to it. I can remember her being angry, but not angry at them, angry at me for thinking that. And how could you say that about this person?

From this one person, it was fairly consistent. Remember when the Miss America lady came out, and she was in a real rich family, and she talked about her father having assaulted her all her life? One of the things that struck me was that she said she was a daytime daughter and a night-time daughter. When she woke up in the morning her relationship with her father was father-daughter, and she never thought about what he did to her at night. But then at night, she knew when he was coming to do it. She had the ability to completely block it out. Well, it was not my father, but I had the same situation with this particular relative, where I could see them in a totally different footing and react to them in the way that a relative would—day and night, same thing.

.   He is still alive and I do speak to him, but I have never confronted him. It's weird. For the longest time, I wondered if it hampered my sexuality and the way I saw myself. Also, I do a lot of reading, and the books talked about how people who have been sexually abused can be sexual abusers, and so there was a point in time in my life when I was afraid and wondered as a young adult if I would do that to a child because it had been done to me. And I was very angry about that, but somehow by the grace of God, I think I've actually become more protective of children. I was very angry, very angry because he knew better and I didn't. I loved him and respected him a lot, and there were a couple of times when I really wanted to confront him about it and I just never did. What would it have helped? It would have helped me because I could have said to him—if I had done it earlier, I might have saved some other people from having it happen to them. He probably wasn't only doing it to me. But the thing is, when I was growing up, nobody was talking about it out loud, so what could you say? The one person that I felt I could go to and say something to freaked. It's sad to know that men do that to little girls, and that they take pleasure in it and somehow forgive themselves for it and continue to do it—that's the part that makes me angry. Most especially when I think about little girls who don't know. I was very specific with my children and said to them, "If someone tries this or this, it is inappropriate. I don't care who it is, your father, your uncle, your brother, your cousin, I don't care. You come and tell me." Now they know they could tell somebody. I was brought up to believe that things like that don't happen in families with a kind of picture-perfect look.

When it came to my menstrual cycle, my mother gave me a little pamphlet and said, "Read this, and if you have any questions, ask me." And I can remember that I was married before I ever heard my aunt even refer to sex as an act. I mean, the word never came out of her mouth. And my mom's conversation about sex was more about what not to do. Not what to do. And because there was no man in the house, I never saw the affection. The couples that I came in contact with were affectionate, but we never saw it. They talked in affectionate ways to each other, but they never touched, they never kissed, they never hugged in front of us. They hugged us; they didn't hug each other. But I also came up at an age where women were fighting to be able to be sexual and to enjoy their sexuality, so there was a lot of information coming out. I loved to read—that's one of the gifts my mom gave me. So there were a lot of magazine articles and books about women's sexuality. I'd say I was about fifteen in the late 1960s when I started reading the articles and magazines. That's how I began to see more about it.

I never had any questions. Back in those days, they were hiding *Peyton Place* because there was one thing where somebody gets raped. Sexuality was very tough to talk about, especially to a daughter, because she's not supposed to have it till she's married. I knew my mother wouldn't talk about it, so why ask? I didn't really find the need to talk about it because really I knew I wasn't going to. I was very slow in developing because of my self-esteem. I had a little-girl persona because my mom dressed me like a little girl. So when other girls were having boyfriends, like eighth or ninth grade, that was not a problem for me. I never thought about it, never cared about it. I more cared about having friends, and having guys who were friends, and I liked to be invited to stuff. I was in the tenth grade before I really cared about having a relationship. Because, you see, in your fantasy relationships, they come out perfect. So I did a lot of reading. Romance was more important to me than sex. It just so happened that in order to get the guys to romance you, you gave them sex.

The words "penis" and "vagina" were never mentioned in our house. It just was not something that you needed to talk about. Because when it was time, you would know. And the only way you'd find out about it is, we would talk about it in the seventh grade among ourselves. And now these children are talking about it in the third grade. So I started talking to my children about it early, using terms like "penis" and "vagina," and of course there were snickers. And now they can think of "vagina" and "breast" and they don't have to laugh.

With my daughters, I sat down and we had a club, everybody was equal, nobody was a child and nobody was an adult, and any question you wanted to ask me you could ask and it couldn't go outside of the club meeting. And they really felt comfortable talking to me about the things that they had heard at school or someone had said, or they heard a friend talking about having sex, and asked me what I thought or felt about it. And asked any questions that they had about the birth process, about relationships between men and women. The only questions that was off limits was anything that had specific things to do with my sexual relationship with their father. I explained that was personal. If you have general questions, I'll answer those. They were fine with that. I guess one was fourth grade, the other fifth grade when the club started. We talked about sexuality later, when they had something to contribute and ask about it. And they loved it. Any member could call a club meeting, if there was a question or a concern.

I didn't wait until I was married to have sex. It was after high school, but it was somebody I'd dated in high school. It was during my first year of college because I was completely afraid when I was in high school. I was guessing that my mother was everywhere I was, that it would just be written all over me if it happened. For some reason when I was a freshman in college, I felt that I had passed the threshold of total embarrassment because I got out of high school, I wasn't pregnant, and I did not have sex, so at that point I was safer.

When I think about it, I don't think about the actual act of it. I think about the closeness that the intimacy brought the two of us, and how we felt more connected. But not only that. For me, I was monogamous, and I think he was, too, at the time.

We found out about contraceptives from some girls at my school. There were girls at my school who were sexually active in the tenth grade, so they knew all the things and all the ways. And then there's just plain reading. You go to the drugstore and you stand around and read. And to be honest with you, there was probably some things I was doing completely wrong. I probably used the wrong products for the wrong thing. I felt that God was just with me at the time. I had to deal with the guilt of what I'd done, so it didn't happen every date. This worked because in that day and age it meant I wasn't loose, so he was proud of that. He was having his needs satisfied, but he didn't have this slut he was dealing with. There's that protocol: you knew the fast girls, and you did what you did with them, but you weren't supposed to go with them. Don't have way too much fun at it because then that's your fault. We thought we were in love. So if you loved, you wanted to have sex, but you didn't want her to like it all that much. I think in the beginning it was more to satisfy his needs than mine.

For me there was a closeness, but it wasn't so much the act of sex. The foreplay of it was actually more important to me than the actual sexual act. Fondling, the holding, the hugging, the talking, the being very close and intimate, the part that led up to that. And then the energy of making my own decision about that. That was kind of exhilarating. So all of that was just as important to me as the actual sexual act. I didn't even understand what an orgasm was. Not till I was a lot older. I'm pretty sure I was having them before, but I didn't know because everybody had a different definition of what it was and how you would know you were having it.

I was very happy about it. There was some sense of liberation to it because for me, relationships were more about what he needed. The guilt didn't go away until I felt I had fallen in love, and then I wasn't just having sex, I was making love. Which was very important. It was still a sin, but a forgivable sin. Just the act of sex was a sin, and the guilt was still there. The pleasure was there—the guilt came after.

Looking back, I got married for the wrong reasons. But my mother was a very dominant force in my life. I loved her and respected her so much, I didn't realize how much her approval did and still rules my life sometimes. And I wanted to leave home and go to college. She was scared to death of that. She came up with every excuse in the book. I was offered an opportunity, because you remember I'm coming up in the age of integration, so the Ivy League colleges were trying to find some of the best students across the country, the best Negroes to educate. My counselors were very excited about that because they lived through an age where there was no integration. So for some of their students to go to an Ivy League college was just incredible. Some of those colleges offered scholars to spend the summer at the college to see if you liked it, and they'd write the full scholarship, with room and board, and books. And for my mom, that was just mind-boggling. It was just an incredible amount of money. She did everything in her power to discourage me.

I got married to get out of college. It was okay to get married and leave home, but it was not okay to go to school, leave home. It was definitely not okay. Nice girls don't do that. My mother was very angry about the divorce—she was more angry longer than I was. Because in my family, I was probably the second person to get divorced. He was abusive. She could not stand him. But what I found out later was there was no man good enough. The man that would have been good enough for me didn't exist. Because it was so hard for her to lose my father, and she told me that she sacrificed so much—her light went out of life. The way she put it to me was because she had children, she did not want to remarry. But in my mind, it was a real miracle that she found that man once. To find it twice would have been impossible, she thought.

So, my ex-husband, he's staying out, he's going out partying supposedly with the guys, which I mostly believed. See, I didn't understand the definition of an alcoholic. I now know he was an alcoholic. Back then people drank all the time. It was part of just a social thing. There's a whole side of my family that parties and they don't mind having a drink to be social. So in my mind the fact that every time he came to pick me up he had something to drink with him did not mark an alcoholic to me. I was rebounding from a previous relationship, I meet him, we get married in about a year. He never slowed down, he never stopped going out. The weekend after we came back from our honeymoon, he goes out and stays out all night. I'm so young and so thrown, I'm sure he's dead because people just don't do that. Because the men in my family, some of them were not the most charismatic people you'd ever meet, but they came home and they worked every day and they did not drink and they did not hit their wives. They might have been emotionally abusive in that they shut themselves down. But to all appearances to me, they were very respectful to their wives and their families, and they provided well for their families. So, I thought he was dead. I called a girlfriend of mine because I was just two steps away from calling the police and the hospital. And she laughed. She had a husband who stayed out all the time. So she said, "I'd give him till tomorrow morning before you call, if I were you." Sure enough, just before dawn he came in. Been drinking all night, stayed out playing cards, and he did that every day—he would come in from work, take a shower, get dressed, and go out. And I realized about three months into the marriage, if that long, that we had not a single thing in common. When we sat down at the breakfast table, we had nothing to talk about. I loved movies. He couldn't care less because he couldn't drink in a movie. Any activity where you could not drink was boring to him.

I was so miserable. And for some reason I had growing up in my life, I didn't have to carry that family tradition on. I was miserable, I was young, and I wanted out. Leaving was one of the best things I did in my life. One of the absolute best things. And the turning point was at that moment my mother said to me, "Come home, save up some money. And then you can get you a really nice place." And because the house was his, I left the house, I left most of the furniture, I took my things and a few pieces of furniture and I was out of there. I sat down and I spent one solid week, day and night, looking for a place to live because I had one week of vacation to move into my own place. And she kept saying to me to stay. I just don't understand why, but to me it was like having a cell door shut. As much as I loved her, I knew that if I went home, I'd never get out.

I had a real good friend at work, and I called her because I made this decision to leave. I had found a place, and I wanted to tell her because she was real concerned about me. She knew there was a lot of emotional abuse and I was having a really hard time. She'd been single a long time and had moved to two or three different cities, so it wasn't a big deal to her. She was very supportive. She said, "Come on over," took out the wine. "We could have some wine and cheese, and if you don't think you'd be able to drive, you could stay the night." It was not in my mother's vocabulary, "spend the night." As a young child, I did not go out and spend the night partying, of course. So I went and talked and laughed for hours, and it was the first time in my mind that I was having an adult relationship, friendship. And we started then, that friendship started that night. So after I got divorced, we started hanging out.

I had said I didn't want to be in any kind of relationship for a long time because I really didn't know what to look for. But I also had the self-esteem problems that come of all the abuse, sexual and otherwise, in my life growing up. So I didn't even have a clue what kind of problems to look for. The city was just starting to open up then and get all these hotels and have all kinds of openings, and we were going from restaurant to restaurant and club to club, and I was seeing life there in a whole different way. If I started seeing someone, it really was not a big deal. We'd have sex, but it wasn't this need to be in love. We just wanted to have sex, so that was kind of fun. Of course, there was still the guilt. But I still managed to work past it because it was an exciting time, and it was a freer feeling that I had never experienced in my life.

And then all of a sudden, I started to feel a little empty. It was time. Because I can remember from the time I was ten or eleven years old not seeing myself in a career, but seeing myself as someone's mother. And a parent and a wife. I worked because I was good at it, and since I wasn't in love or married, I might as well continue to get better and better at that. So that's how that happened.

———

I never masturbated. That made me feel that the actual sex act, the actual orgasm, was more important than the intimacy. See, for me, it's always been combined. Even though there was not love, there was intimacy. So it was almost as if you had an instrument and you were creating this sexual orgasm as opposed to having the intimacy. Because there was some sort of connection with me and anyone who I had sex with. It may not have been love but it wasn't just sex. During the separation, I thought about how it was; my feelings were so strongly connected to it that even when I'm hurt in a relationship, it just kind of heals itself. I don't even think about sex anymore. So I don't even think about orgasms because I don't think about sex. It's almost as though I open up a cabinet, put it in the cabinet, and close it. And I was just thinking about this last week, how much I miss having sex. When you're married, it's always there if you want it. And all of a sudden, since I've been separated, there's been no sex. And I was thinking, Gosh, it's been awhile. I'm starting to miss that intimacy and just the actual sex itself because I enjoy it.

At one point, I was scared to count how many partners I had, only in that there was this stigma. Let me see—going through the Rolodex in my head. I would say six. It's not fifty. If it were fifty, I think I would have known fifty. I wouldn't have had to count. It's always been black men, and only almost once in my life, was it not, and I panicked. So I said, "No, I can't do this." I don't know, for me, there's always got to be some sort of connection, and there wasn't. I consider myself one of the least prejudiced people, but I think all of us carry some prejudice in us. But as I think about it—especially at this point in my life as I think about sexuality, most especially because of HIV and AIDS, which is like a number one fear for me—for me, at this point, it has to be a commitment. Then, there wasn't one.

For white men back then—I'm not saying that a white man never made a pass at me—but I saw it so much as a notch in their belt because it's now this new freedom: we can now say we sleep with black women. So it wasn't so much an emotional connection as a being conquered, like being a mountain they conquered. Even in my workplace, one of the things that I found very funny that people don't think about a lot is that if you are in a workplace where the majority of people are not African American people, the sexual dynamic is really different. So, unlike my white female coworkers, I didn't have to deal with flirting. I'd go to work every day, and not a single soul would flirt with me. So I never even had to think about it. Just cute little things or brushing up against you or touching you in an inappropriate way—never happened. Never even had to think about it happening. So when I talk to women who were aggravated because a man was talking to them, and they were trying to talk business and felt they weren't taking them seriously, I thought, "Oh well." Or when I heard men talk about a new woman who came to work who was very pretty—they never talked that way about a black woman.

Emotionally, most especially since I was in corporate America for so long in my life, there were moments when I did think to myself, I'm being cheated of something here. You know, you really feel good about the way you look, but nobody says, "You look really pretty today." I mean, I'm not saying I want to be sexually harassed, but I would like someone to acknowledge me on a level other than harassment. I'd just like to feel some appreciation and that electricity, those little sparks that go with it, knowing I can't do anything about it, but I can look at it and see it in that way. You spend eighty percent of your day in a world where nobody looks at you in an adoring, sexual way. What does that say to you? It says that something was missing, something that a whole other ethnic group of people got to enjoy that I didn't. I felt as if I were living in the big house when it came to that. I was respected for the knowledge that I had but almost treated like a child when it came to adult personal stuff, which is how slaves were treated. You know, we respect the fact that they can cook, she's a great cook or she's great with the children. But when it comes to other things, then we're talked about almost in a childlike manner because we're not relating to her on an adult level. Because along with sexuality comes the fact that I'm relating to you as an adult. If I don't even relate to you as an adult, then I'm talking to you as if I'm talking to a child. So there was something missing.

I didn't have sexual fantasies; I acted them out with my partners. I'm just determined to work on this good girl, bad girl kind of thing. When you see yourself as the wife and the mother, you're wearing all white, and you have this very virginal thought of yourself. There's a whole lot of love and a little bit of sexuality. But then when you're dressed in red you can just feel it and do it for hours. So I liked to dress myself up in very sexy clothing. And have the whole sexual act take a long, long time. There's a sense of almost a drama going on from the beginning to the end. So mostly that's what my fantasies are, seeing myself very clearly sexually and to be lost completely in the sexual act and just feel it as if your whole body is just feelings, as opposed to thinking and feeling. That is hard to get to; it takes a lot of trust, a long time.

I have never been pregnant and wish I had been, more than life itself. It's one of the struggles I am having as we speak today. I've had a hysterectomy, so I won't ever be able to have children. It's been very hurtful for me. I have raised my stepchildren for some of their lives. I threw myself into the whole thing and tried to erase the "step" off of it. I became very emotionally attached to the children; I became very involved in their lives. I decided to treat them as though they were my biological children. So I worked very hard to have a relationship with their mothers (because there were two mothers), to erase the hesitancy and the jealousy and anger that comes from the separation with the man that you had children with. So that the children could really feel that they had two families instead of just having one family and going to visit this person who is in love with their dad.

For me, the difficulty was that when they looked at me, they knew I was not the only parent. So some of the anger that they had with me, they could dismiss it and be angry instead of working through it, and say, "Oh, that's just my stepmother. I don't have to see her, I don't have to talk to her, I don't have to be with her." Even though they didn't do that, they talked to me and we worked through those things. But that was always there. Plus, I knew that it all hinged on the relationship I had with their father. So the attachment was very vulnerable. Which is exactly what has happened. He's gone; now they're gone.

I guess we grew apart because of self-esteem issues and differences between our ways of being. In the time we had been married, he had four different jobs. He's a recovering addict, which I knew before I married him. He has always accomplished everything, top student, top athlete, educated, and finished college. But then when you start comparing all those things to his life accomplishments, in the real adult world, he's always taken jobs that were beneath the skills and education that he had, and he was frustrated because he was always afraid to have to step out there and do what was necessary to keep his job. I, on the other hand, had the job and was brought up through the jobs—almost mentored through—so I had all those accomplishments. And I didn't have them before in my childhood. I was an A-B-C student. Plus my family was big on manners and class and how you treated things and people, how you worked a little, time to gather things, you didn't have to have a lot, just worked hard together. So morally, we were not in the same place because there's some things I won't do to gain something, and one thing he's had to admit to himself is he doesn't know where that line is. It continues to shift for him. Plus, I made more money. I'd been working and moving up, and he'd been switching, and for the wrong reasons.

I want a partner that has a clear sense of himself so that whatever happens in the relationship, he can communicate those things to me that are really important as we get to know each other. I don't have a problem communicating what's important to me. What I have a problem doing is not losing it in the relationship. Because I continue to use my self-esteem. I find some men with low to no self-esteem, and then I try to work hard with my self-esteem to give them self-esteem. And I normally don't do this until I've really fallen way over, right in. So I need someone with a clear sense of self. If you're poor and you're happy, or you have a clear sense of what you are doing—let us just say you decide you want to teach and teaching is your life's dream and you do it well. You're not going to make a lot of money teaching, but if you know it's your life's dream and you do it well, then you're fine. And if you meet me, and I'm making two hundred thousand a year, then you won't care. You won't mind living the lifestyle that our two salaries will bring. But money matters, only in that I have yet to find a man who is so clearly defined in himself that somehow money doesn't enter that definition.

I can't make enough money, once I decided that the quality of life was important to me. Right now there's some things I don't have because I refuse to buy the lesser quality in order to have it. I will work until I can afford to buy the one I like. So I will always survive, I will always have money, I will always live at a certain standard because my mother worked hard to keep us at a decent standard. Looking back, we were poor, but we didn't know that. Using the economic definition right now, they would consider me poor. But I have been middle to upper-middle class and lived that life very well, and so in my mind, I want to be at least there. Now if I slip up and get rich, there's some things I want to do with that, and help those people who cannot help themselves. But the point is that I will always survive, I will always have money, I will always have the ability to get for me those things that are important to me. I don't need a man to do that, but I do need a man who is so secure in what he is giving me that's something other than economics.

I think that if your environment feeds you a negative, limited sense of who you are, that impacts your relationships. If your environment teaches you that you can actually use the f-word or the act that you are committing is the only plan you know, then you're not going to get a sense of what it takes to bring a woman to orgasm. You're not going to get a sense of intimacy and romancing a woman because, to me, the act of sexuality begins the moment the date begins. You're both bringing each other to that point, and so it may not happen on the third, fourth, or fifth date but it's all in a process. But if your environment says that showing up with a bottle of Ripple, maybe not even bathed, but just because you're a man, and you have a penis, defines sexuality to you . . . and I believe, by and large, that African American men make up the majority of the person I just described, with the bottle of Ripple and the penis, more than any other ethnic group. I'm not saying that every ethnic group does not have someone who falls into that category, but I am saying that I think that it has to do with education and exposure. There are some people who absolutely believe that Steak and

Ale is fine dining. And that doesn't even come close for me. I can remember when I was finding myself after the divorce and I discovered that Steak and Ale, even though it is a very nice restaurant, is not considered fine dining.

I look at people who completely are happy with so little. Some people would call what I am saying classism, but it's not; it's exposure. If you take me to the park with a picnic candlelight dinner, and you took the time to find not an expensive wine, but something nice—or it doesn't even have to be wine, it doesn't have to be based on alcohol—if you found a cider and found a way to heat it over a fire, it's all of those things, and only exposure takes your mind out far enough to research those things. Lack of economic opportunity has been so hurtful to us, and because we are caught in a continuing cycle unlike any other ethnic group. A number of things help feed that, but I think that the media is the most pervasive because, if you think about it, economically, if we are the minority of people still in this country, then we cannot be the majority of people on welfare. We've got to be the minority of people on welfare. But when you see anything in the media and the word "welfare" is being used, the cameraman and the news reporter is standing outside of a black project. And then we feed into that, and not only that, we believe. When a teenager can come to me when they're looking to plan a career and say that they hope they're shooting to make nineteen thousand dollars a year then that's scary. So yes, I think the majority of our minority is set up in that group of people who have no way to dream. Now I try to expose my children by taking them to shop somewhere other than K mart, Wal-Mart. To get exposure.

# Shanice

*I*'LL BE TWENTY-TWO in June, and I am a student at an arts college. I am single with no children, which is a rare trait among black women right now, my age. In my class, there are about maybe five to seven black females—my school's predominantly white—and four of them already have children. I was raised in Newark, New Jersey, with my mom. I went to a Catholic school. I was an only child, a little girl. My dad was on the West Coast, so I went back and forth from East Coast to West Coast, and the South too, to visit him, where I learned that I had two half sisters and a brother. I didn't even know about or meet them until I was in fourth grade, and it was just kind of thrown on me. Luckily, my half brothers and sisters were always very warm towards me, because I've always heard stories where people aren't necessarily liked or friendly in that situation.

I feel like a Catholic school victim, because mad people, when I be speaking to them, say, "You went to Catholic school? Oh, man, the trauma!" But I only went up to eighth grade, so I didn't really get totally conditioned. And I didn't go through the rituals of becoming Catholic, so I just sat on the outside. I'd say I was raised middle class, and that's weird because it's something that I'm dealing with right now, this middle-class syndrome where you feel like your friends are tugging at you. I feel like it's lower-class status that's pulling me to be lower class, and I'm striving to be upper class. So it seems like it's a big hurdle, and I'm not necessarily sure I want to go there . . .

My dad was an ex-offender that founded a nonprofit organization that educated ex-offenders on AIDS and drugs, and he went into the community as well and actually got them the right to vote. So he basically did a 180-degree turn in the community and became very successful. And I just knew him as a businessman who helps all of these convicts, seeing articles on him in books and newspapers, and then when I met my sisters and brothers, that's when they told me the flip side. And I said, "What are you talking about?" There are four kids by my father with three different mothers. My oldest sister is something like thirty-six years old. I am the youngest. My mom was twenty-something and he was like thirty-something when they got together. He was already out of graduate school, the whole nines. He was a drug dealer. He had his own clubs, his own record store, and my mother fell in love with him. It was one of those things. And then she got pregnant when she was in school, and she came back home.

There is a lot of family confusion that lies inside myself because I feel like my family doesn't know enough about our history, and I kept digging. I found Cherokee, Native American, but I also found the story of my great-grandmother, which is amazing. She was stolen from her mom and basically raised by some law officials in South Carolina, and all of our history was lost from there. She was given to them as a real doll, a "real live Negro doll." And her brother was given as a "real nigger doll," boy doll, to one of the sisters.

For me, when it comes to intimacy, I go with my feelings, or my sensations. I don't know. It's like that quiet moment when you're with this guy, and he's looking all good, and it's just like, "Oh, okay." I'm not very comfortable with intimacy. I've only had two sexual partners, so therefore I'm not really comfortable with talking about it now. I think that intimacy is that quiet moment when both individuals are willing to be tender with each other. I'd have to know them for a very, very long time. And so, if anything, I feel most comfortable around my friends from elementary school because they know me so well. They know my good sides and my bad sides. They know when I'm playing and when I'm not playing.

When the other person is not necessarily respecting my personal space and the timing and so on, that is definitely a break in intimacy. When I was a freshman at college, I used to visit this guy all the time in his room, and we used to chill, hang out, comfortable, watching TV. But he didn't necessarily know how to control his feelings toward me, and it seemed like every time I'd get ready to leave, I'd have to be fighting him off of me. I'm here to just be with you, not necessarily in that physical way. I'm here just enjoying your company.

I am closest to my cousin Makissa, but except for her, I feel closest to guys in general. The problem that I have with girls is that they usually tag me. I didn't even hang around girls when I was little. With girls it seems as though you have to sit a proper way, and laugh a certain way, and you have to prop your hair a certain way, little things like that. I feel most at ease when I'm with guys, and I can just be. Even so, it doesn't always work out with guys either. I was really comfortable with my sexuality until this brother who didn't know how to act mistreated me. I thought he was my soul mate. And now, I'm just like all lost in the wind again and not comfortable around people. I don't trust anyone. One bad incident can just mess you up for the rest of your life. It's like trauma.

I found out most information about sex from my half sister, who is five years older than me. She was very, very blunt, and that's where I found out most of the juice, anything and everything you wanted to know. My dad had that organization on sex and drugs, and I had the drama side of like, "Always use a condom; this is your protection." It also caters to homosexuals, so I found out about that lifestyle. Also, when you're little, you watch them little channels, and I would find out about sex and what goes where. I went to Catholic school up to the eighth grade. But I went to a music- and art-oriented high school, and I didn't even fit in that world. Dancers, artists, and drama majors, everyone acting wild and looking very, very weird, as opposed to Catholic school, where everyone was wearing uniforms. My cousin was the first. She was about sixteen when she lost her virginity, and I was like, "God, what the hell are you doing?" So any information I did find out, it was from Makissa, my younger cousin.

For some reason when I speak to my mother about issues about sex, she just closes up. She doesn't really want to listen. She wouldn't even let me date until I was seventeen years old, and she was crying at that point. I said, "Ma, chill out, I'm just going on a date." So any other conversation wasn't going to work with her. I really basically had to learn on my own and come back and just check little points with her. She never said anything about sex except, "Don't get pregnant." At seventeen I had to sit down, with her and her new boyfriend, and be like, "Ma, I'm seventeen now. You told me when I was sixteen I could start going on dates. I waited an extra year. I didn't disobey. You know, what's up?" And so she finally, she said, "I don't know what to say." I wanted to tell her to calm down! Maybe she was thinking I was going to turn out like this wild child, because I feel like there's some gene that runs in my family, this trait, these wild people just chillin', drinking, smoking, all these types of things. And I think that she didn't necessarily want me to go into that arena. I guess she didn't want me to fall into the same predicament that she fell into.

She cried when I got my period. She did very well up until then. She did very, very well with explaining all of that. She got me a book on menstruation. I want to say I was fourteen—it seems so long ago. And I called her up at work and I said, "I got my period." She said, "No you didn't." I said, "Yeah, I did. I know what it is, so when you get home, just bring me some pads and stuff." When she got home she started crying. [*Imitates a big sigh.*] "Don't get pregnant." And that was primarily it. I think the silence made me feel saucy, you know, bitter.

I think I laugh because I'm salty.

If I have a daughter, I will definitely thoroughly explain those things because I don't see why you should have to basically prance around and dance around issues that are normal and natural. I don't know, that's my mother. I really don't know how else to talk about it. I remember being as closed about the issues as she was. My cousins and my aunts were, "Oh, congratulations." I was like, "I don't want to talk about it." So I basically ended up having that same blockage about issues about sex, and my period, and so forth.

Virginity was more about virtue and keeping it until I get married. Actually, I got engaged to Jackson, the first guy I lost my virginity to. I was eighteen, all romantic notions that go along with supposedly losing your virginity. I told my mom after, and she said, "Well, did you see stars?" And I was like, "Oh, not necessarily, but I did have a good time." She was like, " 'Kay. Talk to you later." She didn't cry that time.

As far as my religious background, I got most of my education from my aunt. She's a born-again Christian, and so that's where I got the notion of the need to maintain my virginity until I get married, because the secular man, or the man who's in the world, is not going to treat me as well as the man that's been to church. I told my aunt about losing my virginity and my cousins couldn't believe I told her. My aunt said that she didn't necessarily know if that was the right decision. I thought it was fine. I was chillin', had a good time. I was with someone that professed his love for me, treated me very, very nicely. He was very respectful, and I was cool with it. It was a decision that I thought that I was mature enough to make. I cried, too, you know. I was like, Oh, my God, I waited all this time, I gave it up, and . . . but I got over it, and I was fine. I think it was just that first fear.

Before losing my virginity, I experimented one time with this guy Darryl. He was like this thug a mom would not like you to hang around with. He'll get you into smoking and drinking. But he was a really sweet guy. And right before I was about to leave for school, we had made that move, but I wasn't ready. So we stopped, no oral sex. Just rubbing. Clothes on and then clothes off. Then after that, actually we got to where the tip went in, but then I was like, Pain? So I was like, "Forget it, yo. If it's going to be this much pain . . ." because I was the virgin.

When I was dating Jackson, I made him give up all kinds of information. I ran him through the wringer, made him write a list of all the sexual partners that he had before me and who he was with when he was unprotected. I made him get an HIV test. And then I finally decided that I wanted to make the move. He bought me some red PJs, and it was cool. I had a good time. I was very, very nervous, very, very jittery. I got the giggles because whenever I'm nervous, I always laugh a lot. It seems so long ago. It hurt, and then I bled a little bit, and then I changed sheets, and then I had a good time. I was like, Oh, yeah, this is fun. There was no oral sex. I don't know why, I didn't get into oral sex until later on in the relationship. He was trying to be easy on me, not rock my whole world. But there was a lot of foreplay, which I did like about him, but I didn't like about my next boyfriend, who was straight to the point. I was not enthused. He didn't make me feel enthused. He was a total asshole. But with Jackson, there was a lot of foreplay. I don't know, I just remember doing it over and over again, after I finally got used to it. I mean, like the bathtub, bubble bath. All types of stuff. We had sex the whole weekend.

I would say we had been dating almost a year. And we stayed together for two years after that. He proposed to me. I had a little engagement ring. And Mom was like, "Oh, that's the proper way." I was very, very excited. Then I met this other dude. Martin. And I don't know why, he had this tough exterior that I was really, really attracted to, the roughneck type, the anytime, anyplace type of feeling. But Jackson was West Indian and he was really sweet and cordial. And wanted me to play the wife role, and I wasn't into cooking. I was just eighteen going on nineteen or something like that, and I was like, "Look, I came to college to have fun." So I copped an attitude. For real. I copped an attitude and was like, "We need to separate." I think we were both very much in love with the idea of being in love. We were supposed to be married probably about two months from now. But I knew that wasn't the right choice because I wanted to go to Africa, I wanted to go to this program, and he didn't want me to go. I said, "You're too possessive" or something.

I got pregnant with Jackson. It was after I broke up with him and he was still trying to get back with me. Martin thought Jackson was probably trying to get me pregnant on purpose, which I do believe. I broke up with him partly because of how he acted when I decided to get an abortion. Up to that point, I just didn't believe in abortions, me being the religious type. But that idea I had got kicked to the curb because I was like, "Hell, no, I'm not having any kids," and I just didn't like his reaction to it. I felt like he acted like a punk. That's my personal opinion. He acted as though his world was about to crumble. He treated me as if he didn't know me, as if to say, "Who is this person that I'm sitting next to?" He basically didn't communicate how he felt inside, and I felt that I went through so much trauma with just an abortion and all that shit.

I could have sworn he was wearing a condom. I had broken up with him and I didn't want to be with him, but still something happened. Martin was in Texas at the time and we weren't dating yet, just like talking back and forth, and at that point we did have somewhat of an open relationship. So I was honest enough to tell him that this is what's going on. He was pissed and hurt, but he was just like, "Well, do what's best." He was much more consoling. He comforted me completely, I guess because he wasn't in the situation, but who knows. Or maybe he was just trying to get with me, I don't know.

Now that I look back on it, I can talk about it much, much more. I'm open about it. I feel like I'm not the only one in the world who has been in that situation. When I was in it, though, it was very traumatic. I was angry because this wasn't supposed to be happening to me. Like, Miss Educated Woman about protection and so on. And I didn't want to have to go home with that bullshit to my mom or my sister. I'm bound to be the first to graduate from college and go on to graduate school. It was fucking up my plans, basically. I was like, "Here, take the ring back." He didn't understand that it was not the time and place. I had other stuff I had to do.

But the sex was good. Until I met Martin. The sex was way better with him. The first time I came, I was like, "Damn, I didn't know that was possible! What was wrong?" He wasn't into kissing and so on, which is part of my expectation in foreplay, just like kissing and touching on the breasts, all that good stuff. He was into orgasm, and what could he do, and how could he get me open, and how could he make me come. So he was experimental. I made him go through the wringer too, the test. Who were his past relationships. But I did not believe him. I refused to believe him because when his boys came over, I was hearing about other girls who were not on the list! With Jackson, I believed him; he was very, very sincere, the wholesome-boy type. But with Martin, I'm still pulling skeletons out of the closet.

Before Martin, I had not even heard about an orgasm for women. He said, "Oh, my God. I'm gonna do some favors for you." It was fly, it was awesome. I was wanting more. All right, it was dope. I realized, Damn, I was missing out. And I'm glad I broke up with Jackson. I had never masturbated either, until Martin. As long as that person is committed to me, I am pretty much open-minded about anything that could come up in the bedroom. I actually moved in, and we had an apartment together, so we were doing all sorts of stuff. Masturbating was sort of a joint thing—I would help him, he would help me. I don't know if I have masturbated to orgasm by myself. I want to say no. Maybe it's because I don't want to talk about it, I don't know.

After a while, oral sex got upsetting to me. It's just like, "Wait, I don't want to do that no more. Let's try something else." It just depends on what mood I'm in. I think that he felt that I had all types of inhibitions. And that was his goal, to break all of that stuff. Then he did, and then he acted like an ass, and now I'm right back at square one. I was doing some wild shit in my life, locked my hair, moved out, ran away from home, moved in with him. We were together for going on a year and a half or so.

I daydream about just the times that I had with Martin. Because that motherfucker was tight. I think that the relationship was primarily based on sex. He did try to do right by me, you know, a little life and love. But the main part of the relationship was the sex, and now it's just like, Damn, can I find someone else who can do it just as well? That's what I primarily daydream about, those past experiences. We did the whipped cream and strawberries, the pomegranate, herbal tea. All natural stuff. I think that the fantasies that I had I'm already pretty much done, whether it was the fruit or whatever. But I'm young—I'm sure I'll have some more.

I've decided that I'm not dating any more black men. I've already decided. They don't know how to act. I think they're too possessive. I feel like when sex comes into play with black men, they feel like they own you. And I'm going to experiment with other races. I'm trying to date this other kid that's, I think, from Spain. It's an experiment, so I've already told my mom that I'm not dating any more black men and for her to just get used to it. I actually had a discussion on that yesterday. From growing up, seeing my father, my mom's boyfriends, my aunt's boyfriends, the scrapings of black men that are trying to be responsible, that are not being responsible, that don't know how to handle their business, don't know how to handle violence, don't know how to handle anger—I don't have time for that. I'm not necessarily saying that other races are not the same way, but I'm about to find out.

Both Martin and Jackson were abusive to me. Definitely Martin, and I want to say even Jackson, because I feel like if you put your hands on me, that is abusive. I feel like if you try to prevent me from doing something, physically, mentally, verbally, that's still abusive, and so I have had those situations with the two black men I've been with. I have a little scar right here on my arm because the motherfucker ain't know how to act. Now, mind you, I feel like they are intertwined because Martin gets upset about other guys. And Jackson was my first love, so Martin could not deal with the fact that I had very, very strong feelings for Jackson. I was downstairs talking to Jackson, just talking. And this motherfucker calls me upstairs, and I felt stupid because I saw the signs and I still was like, No, love and trust and all that good stuff. Called me upstairs and was like, "What the fuck are you doing? I told you not to go downstairs." And I was like, "I know what you told me, but I told you that I have to have a conversation with Jackson." So I don't know what happened. I just started screaming, and I guess the whole building had to hear it, so I went upstairs, and I was just like, "Are you feeling okay?" There was scrapings on the wall, like a knife. And a hole in the wall. And I was like, "Damn, what is this? Are you that angry? Can it really be that bad? I was just downstairs talking." So he went walking around, said he was cooling off, that'd never happened to him before, he needed to calm down, etc. I said, "Cool, one slipup, I'ma allow you that."

Then after that we were sitting on the couch, and we got into an argument about some shit, could've been about Jackson who had just moved to where my grandmother lived as well. I don't know what it was about. But he got all hostile, had thrown my shit out the room, threw it at me, and I was like, All right, cool, no problem. I got myself a home, with my best friend at the time. I was like, Shoot, no problem. Everything was cool. Whatever, you ain't affecting me. He was on the phone with someone talking about "this bitch." Now, mind you, disrespecting me completely and threw iced tea in my face, and said, "Take this with you, and tell your friends I threw this . . ." I was just like, "I know he didn't throw tea in my face." So I maintained my composure, kept on walking out the door, got my shit together. I was like, "I'm not going to fuck with this nigger no more." So I was like, "I'ma go to church. That's the reason why I'm in this mess." I went to church, stayed in that little sector for a while. Then after that I went back to Jackson, but the sex wasn't good. That was the only part he was lacking. He was all tight, up until the sex. He had his own apartment. He was respectful, was doing stuff for himself. But it wasn't about him anymore. So I realized that and went back to Martin. We had another argument. I was in the apartment, and we were building this artist team together, and he was upset because I gave him a title that he felt he did more for and so on and so forth. I don't even know how it got physical, but I got a scratch on my arm, and he says he got a scratch on his arm. I don't give a shit about his scratch—all I care about is the scratch on my arm. I mean it's a little tiny scratch, but that's a lot to me.

Then after that I decided, All right, I'm going to be honest; I love this brother. So I said "Yo, you know, when you threw tea in my face? After that, I went back to Jackson." I don't know why I did that, because after that the motherfucker went crazy. He said, "Okay, you're schizophrenic, you're a bitch, you're a ho." He was telling all of our friends this, too, leaving me in the house. And then after that, my friends, which are his male friends, would call me back and he would say that I wasn't allowed to speak to them because I was his girl with no rights. This shit was beginning to get on my nerves. It was like a saga, Mafia type of shit. They're calling me back asking, "What the hell's going on?" I'm like, "Yo, I don't know, he trippin', yo." So then I had to pack up my shit undercover. My friends came and got me out. My grandparents brought me back the next day with a U-Haul, got all my shit out the apartment. Then, he shot off a gun and broke my grandmother's mailbox. Now, I don't know for sure it was him. He claimed he didn't do it. But after that I got a restraining order against him. He doesn't say shit to me, I don't say shit to him, he ain't talking about me no more. So that's how it ended. But you know, I look at positive things, and he just didn't know how to handle himself. I just leave it alone and say, No problem. I'm at another level, and I'm more mature than him, and just move on. That's why I'm just like, Black men, no. It could have been just a bad choice. I'm sure it was.

To be very honest, I think I stayed in it because of the lack of role models that were there for me when I was little—the fact that my mom stayed in those types of situations, the fact that my aunt stayed in those types of situations. The fact that I was the only one sticking up for them when they weren't sticking up for themselves. And when it came to me, I didn't know how to stand up for myself. So that's why.

There was one particular one that is still in my mom's life and probably has been since I was five. He's married to someone else. You know when you become old enough to realize situations that are there in your face. What makes me upset about that whole situation was I tried to talk to my mom about what happened with Martin, thinking she could understand, and she said, "I don't want to talk about that." I said, "What do you mean you don't want to talk about it?" I tried to talk to my mom about this, I tried to talk to my grandmother about it. I'm like, "Here's the restraining order." They were like, "No, Martin couldn't have done that."

It reminds me of the time that my aunt was about to get married, and it was the day before her wedding and her and her husband-to-be were fighting in the bathroom. And my cousin who was a dude—so I felt, yo, he should have been out trying to help my aunt—was chillin'. So I called my grandma: "Oh, it'll be all right. Don't even stress; I'll talk to them." That doesn't stop, you know what I'm saying? When I went to stay with them in New Mexico, sometimes that shit was still on. I don't understand why people put up with shit like this. I know I'm not going through that shit no more. And the little scrape that I got, that was fine enough. The tea in my face, that was fine enough. I'm not doin' it. Fuck it. Black men are not worth that shit, I'm sorry. And like West Indian men, nope, I'm not even dealing with none of them. Close the whole door off until maybe I meet that one that's gonna do right.

Maybe racism has something to do with it, but I don't care. I'm tired of the structure that African Americans have, in that they don't want to do shit. They're either lazy, but yo, I'm out there working, I can afford the shit I got, so why can't you? And don't take your frustrations out on me. Because I think it's a syndrome they get caught in. I understand that you have to deal with the fact that, yeah, we were slaves, and there's racism, but there has to become a point where you can move past that and do something for everyone and for yourself.

In that situation with Martin when we were in the heat of drama, he'd be like, "Don't try that feminist shit with me. Don't become gay." I was like, "First of all, how you gonna draw those two conclusions?" And then it's like, "Don't bring my work into it just because I'm an artist that speaks out on female issues." I don't know, I just think he was stupid. Black men are not necessarily educated on female issues. I think they draw parallels that don't necessarily have anything to do with each other, and therefore I can't even approach them when issues like, just because I'm wearing this short skirt doesn't mean I'm a ho. Even when I bring up those issues, it's like, girls conduct themselves like that, so that's what they should be. Just because I wear a small skirt or I wear a little tennis skirt and sneakers and I think I'm the bomb, whatever, doesn't mean I conduct myself openly with like whoever I sleep with. Then I think it's a class difference. That's probably why I'm not trying to deal with anybody like that anymore.

Images of black women only add to the problem. What's really weird is when I became a lock [wearing dreadlocks], men look at me more, and they expect me not necessarily to have short skirts. I'm supposed to be this religious type figure. I'm supposed to be this mythical queen goddess kind of individual. I don't think I'm attractive when I don't wear anything that's not fitted. This is contradictory as well because then I feel people are watching me because I have locks and I should be three fourths covered up, including my mouth. Do I always have to walk around just representing for my race, and for a political movement, or all that other junk that's in there?

Can I not just chill, just breathe, just walk, just paint, just eat? Do those human things? And I think because those images are constantly out there, that every time something like Freaknik comes around, I could have on jeans and a T-shirt, and I'm still getting mauled. And just guys. I'm sorry to bring it back to black men, but the images in black music, like rap music, really make it hard for us.

Images that come to mind for me—I'm gonna say actresses like Nia Long, Josephine Baker, Foxy Brown—these images are the reasons why I'm being treated the way I am treated right now. When I try to bring those up to black men or just in general, I feel like I'm the last of the Mohicans. To be able to talk for myself and not have a child makes me rare. To be honest, I'm trying to not be associated with African American and black culture anymore. I'm trying to just be on my native tip and just find out about the Cherokee side of me.

But overall, I think I've had a good time, and I'm just waiting for my next partner, the next guy. I just want to be in love with the person, and that's good enough for me. I want to have a lot of children. I want to have, actually, three or four. But I don't want to have them until I'm going on thirty. I want to have my own land, and I want to raise them with the views of ancestors. I want to raise them with views that stress the importance of having communal values. But it's hard because my grandparents and my mother don't quite understand who I am now and don't necessarily respect that. I'm like, "No, Ma, I'm not eating pork anymore. No, Ma, I'm not wearing those shorts anymore." She does not accept certain things because she just thinks I'm doing this on a whim. It is a necessity to my race to have children. And they will be mixed because I'm not going back to black men.

I think right now, I'm just getting used to the fact that all those incidents where I was harassed on the street, even with Martin and Jackson, happened because they were all just ignorant. One particular incident comes to mind now. In my sophomore year I was working in college at this art gallery shop and this guy came up to me in the store and said, "I'd rape you if I wanted to, and how I want to." Just niggerish. And then he came back two other times to reinforce his words. I ended up quitting that job.

When I told my family they went hysterical. I felt like I could handle it. My friends were like, "No, you don't have to work there." I don't think it's fair for men to have so much power in our society. I think that, if I get there, to a place with power, they're going to be upset with me because I'm going to have to set some standards. Like the power is in politics. The power is in making those major decisions as far as education and so on. The only way to break the chain with that sort of mentality is through education. And I'm going to start that within my home, but I'm also going to start it within my community.

# Epilogue

*W*E DO COMPARE our lives to the stories we know. We listen to the stories that surround us hoping to find in them reflections of our own feelings, experiences, and perceptions.

Though the stories we've read in *Longing to Tell* touch on many issues that seem familiar—the gender double standard, the social acceptance of physical violence against women by the men in their lives, the painful color hierarchy in black communities that compound the injuries endured in a society that elevates whiteness as the normal standard for beauty, the expectation that black women should compensate for the pain suffered by black men in society, the issue of dating outside the race, the impact of conflicting sexual expectations for women, and excessive judgments attached to women's sexual behaviors—these women talk about them in a far less polarized manner than is often portrayed.

Thus, many women interviewed for this book asked why behaviors for which women are brutally judged and derided, such as cheating or changing sexual partners frequently, are accepted and often celebrated when practiced by men. Yet they did not conclude that "all black men are dogs" (as the expression goes) and that they themselves were above reproach.

Rather, their detailed, sometimes incriminating, accounts of events and the moments of self-reflection throughout indicate that more often than not they simply wanted enduring and just bonds.

The vulnerability that all these women share is compounded by the many ways racial and gender injustices affect them every day. It would be easy to let rage, despair, and feelings of powerlessness flourish when the difficulty of their circumstances is more compounded by injustice. But by accepting the unbreakable links between intimacy, vulnerability, and risk these women are redefining the way they think about their sexual and intimate futures. Instead of wondering how to find love without struggle or how to win the battle between the sexes, they are focusing on setting up terms for intimate engagement and reciprocal understanding—terms that accept the reality of risk and vulnerability. There is real possibility in the strategies we find here for dealing with, rather than hiding from, the risks associated with sexuality and intimacy. Hope lies in our commitment to build on the courage of these women to tell and our resolve to listen anew.

# Afterword: *The Past as Prologue*

" 'Here,' she said, 'in this here place, we flesh; flesh that weeps, laughs; flesh that dances on bare feet in grass. Love it. Love it hard. Yonder they do not love your flesh. They despise it. They don't love your eyes; they'd just as soon pick em out. No more do they love the skin on your back. Yonder they flay it. And O my people they do not love your hands. Those they only use, tie, bind, chop off and leave empty. Love your hands! Love them. Raise them up and kiss them. Touch others with them, pat them together, stroke them on your face 'cause they don't love that either. You got to love it, you! . . . More than your life-holding womb and your life-giving private parts, hear me now, love your heart. For this is the prize.' "

—*Toni Morrison*, Beloved *(1987)*

*I*N THE INTRODUCTION I wrote that it is impossible to understand a woman's coming-of-age experiences without having a sense of the larger contexts that shape them, such as family dynamics, expectations surrounding gender and sexuality, economic and educational circumstances, religion, race, color, and weight. But if we are to understand more fully the portraits of the women presented here, we must also know the history of black women in America and its legacies. We are all deeply shaped by our histories in this world; histories that have seeped into places many of us find it difficult and painful to go. The personal lives of these women who stepped out on faith—and all of our lives—are shaped by the legacies of racial slavery and the diffused but nonetheless entrenched ideas about black people's sexuality that grew from them.

In *Beloved*, one of our most treasured writers, Toni Morrison, explores the painful connection between the brutality of American slavery with its hatred of black flesh, and the urgent need for black self-love as a survival strategy and form of resistance. Finding ways to love ourselves is undoubtedly a human struggle for us all, but for generations of African Americans it has been a matter of spiritual life and death. Our commitment to remembering and acknowledging this history and its contemporary manifestations is the way beyond it.

Sexual ideology, domination, and violence were central components of slavery. Plantation owners widely used black women as breeders—by forcing them to have sex with male slaves and by raping them. These and other forms of violence were justified by the reasoning that black people were only three fifths human and were sexually debased creatures. After emancipation, control over black sexual activity was substantially reduced, and thus many whites feared black men seeking sexual access to white women (partly a projection based on white male behaviors during slavery). This reinforced the widely held beliefs that black men had a propensity for sexual violence, and that black women's sexual deviance made them less desirable and therefore heightened black men's interest in so-called "pure" white women. These beliefs, in turn, justified the widely accepted use of lynching and castration as forms of racial and sexual terror.

Key sexual myths established during and immediately after slavery have given rise to widely entrenched images of black women. The Mammy, Jezebel, and Sapphire stereotypes are defined primarily by their "dysfunctional" sexuality and motherhood. The Mammy is generally an asexual, overweight, and middle-aged figure whose maternal qualities are expressed through her expert care for white women's children (at the expense of her own). The Jezebel is defined by her excessive, exotic, and unbridled sexuality. The Sapphire is the symbolic antithesis of the "lady": loud, excessive, and irrepressible. She refers indirectly to sexuality by signaling black women's supposed unladylike status.

Coined by policy pundits, the more recent Welfare Queen is characterized as the single black mother who supposedly uses her sexuality irresponsibly and excessively (like a queen bee), producing many children by many different men to get money from them and the welfare state. This term also seems to mock black popular references to black people being the descendents of kings and queens to boost black self-esteem by reminding African Americans that despite their history of enslavement, many African Americans descend from royalty.

Such ideas about black sexuality had an impact on the direction of post-emancipation black activism that, while seeking to defend the community, controlled and defined black women's sexual agency in new ways. Many black intellectuals and social and political leaders attempted to protect the entire community from violence and discrimination by calling on black women to treat their own sexual propriety as a form of race work. Late-nineteenth- and early-twentieth-century racial uplift movements worked to show how morally upright and "normal" black women *really* were. If black women were to be unassailably "sexually pure" and morally upstanding, the argument went, then black men (whose patriarchal masculinity, it was widely believed, had been deeply damaged by slavery) would be restored, and the race would be protected and enhanced. Such racial uplift movements adopted Victorian notions of women's central role as sexual and moral guardians for the race. For black women, this meant that being sexually "inappropriate" was not only a personal stigma, but also an act against an already embattled and despised black community. More recent efforts to illuminate the abuses black women faced as racial/sexual victims in service of slavery and beyond have had the effect of especially negatively branding interracial desires involving black women and white men, while reverse interracial unions (black men with white women) have been seen as a form of political radicalism.

In the early to mid-twentieth century, as millions of blacks migrated to cities in search of work and a better life, the idea of black people's and black women's sexual deviancy took on an urban dimension: black single women were seen to be "loose in the city," "wreaking havoc" in black and white communities (as "enticing" live-in maids, neighbors, and coworkers).[1] Since this migration, and after the disappearance of the industrial jobs that drew black migrants, poor black mothers unable to find work have been targeted as matriarchs whose so-called wanton sexuality has been the cause of their poverty. This reasoning is the hallmark of the anti-welfare debates. Why, some conservatives ask, should "we" pay for "them" to have babies?

In the mid-twentieth century, urban sociological studies on race (such as the infamous Moynihan Report) relied on myths about black women's sexual dominance (e.g., matriarchy, when viewed from a patriarchal point of view) as the reason for the decline of the black family, and gave rise to the same kind of self-censorship in service to the race. Such political strategies discourage black women from expressing desires or sharing experiences that might prove racist sociologists right. Most responses to these studies that delineate the "problem" of the black-female-headed household also take a decidely patriarchal view. Black nationalist patriarchal rhetoric has supported black motherhood and reproduction (making babies for the race), while maintaining the significance of reestablishing a patriarchal family model. This has had the troubling effect of limiting black women's support for abortion, as well as adding to the social stigma of black lesbians and subjugating black women's sexuality under a patriarchal vision of racial justice.

On another front, black women's distinctive sexual concerns are often obscured under a feminism that defines the experiences of middle-class white women as those of all women. Even heartfelt white feminist narratives about the strength and resilience of black women praise them for their superwoman-like capacity to carry overwhelming burdens. This kind of affirmation discourages them from expressing vulnerabilities or acknowledging their pain and mythologizes their strength.

All of these myths—although frequently perceived as outmoded and no longer resonant—remain embedded in our everyday lives and continue to influence legal, medical, and public policies. Until about thirty to forty years ago, it was a commonly held belief in legal courts that black women were too sexually loose to be raped. This made charges for raping a black woman virtually impossible to prosecute successfully. As late as 1971, a judge admonished the jurors not to apply ordinary presumptions of chastity to black women.[2] Throughout the better part of the twentieth century, well-respected doctors have consistently performed more hysterectomies on black women than on other women, even going so far as to perform them on black women without consent or previous announcement. This documented practice frequently took place under the medical and social assumption that the doctors were helping the human race by limiting the reproductive capacities of black women. Early unapproved versions of birth control pills were tested on black and Latino women in the Caribbean before being made widely available to middle-class white American women in the 1960s.[3] Recent efforts to force women who receive welfare to use Norplant, the five-year birth control implant, was on its way to becoming commonplace for black and brown welfare recipients before legal challenges were made.

In October 1989, the Medical University of South Carolina, a state hospital serving an indigent minority community, instituted the Interagency Policy on Management of Substance Abuse During Pregnancy (Interagency Policy). This policy, which was developed in collaboration with the Charleston police and prosecutors, was designed, as they put it, to "ensure appropriate management of patients abusing illegal drugs during pregnancy." They relied on nonconsensual drug testing of pregnant patients, the subsequent reporting of the test results to the police, and the arrest of patients in the hospital. In a few cases, arrested women were transported—in handcuffs and leg irons—from the jail to the hospital for weekly prenatal care appointments. One of the women went into labor three weeks after her arrest and was kept handcuffed to her bed during the entire delivery. All in all, about four dozen pregnant women were arrested in the hospital through this policy before pressure from the federal government led to its being abandoned. Although the language used in the Interagency Policy was race neutral, the results made starkly clear that it was black women's reproduction that was being targeted. Interagency Policy overlooked a much larger, predominantly white group of pregnant cocaine users—who were known to seek medical treatment elsewhere—by locating the policy in a poor minority hospital.[4]

In 1998, Cathy Harris, a black female U.S. Customs Service agent, blew the whistle on the unjustified and excessive search and detention of black female travelers at U.S. airports. Her findings were confirmed by the U.S. Customs' own data, which showed that black women were singled out more frequently than any other racial or gender group of travelers, even though they were the least likely to be found holding drugs or other contraband. How significant is this gap? The General Accounting Office looked at 102,000 searches done in 1997 and 1998 and found the following: black female citizens were almost two times more likely to be strip-searched by U.S. Customs officials on suspicion of drug smuggling than white women or men, and three times more likely to be searched than black men. Black female citizens were nine times more likely than white women to be x-rayed after already having undergone pat-downs and strip searches. Yet black female citizens were less than half as likely to be found carrying contraband as were white female citizens. U.S. Customs agents systematically skipped over other groups of men and women who were actually far more likely to possess drugs and contraband, and did twice as many physical searches on black women travelers.

In both cases—drug testing in South Carolina and strip-searching in airports—black women's bodies were systematically denied rights to privacy and equity of treatment typically afforded white women and other citizens. Both involve hundreds of people operating independently and collectively and, in the first case, doing so across the diverse fields of medicine, law enforcement, and the judicial system.

Such policies are driven by embedded and reinforced stories about black women's sexuality. These stories give rise to a devastating circular logic: they create "commonsense" beliefs that affirm and propel what appear to be "commonsense" policies partly because of the easy and frequent circulation of stories that support them. Sexual stories about black women are all around us, but they almost always rely on key myths, while few stories told by black women about their own sexual lives are available. Stories that do not conform to such highly recognizable but terribly distorted representations are marginalized and frequently perceived as not "really" black. Black women's sexual experiences, when they don't fit these expectations, are extremely hard to find, a condition that reinforces the legitimacy of the ones we've been fed.

If we compare our lives to the stories we know—and I think we do—then what kinds of comparisons are black women drawing to the stories we know? Telling *these* stories is not an easy task. The association of black women with sexual deviance and excess has discouraged many from speaking openly about their sexual desires and experiences for fear that whatever they say will also be distorted. Unlike other stereotypes, negative sexual images can't be dispelled by openly challenging them. Sexual labels have a special power over women's social reputations; adding racially pejorative labels only makes this worse. Rather than risk attacks on their reputation and their self-esteem, many black women have retreated into silence, while some have decided to cash in on the power and profitability of these images by representing them in popular culture. Black women's complex sexual lives are caught between a racial/sexual mainstream cultural rock and a counternarrative hard place.

It is not, then, so easy just to speak—to say what is most important about black women's sexual lives. How will what is said be heard? Will the existing hostile or sympathetic interpretive lenses further distort matters or shed light? Over the past fifteen years, black women critics and scholars have grown increasingly vocal about these various claims being made on black women's sexual worth and the continuation of sexual silences by living, real black women. They have wondered if the risks and fears associated with speaking autobiographically about sexuality have made fiction the only semisafe space from which black women can indirectly speak. Hortense Spillers has noted that black women's "sexual experiences are depicted, but not often by them." In an oft-quoted line regarding the absence of black women in sexual literature, she described black women as the "beached whales of the sexual universe—unvoiced, misseen, not doing, awaiting *their* verb."[5] Audre Lorde argued that the shattering of sexual silences among black women was both a crucial political and personal act of survival and the key to liberation. Darlene Clark Hine has written that the history and threat of rape "influenced the development of a culture of dissemblance among black women." By dissemblance, she means that black women created "the appearance of openness and disclosure, but actually shielded the truth of their inner lives and selves from their oppressors . . . Only with secrecy, thus achieving a self-imposed invisibility, could ordinary black women accrue the psychic space and harness the resources needed to hold their own in the often one-sided and mismatched resistance struggle."[6] This culture of dissemblance is an effective strategy for immediate survival, but some feminists argue that its very nature makes it difficult to develop recognition of lived experience.

This silence is especially troubling in light of the abundant publication of oral histories and studies on sexuality and sexual experiences. Sexuality studies about teenagers, general sexual narratives, and popular books on whether the women's movement and feminism have been helpful to middle-class, predominantly white women have become a field unto its own, while a field of published narratives of black women's sexual lives barely exists. Many of the books on sexuality in modern American life feature a sprinkling of black people, or they subsume a racially and ethnically diverse group of women under a nonracial theme, but do so with a decidedly white dominated majority representing this "diverse" whole. Ultimately, this sometimes well-intentioned strategy to show how all women are connected does not allow us to see what things connect women of color to each other that might not be experienced by white women. And it often sees all women's experiences through a subjective filter.

The books that directly address black women and sexuality are generally aimed at helping black women get and keep relationships and to foster personal growth. Thus, they rarely feature black women's own sexual narratives in any depth. Once we subtract these self-help-oriented books, the selections grow astonishingly thin. Important exceptions to this rule are Charlotte Pierce-Baker's book on rape and black women, *Surviving the Silence: Black Women's Stories of Rape*, and Traci C. West's *Wounds of the Spirit: Black Women, Violence and Resistance Ethics*—two books that explore black women's sexual experiences explicitly, but focus primarily on violence and trauma.

Black women novelists have produced eloquent narrative portrayals of black women's sexual lives. Brilliant, landmark novels such as Toni Morrison's *The Bluest Eye*, Zora Neal Hurston's *Their Eyes Were Watching God*, Nella Larsen's *Quicksand*, Alice Walker's *The Color Purple*, Sapphire's *Push*, and many other works poignantly explore the sexual lives of black women in all their joy, brokenness, discovery, and sorrow. These novels, by making room for and bringing voice to black women's sexuality, represent a crucial breaking of the silences. Black and other women readers enthusiastically embraced these novels, although many of these books were met with contempt, censure, and challenge. Toni Morrison's afterword to the 1992 edition of *The Bluest Eye* closes this way: "With very few exceptions, the initial publication of *The Bluest Eye* was like Pecola's life: dismissed, trivialized, misread. And it has taken twenty-five years to gain for her the respectful publication this edition is." Women writers who have exposed sexual oppression and violence as experienced by black women—for instance, through social and legal custom, police practices, and the sexual characteristics of white supremacy—have consistently encountered this type of response, even when they render the issues fictionally. Despite these troubling responses, black women writers and poets continue to write about matters of intimacy. Fiction, in many ways, has been left to carry the weight of lived sexual experience, perhaps because the characters can say things and show us things without fear of reprisals—and black women can talk about this complex issue without speaking about themselves directly.

Films by and about black women's sexuality have been produced, but few (especially if we subtract those adapted from black women's novels) have had a prolonged impact in the public imagination. Popular music has a much more sustained impact, but has not been nearly as dynamic a place for a progressive female-centered sexual conversation. Several black women artists, such as Lauryn Hill, Jill Scott, Eryka Badu, Eve, India.Arie, and Angie Stone, as well as some underground artists and black women in the spoken word community, have been telling incredibly powerful, rich, and sometimes explicit stories about intimacy, love, betrayal, sex, and desire.

However, since the early 1990s, after black popular youth culture emerged as the defining and highly profitable element in American youth culture, the visual exploitation of black women in music, video, and film skyrocketed along with black music profits. For many black women artists—and women artists generally—being sexually explicit in ways that mirror trite patriarchal sexual fantasies has remained the most reliably profitable motif. This explosion of sexually explicit expression by black female performers simply represents the music and film industry's profiting from the long-standing sexual ideas about black women to which I referred earlier. It does not generally represent, as some have argued, a new black feminism. Since the mid-1980s, black female musicians and dancers have been increasingly pressured to participate in highly visual and sexually exploitative marketing strategies for selling mainstream popular music. They are often required to be sexually explicit and stereotypical in ways that reflect the profitability of racially distinct sexism rather than given the freedom to make their own decisions to explore sexual issues.

Many very sexually explicit artists, such as Lil' Kim, Trina, and Foxy Brown, reinforce both the history of black women's sexuality as deviant and illicit and the primary role of black women in male hip-hop music videos as exotic sexual playthings and strip-club dancers. Unfortunately, some middle-class and conservative representatives tend to call for a reduction in sexual explicitness across the board, in the service of patriarchal notions of female propriety, not to make room for a wider range of black female sexual expressivity. This conservative public criticism has made it difficult for a sexually progressive critique of these images to establish a public footing.

The racial and sexual myths, stories, and practices established to justify the brutalities and exploitations of slavery do not exist today exactly as they once did. Over the past 150 years or so, they have been altered by the impact of vast changes in cultural, political, economic, and social spheres. Although they cannot be explored here, it is important to note the importance of changes such as post-emancipation Jim Crow segregation, early-twentieth-century black urban migration, the civil rights and black power movements, feminism, integration, gay and lesbian activism, deindustrialization, globalization, and the proliferation of consumer capitalism. These have all played central roles in changing our notions of race, sexuality, and gender. The changes are significant; many of them signal important movement away from dehumanization toward racial, sexual, and gender equity and justice. However, some of these changes have produced mutations of the old racial and sexual myths and stereotypes, whose power lies in reinforcing while seeming to eschew them.

The women in *Longing to Tell* speak as both individuals reflecting on their personal lives in this moment and as women who are part of a larger story. So, when they repeatedly speak about the fact that dark-skinned women are still considered less attractive—by many black people and others—this is a direct result of the hatred of blackness fostered by the ideologies of slavery. When many of them speak about dating outside the race, the tone and disposition expressed has a great deal to do with the once formal and now informal systems of racial segregation that shape the kinds of access black people have to other groups, especially to whites. Some women's concerns about being desired as "exotic" cannot be fully appreciated without some sense of the long history of black sexuality being perceived as deviant, different, and therefore sometimes exotic. While many women protect people who abuse them, when black women protect some of the abusive black men and women in their lives, this is far better understood in the context of racial profiling, police harassment, and judicial sexism and racism. Surely their immense frustration about the sexual double standard they face is shared by all kinds of women, but how is this double standard compounded by the racial one to which they are also subjected? When the women speak of their struggle to make it, to discover and then arrive at where they want to go—no matter what obstacles have been put in their path—the courage and fire in these pronouncements can be appreciated when we understand the historical struggles that have shaped them. If we continue to downplay the importance of these powerful histories and social forces, we will keep them alive; we will mask and sustain their impact on our lives. Intimate justice comes from our working through, not around, these histories. It comes from our listening with self-awareness and making a steadfast commitment to nurturing space for new stories and new ways of telling them.

# Notes

## INTRODUCTION

Epigraph: Mary Romero and Abigail J. Stewart, eds., *Women's Untold Stories: Breaking Silence, Talking Back, Voicing Complexity* (New York: Routledge, 1999), p. xvi.

1. Richard Delgado, "Storytelling for Oppositionists and Others: A Plea for Narrative," *Michigan Law Review* 87 (1989): 2411.
2. E. Frances White, *Dark Continent of Our Bodies: Black Feminism and the Politics of Respectability* (Philadelphia: Temple University Press, 2001).

## AFTERWORD

1. Hazel Carby, "Policing the Black Woman's Body in an Urban Context," *Critical Inquiry* (Summer 1992): 738–55.
2. Kimberle K. Crenshaw, " 'Whose Story Is It Anyway?': Feminist and Antiracist Appropriations of Anita Hill," in *Race-ing Power, En-gendering Power: Essays on Anita Hill, Clarence Thomas and the Construction of Social Reality*, ed. Toni Morrison (New York: Pantheon, 1992), p. 413. See also Paula Giddings, "The

Last Taboo," and Wahneema Lubiano, "Black Ladies, Welfare Queens and State Minstrels: Ideological War by Narrative Means," in the same volume.

3. Linda Grant, *Sexing the Millenium: Women and the Sexual Revolution* (New York: Grove Press, 1994), chapter 3.

4. Dorothy Roberts, *Killing the Black Body: Race, Reproduction and the Meaning of Liberty* (New York: Vintage, 1997), pp. 164–67. Also, special thanks to Kimani Paul Emile for her research on the Intragency Policy, which brought this policy to my attention.

5. Hortense Spillers, "Intersticies: A Small Drama of Words," in *Pleasure and Danger: Exploring Female Sexuality*, ed. Carole S. Vance (New York: Routledge, 1984), p. 74.

6. Darlene Clark Hine, "Rape and the Inner Lives of Black Women in the Middle West: Preliminary Thoughts on the Culture of Dissemblance," in *Words of Fire: Anthology of African-American Feminist Thought*, ed. Beverly Guy-Sheftall (New York: The New Press, 1995), pp. 380, 382.

# Selected Bibliography

The following books and essays are suggested readings that explore issues of race and black women's intimacy and sexuality. They have been important to my thinking on the subject. It is by no means intended to be exhaustive, but rather suggestive and generative.

Davis, Angela. *Blues Legacies and Black Feminisms: Gertrude "Ma" Rainey, Bessie Smith, and Billie Holiday.* New York: Pantheon, 1998.

duCille, Ann. " 'Othered' Matters: Reconceptualizing Dominance and Difference in the History of Sexuality in America." *Journal of the History of Sexuality* 1, no. 1 (1990): 102–27.

Golden, Marita. *Wild Women Don't Wear No Blues: Black Women Writers on Love, Men and Sex.* New York: Doubleday/Anchor, 1994.

Guy-Sheftall, Beverly. *Words of Fire: An Anthology of African-American Feminist Thought.* New York: New Press, 1995.

Hammonds, Evelyn. "Black (W)holes and the Geometry of Black Female Sexuality." *Differences* 6 (1994): 126–45.

Hill-Collins, Patricia. *Black Feminist Thought: Knowledge, Consciousness, and the Politics of Empowerment.* New York: Routledge, 1991.

hooks, bell. *Salvation: Black People and Love.* New York: Harper Perennial, 2001.

Hurston, Zora Neal. *Their Eyes Were Watching God.* 1937. Reprint, New York: HarperCollins, 2000.

Lorde, Audre. *Sister Outsider.* Berkeley: Crossing Press, 1984.

Morrison, Toni. *Beloved.* New York: Alfred A. Knopf, 1987.

———. *The Bluest Eye.* New York: Holt, Rinehart & Winston, 1970.

Pierce-Baker, Charlotte. *Surviving the Silence: Black Women's Stories of Rape.* New York: W. W. Norton, 1998.

Roberts, Dorothy. *Killing the Black Body: Race, Reproduction and the Meaning of Liberty.* New York: Pantheon, 1997.

Sapphire. *Push.* New York: Vintage, 1997.

Wallace, Michelle. *Black Macho and the Myth of the Superwoman.* 1978. Reprint, New York: Verso, 1990.

West, Cornel. *Race Matters.* Boston: Beacon Press, 1994.

West, Traci C. *Wounds of the Spirit: Black Women, Violence and Resistance Ethics.* New York: New York University Press, 1999.

White, E. Frances. *Dark Continent of Our Bodies: Black Feminism and the Politics of Respectability.* Philadelphia: Temple University Press, 2001.

# Index